LITERATURE AND DISSENT IN MILTON'S ENGLAND

The England of John Milton's great poems was the England of Dissenters, those who refused to join the state church after the return
of monarchy in 1660, seen as dangerous outcasts and rebels. Sharon
Achinstein's book shows how a literary tradition of Dissent was produced by those who suffered political defeat and religious exclusion
in Restoration England, bringing to view a range of writing that has
been largely, and unjustly, neglected. Considering authors both inside
and outside the Dissenting tradition, including Milton, John Bunyan,
Richard Baxter, Mary Mollineux, John Dryden, Andrew Marvell,
Elizabeth Singer Rowe, and Isaac Watts, and other little-known Dissenting writers, Achinstein shows how a distinctive, Dissenting cultural legacy challenges our current notions of literary history, aesthetic
value, and the relation between literature and politics. This important
study will be of interest to students and general readers interested in
England's turbulent seventeenth century, as well as Milton scholars
and seventeenth-century literary and religious historians.

SHARON ACHINSTEIN is Lecturer in English at Oxford University
and a Fellow of St. Edmund Hall, and has previously taught at the University of Maryland and Northwestern University. She is the author
of *Milton and the Revolutionary Reader* (1994), which won the Milton
Society of America's Hanford Prize, and edited *Literature, Gender and
the English Revolution* (1994).

D1808925

LITERATURE AND DISSENT IN MILTON'S ENGLAND

SHARON ACHINSTEIN

St. Edmund Hall, Oxford

CAMBRIDGE
UNIVERSITY PRESS

CAMBRIDGE UNIVERSITY PRESS
Cambridge, New York, Melbourne, Madrid, Cape Town, Singapore, São Paulo

Cambridge University Press
The Edinburgh Building, Cambridge CB2 8RU, UK

Published in the United States of America by Cambridge University Press, New York

www.cambridge.org
Information on this title: www.cambridge.org/9780521818049

First published 2003
This digitally printed version 2008

A catalogue record for this publication is available from the British Library

ISBN 978-0-521-81804-9 hardback
ISBN 978-0-521-05070-8 paperback

To David

The shadow of history
is the ground of faith

A question of overthrowing

Formulae of striking force
Vision and such possession

How could Love not be loved

Susan Howe, *The Nonconformist's Memorial* (1993)

Contents

Illustrations

Acknowledgments

This project was supported by a research fellowship from the National Endowment for the Humanities for 1997–98. I also received material support from Northwestern University and the University of Maryland. The scholars of Dissent who have come before me have been a vital community. I am enormously indebted to the supreme generosity of Neil Keeble, and have been graced by the inspiration of Christopher and Bridget Hill over a long period. At crucial stages in this work, Geoffrey Nuttall and Richard Greaves pointed me in the right directions. For their having read with minute care the entire manuscript, I also thank David Loewenstein, Nigel Smith, an anonymous reader from Cambridge University Press, and the wise Annabel Patterson. For reading drafts of individual chapters and earlier material, I have learned much from the advice of Tracy Davis, Jules Law, Kathleen Lynch, Barbara Newman, Richard Strier, Nicholas von Maltzahn, Wendy Wall, Steven Zwicker, and members of the Folger Shakespeare Library seminar "Puzzling Evidence," imaginatively led by David Kastan and David Armitage. For my colleagues at the University of Maryland, who generously commented on early material, Marshall Grossman, Ted Leinwand, Donna Hamilton, and Jane Donawerth, I give a special thanks as well as to the rest of the early modern group, Bill Sherman, Kent Cartwright, and Gary Hamilton, for their intellectual rigor, kindness and friendships. I would like to thank the students who took part in my seminar "Theorizing Religion in Early Modern Britain" at the University of Maryland, and my department chairs Betsy Erkkila, Theresa Coletti, and Charles Caramello, who helped me along while I was researching and writing this book. For discussing matters ecclesiological and political and more, I thank Judith Maltby, Nigel Smith, Steve Pincus, Elizabeth Clarke, Lori Ann Ferrell, William Lamont, and Kevin Sharpe; Kathleen Lynch and Judith Maltby for sharing work in progress; and the late Don McKenzie and Jeremy Maule for bibliographic help. I benefitted from testing my ideas at Harvard University, Warwick University, Sheffield University, Northwestern

University, the Huntington Library, and the East Coast Milton Seminar. The assistance of staffs at the Bodleian Library, the Huntington Library, the William Andrews Clark Memorial Library, Dr. Williams' Library, the British Library, the US Library of Congress, and, especially, the Folger Shakespeare Library, has been invaluable. My ongoing dialogue with Nigel Smith about early modern radicalism and religion has been intellectually and morally sustaining. Friendship over a long time and much intellectual support have been given by Earl and Jinny Miner, Tom Corns, and especially Annabel Patterson, who prodded and replenished my energy by her own. While at Cambridge University Press, Josie Dixon encouraged me by her early interest in the project and Ray Ryan deepened that interest. Finally, my greatest debt is to David Norbrook, who warmly understands, and who keeps encouraging in this and in so much else.

Earlier versions of some material have been incorporated from the following articles, whose publishers I thank for their permissions:

"Milton's Spectre in the Restoration: Marvell, Dryden, and Literary Enthusiasm," *Huntington Library Quarterly* 58,2 (1997), 1–30.

"*Samson Agonistes* and the Drama of Dissent," *Milton Studies* 33 (1996), 133–58.

"Honey from the Lion's Carcass: Bunyan, Allegory and the Samsonian Moment," in David Gay, James R. Randall, and Arlette Zinck, eds., *Awakening Words: John Bunyan and the Language of Community* (Newark: University of Delaware Press, 2000), 68–80.

"Romance of the Spirit: Female Sexuality and Religious Desire in Early Modern England," *English Literary History* 69 (2002), 913–38.

Abbreviations

All place of publication London unless noted. Citations to Milton's poetry (Hughes, *John Milton*) are to Merritt Hughes, ed., *John Milton: Complete Poems and Major Prose* (Indianapolis, 1957), unless otherwise noted.

BL	British Library
Bodl.	Bodleian Library, Oxford
Bunyan, *MW*	*The Miscellaneous Works of John Bunyan*, gen. ed. Roger Sharrock, 13 vols. in progress (Oxford, 1976–)
Columbia Milton	*The Works of John Milton*, gen. ed. Frank Allen Patterson, 18 vols. in 21 (New York, 1931–38)
CPW	*The Complete Prose Works of John Milton*, ed. Don M. Wolfe et al., 8 vols. in 10 (New Haven, 1953–82)
CR	A. G. Matthews, *Calamy Revised: Being a Revision of Edmund Calamy's Account of the Ministers and Others Ejected and Silenced, 1660–2* (Oxford, 1934)
CSPD	*Calendar of State Papers, Domestic Series*
DNB	*Dictionary of National Biography*
Dryden, *Works*	*The Works of John Dryden*, gen. eds. Edward Niles Hooker and H. T. Swedenberg, Jr., 20 vols. in progress (Los Angeles, 1956–)
DWL	Dr. Williams' Library, London
Folger	Folger Shakespeare Library, Washington, DC
Greaves, *Deliver*	Richard L. Greaves, *Deliver Us From Evil: The Radical Underground in Britain, 1660–1663* (New York, 1986)
Greaves, *Enemies*	Richard L. Greaves *Enemies Under his Feet: Radicals and Nonconformists in Britain, 1664–1677* (Stanford, 1990)

Henry, *Diary*	Philip Henry, *Diary and Letters of Philip Henry*, ed. Matthew Henry Lee (1882)
Hill, *Bible*	Christopher Hill, *The English Bible and the Seventeenth-Century Revolution* (1993)
Hill, *Defeat*	Christopher Hill, *The Experience of Defeat: Milton and Some Contemporaries* (1984)
Keeble, *LC*	N. H. Keeble, *The Literary Culture of Nonconformity in Later Seventeenth-Century England* (Athens, GA, 1987)
Milton, *PL*	John Milton, *Paradise Lost*
Milton, *PR*	John Milton, *Paradise Regain'd*
Milton, *SA*	John Milton, *Samson Agonistes*
Rivers, *RGS*	Isabel Rivers, *Reason, Grace, and Sentiment: A Study of the Language of Religion and Ethics in England, 1660–1780* (Cambridge, 1991)
Watts, *Dissenters*	Michael Watts, *The Dissenters: From the Reformation to the French Revolution* (Oxford, 1999)

CHAPTER I

Reading Dissent

Consider the career of Edmund Calamy. A leader of the Presbyterian ministry during the English Revolution, co-author of the anti-episcopal tract, *Smectymnuus*, parliamentary preacher, licenser of the Cromwellian press and called by Anthony à Wood, "a great evangelist of the new way, [who] encouraged the people to rebellion," he had been indicted by Charles I for high treason in 1642.[1] A reluctant Cromwellian, Calamy vigorously opposed Pride's Purge and the trial of the king, and he offered his services to the martyr king on the day of his execution. In the 1650s, still licenser of the press, and now President of Sion College, Calamy urged Oliver Cromwell not to accept the crown. After the death of the Protector, he threw his lot in with his son Richard, but with the suspension of Parliament in 1659, turned to George Monck, whose actions helped to bring about the Stuart Restoration, and whose chaplain Calamy became in 1660. Present at negotiations to bring back the king in a delegation to Charles in Holland in May of that year, Calamy was appointed one of the returning king's chaplains-in-ordinary at the Restoration.

By August 1662, however, Calamy was preaching his farewell sermon at St. Mary Aldermanbury, the congregation he had served since 1639, and by January 1663 he was in prison. Calamy was the first nonconformist to be subject to the penalty of the Act of Uniformity, committed to Newgate under the Lord Mayor's warrant on 6 January 1663 for having preached illegally on 29 December. To many he was a saint testing the government's strength of commitment to Uniformity and the king's resolve; to Clarendon he was seditious. Outside Newgate prison, the street was blocked by the coaches of his visitors, and he was apparently visited by one of the king's mistresses. A cause célèbre for tolerationists, as Richard Baxter reported, "many daily flocking to visit him," Calamy attracted contemporary public comment in the press, with the proceedings of the trial recounted in a pamphlet.[2] There was a printed rebuttal by an Anglican minister who accused Calamy and others of conspiring to "inflame and engage the people

I

unto rebellion."[3] Much comment and poetry appeared as a result of the affair.[4] Calamy's preaching was taken as part of a broad conspiracy of non-conformists to topple the government.[5] An anonymous satire was published under the name *Hudibras*, the title of Samuel Butler's enormously successful mock-heroic poem caricaturing Presbyterians and sectaries. The would-be *Hudibras* complained that "'Tis He who taught the *Pulpit* and the *Press* To mask *Rebellion* in a *Gospel-dress*."[6] A competing poem praising Calamy was written by the Presbyterian Robert Wild, perhaps the most widely read top-ical Dissenting poet, his works repeatedly attracting satirical response and also surviving in commonplace books of verse miscellanies of the period.[7] Wryly noting that the figure of the unjustly incarcerated was now a cliché, still Wild had sympathy for the victim:

> *Newgate* or *Hell* were *Heav'n*, if Christ were there,
> He made the Stable so, and Sepulcher.
> Indeed the place did for your presence call;
> Prisons do want perfuming most of all.
> Thanks to the Bishop, and his good Lord Mayor,
> Who turn'd the Den of Thieves into a House of Prayer:
> And may some Thief by you converted be,
> Like him who suffer'd in Christs company.[8]

On Calamy's behalf, Baxter interceded with the king to obtain a release, which was granted on 13 January 1663 on the grounds that Calamy had preached "with the privity of several lords of the Council, and not in contempt of law."[9] The news journal *Mercurius Publicus* was outraged "to see so high an affront" to king and Parliament offered such clemency. The Commons on 19 February referred it to a committee to inquire further, and addressed the king against toleration.[10] The new Surveyor of the Press, Sir Roger L'Estrange, castigated Calamy's sermon as highly objectionable.[11] In October 1663, however, there was a neighborhood movement to reinstate Calamy to the pulpit at Aldermanbury, "the good people thire very much desiring him."[12] Calamy never regained an official ministerial post, though he preached every Sunday evening from his house. He was buried in the fire ruins of his beloved St. Mary Aldermanbury in 1666.

Whether he was considered a dangerous rebel or a sober Protestant martyr, the Restoration Dissenter was caught between two opposing rep-resentations. Yet Calamy's case shows the complexity of reducing religious positions to political factions. Royalist yet willing to test his king, Calamy remained true to his convictions regarding church ceremony in times when differing political leaders made varying political demands; he was willing to go to gaol for his beliefs. Writers took up Calamy's case as a means to discuss the nature and scope of community; through him they represented powerful conflicts within the polity over how to accept religious difference. A symbol of political energies which were dangerous to unity, Calamy embodied a threat to the social order. An emblem of the steadfast nature of the godly, Calamy was a martyr in the dissident press; as one commentator remarked on his case, "But precious in the sight of the Lord, is the Blood of his holy ones."[13] Blood was, after all, recently washed from the battlefields of the English civil war. Although there was no actual blood in Calamy's imprisonment, the stakes seemed just as high.

This is a book about Milton's England, that is, about the cultural, religious, and political currents in England that gave rise to Milton's great, lasting works of poetry, *Paradise Lost*, *Samson Agonistes*, and *Paradise Regain'd*, all published in the Restoration when Milton was a political outcast. I use the title *Milton's* England rather than *Restoration* England or *Dryden's* England, in order to challenge how we perceive this period in literary history, and to bring Dissent (with its English Revolutionary past) to the fore. The book shows how Milton's England was also Calamy's England; how through works of literature, the defeated and excluded produced a vibrant culture, made sense of their experience of loss, and how their literature was embedded in significant social action. For many Dissenters, Calamy and Milton included, the prime challenge was to maintain commitment to God despite persecution. In Dissenting literature, these outcasts constructed shared memories, a powerful force in the service of this task of faith. We will see Dissenting ministers' funerals as sites for the performances of survival of an endangered community; hymns as a means of sharing in social practice; and poetry as a means to reconcile self and world.

This book has two central aims. First, it observes how, as a community and a political concept, dissent was created through cultural forms arising from an experience of social exclusion. Beyond "The Age of Dryden," it will be shown, the period 1660–1700 encompassed a range of writing that has been largely, and unjustly, neglected. Dissenters' literary and cultural legacies helped to assure the vitality and coherence of their invented tradition.[14] Milton, it will be shown, was no mere holdover from the Renaissance. Rather, his preoccupations were absolutely in tune with his contemporary Dissenting writers. Their distinctive, Dissenting cultural contribution challenges the current periodization's conceptions of literary history, aesthetic value, and the relation between literature and politics. The literary historian Neil Keeble has investigated how "literary creativity, composition and reading were vital not merely to the survival of nonconformity has been driven by my observing intolerance and religious fundamentalism restored around the globe today. I began this book well before the dramatic events of September 2001, and yet its completion I hope might shed some light on a quite different cultural moment where religious violence was both feared and welcomed.

In the United States, the country of my birth, I have long worried over the degree to which religious arguments undergird political life, seeking to understand the origins of the possible violent subtext of some theocratic world views in England's Puritan past. On the one hand, I see the noble tradition of conscientious religious activism in the United States, its importance in struggles to confirm the rights of oppressed minorities when civil laws were unjust; on the other hand, I have also worried about the violent antinomian or "enthusiastic" elements of an outlook that prizes the hereafter rather than the worldly here and now, its tendency towards intolerance in the name of Truth. Seventeenth-century Dissenters make a powerful case for the workings of the spirit in the world and speak most sympathetically for a higher justice. Just so, the Enlightenment confrontation with Enthusiasm is an important legacy to recover in order to understand the dangers and benefits of the intertwining of religious authority with political action.

POLITICAL MEANINGS

Restoration Dissent came into existence by an act of state, though not with the return of the monarchy. Many nonconformists, like Edmund Calamy, were heart-felt royalists, and it is a mistake simply to equate anti-royalism with Dissent. Although Charles' installation as monarch after the English Revolution had brought hopes for wider latitude for religious practices, these were undermined by the Anglican royalist Parliaments, which pursued instead a policy of religious persecution in order to secure their goal of uniformity of religious belief and worship. Beginning in 1662, with the Act of Uniformity Parliament legislated a strict penal code, and followed this with other legislation of increasing severity over the next decade. The Book of Common Prayer, in abeyance during the Cromwellian era, was reinstated, and repressive laws passed in the 1660s and 1670s defined those who provided or attended services outside established churches as nonconformists and therefore criminals.

Persecution of Dissent, moreover, was discontinuous across the period. There were several bursts of punitive activity: at the beginning of Charles' reign; following the passage of the Second Conventicle Act in 1670; during the Tory reaction and the defeat of exclusion (1681–86), especially in the aftermath of the Duke of Monmouth's rebellion against James II in 1685.[16] Charles II signed a Declaration of Indulgence in 1672, and within ten months more than 2,500 licenses for nonconformist preachers were issued. The declaration was soon revoked, however, and nonconformists once again met in private houses or in secret. Bringing an awkward alliance between some Dissenters and Catholics, James II suspended all laws against nonconformists and Catholics in 1687 and issued a second Declaration of Indulgence in 1688. The Quaker William Penn welcomed James II's toleration, while many other Dissenters hated it.[17] The Toleration Act of 1689 came with William III, still excluding Catholics, but permitting varieties of nonconformist worship if not office holding. During the period 1662–89, then, Dissenters' resistance to the state church varied according to politics, no less than theology and status. There were significant differences between, for example, the Presbyterians' search for an accommodation within the Anglican orthodoxy and the Quakers' flagrant rejection of it. All nonconformists, however, raised significant theological and practical challenges to the normative state church, and many maintained unorthodox and outlawed practices of worship, whether surreptitiously, privately, or by skirting technicalities of the law in these uneven periods.

Who were the Dissenters? This general nominative includes such a range as the self-educated Baptist preacher John Bunyan, with his long-suffering in prison, his poor-man's ardent Calvinism, his robust apocalypticism, and the Cambridge-educated Latin Secretary to Oliver Cromwell John Milton, whose friends procured his release from prison, a figure who moved towards Arminianism in belief, of whose public worship we have no record, and whose declining years were spent composing a poem meant to outshine all other poems before it, and who was buried in an Anglican parish church. Dissenters after the Restoration were a heterogeneous lot, radical Quakers as well as conservative Presbyterians, sometimes royalists like Calamy, with antimonarchist Independents (Congregationalists) and Baptists in between.[18] Children of the great religious upheaval of the early modern period, Restoration Dissenters were heirs to Puritanism, a movement within the Elizabethan church that sought to reconstitute the national form of religion, and that had reworked the relationship between God and man and the shape and scope of a national church.[19] During the English civil war period, a range of experiments in ecclesiastical organization was undertaken by the new regimes; during this period sectarian activity flourished.[20] Honed by civil war violence and apocalypticism, Restoration Dissenters comprise the remnants of the radical wing of the Reformation.

In 1660 the returning monarchists sought to eliminate this complex legacy of religious and political activism. With the noise of the recent civil wars still echoing in their ears, many Anglican royalists vigilantly opposed religious diversity, and, amidst rising fears of international popery and domestic sedition, they hardened religious nonconformists into the political figures of Dissenters. Their policies of religious uniformity led to the expulsion of over 2,000 ministers, clergy, and lecturers – at least one in five – from livings between 1660 and 1662 for refusing to conform to the newly defined orthodoxy, pushing even moderate Presbyterians, who would have supported a national church, into separation.[21] The nonconformists' resistance was warranted by a fundamental perception of Christian liberty that was at once belief and action.[22] The Act of Uniformity was followed by a series of laws, enforced to a greater or lesser degree over the next decades, which diminished civil liberties and due process of law for Dissenters on a massive scale. A thorny problem was "occasional conformity," which was taken by the authorities as dissent, apathy, or irreligion, seen in a census of 1676 as a threat to the Anglican interest.[23] Numbering something over 340,000, in the late seventeenth and early eighteenth centuries, Dissenters made up about six percent of the population as a whole.[24] Despite the 1689 Toleration Act, when the Anglican church turned away from outright persecution of nonconformists, England suffered resurgent crises over theology and loyalty, with Test and Corporation Acts, not rescinded until 1828–29, signs of Dissent's ongoing political volatility.[25] From the Restoration until the Reform Bill period then, over one hundred and fifty years in English social life, those who remained outside of the Anglican church were Dissenters, officially excluded from office and university, denied legitimate burial in parish churchyards and marriage in their own meeting houses, even though many found ways of bending the rules. Nonetheless, Dissenters carried on a tradition of freedom of thought, self-government, and political radicalism, and, in their literature, sought to transform the world and to find a place in it.[26]

After the massive failure of political and godly reform in the English Revolution in the mid-seventeenth century, the English Dissenters, the subjects of my study, found themselves excluded from political society and subject to religious persecution.[27] With the challenges to royal succession during repeated crises, many nonconformists assisted in formal political opposition to the Crown.[28] But the majority of nonconformists were not willing to participate in seditious plotting; after 1660, Quakers abjured violent uprising, and, from prison, the Baptist John Bunyan counseled patience to his frustrated and persecuted parishioners. Presbyterians hoped for a comprehensive church settlement which would widen the scope of religious practice; in calling for this political solution they eschewed rebellious uprising. This majority of peaceful souls nonetheless resisted state authority by refusing to come into a state church.

This book understands radical action not simply as overt or covert political intention, then, but also through the social settings in which Dissenters produced their resistance; in the theologies that underscored the role of God in human action; and in the imaginative resources from which they built schemes of apocalyptic revenge. The social meaning of the nonconformist funeral, for instance, went far beyond the stated political content of those preaching the sermons, as those in attendance found themselves gathered in an assembly that challenged the state's ban on nonconformist worship. Likewise, we may search in vain for radical political content in the many hymns produced by Dissenting writers; instead, we must look to the situation of the hymn in nonconformist worship, its coded references to anterior biblical moments, to understand how it flaunted the Anglican service and organized people to express solidarity and protest. How did religious commitment gird political activism and redefine it?

Indeed from an experience of dispossession and social exclusion, many nonconformists who gave up on earthly political solutions expressed their radicalism through imaginative writing filled with dreams of apocalyptic revenge. In their political counsel, even as some Dissenters refused outright rebellion against the state, still they recused themselves from the uniform church, and embraced hopes for apocalyptic change. In revaluing violence, they also raised theological questions about the role of the Holy Spirit. Though this may have seemed like a political withdrawal into a "paradise within," ruminations on divine agency through doctrines of the Holy Spirit, such as those of the Independent John Owen, who devoted a lengthy treatise to the subject, can be seen as a strategic revaluation of the nature of human action.

After the return of monarchy in 1660, many of the Puritan godly retreated from the radical activism of their Revolution experiences, forsaking the quest for the reign of King Jesus in this world. And yet beliefs in radical millenarianism, the hopes that end-time was near, were hardly quiet.[29] Out of their experience of political defeat, nonconformist writers sought in withdrawal a construction of a radical political identity. We might think of these consequences not solely in terms of a tremendous outpouring of writing – and superb writing at that (*Paradise Lost*, *Paradise Regain'd*, *Samson Agonistes*, *Pilgrim's Progress*) – but also in terms of poetics. The theological and political radicalism of the Revolutionary years as well as the failure of political hopes with the advent of Uniformity in 1662 gave new urgency to Dissenting writers. They wrestled with authority in their concern over imitation and originality; they experimented with poetic form, voice, figuration, genre, and metaphor; and they politicized the aesthetic categories of inspiration and the sublime. These are consequences of the experience of Puritanism in the seventeenth century, in short, a legacy of the English Revolution.

Just as the Restoration state did, however, by using the term Dissenter, so do we risk reducing an important complexity, a range of positions, to a singular nominative. As Neil Keeble, the foremost scholar of the literary culture of nonconformity, points out, the effect of persecuting laws "was to forge the corporate identity of dissent."[30] There is a risk in overstressing the variance of Dissent from Anglicanism at a time when the practice of "occasional conformity" was common, when many nonconformists were hard at work to find reconciliation with the state church through policies of "Comprehension," and when Anglicanism itself was undergoing significant transformation.[31] It is true that some nonconformists and Anglicans were often not far apart in belief, politics, and worship; nonetheless the often sharp polemical divides do tell us an important story of perceptions and cultural meanings. Doctrinal differences within English Protestantism during the early modern period were indeed significant motors for conflicts over ceremony and ecclesiology. This book is not a study of the denominational differences between various groups of nonconformists, nor a literary history of particular theological or sectarian traditions. I have not separated the various strands within Dissent to tell a history of the changes within various sects over time. Those kinds of histories are available, and more are needed.[32] In order to assess the broad meanings of religious opposition in a society just newly washed of the blood of civil war, here I am more interested in the common characteristics of the "unorthodox" than in their differences. Dissenter, in short, is the loose way I designate what can be generalized in habits from those who embraced many different themes, but who all lived out variations on these two: a Protestant belief in the immediate apprehension of the divine; and a refusal to partake in compelled religious ceremonialism, exemplified by unwillingness to join the English state-sponsored church after the Restoration government's legislation of 1662.

CONSTRUCTING DISSENT

The stories told about Dissent are multiple, and contradictory. To those outside the tradition, Dissenters were dangerous radicals who resisted not simply the state religion, but politeness and civility *tout court*. This is the point of view still tacitly adopted by the literary periodization of the era as the "Age of Dryden." Conventional literary history has observed that the Restoration period brought with it a search for poetic order and decorum, a revival of classical modes in a bid to leap over recent history in appeal to a shared – allegedly neutral – past, one remote in time and place. In the realms of architecture and urban design, with the splendors of Christopher Wren, the efflorescence of the London stage, in painting, the decorative arts, and in the shapely music of Handel and Purcell, English cultural production after the civil wars exalted the values of the ancients, rewritten as imperial order, balance, openness, cosmopolitanism, and publicity. This Restoration mode was a public, sociable mode, with the lashings of satire's whip leaving lasting marks on the literary imagination. Even the heroic couplet, rising to a prominence it would hold until Coleridge and Wordsworth's dismantling, marks that balance, harmony, and hoped-for reconciliation of opposites.[33] This literary characterization of the period leaves the writing of Dissent invisible.

To accept that invisibility, I suggest, is to concede that the English Revolution was indeed a failure. It is a main objective of this book to show how the writing by and about Dissenters was – and is – politically motivated and still doing important cultural work. Reformed religion had produced an iconoclastic sensibility, and with it forms of literary expression, which did not go away. Indeed, both Anglican and nonconformist poets continued a devotional literary tradition that was at odds with both the decorous neo-classicism and the libertinism of the Stuart court.[34] The poetry of writers such as George Wither and George Herbert gave to English writers a lasting interest in recording the multitude of inner states, whether contemplation, repose, or chastisement. A literary tradition, just as had a radical political tradition, vaunted the workings of conscience – a conscience that could only be observed in the inward reflection of God and the individual soul.[35] As they resisted mandated church forms in their religious practice, so too their literary practice was one of devotional iconoclasm. In objection to and in dialogue with the public modes of satirical poetry as well as with the libertinism of courtly verse, the Dissenting muse after the Restoration seemed to live in the shadows, perpetually wedded to the dark notes of elegy, fastidiously cultivating an almost-impossible otherworldliness.

Even if orthodoxy sought to silence them, Dissenters were nonetheless all too visible in the imaginations of their enemies. The conservative Anglican apologist Samuel Parker called Dissenters "Brain-sick People," "morose," repeatedly contrasting their irrational or "fanatique tempers" to his own "sober," "rational," and "civil" approach to religion. Nonconformists' irrationality extended to their writing style, as Parker accused them of "hiding themselves in a maze of Words... rowling up and down in canting and ambiguous Expressions."[36] Parker linked these communicative failures with unstable politics, stressing "the natural tendency of Enthusiasm and Superstition to public disturbance."[37] Thomas Hobbes, writing in *Behemoth* in 1668 of the causes and consequences of the civil wars, faulted crafty preachers: the people "admire nothing but what they understand not"; and were "cozened" with "words not intelligible."[38] For Samuel Parker, the source of all this muddle was Dissenters' emphasis on individual conscience: "their Consciences are seized on by such morose and surly Principles, as make them the rudest and most barbarous People in the World; and that in comparison of them, the most insolent of the Pharisees were Gentlemen, and the most salvage of the *Americans* Philosophers."[39] Their reliance on conscience rendered nonconformists no better than savages, unreliable as preachers, teachers, office-holders, and citizens. The printed frontispiece to the anti-Dissenter pamphlet, *Cabala: Or, The Mystery of Conventicles Unvail'd* (1664) shows the powerful connection between nonconformist religious worship and feared violent insurrection (see Figure 1). In the upper half of the diptych an armed band cries "No Bishops." The lower part depicts the discovery of their "conventicle," where knives, swords, and pistols are laid on the table whilst the leader of prayer presides over a sectarian congregation including women and men. Dissenting religion is one and the same as rebellion.[40]

To many Anglican royalists, Dissent also became the sign of the unlawful and unlicensed dispersal of information and ideas to the wrong sorts of people. For instance, in his portrait of Dissent, John Dryden offers a special case of the worry, present since the Reformation, about scriptural exegesis by the all and many. Dryden offers perhaps the most brilliant portrait of the Dissenter as the dangerous and uncivil subject, and his ideas help us see how Dissenters posed serious threats not simply to political and religious stability, but how their social practices heralded a major shift in English cultural life as well. Dryden repeatedly took digs at nonconformists through the 1660s and 1670s from the perspective of an Anglican Tory. Even when turned Catholic, Dryden barely withheld his contempt. In *The Hind and the Panther*, the sectarian radicals are the lowest of the low; as "A slimy-born and sun-begotten tribe," they are barely discernible as creatures vested with God's care. To figure his human concerns in bestial form, in fable, is to denote their degradation. But these fanatics are beyond artistic representation, "nor will the Muse describe" them, he writes of these "Gross, half-animated lumps."[41]

Figure 1 Title page to David Lloyd, *Cabala: Or, The Mystery of Conventicles Unvail'd*
(1664).

Dryden's opposition to the swarm of interpreters newly empowered by Protestant bibliolatry is often confused with antipopulism: yet his is not antipopulism in any simple sense. Rather, Dryden's terror of the Many-Headed Reader is linked to a cluster of associations in the economic register which evoke the dangers of fungibility, interchangeability, and, in short, warn against commodity consumption. Dryden's strategy of distinguishing authority from its opposite governs the prospect of social order in his poems, and his political ideas take the specific form of an observation on the excess of social mobility advanced by a particular historical mode of religion, for which Dissent becomes the sign.

Dryden is right in seeing that Dissenters' reading and writing habits did sap authority from elites in power. In *Religio Laici*, Dryden uses economic metaphors to narrate the history of how people wrested religious authority away from the priests: "That what they thought the *Priests'*, was *Their* estate," Dryden writes in evoking the specter of the great transfer of church wealth into private hands. He describes the motive to consume directly what had before been mediated by authorized figures: "every man who saw the Title fair/ Claim'd a Child's part, and put in for a Share."[42] The people's assuming an economic agency does not represent a triumph of right, however; rather, it is Dryden's nightmare of unbounded consumption. Again, *Religio Laici*: "The Book thus put in every vulgar hand,/ Which each pre-sum'd he best cou'd understand,/ The *Common Rule* was made the *common Prey*/ And at the mercy of the Rabble lay" (400–03). The "common rule," perhaps the "Golden rule" of the Bible, that doctrine of the reversibility of good acts, has disintegrated into a terrifying fantasy of social leveling. The double sense of the word "common" articulates a double threat: that of accessibility through dissemination, and that which is low or vulgar. With the pun on "common prey," or common prayer, the language of predatory relation depicts reading in all its brutal carnality. If the language is that of commodity consumption, then indeed the voracious, hungry, physical need-driven acts classify the consumers as rank sensualists "preying" on their victims:

> The tender page with horney Fists was gaul'd;
> And he was gifted most that loudest baul'd:
> The *Spirit* gave the *Doctoral Degree*:
> And every member of a Company
> Was of *his Trade* and of the *Bible free*.
> Plain *Truths* enough for needfull *use* they found;
> But men wou'd still be itching to *expound* . . .

This was the Fruit the *private Spirit* brought;
Occasion'd by *great Zeal* and little *Thought*.
While crouds unlearn'd, with rude Devotion warm,
About the Sacred Viands buzz and swarm,
The *Fly-Blown Text* creates a *crawling Brood*;
And turns to *Maggots* what was meant for *Food*.
A Thousand daily sects rise up and dye;
A Thousand more the perish'd race supply.
(*Religio Laici*, 404–22)

These class attacks resolve into a quotable aphorism, a linguistic normalization, impersonally marking an allegedly universal truth to which all can assent. By comparing this disturbing social arrangement to corrupted nature, Dryden makes the rejection of dissenting bibliophilia, with its "private reason," seem inevitable. Likewise, Samuel Butler's *Hudibras*, in attacking radical sectaries and Presbyterians, gives a similar image of texts and maggots:

Religion spawn'd a various Rout,
Of Petulant Capricious Sects,
The Maggots of Corrupted Texts,
That first Run all Religion down,
And after every swarm its own.
For as the *Persian Magi* once,
Upon their *Mothers*, got their *Sons*,
That were incapable t'injoy,
That Empire any other way;
So *Presbyter* begot the other,
Upon the *Good Old Cause* his Mother.[43]

There, the accusation is corrupt genealogy and incestuous generation, twin problems of the Stuart succession after the execution of Charles and the installation of Commonwealth and Protectorate regimes.

Dryden's accusation, as the contrast with Butler makes clear, is very much a reflection upon private zeal and public access. Dryden charges that the unlearned were coming to see themselves as possessing authority, here authority to interpret the Bible. This is felt as repulsive; the reader is called upon to alter that situation, to defend that precious victim, the "tender page," from such a rude assault, rude in its class origins, rude in its mannerless and disgusting corporeality (itching, horny fists, warm devotion), and corrupt in its effects, turning into maggots – putrefied meat – what was before good food (in a twist on the traditional meaning of the eucharist). The Anglican royalist Robert Whitehall, celebrating the

coronation of Charles II, ridiculed the spiritual and political usurpation of
the lower orders during the civil war period:

> See, and admire, this Fellow laying down
> His Awl and Stirrup, is no longer clowne;
> But sit's upon the Bench, and winks and nods,
> As gravely, as if sent us by the Gods.[44]

Dryden and Whitehall are thinking of the ideas and social position of a
writer like the self-educated Baptist Samuel How, who was a cobbler by
trade, and who published his *Sufficiencie of the Spirits Teaching without
Human Learning* in 1640, admired for "The *Spirits teaching* in a *Coblers
shop*."[45] This book became a runaway bestseller, reprinted seven times
through the seventeenth century, and nine times in the eighteenth.

The promises of freedom; of equality of interpretation; of claims to
innate authority; and of the rule of conscience, are all axioms of democratic
ideology, including the belief that anyone, including Dryden, can read, or
change places, or succeed. But these axioms are also the age's chief sources of
social anxiety. Dryden's nightmare of biblical access reveals the functional
instability of social hierarchy in his time. His condemnation of dispersed
authority is at every moment dependent upon the resources of literacy and
education, forms of cultural capital, as John Guillory has called it, which
are paradoxically the enabling condition of Dryden's poem. Early modern
Puritans had been great endowers and patrons of educational institutions,
and with their loss of power, there was a loss of such charitable bequests.
With suspicion of popular education, there was also a sharp decline in the
growth of basic literacy after 1680, a marked slowing in classical secondary
and university education, closing routes to advancement following those
means. "In quantitative terms," the historian Lawrence Stone has written,
"English higher education did not get back to the level of the 1630s until
after the first World War." That educational depression began in the second
half of the seventeenth century.[46] Enough education, but not too much,
will hold the precarious social order in balance.

As his *Religio Laici* makes clear, Dryden acutely saw that education
had caused destabilizing social effects, particularly education of the wrong
sort; these are, after all, "crouds unlearn'd" for whom "The *Spirit* gave
the *Doctoral Degree*." If non-institutionalized learning had created opportunities for social mobility, then Dryden synecdochally indicts the wider
processes of communication and dissemination of cultural authority in
his own time. Those would include a public eager for a nontraditional,
lay, education: coffeehouse culture; formal evening lectures by leading

nonconformists: other non-orthodox sites of education were Dissenting grammar schools and vocational academies.[47] The wide availability of printed matter was a process from which Dryden himself benefited, but it also created and responded to an uncontrollable audience for that literature. All these are forms against which his defense of the established church in *Religio Laici* is meant to be braced.

By blaming the mid-century civil war on radical religion, Restoration apologists such as Dryden and Butler discounted the idea that private spiritual authority had any kind of role in political legitimation. The success of Samuel Butler's *Hudibras*, running to three parts, and provoking many imitators and an execrable literary legacy, tells us how much those having lived through the civil war period wanted easy targets: but he hit upon the right target. As we shall see, doctrines of the Holy Spirit did indeed challenge civil and ecclesiastical authority; further, they authorized violence. Butler's poem saw how irrational forces, ridiculed as spasms of popular revolt, humans' foolish adherence to their spiritual hunger, and power-lust, were the causes of civil war. At heart what the poem recoils against is the danger of fanaticism. Ralph, Hudibras' squire, is of the company of those who "speak by this *new Light*" (497): with a charismatic authority, "A Light that falls down from on high,/ For Spiritual Trades to cousen by";

> For Spiritual Men are too Transcendent,
> That mount their Banks, for Independent.
> To hang like Mahomet, in th'Air,
> Or St. Ignatius, at his Prayer,
> By Pure Geometry, and hate
> Dependence, upon Church, or State.[48]

The problem with inspiration was not only that it spoke from within the individual, but that it heralded its authority as coming from the realm of the divine. Recognizing the political dangers of this transcendent view, Dryden likewise repeatedly represented sectarians' prophetic utterances as dangerous misapplications of individual intention. In his satire against the Whigs, "The Medall" (1681–82), Dryden persistently sought to devalue the Dissenters' authoritative claims from the Bible:

> 'Twas fram'd, at first, our Oracle t'enquire;
> But, since our Sects in prophecy grow higher,
> The Text inspires not them; but they the Text inspire.[49]

In a similar vein, the conservative Anglican minister Benjamin Laney, preaching to King Charles in 1664, rejected the claims of those defending liberty of conscience. Like Dryden and Butler, Laney adopts a language of mistaken perception, false illumination, and here we can see how the critique of religious enthusiasm is also a critique of antisociality:

Let loose to the prejudices and fancies of every man; for then it will fall out, as with those that look in a Glass, in which every one sees his own face, though not anothers; the reason is because he brings his face to the *Glass*, not because it was there before. So every Sect sees the face of his own Religion in the Scripture, not because it was there before, but because his strong fancy and prejudice brought it thither; he thinks he sees that in the Scripture, which in truth is only in his own imagination.⁵⁰

To Laney, to refuse mediation of the professional priesthood is to indulge in a dangerous solipsism. Those defending the Restoration state and church found themselves, like Laney, reaching for principles of communicative rationality, a secular alternative to the individualistic, charismatic authority of the prophet.

The uncivilized prophet vs. civility of rational norms: in these conservative accounts of civil war politics, then, we have an Enlightenment binary pair. Defenders of the Restoration church thus posited communicative norms as a brace against the violence of prophecy or the inner callings of conscience. The Anglican diagnosis of radical prophecy bore a political imprint, transforming the radical opposition between earthly/otherworldly into a neater civil/uncivil binary pair. The binary opposition between ecstatic prophecy and rational conformity was one fiction created to attempt the control of the unruly subject, and to combat an opposition between World and Truth by secular means. But at a deeper level, the Anglican response was an accurate assessment of some of the implications of wide biblical access, antinomianism, and inspired religion.

To those inside Dissent, on the other hand, their story was one of heroic martyrdom, stoical suffering, and patience, relieved by divine providence in the Glorious Revolution of 1688. The generation of 1662, those ejected from their posts by the edict of Uniformity, were written about, pictured in frontispiece portraits, had their works reprinted in pirated and official editions, and their sayings excerpted to be hung on household walls for inspiration. The political stakes of the Dissenting martyrologies proliferating in the press were clear. A contemporary squib marked how clichéd the genre of Dissenting martyrology had become: "And whereas Mr. *Fox* that good man hath written the suffering of such as held the Word of God patiently under the great Tryal in Queen *Maries* days... That eminent Patriot Mr *Prynne* hath taken great pains to publish his own and his

Brethrens sufferings in thos elaborate pieces." The press, it was once again noted, was a chief ally of Dissent, as this observer remarked, "about this time [1 September 1663] Mr. *Baxter* moved, that seeing he and others were silenced, their soul-saving Works might be immediately reprinted," and the list of reprinted works includes the politically radical civil war period tracts, *Smectymnuus, Lex Rex, Holy Commonwealth*, "most of *Milton* and Mr. *Goodwyn's* Papers," along with works in Protestant hagiography and controversy from the time of Queen Elizabeth.[51] Dissenters to be sure elicited sympathy by casting their experiences in a heroic light, relying upon known habits of interpreting suffering after the model of Christ. Their printing and disseminating such models was recognized as a primary mode of survival.

Dissenters, barred from pulpits and forbidden to assemble in public, sought a means to construct and maintain community through writing, as Neil Keeble has shown. The impact of this culture of publishing and disseminating their material was greater than their particular cause; indeed, Dissenters contributed to a fundamental change in political culture in early modern England. By their repeated appearances in print, Dissenters would simply not go away; and by their commitments to publicity, openness, and generative dispute, they wrote for the many, barely literate included, expanding the culture of political knowledge at a time when there was a general expansion of the public sphere.

From the moment of their exile from the national church, nonconformists thus created an alternative characterization to that of dangerous fanatics by which they were stereotyped by their enemies. Building on the paradigm of heroic martyrdom enshrined in John Foxe's *Actes and Monuments*, they attracted sympathy for themselves as victims and celebrated their depredations through copious publication. Joseph Besse's *A Collection of the Sufferings of the People Called Quakers* arouses sympathy by its title.[52] Sympathy was only one intention; creating a tradition was another. Richard Baxter's autobiography was transformed into a heroic and collective story of many Dissenters by Edmund Calamy, reworked as Samuel Palmer's list of ejected ministers, *The Nonconformist's Memorial* (which remains a chief reference tool in the study of Dissent).[53] That title bears a name which fuses the genres of funerary commemoration and history. This cult of heroic victimhood marks later historiography, from the Victorian studies whose sentimentalism about suffering saints helped to push through Reformist legislation, to the primary modernist account, Max Weber's *Protestant Ethic and the Spirit of Capitalism*, which is based upon

Figure 2 Frontispiece to Benjamin Keach, *War with the Devil* (1683).

that magnificent and partisan Victorian historiography.[54] This archetype of a tragic Puritan dissent has made it hard to perceive Dissenters on any other terms.

Dissenters who resisted state persecution on the grounds of conscience during the Restoration period prominently made a structural divide between civil and spiritual, a binary pairing of World and Truth. The two images fronting Benjamin Keach's *War with the Devil* (1683; see Figure 2) offer a striking instance of this habit of mind. There the embattled sixteen year old in his "converted state" combats the devil and an armed band by means of his Book; but he also opposes worldliness, the public standards of civility and taste of a fine doublet and feather cap, ruffles and curls, dancing townspeople, trappings of his former, "naturall" self. Indeed, breaking away from the here and now was at the heart of many Dissenters' experiences, and the phenomenology of conversion illustrated here rigorously asserted this split. Scholars hold that after the return of monarchy in 1660, the Puritan godly turned inward, retreated from the radical activism of their revolution days. The "paradise within thee, happier far" vaunted by *Paradise Lost* defines this post-Restoration quietism. Yet, Puritan rejection of worldliness by the authority of conscience also became the basis of a kind of political radicalism that threatened the legitimation of the Restored regimes.

By examining literature and Dissent – literature by and about Dissenters – this book explores how the discourse of charismatic authority, and its opposite, the self-disciplined political subject, registered an important engagement with the complex political consequences of religious radicalism. However much Anglican Tories constructed all Dissenters as prophetically inspired or as dangerous interpreters and disseminators of unorthodoxy, that construction also became a problem for Dissenters in contests over rationality, voluntarism, authority, and community raging across the period. The civil war period inaugurated a series of responses in the political and religious registers that gave rise to discourses of secularization by various means, from within as well as from outside Dissent. One consequence was the opposition between religious enthusiasm and civility; another was the creation of a private sphere of uncontaminated conscience. Paradoxically, the processes of secularization made Dissent a functional part of the polity.

Literature, as I hope to show, was a primary means of effecting this transformation. In their literature, Dissenters suggest early modern paradoxes: as they warred against the world in an intense desire to communicate with the divine, they also forged lateral bonds to their living communities and diachronic bonds to their projected heirs. As they delighted in their superiority to the vanities of this world, they doubted their very worthiness as objects of God's care. They proposed a radical understanding of the relationship between writing and action in the world, often maintaining a tradition of iconoclastic radicalism by means that were not simply challenging state authority. Writing and publishing a democratic literature, hoping to reach to the very least capable in society, they participated in a number of specific assaults on traditional society: they numbered women and the poor among their authors; they depended on the new resources of printing to communicate over large distances; they prized direct access to the sources of authority, both scriptural and political. In these matters, Dissent shares in the successes of the English Revolution. Milton's great poems track the complex states of mind as well as the political consequences of living through bloody civil war, political experiment, loss and deprivation, and reflect upon the possibilities and dangers of religiously inspired action. His were among the many powerful works of commemoration and calls for renewed faith. The mid-century crisis left a remainder, registered by some as an urgency over the problem of civility, figured as a contest between fanaticism and cultural advance. In spite of a campaign to barbarize nonconformity, nonetheless, Dissenters did not simply retreat into political quietism, or even what E. P. Thompson has called a "slumbering Radicalism."[55] On the contrary, their primary assaults on the integrity of the authoritarian state took many creative forms, not all of them outrightly seditious: their robust imaginative voices are the subjects of the following chapters.

CHAPTER 2

Memory

"I desire to dye in the true faith of Christ in the truth contained in
the Scriptures and in the Religion of the Right old English Puritan."
Richard Thorp (d. 1671), Will, 19 May 1663[1]

The year 1660 brought to England the return of the exiled royal heir, and
with him, a terminus of one era of political and ecclesiological experiments and a starting point for another. Ended were structural revolutions
of non-monarchical government and a dis-established church, twin radical
innovations wrought of rebellion, civil war, and regicide. In 1660, the gov-
ernments of this "Restoration" wished to hasten a grand forgetting of that
recent, turbulent past, condemning the "Good Old Cause" to ridicule
at best and ignominy at worst. A statute within two months of the new
monarch's coronation, called a bill "Of Free and General Pardon, Indemnity and Oblivion," spoke of the king's urge to forget: "out of a hearty and
pious desire to put an end to all suits and controversies that by occasion of
the late distractions have arisen and may arise between all subjects."[2] The
act fudged as much as it wished to forget, however, blunting the assignment
of agency and responsibility and instead blurring recent history in innocu-
ous language. On the other hand the general representational matrix of
"Restoration" – which included not only poetry but the state policies of re-
establishment of pre-civil war institutions – took sides on the issue of what
should be forgotten and what remembered.

The return of the Stuart heir to British shores in 1660 may have signaled
the end of the English Revolution, but that year did not close the war over
how to interpret the events of the previous twenty years. The destruction of
civil war residue was, indeed, a central mode of the Stuart political quest for
legitimacy. "Now our sad ruines are remov'd from sight,/ The Season too
comes fraught with new delight": so wished the future laureate John Dryden
in celebrating the coronation of Charles II. After the return of monarchy
to England in 1660, many like Dryden wished to put the past, especially

the immediate past, behind them.[3] Charles changed the names of all the
ships in the fleet that might be associated with the Commonwealth, and
soon after his first entry into London on 29 May, the effigies of Oliver and
Elizabeth Cromwell and the arms of the Commonwealth were burned in
huge bonfires in Westminster. On the date commemorating the execution
of Charles I, 30 January, the actual bodies of Cromwell and the regicides
were unearthed from their resting places and dismembered at Tyburn, their
bodies and heads impaled on pikes for all to see in the City of London,
where they remained, rotting, for months.[4] But the revival of memory was
not without backlash. Revolutionary conflicts also returned in repeated
plots and rebellions against the Stuart regime. Historians, then and now,
have disputed how to write a narrative of the previous twenty years, whether
it was an unfulfilled period of godly reform and divine punishment; or a
perfidious and Satanic rebellion: this interpretive dispute still rages today
in contests over whether to name it the English Revolution, the Great
Rebellion, or the apparently neutral "The English Civil Wars" – which
last designation seems to gloss over the period of Commonwealth and
Protectorates. The contest over memory was there from the first, nowhere
more urgently waged than over the bodies of the dead.

In September 1663, three days after the Baptist preacher Henry Jessey
died, his body was taken to Bethlehem new churchyard, "whereof several thousands of persons of several perswasions assembled." Because of
laws passed against nonconformist assembly, these four or five thousand
mourners had no legal grounds on which to assemble, in what can only
have been felt by those present as a dangerous show of Dissenting strength.
His biographer saw Jessey as a martyred saint: "to accompany him thither
many weeping bitterly, and making great lamentation, complaining of their
loss, according to that wherein he was most useful to each of them, whether
in council, comforting or releiving [sic] their necessities: And as it is said
of *Stephen, Act* 8.2. Devout men carried him to his Burial, and made great
lamentation over him."[5] The funeral gathering was perceived by authorities
as especially threatening since unrest was boiling: there had been risings in
the North during the spring and summer of 1663; Venner had rebelled;
government military upsizing was putting pressure against all forms of opposition. That year saw yet more stringency in Anglican persecution, with
the renewed enforcement of church attendance. Parliamentary legislation
had outlawed Dissenting meetings, and its agents were in the process of persecuting not only ministers, but punishing ordinary nonconformist citizens
for nonattendance at Anglican church meetings. Since Parliament was pro-
rogued on 27 July, further legitimate political resolution to the question

of Dissent would have to wait until the following spring. Rumors of impending revolt spread through the countryside, from the North to London all through the summer and fall of 1663, and Baptists and Quakers were particularly singled out by the authorities for arrest and investigation; the northern insurrection was to have begun 13 October. Some of most radical anti-Stuart pamphlets to make it into print were probably published in time for this funeral, moreoever, available for sale to a large gathering of potentially sympathetic readers.[6]

The Calvinist Baptist Jessey, it was known, remained loyal to the saints' cause even up until the moment of his death. He was a potent reminder of the radicalism of the English Revolution, an associate of the prominent Independents Thomas Goodwin and John Owen, and an extraordinarily active figure in London ministerial politics during the Commonwealth years. He had translated the Bible, worked for the re-admission of the Jews to England, and, after the Restoration, was most likely one of the authors of the anti-royalist interpretation of providences, *Annus Mirabilis* (1661), a work deemed significant enough to merit a negative response from John Dryden, and for which Jessey was tried and imprisoned.[7] His "conventicle," an illegal church at Allhallows the Great in London, was, as one historian puts it, "a showcase for proven sectarian talent."[8] Twice arrested in the Restoration for seditious plotting, Jessey was at the center of nonconformist radical publication and politics. His death was understood to be due to scurvy contracted during his imprisonment.

On his deathbed, Jessey is said to have called on God to begin the destruction of his enemies in a Fifth Monarchist revolt. Authorities noted that Jessey's "dying words were that the Lord would destroy the powers in being, and he encouraged the people to help the great work."[9] Jessey himself had been outlawed from preaching under the Uniformity act of 1662, and he had himself been arrested twice for seditious activity in the early 1660s. At his funeral, at the explicit instructions of the deceased, Jessey's will was read aloud, which reiterated his refusal to conform to those ritual practices of the Anglican church he deemed offensive. It also issued a threat: "Remembering 2 King 23.5. Josiah caused to cease, the Idolatrous Priests."[10] If Jessey's will insisted on the parallel between his own day and that of the reign of biblical King Josiah, descendent of David, who purified the Temple from the idolatrous worship of Baal, and who, since Edward VI's day, was the type of true piety evoked by Protestant reformers, then his words demanded a renewed commitment to purification. Josiah's renewal of the Temple led not only to the removal or breaking of idols and false gods, but also to the slaying of priests. Though his words reflected a traditional attack on ceremonies long familiar to Protestants, in the Restoration, such words would have had double resonance and been interpreted as an assault on the Anglican church.

The historical context of this funeral gives us a key to its political meaning. For Jessey's own words to appear in public, for his will to be read aloud to this assemblage, were acts that worked against the law barring nonconformist ministers like Jessey from making public utterance. Those who attended Jessey's funeral in 1663 were labeled by the conservative press a "strange Medly of *Phanatiques*," a term of abuse used by the Anglican royalist authorities in the Restoration to discredit Dissenting religious groups.[11] Such name-calling was an instance of the deep social and political division left over from the civil war and Revolutionary period, division that focused on the question of the scope and latitude of religious toleration in the Restoration. Religious disorder, it was thought, masked political disorder. This context – with its tense relations between civil and ecclesiastical authority, loyalism, and disobedience, which were being played out over the bodies and in the hearts of the persecuted nonconformists – gave this particular funeral political meanings that went far beyond Jessey as an individual.

Embracing a wider conception of radicalism during a period of political backlash against English Revolutionary activism than we currently possess, this chapter addresses Restoration contests over memory. By exploring the cultural shapes of memory, including funeral, eulogy, tombs, and commemorative verse, this chapter shows that dissent is made not only by words, but by the social exchanges and the social spaces in which the Dissenters produced their resistance: in private chapels, illicit gatherings in fields, and at funerals. The social meaning of nonconformist funerals will be shown to press further into the heart of opposition than the words of the sermons preached at them; for instance, those in attendance found themselves gathered in an assembly that challenged the state's ban on nonconformist worship; they performed rituals denied by the orthodox prayer book; sometimes they heard (or read) radical utterances expressed in the wills of the deceased. In gathering, in commemorating their martyrs, Dissenters forged common experiences that would comprise a memorial legacy of Dissent. Milton's final work, *Samson Agonistes*, will be brought into this context in order to explore how one thinker meditated on the politics of memory.

This chapter sets up several preoccupations of this study: how political action operates at a register other than topical political content; how people maintain solidarity with larger groups despite their dispersal and differences; how innovative uses are made of traditional forms; how context serves content. We may search in vain for radical political content in the many writings produced by Dissenters. Instead, we must look to the situation of the poetry in nonconformist experience, for example to understand how their hymns flaunted the Anglican service; how calling upon biblical history justified continued resistance and organized people to express solidarity. The structure of typology is a central hermeneutics driving the Dissenting construction of community and memory. In English Protestantism, typology was a sanctioned way of making sense of individual and collective experience within a cosmic framework. Through biblical typology, a metaphorical reading of the Bible whereby literal and figurative levels of meaning were condensed, "types" from the Hebrew Bible were matched to antitypes from the New Testament: this was extended to encompass a way of reading history allegorically through a providential and apocalyptic narrative. History, the Fall, the eternal struggle between Christ and his enemies, the Redemption, were all an unfolding pattern of meaningfulness that voided differences in time and place; for Dissenters, the relation between type and antitype was a fundamental structure of knowing. How did Dissenters continue to be Dissenters amidst persecution? I have found their cultural forms doing the work of constructing shared memories.

ACTIVIST MOURNING

From the psychic and political needs of those suffering political and personal loss emerges one of Dissent's most powerful genres in a post-Restoration landscape, the funeral. Along with the social performances of writing, publication, illicit worship, private study groups, private libraries, coffeehouses, booksellers' stalls, as well as other communicative practices along a spectrum of activities through which Dissenters imagined themselves restored to social esteem, the funeral transmitted memory. A martyrological tradition from John Foxe found vitality in heroic commemoration – political as well as personal – and Dissenters made funerals into occasions to recollect individual virtue, to sustain a contract with God, and to consolidate powerful social bonds. Years later, Daniel Defoe built upon this commemorative tradition in recounting the life of the Baptist author Thomas De Laune, who had died in prison, persecuted for publishing a defense of nonconformity in 1682: "The Treatment the Reverend and Learned Author of this Book met with, will for ever stand as a Monument of the Cruelty of those Times." The genre of heroic martyrdom does political work in the realm of memory. Here "lies a Monument of *English Tyranny* on One Hand, and *Selfish Principles* on the Other, both which make Nations blind to Men of Merit," Defoe wrote, and explained his paper eulogy so long after De Laune died: "since no Man will build a Monument upon his Grave, I thought it a Debt due to his ill-rewarded Merit, to write this as a Monument upon his Work, and I am sorry it is perform'd no better."[12] Through funerals, nonconformists placed their individual experiences of suffering into a common fund; they assimilated collective trauma into a positive framework; they presented a memory for the future. The space of the graveyard, too, would be a space of fellowship, a distinctive nonconformist locus of identity. Not simply through words, but by their refusal of state-mandated forms of worship and in their assembly in special spaces outside the authorized church, did Dissenters recognize themselves, and were recognized, as fomenting resistance.

What happened in these Dissenting ministers' funerals was the making and sustaining of a Dissenting community, a construction through mourning of a community out of the loss of the individual member. The work performed by these funerals refutes much current scholarship which gives that the history of death in the early modern period is a story of individuation and privatization.[13] As modernity advances, runs this account, death becomes more private – the beautiful Victorian cemeteries display the ideology of death as pastoral, personal, and to be commemorated through sentimental act and artifact. Though death may have in fact over the course of the early modern period become more commercialized, more commodified, and more bureaucratized, social attitudes towards personal grief and mourning have projected a fantasy that death belongs to the individual.[14] The history of Dissenters' communal actions in funerals however offsets that individualist narrative; on the contrary, their funerary activities shaped communities around potent symbols of collective loss.

After Uniformity, with the abolition of any religious organized meeting outside the Anglican church, funerals were rare occasions when nonconformists did meet in large numbers in public. Whether the funeral was Presbyterian, Independent, Baptist, or Quaker, and despite particular differences in ritual and theology, Dissenters did innovative political work, defying the state by their significant social action. At funerals, mourners often departed from the mandated prayer book's Service for the Dead, with Presbyterians, Independents, and Particular Baptists often returning to the civil war prayer book. Many of the dying requested non-Anglican rites in their wills. Philip Henry reported that between 100 and 120 mourners were in attendance at an Islington funeral for ejected minister John Burgess in

1671, and these different groups of mourners behaved differently, some staying for the "office for the dead," and "part going out."[15] Quakers pushed even further against prayer-book religion in their funerary modes. Amidst the different traditions of funeral practice, the political stakes of Dissenting funerals were remarkably uniform.

The funerals of nonconformist ministers were usually not riotous occasions nor were they often moments of large-scale violent resistance, though they were feared to be so by the authorities. The burial of the Buckinghamshire Quaker Edward Perot or Parret on 1 July 1665 is a case in point. This was a rare recorded instance of physical violence or disruption of a Dissenting funeral; it was forcibly broken up and many of the mourners, including the Quaker Thomas Ellwood, were arrested, following which the coffin was left lying all day in the public road and finally interred in a far corner of the steeple-house yard in Amersham, Buckinghamshire. As Ellwood described it, "most of the Quakers in the country [i.e. county] were come thither to the burial." As the assembled mourners – and there were many, "the deceased having been well-beloved" – gathered up the body on their shoulders to be taken up to the burying ground in an orchard belonging to the deceased, they were violently interrupted. What ensued reveals the way that gatherings could be misconstrued by the authorities. Ellwood describes the interruption of the solemn gathering in a painful scene, where the local JP, one Ambrose Benett, led the charge, rushing out of his inn with his constables with his drawn sword, and "struck one of the foremost of the bearers with it, commanding them to set down the coffin." The Quaker was so frightened that he froze instead of complying. He "held the coffin fast; which the Justice observing, and being enraged that his word (how unjust soever) was not forthwith obeyed, set his hand to the coffin, and with a forcible thrust threw it off from the bearers' shoulders, so that it fell to the ground in this midst of the street, and there we were forced to leave it."[16] Ellwood, Isaac Pennington, and eight other Quakers were held in prison for a month after this event. Those participating in such funerals were taking actions that were read as subversive – they gathered in assembly; they consciously bucked the Anglican prayer book, itself a symbol of the persecuting orthodoxy; and they chose burial places outside local parish churches.

The publication of funeral sermons preached at the burial of nonconformist ministers reveals a record of piety and reflection, not calls for revolutionary protest. Censorship is only partly to blame, since oblique or allegorical writing often served political needs. Many nonconformist writers in the Restoration adopted indirect modes of writing in order to evade persecution; and this meant a proliferation of "coded" writing.[17] Yet seemingly apolitical words, when taken into consideration along with the occasion and setting in which they were spoken, did carry explicit political content. To meet as an assembly, in no matter how orderly a fashion, was to participate in overt political action, for instance, to organize against Anglican Uniformity. Dissenting funerals thus performed ideology without saying so exactly.

At the funerals, not only were Dissenters disobeying the legally prescribed service for the dead, they also powerfully evoked the memory of conflicts and riots over the official prayer book.[18] Presbyterian and Independent ministers, for instance, adhered to the Westminster Assembly's 1644 *Directory for the Publique Worship of God*, thus disobeying the present requirements of Uniformity. Specifically aiming against "popish practices," the *Directory* had banned as "superstitious" such customs as "kneeling down, and praying by, or towards the dead Corps, and other such usages, in the place where it lies, before it be carried to Burial." In contrast to these performances, the *Directory* stressed the meaning of the funeral for the community, and suggested that the collected "friends" "doe apply themselves to meditations, and conferences suitable to the occasion: and, that the Minister, as upon other occasions, so at this time, if he be present, may put them in remembrance of their Duty."[19]

Though simple in interment, Dissenters' funerals were often surprisingly well attended. Anthony à Wood noted that 3,000 had attended one nonconformist burial in 1675; and in 1691, 5,000.[20] Benjamin Keach, a leading Particular Baptist, justified publishing his funeral sermon for John Norcot by reason of the great crowds which made hearing it difficult.[21] One hundred and fifty coaches brought mourners to William Jenkyn's funeral at Bunhill in January 1685.[22] From the vantage point of the authorities, these were dangerous performances, signs of opposition to the government's religious policies. *The Newes*, which usually restricted itself to foreign affairs and the king's actions, took a rare detour to describe the funeral of Henry Jessey in September 1663, calling the departed minister, the "*Oracle* and *Idell* of the *Faction*."[23] That such a gathering attracted notice by this official publication tells us that these funerals were being watched. Protestants of different stripes appeared together at these funerals. Ralph Thoresby recounts the burial of the Presbyterian luminary Dr. Manton, a funeral at which Pepys was in attendance, at Stoke Newington on 22 October 1677. Manton, he writes, "being deservedly styled the King of Preachers, was attended with the vastest number of ministers of all persuasions, &c that

I ever saw together in my life," nonconformists and orthodox clergy walking side by side.[24]

Those supporting uniformity saw the Dissenting funerals as part of a full-scale campaign to incite citizens to rebel against the government and thus acknowledged their performative power. By labeling funerals "riots" or "plots," the authorities cast funerals into the category of subversive acts. The author of *Cabala, or an Impartial Account of the Non-Conformists Private Designs* (1663), claimed that ministers were bribed with £5 to give funeral sermons; 20s to bury without the Book of Common Prayer; and £10 for the dead to be buried at known Dissenting grave sites.[25] The funeral arrangements are seen as an important tool of propaganda for nonconformist activity. A mock-elegy for the London Independent minister Joseph Caryl, published after his funeral at College Hill in 1673, conveyed surprise at the "motley throng" and "rabble" that had assembled to pay respects to a man who had been a leading minister under the Commonwealth:

> Right Hypocrites! All's for a show.
> How came all sects thus to combine?
> Oh! I can tell you, 'tis designe
> Which makes them All agree in one,
> In what d'ye think? In Sedition.[26]

In their bodily practices, then, those leading the ceremonies, as well as those in attendance, were observed defying the state church, transmitting a counter-tradition.

In writing their wills or in other explicit instructions, Dissenting ministers themselves often specified their own resistance to the new prayer book.[27] Jessey wished his burial to be without ceremony: "Nor any mourning worn for me, or given, or complemental in any pompous way."[28] John Hutchinson desired his body removed from the place of his death and inconveniently returned back home, "though it was about eight score miles distant from the place where he died. What moved him to it he declared not, but I am apt to believe one thing was because he would not have any of those superstitions exercised about him, being dead, for the opposing of which he lost his liberty and life." Hutchinson was buried in 1664 in his parish church, where presumably there was enough family control over patronage to be sure there was no idolatry.[29] In opposing those "superstitions," in refusing the prayer book service, this political radical who had signed the death warrant of Charles I was continuing the work of resistance that had taken him to gaol where he died, possibly murdered by poisoning. His memorial was placed in a private chapel by his wife.

Though rejecting pomp or ceremony in burial practices had been a habit of Protestants in England since the Reformation,[30] during the Restoration, injunctions for simplicity took on a special political force, as in their simplicity, ministers requested now-illegal procedures: Edmund Colby requested "to be decently buried without Common Prayer, if it may be," and the Presbyterian minister William Bagshaw wrote, "I desire that my body shall not be admitted into a place stiled consecrated." The Westminster Assembly member Philip Anderton, who was ejected in 1662, requested in his will that "Nothing to be given at my funeral but a sprig of rosemary only half a dozen pair of black gloves to 6 nonconforming ministers whom I desire may privately inter my corpse without any funeral sermon from any conformist."[31] Keepsakes could voice protest: at the Presbyterian William Jenkyn's funeral in Bunhill his daughter distributed mourning rings inscribed, "William Jenkyn: Murdered in Newgate."[32] On occasion, as with Henry Jessey, the will was to be read aloud to the assembled auditory, making public a resistance few of the living dared to speak.

As well as serving as a keepsake for mourners, the published will – for example Henry Stubbes' – could rage against current practices.[33] The Presbyterian Richard Steele wrote a will also indicating how this unusual medium could be a forum for radical action, as the author wrestled with earthly politics and those commitments of the spirit. A close friend and Chester associate of Philip Henry, Steele had been several times imprisoned during the 1660s for not complying with Uniformity and for his alleged complicity in a plot; he was later licensed to preach in London in Bartholomew Close in 1672. Fined for conventicles there in 1683, he was buried at St. Bartholomew the Great in 1692. In his will, Steele defended his Dissent in his particular burial instructions: "declareing my non-conformity to proceed from my feare of sin and not from disloyalty or singularity," and he asked, as was customary for these ministers, "to be privately and decently buried without pomp."[34] Steele insists upon his faithfulness to his Crown, but dissents out of fear of sin: of the two claims on his loyalty, conscience, then, is the stronger.

In their bodily practices, those leading the ceremonies along with those in attendance confirmed their aversion to the state church. These bodily practices make visible – and were read as – a challenge to legislated orthodoxy. Resistance here can be read not solely in the texts of the funeral sermons, but in how Dissenters comported themselves. Philip Henry was asked to officiate at several burials before his ejection, and his diary recounts how controversial matters of ceremony could be. He remarked on the first burial of which he was supervisor in March 1662, that of his aunt: "I was forc't in some things to submit to custom, tho' against my own inclination...I desired shee might be buried before the sermon, but it was not granted... At Worthenby in the morning I rather permitted than desired the ringing of the bells, but after a peal or two they were forbidden to proceed."[35] In a letter to Sir Edward Harley in August 1677, Andrew Marvell noted one instance of defiance at the funeral of a child of a Dissenting minister. The funeral in Glasgow drew a crowd of about 3,000 "to spight the Bishop of Argyle who is also Parson of Glasgow," who had refused to let the "Bellman to publish the buriall after the usual manner." A woman, spying the bishop at the funeral, cried out in mockery, "Ha Theefe thou wilt never haue so many at thy buriall except thou be hanged."[36] Marvell's description reflects a period after the Declaration of Indulgence, but shows how high tensions could be. Such colorful incidents are rare to find in the accounts of these funerals.

The funeral was therefore an occasion not merely to remember a beloved minister or friend, but to keep up the faith by making significant verbal and physical gestures. Stating commitment not only to that minister, but to the collective enterprise represented by that minister, at the funeral of his friend Zachary Thomas in Nantwich, Cheshire, in September 1670, who had been forced out of his curacy in 1663, Philip Henry took the minister's funeral sermon to heart. He noted in his diary: "Mr. Kirk preacht, gave him a worthy character, for uprightness, humility, moderation, prayer, faithfulness in reproving, patience under Affliction, and in saying hee was a true Israelite without guil[t], hee said all; lord make mee a follower! Amen!" It is unclear whether Henry's "amen" is that of the preacher Thomas, or his own written assent to that preacher's words.[37] Either way, Henry vouches his support for the outlaw approach. Richard Baxter explained this work of memory was important since "funeral sermons are not for the benefit (though for the due honour) of the dead, but of the living, to teach us all to prepare for death," yet the arts of death took on a special contour under persecution, where praise of a minister's virtues also entailed endorsing their resistance to state policy.[38] Philip Henry in his diary from June 1667 tells of the funeral of the ejected Presbyterian minister Thomas Porter, and he takes pains to record that the dying man's last counsel: "to the lords people was, to stick to Christ & not let him goe, tide life, tide death."[39] Henry's notation allows us to see the importance of a dying man's words for "the lords people," and could be read between the lines to confirm allegiance to Dissent.

Through remembering significant leaders, writers portrayed their ideal fellowship, voiced unorthodox opinions, and offered implicit critique of current ecclesiastical or political leadership. Most of all, their funerals themselves kept the collective aim in view. As Presbyterian minister Thomas Watson put it in his sermon at the Bunhill funeral of Henry Stubbes, "we must...continue firm to the end...To finish the course and keep the faith."[40] The ejected Presbyterian vicar of St. Giles Cripplegate, who had been several times convicted for holding illegal meetings, was Samuel Annesley, who preached at the funeral of the ousted Presbyterian William Whitaker. Annesley stressed to the assembled that mourning was not enough: "'Tis not enough to breathe out a sigh, or to squeez out a tear, 'tis not enough to come see a faithful Minister buried, as those went to see Christ crucified...I will not clog your memories, but press upon your conscience this one thing, *Live over what you have heard from him.*"[41] Remembering those qualities she wished to keep alive, Theodosia Alleine, daughter of one ejected Presbyterian minister (Richard Alleine), and wife to another, Joseph Alleine, amplified her husband's virtues not simply on account of her wifely role, but to contribute to a literary culture of Dissent in which the portrayal of significant figures was a means to consolidate political and spiritual unity among the dispossessed. Theodosia Alleine, who kept a school at Taunton, with pupils boarding at her house, had offered to remain with her husband in prison after his arrest in 1663 at Ilchester for his religious activities. As did many wives during their husband's imprisonment, she stayed nearby to assist him, later joining him at Bath prison, where he had been removed because of ill health, and where he died because of the miserable prison conditions. Her *Life and Death of that Excellent Minister of Christ Mr. Joseph Alleine* was first printed in 1670, and was such a success, it had seven printings up until 1693: others were hungry to read this exemplary tale of righteous courage and domestic fidelity under persecution.[42]

Even though on occasion a minister ran into trouble with the authorities for the content of a funeral sermon, as did the Independent Christopher Ness in 1684, who received a warrant for his arrest on the charge of publishing an elegy on the death of a Dissenting minister friend, usually the highly conventional formats in the nonconformist funeral sermons or hagiographic literary biography are not exciting chapters in the history of radicalism. Peaceful and somber for the most part, the funerals may be seen as opposition acts nonetheless, speaking in metonymic form the mourning for the failed hopes of reform after the Restoration regime began publicly to silence Dissent. Samuel Palmer catalogued ejected ministers in a work he entitled *The Nonconformist's Memorial*, revealing the importance

of memory in forging a tradition. The commemorative poem included in
The Life and Death of Mr. Henry Jessey insisted on the worldly presence of
Jessey's own heirs, the survival of his "root," alluding to the biblical "root
of Jesse" that would give rise to Christ:

> What if deaths dart did us in Jessey wound,
> The root of Jessey grows not under ground;
> The root doth grow, above, there all is found:
> That doth with everlasting fruits abound.[43]

Not to be found in some mystical otherworld after death, what lasts is
"above ground," in the community Jessey leaves behind. Members of that
community feared for its existence; in its commemorative poetry and in
attending funeral ceremony, Dissenters insisted they were still there.

Tearful and at the same time enjoining hope, the commemorative material that often accompanied the nonconformist funerals often simply
asserted the community was surviving, even though it looked as if numbers were thinning out, especially those of notable leaders. The elegy on
the Independent leader John Owen, published in broadside folio, worries
what omen the loss of such an eminent man would mean to the community as a whole; and here Owen's departure is surrogate for the feared end
of the world: "When such a *Pillar* of the *Church* is taken/ Away, we've
cause to fear the *Fabrick's* shaken."[44] Indeed, the many deaths of leaders in
the period of persecution prompted fears that godliness was disappearing,
and God would bring imminent destruction. The mourned minister, then,
became the means by which to project diverse fears and hopes about the
community's survival.

The life being mourned may have been that of a lost minister, but in a
sense, it was also a social body which was being mourned. The mourning
thus became the occasion to make visible individual losses and those within
the social polity, to make a community present despite public exclusion. An
elegy for the Presbyterian minister William Taylor registers that his death
in 1661 compounds the general loss, heightens the community's fears that
it will not itself survive. Public grief turns into a lament for the sorrowful
existence of the community as a whole:

> Is't not enough that wicked men doe thrust
> Out teachers into corners, but thou must
> Fling them into these graves, oh! death forbeare,
> dont make such havock, ministers are rare,
> We cannot spare them at soe low a rate,
> We have but few, and now it's growing late;
> The night is nigh we feare.

The author rebukes death for colluding with the Anglican orthodoxy in silencing ministers:

> Ah cruel death! the Bishop sure and thou
> did lay your heads together, plotting how
> To throw him downe, and thus you end the strife,
> He tooke his living from him, you his life.[45]

As the minister's death becomes a symbol for the social deaths of members of a community, the work of commemoration takes up significant psychic functions for mourners. Joseph Roach, in his *Cities of the Dead*, analyzes the "three-sided relationship of memory, performance, and substitution," observing "how culture reproduces and re-creates itself by a process that can be best described by the word *surrogation*."[46] By surrogation, Roach indicates the means by which a community substitutes alternatives for that which has departed, answering the psychic needs of those who feel abandoned. Protestant habits of typological reading ensured that any individual could be assimilated into a timeless, but always timely story. Dissenters did not simply surrogate their departed ministers for the social deaths they were experiencing in the wake of civil war, nor merely did their commemorations protest against the forced forgetting of the Restored regime. Their focus on significant losses was also their means of constructing a tradition, of conjoining the past, present, and future.

This work of memory would prove especially complex for a culture that had recently radically altered its relationship to the dead. Protestant Reformers had reconceived the meaning of mourning and commemoration by denying the existence of purgatory. Protestant Reformers focused attention on personal experiences of the dying, and placed emphasis on the quality of the last moments of the dying person's life – his "good" death or "bad" death. Further, the Reformation brought with it a changed attitude towards commemoration. When the transubstantiate power of the Host was denied, Reformers took the sacrament as a "memorial," observing its rituals not as transubstantive but as commemorative. The tension we can see between the memorial functions of the funerals and their actions as political work as constitutive of identity, resonates with conflicts over that central paradox of the eucharist: was to worship it to endow it with divinity, or simply to recollect a scene of divine instantiation? In Protestant readings, the meaning of the sacrament was to be commemorative, and typological, and Protestants insisted upon *figural* readings, defending a linguistic theory of parabolic signification. Dissenters, with their cult of commemoration, deepened this commemorative approach to the eucharist; however, even as they used allegory and types to do political work, whether evading censor-ship or supplying needed braces for assaulted identities, they also verged on the signification practices of investing Real Presence by conjoining prophecy with commemoration.

Apocalyptic thought rendered significant figures not only as mnemonic devices, metaphoric markers, but as metonymic for the whole of suffering Christendom and prophetic of the downfall of the unjust. In preaching a funeral sermon on the eve of the "Great Ejection" for Simeon Ashe, a leading London Presbyterian minister, Edmund Calamy the Elder reminded his gathering that the loss of Ashe would be like the loss of all the ministers who were to be the next day forcibly silenced by the Anglican church. Ashe's death becomes an emblem for the scattered condition of the faithful under those particular times. "Of consolation to all the people of God in reference to evil times that are coming upon us," Calamy suggests, "or to the evil of times. Whatever befalls a child of God in this life, though he be scattered by wicked men, from *England* into Forraign countries, though he wanders up and down in Desarts, and Wildernesses, though he be scattered from house to prison." There is nonetheless consolation to be found:

Yet there shall be a gathering time shortly: there will a time come when all the Saints shall be gathered to Christ, and to one another, never to part any more. The death of God's people is not a perishing, but a gathering: comfort your selves therefore with these words against the fear of death: look upon death as a gathering, as a gathering to Christ: you are here as *Daniel* in the Lyons Den, as *Jeremiah* in the Dungeon; yet there will come a gathering, and if you die in a good cause, you shall not perish, but be gathered to Christ, to his Saints and Angels.[47]

Biblical typology rendered the prison examples of Daniel and Jeremiah as common figures to rally hopes among the persecuted, many of whom were to be imprisoned for their beliefs and actions.[48] Daniel's was a story of divine vengeance on behalf of the persecuted, furthermore, as John Goodwin, once minister at Coleman Street, expresses his Fifth Monarchist beliefs in the "*New Heaven*, and the *new Earth*, the *Kingdom of Christ*, and of the *Saints*" in which the "first fruits" shall rule the World to come, he prophecied violence: "that they shall rule the Nations, as it were, with a Rod of Iron, and break them in pieces like a Potters Vessel." Quoting the book of Daniel, 7:18, he foretold, "But the saints of the most High shall take the kingdom, and possess the kingdom for ever, even for ever and ever."[49] Memory in this case was a spur to violence, divinely authorized by past experience, in a bold assertion of saints' political action.

ABEL'S SPEECH

The last sermons of ministers before ejection were often likened to funeral sermons, and when published in 1662, they were deemed seditious speech acts. The frontispiece of one collection of these farewell sermons represents the crude likenesses of the ministers, an assembly of portraits showing their collective, grim perseverence. The twelve heads appear as a jury, perhaps indicting persecutors, perhaps just asserting they are still there (see Figure 3). *A Compleat Collection of Farewel Sermons*, texts of thirty-one of the ejected ministers, was seized in November.[50] Simeon Ashe's death coincided with Ejection, and he became a potent symbol of the collective suppression of dissenting voices. In his sermon on Ashe, Calamy gives a brief portrait praising the worthy's ethical character (there is, characteristic of this genre, no mention of a home life or family) only insofar as it might be exemplary: "not so much for his commendation; he needs it not, but for our imitation; it is pity great pity something should not be said that this reverend Minister though dead, may yet preach this night."[51] This seems a rather pedestrian pedagogy. However, Calamy chooses as his biblical proof-text the fratricidal struggle between Cain and Abel. Abel had long been understood as a type of Christ in the typological way of reading; this was a story that lay behind many Dissenting calls for violent retribution against persecution, and which summoned to mind recent civil war history:

For as *Abell* being dead, yet speaketh; so shall the Sermons of this worthy Minister at the great day, speak for you, or against you; for they are spiritual talents that God hath betrusted you with, and you must be accountable; both he and you shall appear before the Tribunal of God ... Whatever was good in this Reverend Minister, let it live in you; and though he be dead, let not his Sermons that he preached die with you, but let them be in you.[52]

"Be in you": this is more than simple commemoration, with the dead speaking to the living; it was a summons to potent action. "I pray God give all who are concerned in this loss, wisdom to improve this present stroke," Thomas Watson preached on the death of ejected Presbyterian minister Henry Stubbes in 1678, "and make a living Sermon of their dead Minister."[53] To make a "living sermon" was to participate in a kind of transubstantiation, to revive in one's own actions and person those of the departed minister. One collection of ejected ministers' sermons was titled *Saints Memorials*, with the title-page epigraph Hebrews 11:4: "Who being dead, yet speak."[54] Those silenced ministers were "dead," even if physically living. As Lazarus Seaman put it, "what can be expected from those who are dead, and yet not free among the dead?"[55] Beyond commemoration, then,

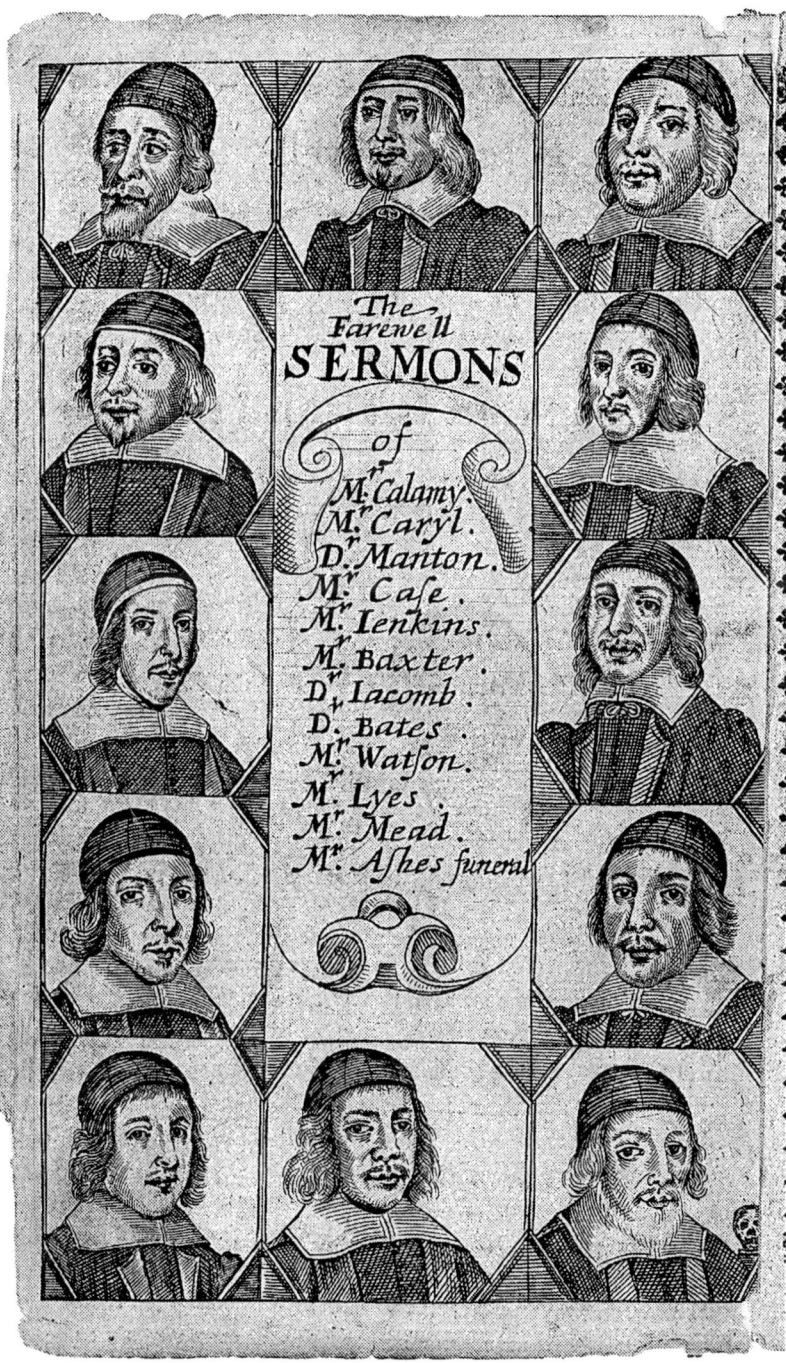

The Farewell
SERMONS
of

Mr. Calamy.
Mr. Caryl.
Dr. Manton.
Mr. Case.
Mr. Ienkins.
Mr. Baxter.
Dr. Iacomb.
D. Bates.
Mr. Watson.
Mr. Lyes.
Mr. Mead.
Mr. Ashes funeral

Figure 3 Frontispiece to Edmund Calamy, *The Farewell Sermons of the late London Ministers* (1662).

reflections on the recently silenced, as the recently departed, uncannily provoked metaphoric substitutions.

"Living over" the lives of dead or silenced ministers would complicate the story told by typological or strictly commemorative readings of the Bible. As sermons recalled significant figures and linked them to biblical types, they made the Bible's history present. Typology gave meaning to current events and situations; so too did it promise God's participation in current history. This dimension made room for powerful topical political intent, and because of this, it is worth exploring some instances of this regenerative memory-practice. To cite stories from the Bible, as did Calamy in his text on Ashe (Heb. 11:4: "He being dead, yet speaketh") could bear red-hot political meaning. Long used by radicals to exemplify the near relation of persecutors and persecuted, Cain and Abel were biblical types evoked again and again during the period 1640–60 to describe the fratricidal civil wars. During the Restoration period, not only were Cain and Abel the first of the visions Adam viewed in his run-through of history in *Paradise Lost*, as he learns the history of human vice (*PL*, 11:429–65); but in Bunyan's *Holy War* the godly blood of Abel cried out for vengeance against the tyrannous persecution by Cain and his offspring; Richard Baxter would write his tract *Cain and Abel Malignity* using the story to analyze the recent history of the struggle between the godly and ungodly. These brothers came to be written as types of the repeated struggle of Christ with Antichrist. The trope of fratricide alluded both to the trauma of recent civil war and to Restoration ecclesiological strife.[56] The eminent Independent divine John Owen wrote of the bloody brothers in his commentary on Paul's Epistle to the Hebrews: "here we have the *Prototype* of the *Believing* and *Malignant* Church in all Ages...This was the first publicke visible acting of the *Enmity of the seed of the Woman, and the Seed of the Serpent*."[57] The republican Independent Lucy Hutchinson gives the murderous brother a topical polemical spin in her biblical epic, using Abel's curse as an occasion to condemn the overweening power of magistrates and ministers, figuring Cain in the image of the "formal hypocrite."[58]

During the period of Restoration persecution, Abel's suffering signified more than a type of Christ; his suffering "speaks." John Bunyan wrote of God's remembrance of the death of Abel at the hand of Cain in his commentary on Genesis, "*When he maketh Inquisition for Blood, he remembreth them: he forgetteth not the Crie of the humble* [Psal. 9:12]. Blood that is shed for the sake of God's Word, shall not be forgotten or disregarded of God." As was common among the radical reformers, Bunyan took the story of

Cain and Abel to illustrate the types of persecutor and victim that had particular relevance to his own experience of Restoration Dissent: "Beware Persecutors," he continues,

you think that when you have slain the Godly, you are then rid of them; but you are far wide, their Blood which you have shed, cries in the ears of God against you. O the Cries of Blood are strong cries, they are cries that reach to Heaven; yea they are cries that have a continual voice, and that never cease to make a noise, untill they have procured Vengeance from the hands of the *Lord of Sabbath*.[59]

Memory of God's powerful acts could repair hope of justice for those members of a community that had been abased and fractured by persecution. "The Apostle makes this Voice of the Blood of *Abel*," continues Bunyan, "a Type of the Voice of the Justice of the Law" (*Exposition*, 166). God's remembering would assure that all would be righted by justice in the end. By forming a communal identity out of disparate instances of suffering in the type of Abel, those persecuted could remember God's memory, and thus protest against the unjust regime.

Bunyan is careful to interpret the story of Cain and Abel as a story of divine – not human – retribution. Writing almost in a personal note of his own experience, Bunyan explains, "the quarrel is in special between the Persecutor and God himself: For we are not hated because we are Men, nor because we are Men of evil and debauched Lives; but because we are Religious; because we stand to maintain the Truth of God. Therefore no Man must here intercept, but must leave the Enemy in the hand of that God he hath slighted and condemned" (172). Rather, "Let *Cain* and God alone, and do you mind Faith and patience; suffer with *Abel*, until your Righteous Blood be spilt: Even the Work of Persecutors, is, for the present, Punishment enough; the Fruits thereof being the provoking God to Jealousie" (173). Yet the plea for punishment in the name of Abel had topical political import as well. The fiery funeral sermon of Sir Edmundbury Godfrey, the JP whose murder in 1678 touched off a wave of anti-papist prosecutions, added fuel to the flames. "Here's a subject that makes it's own Sermon and its own Prayer," exhorted William Lloyd: "*The Blood* of *Abel* speaks, saith the Apostle... This Innocent Blood speaks and cries in the Ears of God... it speaks and cries aloud to him for Vengeance: *How Long, O Lord, holy and true, dost thou not Judge and avenge?*"[60]

To speak as Abel's blood did was to call for violent justice, and particularly to direct that summons to the actions of human, and not just to divine, ears. "*There is a Voice in all innocent blood shed by Violence*," writes John Owen on this passage, "There is an *Appeal* in it from the injustice and cruelty of men, unto God as the Righteous Judge of all."[61] The Presbyterian John Fairfax used Abel for overtly subversive purposes in a funeral sermon, where he was reported to have spoken "dangerous words."[62] In exile in Holland during periods of the 1660s, his sermon commemorated the Smectymnuuan Matthew Newcomen, who died in exile in Leiden in September 1668 or 1669. The preface by John Collinges states that this was a sermon preached before a gathering in Newcomen's church in Dedham in 1668 or 1669. Though Fairfax cited the New Testament text, he pulled his interpretation out of the Old Testament account, and daringly called for a revenge for Abel's murder at the hands of Cain: "*Abel* being dead, yet speaketh unto God *by his blood*. When he was dead, said God to Cain, *The Voice of thy brothers blood crieth unto me from the earth.* The Martyrs blood, it crieth against Cain for vengeance, which is not yet fully executed." The sermon, not printed until 1679, safe perhaps in the heightened pitch of the Popish plot when censorship lapsed, must have sounded a radical note when it was preached aloud in 1668 or 1669. Fairfax pursues his bloodthirsty revenge motif:

Abel's blood yet crieth unto God; not only against *Cain*, but it cryeth unto God against all the *generation of the Cainites*, against all the persecutors of the Church of God; for all persecutors, following, in respect of *Abel*, are as *Saul*, in respect of *Stephen*, they are consenting to his death. For had the present generation of persecutors lived in the days of *Abel*, they would as well as *Cain* have imbued their hands in the blood of *Abel*. Tremble at this then, oh ye generation of persecutors! *Abels* blood crieth unto God from the earth against you.[63]

Fairfax's repetitious phrases, the peaks and valleys of his spoken prose, culminate in a question that is a rousing charge: "*How long, Lord, holy and true, dost thou not judg and avenge our blood on them that dwell on earth?*" (11–12). "How long, O Lord" alludes to Revelation 6:10, a persistent and oft-quoted call for the apocalyptic Judgment to accompany the Second Coming.[64] Fairfax was soon to spend five more months in prison in 1670–71.

For the auditor of the funeral sermon, the work of the living was active and political memory-work. Hearers were enjoined to remember the words and lives of their departed ministers; they were encouraged to repeat the deeds of their leaders in their own lives; they were consoled to bear up under suffering for the sake of those memories; and, in the case of Abel's speech, they were to prepare for their role in a militant cosmic drama.

SITES OF MEMORY

If the work of mourning was incomplete, fractured, and dissipated by the Anglican regime, then the nonconformists' funerals, notwithstanding their sectarian differences, gave voice to other points of view. Just as communal mourning spoke of a loss that could not be confronted with political protest, so the topographical unity of the graveyard also gave symbolic fullness to the longing for a place called home for those experiencing social exclusion and dislocation. Some nonconformists did choose to be buried in conforming churches, even if they had been ejected from the pulpit or had themselves refused membership; John Milton (d. 1674) was buried in St. Giles Cripplegate; Edmund Calamy the Elder (d. 1666) asked to be buried in the ruins of St. Mary Aldermanbury, out of whose pulpit he had been ejected.[65] We do not know how many suffered the fate of the Baptist Samuel How, the autodidact author of a popular tract challenging the priests' monopoly on education, who was refused a Christian burial, and whose "Friends were forced to lay his Body in the High-way, as one which was numbered amongst the Transgressors."[66] Quakers from the earliest times provided their own burial grounds, which often preceded the building of their meeting houses, as they were not in the practice of burying Friends within the walls of a meeting house. The burial ground at Chalfont St. Giles, purchased by Thomas Ellwood and others within the Quaker community in 1671, contains nearly 400 burials of the early Friends; the adjacent Jordans meeting house would not be built until 1688. The graveyard includes the Penn family, Isaac and Mary Pennington, and the Ellwoods: in line with strenuous Quaker reforms, in 1766, all headstones were removed as ostentatious, only to be replaced in 1862.[67] There is a tension between the sign and the meaning of commemoration; many dissenting memorials were in a plain mortuary style. The tombs at the graveyard at Bunhill Fields appear without figural representation or decorative art; classically plain, they are the aesthetic equivalent to purification and rejection of ritual.

It was the Dissenting burial ground at Bunhill Fields that became a powerful rallying point and symbol for high-ranking nonconformists – Presbyterians, Baptists, and Independents – in the Restoration. Opened as a burial pit for use in the Great Plague, Bunhill was enclosed by a brick wall and gates in 1665–66. Since there was no consecration of the ground, nonconformists were here able to bury their dead without the official prayer book. The cemetery of Puritan England, Bunhill boasts monuments to John Bunyan (1688); the Independent divines John Goodwin (1665) and

John Owen (1683); Major-General Charles Fleetwood (1692), son-in-law of Cromwell; Jane Lead (1704), the founder of the mystical theosophist society, the Philadelphians; Daniel Defoe (1731); Susannah Wesley (1742), mother of John and Charles and sixteen others; Isaac Watts (1748); and William Blake (1827). "In Bunhill Burial Ground crumbling to Dust/ There lies two Generations of the Just," crowed a poem published in 1745.[68] In Bunhill, in a way that they were not able to do in their lives, Dissenters of different sectarian leanings gathered together. Burial sites were places of gathering for the living and for the dead. The popular preacher, "Eternal" Robert Bragge, was buried in the same vault as John Bunyan. Ann Overton's express wishes were to be buried "as near ye olde Prophet, Mr Jesse, as could be," thus making her burial into a public statement of loyalty through proximity; this was indeed enacted in a confirmation of the symbolic power of Dissenting space.[69] That unified space formed an emblem for the collective legacy of Dissent and also was a symbol for their longed-for gathering in heaven.

Today little is legible in the acid-rain washed tombstones in Bunhill cemetery in east London, just down the lane from Bunhill Row, where Milton composed *Paradise Lost, Samson Agonistes*, and *Paradise Regain'd*. Access to the grave sites is prohibited due to the sinking ground, but we have the cult of the Dissenting martyrs to thank for the preservation of many of the inscriptions on these gravestones in a 1717 pamphlet. If the physical graveyard was a site of protest and fellowship, then the inscriptions on tombs offer another way to understand the place of commemoration in the making of a Dissenting tradition. In the classical spirit, the poetry of funereal inscription is epigrammatic; it requires brevity and, paradoxically, it insists upon permanence even in the face of the impermanence of life. Yet the Dissenting monument refuses the stoicism and detachment of that classicizing interest in immobility, fixity, and detachment from the ruins of time; instead, there is a gesture of public communication, a search for a living presence. The Dissenting memorials offer another kind of plainness. Poets traditionally think of their own poetry as a kind of monument – think of Herrick's "His Poetry His Pillar" or Milton's sonnet on Shakespeare ("Thou in our wonder and astonishment/ Hast built thyself a livelong Monument"); the poetic inscriptions on the stones of tombs rework that essential link between poetry and commemoration. Dissenting gravestones were also important memory-sites, places to draw visitors and organize their experiences of the past even as they supplied new means to create futures.[70] Open to political contest after the Protestant Reformation, even gravestones were not exempt from the controversies surrounding ceremony. In 1631, when John

Weever linked the contemporary Puritan attack on images to the excessive iconoclasm of the Reformers' despoliation of the monasteries, he sought to restore the beauty of holiness in his Laudian aesthetic by revitalizing elaborate funerary monuments. Thus the politics of the graveyard mirror those of the prayer book, altar, and pulpit.[71] Sir Thomas Browne's *Urn Buriall* (1658) is another entry into the controversy over funeral rites during the period of the English civil war, written and published when the burial rites of the church were banned.[72]

Funeral monuments were major players in the cultural war over memories in the Restoration. In January 1661, on the twelfth anniversary of the regicide, the bodies of Oliver Cromwell, Henry Ireton (Cromwell's son-in-law), and John Bradshaw (President of the Court in the trial of Charles I) were disinterred and desecrated. These three corpses were taken from their tombs in Westminster Abbey and hanged in their shrouds, after which their skulls were impaled in Westminster Hall beside those of recently executed regicides. Other distinguished republican and parliamentary dead were also disinterred from the abbey, as ordered by the Dean of Westminster, and were thrown into a common pit beneath Tyburn, the traditional place of public execution. This treatment has been seen as a symbolic reversal of what these regicides had done to Charles on 30 January 1649; this "finished the tragedy of their lives in a comic scene at Tyburn; a wonderful example of justice," according to the official record.[73] The exhumations of these notable Commonwealth leaders registers the violence of backlash, and tells us about the significance of the dead for contemporary politics. This was not merely political revenge; it was an assault on cultural memory. Even the body of Anne Fleetwood, Charles Fleetwood's daughter who had died as a child, was exhumed with the abbey regicides. When Elizabeth, wife of Oliver Cromwell, died in 1665, she was interred without any monument or inscription.[74] To this day, it is unknown where Oliver's remains lie, although a host of legends has arisen in the absence of a burial site, including the fabulous theory that Cromwell had his own body exchanged with that of Charles I at Windsor to protect it; this was given the lie when Charles' tomb was opened in a later age – that the tomb was opened at all tells us that such a rumor had credence.[75]

Contests over cultural and political memory, and thus social and political legitimacy, were very much fought over recognition of the dead. Charles Fleetwood (d. 1692), son-in-law of Cromwell, has a plain, imposing tomb in Bunhill, unlike his unfortunate parliamentary compeers and his daughter, whose bodies were treated like waste after eviction from Westminster Abbey. Bunhill opened up a counter-place for a counter-tradition.

Funerary monuments, therefore, could tell a disobedient story, insisting with concreteness on the presence of a valued history and making its virtues available for public legitimation. The great Presbyterian preacher Nathaniel Vincent, who had preached to thousands after the Fire of London and had suffered several imprisonments, died in 1697 and had etched onto his headstone, "I have thus made a Pulpit of my Grave."[76] Concrete poetry, there to outlive the thin threads of the persecutors' lives, Dissenting gravestones utter powerful poetic resistance and call for retribution. The headstone of the ejected minister Edward Bagshaw's wife Margaret (d. 1672) tells a tale in its compression. After his ejection Bagshaw became chaplain to the Earl of Anglesey, and in 1662 suffered physically in the Tower and then in Southsea Castle, and in 1671 he was again sentenced for recusancy to forfeit his goods and lands for life and be imprisoned in Newgate:

> Here the Wicked ceace from Troubling,
> And here the Weary be at Rest
> Here the Prisoners rest together
> They hear not the Voice of the Oppressor.[77]

Echoing Job's curse out of his grief in 3:18, "There the prisoners rest together; they hear not the voice of the oppressor," the tombstone justifies the righteousness of the victims.

A Latin epitaph inscribed on John Owen's tomb at Bunhill praised his superior mind and moderating temper, but closed with a protest against Uniformity: "He left the world on *a day dreadful to the Church by the cruelties of men*, but blissful to *himself* by the plaudits of his God. August 24, 1683, aged 67." Owen's date of death punctuated the calendar that would come to mark 24 August as the most dolorous day of the year because that was the day Uniformity went into effect and the nonconforming had to abandon their pulpits. Owen's funeral was a major public event in 1683, attended by the carriages of sixty-seven nobles and gentlemen.[78] His tomb is a very plain stone erection, without ornament or figure; it boasts only words, its stone inscription retelling the story of his intellectual achievements and spiritual warfare as like "Herculean labors."[79] The tomb records for all time not only his extraordinary abilities, but gives narrative shape to them as classically heroic as well as typologically Christian, also marking a social register inclusive of the classically trained.

To visit the tomb is to perform an act of homage, of connection across time by space. The memorial in a church in Whitefriars' Convent for the Baptist minister Thomas Grantham (d. 1692) lists his sufferings,

who with true Christian fortitude endured persecution
Through many perils, and loss of friends and substance,
And ten imprisonments for conscience sake,
A man endued with every Christian grace and virtue.[80]

Potent records of persecution, gravestones signified in an economy of re-membrance that conjoined written and performed, ideological markers as well as sites to visit to remember, and by that remembrance, to carry on a Dissenting tradition.

If a chief fear of the persecuted was that they would be forgotten or that their suffering would be in vain, the concrete inscription bore ineradi-cable witness to the value and legitimacy of their cause. The inscription, quite literally, offered the last word. The Bunhill tombstone inscription for the Fifth Monarchist Vavasor Powell who died while still a prisoner in the Fleet prison, in 1671, after spending almost the whole of the 1660s in imprisonments in Southsea and Cardiff Castles, gives a brief life: "Vavasor Powell, a successful Teacher of the past, A sincere Witness of the present, and an useful Example to the future Age, lies here interr'd, who in the Defection of so many, obtained mercy to be found Faithful; for which being called to several Prisons, he was there tried, and would not accept Deliverance, expecting a better Resurrection." As Powell's poetry sought to remember God and be remembered by Him, as we shall see in the next chapter, so the mortuary words render identity as a counter-narrative to official silencing. Powell's epitaph, by Bagshaw, also speaks a protest:

> In vain oppressors do themselves perplex
> To find out Arts how they the Saints may vex:
> Death spoils their Plots, and sets the Oppressed free;
> Thus VAVASOR obtained true Liberty.
> Christ himself released, and now he's joyned among
> The martyred Souls, with whom he cries, *How Long*.
> (*Rev.* 6:10)[81]

Echoing the call of the despairing for release from persecution, this is an invitation to divine vengeance. Bagshaw's words speak in the eternal present of biblical typology, as the time of Powell's life, whose death he provides with meaning, is linked to the time of the past prophecy of Revelation, and to the time of the future, in which time will no longer exist. The monument, fixed in space, queries the very terms of history, seeking to rise above them.

By listing persecutions, Dissenters composed their public histories, merg-ing personal and communal, challenging those who would silence the voices and suppress the right of the excluded to bequest a socially meaningful legacy. The General Baptist Francis "Elephant" Smith (d. 1691) was given a biography in miniature in his tombstone inscription. Licensed as a preacher in 1672, Smith had been the bookseller and publisher of Bunyan as well as Whig opposition writing:

[He] in his Youth was settled in a separate Congregation, where he sustained, between the Years of 1659 & 1688, great Persecution by Imprisonments, Exile, and large Fines laid on Ministers and meeting houses, and for printing and promoting Petitions for calling of a Parliament, and several Things against Popery, and after near 40 Imprisonments, he was fined 500 l. for printing and selling the speech of a Noble Peer, and three times Suffered Corporeal Punishment. For the said Fine, he was 5 Years Prisoner in the *Kings Bench*: His hard Duress there, utterly impaired his Health. He dyed House-Keeper in the Custom-House, December the 22nd 1691.[82]

Of his publications Anthony Shaftesbury's *Speech of a Noble Peer of the Realm* (1681) is singled out, a revolutionary speech delivered on 23 December 1680 on the exclusion of James II. Smith may have been fined then, but he was vindicated later, reprinting that single-sheet folio text and presenting it to King William in 1689. The publisher and author lived long enough to see his hopes and his place in history restored. The Protestant cause by the time this inscription is recorded was safe for such accounting.

These unornamented tombs, whose distinctiveness or individuality was only visible in the inscribed words, published their simple protests and enjoined visitors to make memory serve the present and the future. Without such memorials, these figures would remain silenced and invisible, lost to meaning. The place of the graveyard, outside any local parish and indeed outside the city walls, could become a refuge for Dissenters' memories, a habitation in which the dead could be made to constitute a counter-community, and where the living could meet each other in recognition, through the dead, of each other.

SAMSON AGONISTES AND THE POLITICS OF MEMORY

Milton's retelling of a biblical life in *Samson Agonistes*, ready for sale in the autumn of 1670, offers up an instance for considering the workings of commemoration, typology, and mourning within a Restoration Dissenting framework. Ideological critics have looked to the author's biography to understand Milton's intentions – to understand both his choice of dramatic genre and his topic. This historical approach has tended to allegorize the play either in terms of Milton's biography or in terms of the

Puritan cause; Milton like Samson found himself blind, in prisons both literal and metaphoric during the Restoration; he, like Samson, was questioning his divine gifts: "What is strength, without a double share/ Of wisdom."[83] Samson has been seen to represent the New Model Army, or the crushed "Good Old Cause."[84] Such a historical approach sees *Samson Agonistes* as Milton's way of writing a political tract for his times in poetry, a message showing how one *ought* to behave by the exemplary (or negative-exemplary) story of Samson's internal growth and final action, an action that resembles – or doesn't – that of the Christian paradigm of sacrifice. When we think of the play as a work of memory, however, we add new contours to the portrait. Through repetition of a known story, Milton commemorates a past hero; but in the drama, he also faces the problem of how an individual mediates a cosmic story. Through *Samson Agonistes*, Milton contributes to the Restoration contest over whose memories should survive.

Samson Agonistes is nothing if not a performance of political memory. In keeping with the expressive forum of tragedy, with the Greek example of public theatre in the service of democracy, the play works out issues of public meaning for a specific community. Typology could construct logics of identity for believers; interpreting the Bible transformed the worldly experience of readers by providing surrogates for their own suffering. Through the process of retelling a known story, Milton not only commemorates a past heroism, but offers a visible proof of the hand of God in human history. In *Samson Agonistes*, memory brings not relief, but violent destruction and collective liberation.

Milton's play looks as much to the present and future as it does to the immediate past. If Milton's drama is "a human tragedy recounting the tragedy of civilization and of its supposedly civilizing religions," as Joseph Wittreich humanely puts it,[85] *Samson Agonistes* may also be seen to express the particular trauma of living after the failed Revolution, voicing out of the depths of post-Restoration mourning an ever-grieving Samson who lives literally in darkness, not only physically blind but also incarcerated, doubly barred from the light of the sun: "O dark, dark, dark, amid the blaze of noon,/ Irrecoverably dark, total Eclipse/ Without all hope of day!" (*SA*, 80–82) – the opposite to the Restored monarchy's self-image of a sun-bringing, sun-dwelling king. Milton's drama stages self-abasement as a prelude to making meaning out of despair, as over the course of the play the virtuous community will be established not on woe but on triumph – "to *Israel* honor hath left/ And freedom" (1714–15). Memory of Israel's heroic deliverance is the means to mediate later losses that are individual and collective, and to generate further action. It is the conversion of Samson's experience to Restoration cultural memory that interests me here. A central question the play asks is, *What form should memory take?* As the play moves from passive remembrance to active memory, the sorry hero ruminates on his past actions and moves outwards to challenge God to remember him.

In *Samson Agonistes* Milton meditates on the contests fought over memory by presenting several alternative narratives, none sufficient to transform the experiences of readers to construct true knowledge nor to seal the identities of the speakers. The dejected, melancholy Samson is the champion of remembrance, in his opening soliloquy brooding upon "Times past, what once I was, and what am now" (22): memory threatens to shatter identity. The play offers various paradigms for commemoration, various means to reroute despair into hope, and though it is a drama, these are effectively portrayed as narrative fantasies. The Chorus in *Samson Agonistes* offers reminders of a heroic past, in the form of biblical stories through which Samson might recollect his own glorious mission, reciting a list of worthies amongst whom Samson's name will be enrolled (277–89). The Chorus prays to God that Samson not suffer the degradation of the defiled outcast, silently recalling the fate of the regicides at the Restoration.

Will history be written by the conquerors? Milton presents the conflict between Samson and Dalila as a conflict over memory: theirs is a battle over whose memories will survive and thus over who will be the hero. It is the trick of Milton's genius that Dalila's bid for feminist heroism is consistent and plausible; indeed, he summons the proof-texts for authorizing women's public voices in the seventeenth century. In assembling her own life-narrative, even Dalila imagines her own commemoration:

> My name perhaps among the Circumcis'd
> In *Dan*, in *Judah*, and the bordering Tribes,
> To all posterity may stand defam'd,
> With malediction mention'd, and the blot
> Of falsehood most unconjugal traduc't.
> But in my country where I most desire,
> In *Ekron, Gaza, Asdod*, and in *Gath*
> I shall be nam'd among the famousest
> Of Women, sung at solemn festivals,
> Living and dead recorded, who to save
> Her country from a fierce destroyer, chose
> Above the faith of wedlock bands, my tomb
> With odors visited and annual flowers.

Not less renown'd than in Mount *Ephraim*,
Jael, who with inhospitable guile
Smote *Sisera* sleeping through the Temples nail'd.
(*SA*, 975–90)

This is the Euripidean heroine – dangerous, sexy, and, finally, fatal. Her autobiographical narrative sings a feminist triumph, and though she anticipates her defamation, she seems to revel in the bad words that will erupt from her enemies' mouths; their maledictions, their "blot of falsehood" only serve to make her glory brighter. Dalila knows history will be written by the victors, as the instances of female biblical heroism give her evidence. In her song are enfolded the key texts of female warrior heroism; the commemorative function of her song is to remember them and to insert her own history between their lines.[86] In her very language, too, Dalila chooses self-production through narrative within a heroic frame of elegy, the *tomb*, a production that will supercede any implicit generative production of her *womb*. As if to tease us with the proximity – and difference – of these two modes of generation, Dalila's words include a cluster of *w* sounds in which the word *tomb* is embedded and framed: "wedlock bands, my tomb/ With odors visited." There is nothing in the text itself that could adjudicate these opposing versions of history. The only clear difference in the two stories is not in their exposition, but in the knowledge of on whose behalf the True God is working, not in epistemology, but in ethics.

Dalila's is not the only bid to enshrine history in song and to construct truth through discursive projection; each participant in the drama contributes a possible story for Samson. As the members of the Chorus enter, however, they have difficulty in making the parts of Samson's life cohere into a continuous narrative. They can only observe, and their mode of description is as disjointed as that life they hope to give shape by words:

This, this is he; softly a while,
Let us not break in upon him;
O change beyond report, thought, or belief!
See how he lies at random, carelessly diffus'd,
With languish'd head unpropt,
As one past hope, abandon'd,
And by himself given over;
In slavish habit, ill-fitted weeds
O'erworn and soil'd;
Or do my eyes misrepresent? Can this be hee,
That Heroic, that Renown'd,
Irresistible *Samson*?　　　　(*SA*, 115–26)

The Chorus wishes not to "break in upon him," but its very words are themselves broken up into astonished and discontinuous reactions, a series of exclamations, as it shudders in its incredulity. Finally the Chorus' doubt gives occasion to render a full account of his past actions. It is as if it seeks to square the present with the past by reciting the past ("whom unarm'd/ No strength of man, or fiercest wild beast could withstand;/ Who tore the Lion" etc.), invoking its specter as a means to pour out the grief over the great change. From the first words of the Chorus, then, we see that *Samson Agonistes* is a drama about the images by which heroes and antiheroes can be known and commemorated. For the Chorus, Samson's heroism can only be constituted as a now-and-then story, without narrative continuity that could constitute a coherent emblem of identity. The shock of those who regard Samson is over the way he has so rapidly exchanged his heroism for baseness: "The glory late of *Israel*, now the grief" (179); they wonder "can this be hee," in a coy echo perhaps of Satan's dim first view of his fallen companion Beelzebub (*PL*, 1:84), but they pose the existential question upon which narrative accounts of identity falter. By repeating the visual and ontological negations that mark these post-fallen situations, Milton's imagination works over the crisis of invalid recognition: Samson is unrecognizable to his mates: is he indeed *Samson*? The Chorus' words, too, fumble. The irregular lines spill out beyond known forms, in a disarray of rhythm that mimics Samson's disheveled appearance; only at the very end of the Chorus' sloppy sentence does it utter his proper name. Identity does not precede narration, but is brought into being through it.

During the course of the play, the character Samson denies several possible narratives of identity, and through these denials, Milton thinks through the political and social problems of commemoration. Samson may already have become a kind of tourist attraction to the Chorus, but through his engagement with visitors who bid to give Samson a legacy, he repels those representations others would thrust upon him. His father, Manoa, offers an ignoble ransom which would leave Samson as the wrong kind of monument, as Samson projects his future into narrative:

> But to sit idle on the household hearth,
> A burdenous drone; to visitants a gaze,
> Or pitied object, these redundant locks
> Robustious to no purpose clust'ring down,
> Vain monument of strength . . . (*SA*, 566–70)

To accept ransom would be to accept the passivity of subjection to the gaze of others, a gaze that can only render him pitiable. Samson chooses not to consign himself to this emasculate role in a feminine space, the household. His long hair, itself formerly the sign and not the agent of his strength, would cluster uselessly, slackly, a limp male member. To be subject to the gaze of others, to be compelled by their narratives, would be to surrender his manhood; indeed to retire to the domestic sphere is also to succumb to Dalila's fantasy as well.[87] But by active engagement with, and against, this fantasy, he is able to project his masculine future of dramatic conflict and battle.

Another chance for projection is offered by the giant Harapha, who, like all the others, has come to observe. His gaze also reconstructs a history of heroism, and it is offered not to emasculate the captive, but quite the opposite. Harapha proffers his heroic manliness in estimating Samson's worthiness as an opponent:

> I come not, *Samson*, to condole thy chance,
> As these perhaps, yet wish it had not been,
> Though for no friendly intent. I am of *Gath*;
> Men call me *Harapha*, of stock renown'd
> As *Og* or *Anak* and the *Emims* old
> That *Kiriathaim* held: Thou knowst me now
> If thou at all art known. Much I have heard
> Of thy prodigious might and feats perform'd
> Incredible to me, in this displeas'd,
> That I was never present on the place
> Of those encounters, where we might have tried
> Each other's force in camp or listed field;
> And now am come to see of whom such noise
> Hath walk'd about, and each limb to survey,
> If thy appearance answer loud report.
>
> (*SA*, 1076–90)

Harapha offers another kind of appeal to remembrance, one in which identity is produced within an economy of heroic fame, in which reciprocal remembrance is the prize for recognition. "Thou knowst me now/ If thou at all art known" (1081–82) he taunts.

Samson takes up the contest of boastful storytelling, embracing this masculine dialogic relation that serves to constitute self as a mode of knowledge. Refusing the passivity of becoming an object to gaze upon, he hurls back a challenge: "the way to know were not to see but taste" (1091). Threats, verbal actions through which mutual relation may be expressed, ground this exchange wherein masculine heroic identity is configured as a collaborative construction of knowledge about the self. Participating in the economies of remembrance incited by Harapha's dare, Samson rebuffs the giant by disputing his story: "Cam'st thou for this, vain boaster, to survey me,/ To descant on my strength, and give thy verdict?" (1227–28). Competitive storytelling, then, is not merely a temptation spurring Samson to action that returns him to his heroic self, but heroic combat is a means to recognize and to be recognized in turn. This is a better deal than that offered to the fomenters of revolution in the "Act of Oblivion."

The last action of Milton's work is an invitation to a funeral. The mourning father Manoa enjoins all those present to attend,

> With silent obsequy and funeral train
> Home to his Father's house: there will I build him
> A Monument, and plant it round with shade
> Of Laurel ever green, and branching Palm,
> With all his Trophies hung, and Acts enroll'd
> In copious Legend, or sweet Lyric Song.
>
> (*SA*, 1731–37)

This invitation is issued in a series of pentametric iambics, affording some somber regularity of meter after a firestorm of the sprung rhythms and irregular verse, the metrical forms that have just fashioned the teeming language of violence in the play. In this invitation is heard the meter of epic poetry; discursive orderliness is met by that literary tradition: both stand here as against the irregular forms that produce this telling of the violence. That violence of memory recedes as commemoration serves to bind it. The shape of this invitation has already begun to forge a laurel tree; it is a column that constructs a classical shape in its verse.

> Thither shall all the valiant youth resort,
> And from his memory inflame thir breasts
> To matchless valor, and adventures high:
> The Virgins also shall on feastful days
> Visit his Tomb with flowers, only bewailing
> His lot unfortunate in nuptial choice.
>
> (1738–43)

This is a classical monument, not a Dissenting one, and its pedagogy induces virtue. Milton's own drama, on the other hand, is the Dissenting monument.

Silence, but knowing silence, is to be the vocal register for that commemoration. Manoa offers to the assembly a paradox: an obsequy that is silent, a funerary ritual without words, humbly connoting obedience in the shadow-term, *obsequious*. The invitation is extended not only to the

Chorus and Semi-Chorus, but to all the people of the Israelite nation who have just been liberated by Samson's final act. The funeral, moreover, is not to be in a temple; rather it will take place in the domestic space of the household. With this silent assent, Milton's *Samson Agonistes* shows how individual experiences of loss could be shaped into a collective experience through reiteration of a known story. Through performance of that concrete instance, commemoration could take place in the Dissenters' world so as to perform a political and psychologically restorative role in the symbolic order of the dispossessed. During the Restoration, as we have seen, nonconformist funerals were indeed modes of dramatic performance through which the assembled mourners brought their community into being, despite legal bars to their constitution. When seen in relation to this larger culture of Dissent, Milton's close to *Samson Agonistes* may be seen to do political work that is radical in shaping memory. Radicalism here may be understood as discursive construction through shared narratives. Thus "the experience of defeat" might also be a triumph for community identity.

While commemoration – and Milton's reworking of the Samson story from Judges is just that – appears to be about the past, memory-work is an active task undertaken for the present and, most of all, for the future. That commemoration, and the recovery of community potency, is only effected through the annihilation of one of its members, a sacrifice echoing the Christian paradigm. Here, it takes place in space and time, through stories that if they evoke past sufferings also conduct prior experience into the present via commemorative gestures.

Samson's return of belief in God, and then his approval by God, and then the violent acts of the Holy Spirit all revolve around a fundamental fact: God watches and remembers. So pleads Samson in the Bible, Judges 16:28: "Oh Lord God, remember me, I pray thee, and strengthen me." But that is not what Milton's Samson says. What happens at the moment of Samson's regeneration is recounted by a witness: "eyes fast fixt he stood, as one who pray'd" (*SA*, 1637). His own words instead promise action, as if he *already knows* that he has been remembered.

The pleasure of the text is not in Samson's solicitation of God's attention so much as it is approval and recollection that, yes, Samson *was* remembered by God in the end. As much is said by the Chorus whose approval ends the drama:

> All is best, though we oft doubt,
> What th'unsearchable dispose
> Of highest wisdom brings about,
> And ever best found in the close.

> Oft he seems to hide his face,
> But unexpectedly returns
> And to his faithful Champion hath in place
> Bore witness gloriously... (*SA*, 1745–52)

The grammatical subject of the sentence is God, "he" who seems to hide his face, and it is God's witness that matters. That witness is a form of remembrance, returning to his beloved unexpectedly. The unexpected return of the deity, of course, recollects the allegorical return of the beloved in the Song of Songs, and the Chorus here jubilates in the contract with God now proven good. The memory-work of the drama is not in Samson's monument but in the monument of *Samson Agonistes*.

As it turns out, the violence and suffering evoked and purged in *Samson Agonistes* merely shift signifiers, as the gathered body of mourners whose repeated actions of homage fashion a compelling fantasy of cultural power and cohesion also urge on a reversal of fate whereby the Philistines are to be the mourners. If the power of commemoration reaches its idealized apogee in Milton's closing passages of the drama of Samson, nevertheless, there must remain someone who mourns: "whence *Gaza* mourns/ And all that band them to resist/ His uncontrollable intent" (*SA*, 1752–54). While the conclusion of the drama promises an end to bloodshed, "calm of mind, all passion spent" (1758), this may be merely a false closure: the economy of suffering is ultimately a fixed one. As the Chorus moves from grief to celebration, its own mourning is displaced onto the former celebrants who now must occupy the same position as the previously debased champion:

> Unwittingly importun'd
> Thir own destruction to come speedy upon them,
> So fond are mortal men
> Fall'n into wrath divine,
> As thir own ruin on themselves to invite,
> Insensate left, or to sense reprobate,
> And with blindness internal struck. (*SA*, 1680–86)

Celebration comes at great cost, adumbrated in the ever-present currents of violence and rage roiling under the action, which are released in a final frenzy of bloodshed of "this so horrid spectacle" (1542), so terrible it can hardly be reported, no less witnessed. The fantasy is that transformation of suffering into victory can be decisive, instantaneous, and immediate. But that transformation requires a bloodshed and violence that if they are beyond human imagining, are also beyond human responsibility. The

political underpinnings of this exchange of mourning to victory are a politics of retributive violence, a holy war.

By showing productive encounters between past and present, the dead
and the living, Milton's tragedy sealed obligations by allowing readers to
proffer active support in the work of memory, in the name of the future.
Rather than being sealed in the past as victims to passively suffer another
round of violence and reprisal, Dissenters could place themselves as pro-
genitors of a tradition and could take the *active* part, effecting agency
through that reversal. Nonetheless, the bloodstained supplement remains –
not Samson's gory body which will be washed but the Philistine nation
which will mourn next.

Memory thus represents an important aspect of public, or community
obligation: finding stories and apt symbols through which to express, and
to experience collective identities. The messenger, Manoa, the Chorus and
the Semi-Chorus all contribute to the telling, this accumulation of symbols
and meanings and narratives. It is now up to the Israelites to "lay hold on
this occasion," and perform acts of their own. Manoa's storytelling is one
such act, and another is his sending for all his kindred to attend a funeral
train, something that might have been forbidden before, but now, "*Gaza* is
not in plight to say us nay" (*SA*, 1729). To tell the story itself is to perform
the play as a drama of the mind, itself an action of suffering, of passion,
of active memory. If the English Revolution was to be legally forgotten in
an "Act of Oblivion" or to be remembered with vengeance as in the Act of
Uniformity, nonetheless revolutionary conflicts re-emerged in new form.
Whether Dissenters went underground or went to prison in the Restoration,
or veered towards end-time with more avidity, their ideological conflicts
took on new forms, and so their acts of commemoration created an arena
in which to conduct political engagement and the restitution of identity.
It is ironic then that Milton's own tombstone was soon obliterated, his
headstone removed in 1679, making way for steps to be built up to the
altar (according to Aubrey). This was part of a process of Anglicanization
of Milton's parish church at Cripplegate.[88] So Milton's own memorial was
demolished in the name of enhancement of ceremony and sacrament.

Funerals across many cultures solicit individuals' affirmation of an abstract entity of the social whole, forging a social imaginary through a
common experience of loss and reconstruction.[89] The memorials of the Dissenters are of particular interest for understanding the ways that members
of an excluded minority sought to create loyalty to its particular traditions,
to challenge in various ways the state-imposed ceremonialism, and to experience themselves as a collective body. These means, rather than outright

sedition, may be taken as the cultural meaning of their action. In their political contours, those who fought in the realm of memory did not just express words that could not be uttered outright; they also constructed social identities for members of a dispersed and excluded community. Through their performances of commemoration, whether in funeral ritual, gravestone inscription, or in the dramatic retelling of an instance of vengeful heroism, Dissenters altered the conditions of their plight. They lived over the roles that were publicly denied to them, negotiated a troubling history, and came to understand themselves as producers of a tradition that could make current experiences recognizable. Indeed, they recovered action out of forced passivity. In the service of memory, commemoration built significant social experiences, and typological habits of reading offered an account of embodied, radical action.

A paper monument, however, could prove to be more lasting than a stone one, as Richard Baxter discovered when the fire of 1666 smashed the marble headstone for his mother-in-law set up in Christ's-Church near the altar, where his wife was also to be buried: "In the doleful flames of *London*, 1666. the fall of the Church broke this great Marble all to pieces, and it proved no lasting Monument." In contrast, he wrote, "I hope this Paper-Monument, erected by one that is following, even at the door, in some passion indeed of love, and grief, but in sincerity of truth, will be more publickly useful and durable than that Marble-stone was."[90] The rest of this book explores these paper monuments.

CHAPTER 3

Prison

Even if Londoners welcomed the return of Charles II in 1660, not all were prepared for the force of backlash. Although Charles' Declaration at Breda of April had promised clemency along with liberty of conscience, regicides who had not been caught went into hiding. Almost 700 Puritan ministers lost their places in parishes across the counties, to be replaced by the sequestered ministry of the 1640s. Milton during the summer of 1660 waited "in darkness, and with dangers compast round" (*PL*, 7:27). Sectarian meetings were heavily watched. Twenty-eight regicides and one alleged executioner of Charles I were placed on trial in October, and ten were sentenced to death and hung, drawn, and quartered.[1] By February 1661 more than 4,000 Quakers and Baptists were arrested and imprisoned in the space of a few weeks following a Fifth Monarchist rising in London.[2] One newsletter writer noted in August 1662 that most of the prisons in London and in the country were filled with Quakers and Anabaptists; in October of that year it was noted, "many was put in to prison persons that sate in Committees in the dayes of Oliver Cromwell."[3] The re-establishment of monarchy took considerable administrative, military, ecclesiological, and social effort. The many who did not comply found themselves in prison.

Retributive punishment may have been absent from the Act of Oblivion, but after the lost opportunities of Revolutionary spiritual and civil reform, many of the godly faced political exclusion and religious persecution over the Restoration period.[4] There were, however, outlets for their expression of formal opposition to the Crown.[5] Topical political writing, often critical of state policies, flourished in an age of satire and polemic. There were plots, real and imagined, all through the period, and yet most noncon-formists did not align themselves with rebellious activity. Quakers after 1660 condemned violence, and most religious leaders, including John Bunyan, looked to the Christian paradigm of endurance to cope with their experi-ence of suffering. Presbyterians were most willing to seek political solutions within existing structures. Very few Dissenters voiced direct opposition to the restored regime. Were they holding their tongues? Or were they instead making some peace with political authority? There is not one answer to this question, as different solutions to the question of earthly and divine loyalty shook the many separating congregations. The Dissenters, however, expressed their opposition by refusing to conform to the legislated state church. Despite their different political commitments, then, Dissenting writers shared a common experience of isolation and social denial.

To be sure, there was a barrage of oppositional political literature in the topical paper wars of the day; indeed the career of John Dryden's political writings no less than the multi-volume collection *Poems on Affairs of State* testify to the abundance of polemic, but that was not the only kind of writing we ought to consider as doing political work. How ought we to understand political radicalism for those who were not violently seditious? How are we to understand people whose deepest beliefs turned them away from worldly solutions to political problems?

This chapter explores how Dissenters restored meaning in times of despair, as they shaped their own personal suffering in imaginative literature, and thus focuses on the psychological needs of victims to regain esteem. Examining a common experience of suffering from disparate political, religious, and personal perspectives, this chapter takes up the prison writings of three significant Dissenter poets, John Reeve, Vavasor Powell, and Mary Mollineux, and Lucy Hutchinson, who did not go to prison, but whose experience of her husband's death in prison shaped her fiery imagination. Despite their theological differences, these authors held experiences in common: imprisonment, social deprivation, and political censure. Melancholy and despair were common temptations. Dissenting responses to earthly opposition were many, although the Bible gave shape and authority to these diverse experiences, wrapping them in a common strand. Writing from or about prison, they weighed the meaning of virtue and sympathy in the world as they went inward to reflect on their own sins. This was no simple withdrawal into isolated personal meditation. Through adapting the Bible, and especially the Book of Lamentations, they fashioned a common textual legacy, soliciting sympathy from readers and forging bonds in the world. In his principled defense of the beliefs for which he was thrown in gaol, for example, John Bunyan began his poem with a singular, personal "I"; he soon shifted to a first-person plural, a collective we: "Though Men do say, we do disgrace/ Our selves by lying here/ Among the Rogues, yet Christ our face/ From all such filth will clear."[6] The social meanings of such laments may be judged by the publishing successes of a number of these volumes; Vavasor Powell's prison poem, *Tsofer Bepah: The Bird in the Cage* (1661), appeared in three different editions in just two years; John Reeve's hymns were published in 1682, 1684, and then again in 1693; George Wither was an unstoppable publishing presence, smuggling his works out of gaol to be printed. Lucy Hutchinson, however, remained in manuscript, choosing to limit access to her politically daring writings by apparently circulating them to family and friends (her published poem, *Order and Disorder*, appeared without her name). The Quaker Mary Mollineux's *Fruits of Retirement* was reprinted throughout the eighteenth century, including several North American editions. Her writings had long circulated in manuscript, drawing attention from a detractor for their ubiquity, "privately spread up and down over *England* and *Wales*, amongst their People, and highly admired as a Piece unanswerable..."[7] These productions, therefore, reached far beyond the individual sufferer to an audience of sympathetic listeners, forging collective solidarity for those separated in space and prohibited from gathering in public.

PRISON-WRITING AND PROTEST

Dissenters made powerful celebrity prisoners. Bunyan, first arrested in November 1660 for illegal preaching, was given leave to preach in the City of London, though this was soon stopped. He was to sit in prison for twelve years, sermonizing and receiving a number of visitors during his time there. When the Quaker leader George Fox was apprehended in 1660 for illegal preaching, a guard of no fewer than fifteen or sixteen kept watch over him, some sitting in the chimney for fear he would escape. At Lancaster Assizes, he spoke to crowds from the window of his gaol.[8] Edmund Calamy, as we have noted, attracted a traffic jam of coaches and pamphlet comment during his brief imprisonment for taking the pulpit after Uniformity went into effect.

Even if prison offered a pulpit, imprisonment was nonetheless a miserable circumstance. Present were the dangers of maltreatment, physical abuse, loneliness, harassment, humiliation, starvation, gaol-fever, plague, or smallpox. Families as well as individuals suffered: bouts in prison could mean the loss of a household's income. The psychological consequences of imprisonment were debilitating: the loss of public presence, social esteem, and personal agency. John Bunyan, an exceptionally long prison-sitter himself, well understood the psychology of suffering behind bars. In *Pilgrim's Progress*, the pilgrim Christian is made to look upon a man in gaol, who sits in the dark, eyes cast down, and sighing "as if he would break his heart." This man unburdens his confession: "I was once a fair and flourishing professor, both in mine own eyes, and also in the eyes of others; I once was, as I thought, fair for the Celestial City, and had then even joy at the thoughts that I should get thither." The pilgrim is puzzled: his is that very same hope; his is that very same journey. "*Well, but what art thou now?*" is his question, one near to his own heart and one which is also directed to Bunyan's readers, those suffering saints who also sit in the darkness that is England's shame. The man answers, "I am *now* a man of despair, and am shut up in it, as in this iron cage. I cannot get out; O now I cannot."[9]

The difference between the Dissenters' plight and that of the wretch in Bunyan's story is that Bunyan's man has abandoned God first; he sits in a prison of his own making. For this portrait, Bunyan's model is thought to be one John Child, silk-weaver of Bedford, a lapsed Baptist who had been a Fifth Monarchist and a leading member of the Bedford church in the 1650s, but who in 1660 conformed to the Church of England and thereby became a sad lesson for the nonconformists. Often visited after his lapse by Bunyan and other fellow Baptists, Child later hanged himself.[10] The Man in the Iron Cage has pushed self-reproach too far, bewailing that he has shut himself out "of all the promises; and there now remains to me nothing but threatenings, dreadful threatenings, fearful threatenings of certain judgement and fiery indignation, which shall devour me as an adversary."[11] Bunyan's Man in the Iron Cage lives in the dark because, though he has remembered all too well his own sins, he has nevertheless forgotten God's promise of salvation, refusing to repent.

His condition reflects precisely that which tempts the bound Dissenter: to despair, to capitulate to the authorities. The lure of despair almost catches Christian and his companion Hopeful who, late in *Pilgrim's Progress*, find themselves in the prison of the Doubting Castle, oppressed by the Giant Despair. They contemplate suicide and almost surrender to their terrors. Prison conditions were certainly propitious for melancholy. *Pilgrim's Progress* would help Bunyan's readers to avoid just that despairing outcome, a prison-text catalyst for his readers to remain hopeful. A long view was necessary to keep the spirits up. In *Prison-Meditations, Directed to the Heart of Suffering Saints and Reigning Sinners* (1663), Bunyan shows prison to be a secluded space in which to experience a vision of a world out of time, in his simple ballad-meter rhythms:

> This Goal to us, is as a Hill,
> From whence we plainly see
> Beyond this World, and take our fill
> Of things that lasting be.[12]

Guilt and hope: twinned in the prisoner's heart, in these emotions nonconformists also yearned to explain recent history. For Bunyan and for others
suffering persecution after the Restoration, the turn of events could seem
very much like judgment against them by the very God for whom radical
action had been undertaken in the first place. The worry was ever-present:
perhaps they had sinned and deserved to suffer. Thus the nonconformist
minister Elias Pledger the younger urged those who were troubled by "the
churches adversity" to "examine how far we have contributed to it by o[ur]
particular sins."[13] As Richard Baxter eyed the settling of the nations on
the eve of legal return of monarchy, he preached his sermon *A Sense of
Repentance* to the House of Commons on 30 April 1660 on the biblical passage Ezekiel 36:31 ("Then shall ye remember your own evil ways,
and your doings that were not good, and shall loathe yourselves in your
own sight for your iniquities and for your abominations"). Baxter linked
remembrance with guilt, demanding his listeners heed the counsel that
"*The Remembring of their own iniquities, and loathing themselves for them,
is the sign of a Repenting people, and the prognostick of their Restoration.*"[14]
Proper remembrance and repentance in this case meant that each admit
culpability, that each sitting in audition of that sermon should flog himself,
"and each man say, *What a wretch was I? What an unreasonable self-hating
wretch, to do all this against my self? What an unnatural wretch! What a
monster of rebellion and ingratitude, to do all this against the Lord of love and
mercy? What a deceived foolish wretch!... to be sold for a harlot, for a forbidden
cup, for a little aire of popular applause, or for a burdensome load of wealth and
power, for so short a time?*" (*Sense*, 27). The crime is forgetting God in favor
of earthly power; the political lesson is equivocal (is Baxter condemning
the Commonwealth? Is Baxter condemning the pre-civil war church?).

In 1660, Baxter still hoped that the restored government would open the
way towards greater recognition to Puritans through latitude in religious
practices; that liberalism was not favored by the new regime. As the search
for an accommodation failed and even Baxter found himself suffering exile
from the heart of power, his rhetoric of remembrance and repentance was
deepened with the colors of self-reproach. Baxter may have encouraged
self-blame in 1660 – "For this *loathing* is a kind of *Justice* done upon our
selves" (*Sense*, 6) – but he also recognized that his theology could lead
to true despair. Baxter was an early exponent of psychological counseling,
what has been called pastoral therapy, and he recorded among his typology
of melancholy the category of those with excessive fearfulness, which led
sufferers to self-accusation, "apprehending themselves *forsaken of God*, and
prone to Despair. They are just like a man in a Wilderness, forsaken of all

his Friends and Comforts; forlorn and desolate, their continual thought is, I am undone, undone, undone!"[15] Recollection of sins could thus be both a cause and a cure of dis-ease. Such reflexive blame about political failure as spiritual failure could also lead to a world of paranoia, where even the tiniest action could be understood as a sign of backsliding. It could also be the response to social and political exclusion.

Prison-sitting may have been for Bunyan an opportunity to reflect and to ponder the hereafter, but it also gave room for violent augury. "A Prisoners verdict" recapitulates prophecies foretelling the fall of the Temple, given contemporary parallel. This author, possibly the Presbyterian divine Joshua Kirby (d. 1676), along with whose anagram this poem appeared, reflects the tenuous position of some conservative Presbyterians during this turbulent era. Kirby had refused the Engagement, the oath of loyalty to the Commonwealth government, in 1650, was ejected by the Cromwellian church, and was a participant in Booth's royalist rising in 1659. After the Restoration he later sat in prison for three months in 1664 for preaching illegally in his house. He died excommunicate in 1676, buried in the garden of Flanshaw Hall, Wakefield. In his poem he reflects on the current condition of persecution and on his own status as a prisoner, recalling the work of the civil war period was not yet complete:

> An army rampant first mee prisoner made
> A Rampant Kirk now taketh up their Trade.
> faln is that army and that kirk must fall
> the Temple wil consume the Cathedrall
> the Stones have been remov'd in wch was found
> the Leprosy: the house was scraped round:
> new Stones are laid: al is new plasterd,
> Yet stil the fretting Leprosy doth spread,
> the Harlots mark cannot be purged with nitre
> Nor can Melchisedeck brook Aarons mitre.[16]

In his scheme of history, succession depends upon destruction. The cry for vengeance carries with it implicit protest against justice transgressed.

In calling for revenge the prisoner made a final plea over the head of the oppressor to a higher authority. A letter from a friend to the Quaker Benjamin Antrobus in gaol commits to a future where injustice would be routed by violence:

> Why do the Nations rage, and still conspire
> Against our God? Think they to quench his Fire?
> False Flames of Holiness they may put out,
> But *Israel's* Armies *Ashur* cannot rout:

> Their Blood's a Conquering Sword, which wounds that part,
> *Galen* can never cure with all his Art.
>> But what's your Crime? dissent from Man's Devotion;
>> O *Luther! Luther!* Didst thou leave this Notion
>> To thy Reformers? Were they to protest
>> Against the Birds, & force into the Nest?
>> Away with such Soul-drivers: O my God!
> Drive out such Merchants with thy Powerful Rod.[17]

Consolation was to be found in the reiteration of the biblical narrative of violent fantasy, but the appeal to Luther reveals another component of this restitution of communal identity. Lamenting his absence as much as asking a question – what will be Luther's legacy? – Antrobus takes Luther as the sign that could unify a nation currently rent by division. Prison was not a stoical retreat in which to balance the passions, rather, a place to ponder and prepare violent action.

Out of abasement would come searing poetry. John Reeve, the Baptist minister who was committed in March 1677 for selling copies of a seditious pamphlet, is a good case through which to explore how personal and religious distress were rapidly converted to political ends. Called by a detractor a "Trumpet blown outright for Rebellion," the pamphlet dispersed by Reeve was *The Long Parliament Dissolved* (1676), an unsigned piece written by the Presbyterian peer, Lord Denzel Holles who, along with Shaftesbury and others, was beginning to mount a Whig opposition to the Crown, here defending "Lives, Liberties and Fortunes from all wrongs of the Government."[18] The extent of Reeve's Whig or radical career is not known; he shared in common with Baxter, Calamy, and Keach one of the leading Presbyterian booksellers, Thomas Hancock, Senior. Publishing his first collection of poetry in 1682, Reeve recalled his time in prison, "being in his own and others eyes, under a sentence of death despaired of life (in an agony of dolour)," at which time he was rescued by a biblical remembrance, "suddenly injected and impress't upon his spirit that place, *Psal. 32.7*, preserve from trouble, and compass me about with songs of deliv'rance. Which makes me say if God has perform'd his part in the former, ought not I to essay to sing thus."[19] Reeve's composition is a contract with God in exchange for his rehabilitation. Yet deliverance is more than just release from despair, or even from prison: his poetry is coded with a political message that would be hard to miss in the fiery polemics of the 1670s and 1680s.

The seclusion of prison was a powerful metaphor for an antisocial purity. For instance, Reeve prefaced his 1684 collection of poems with a description of the half-light that framed their composition:

> These *Hymns* were most composed in the dark,
> When restless hours interrupted sleep:
> With a design to stop that rambling work,
> Ungovern'd fancy useth then to keep.
> Better make Hymns than yield to Melancholy,
> Or take the World to govern by a thoughtful folly.

The compositions are a prophylactic against personal sorrow, and yet they also reached out to an audience beyond the prison walls. Reeve writes his prologue poem "To the chast and pure Virgin-Souls, that love the Lord Jesus," ending with a promise to send his words out into the world, to be understood by those special few: "Nor had this been expos'd to publick view,/ But that the Child was drawn by Cogent hand:/ 'Twas hard to trust it, when there are so few/ Chast Eyes, and pure Minds, abroad the land."[20]

Reeve's book of poetry is ostensibly a rendering of that most favored of Puritan texts, the Song of Songs, yet he laces its lines with powerful political content. Rewriting Canticles 1:6, "They made me keeper of the Vineyards," Reeve produces an anti-episcopal poem that wraps its radicalism in the authority of divine purpose:

> Arise, O Lord, some help afford;
>   To thee my Soul doth moan:
> I cannot hold, I must unfold
>   My grief to thee alone.
> They've gotten Vineyards here and there,
>   Exotick to thy Laws,
> Which by their force they'l make me keep,
>   From which my Soul withdraws.

Though Reeve in a flat-footed way pushes the allegory too far ("Their Figs are naught, their Grapes are sour,/ Their Vintage is not good"), his political position is unequivocal: "Their Winepress is to press the Saints;/ Their Liquor is their blood." The poem boldly challenges the reigning religious orthodoxy:

> They've got a Vineyard strange to thee,
>   No Scripture-rule must guide it;
> And they'd have me their slave to be:
>   O Lord! I can't abide it.[21]

Reeve considered this political condition as a loss of personal identity:

> Alas! When I with them comply,
>   My soul doth suffer loss:

> My Vine doth languish, and my Trees
>> Are overgrown with Moss.
> My Graces they felt a decay,
>> My Plants began to dye,
> My Conscience bled, my Joys were fled;
>> Oh, what a Wretch was I!²²

This heart-broken lament begins the passage with a personal "I," a lone self that becomes Christ's "I" in the familiar vineyard trope. Christ's vine/trees/plants are one and the same as "my" conscience: through reiteration of the archetype, the poet finds a narrative constitutive of his identity that can speak to personal and political bereavements. With the verb tenses shifting from present to past, that metaphoric substitution is incomplete and ongoing. Present compliance to unjust ordinances (1) *precedes* the consequent degeneration figured in the garden (6–7), yet that degeneration, and the resulting wretched feelings and impairment of the conscience, are represented in the past tense, *as if they had already happened*. This confusion about cause and effect, played out in the ambiguous tenses, reveals the ambivalence of deprivation and responsibility, an ambivalence that was heightened by the problem of compulsion which denied personal agency ("they'd have me their slave to be"). Even though physical coercion removes individual responsibility for action, the consequences of forced actions are borne by the actor. The subjected soul, then, takes the loss inside, internalizes the injurious act, and claims it as a badge of his own wretchedness.

A melancholic structure has been seen as central to Calvinism, as in Max Weber's account of the Puritan work ethic, where guilt and unworthiness are found to be constitutive of modern subjects.²³ Even Richard Baxter wondered if the doctrine of predestination had led some to despair.²⁴ Melancholy was a consequence of a precise historical social experience of exclusion and cultural marginalization, however, not simply a result of Reformation Calvinism and its demands for self-scrutiny. That mental anguish was the source of fury that was ultimately political. Fending off the melancholy that threatens him in those dark shadows, John Reeve rouses his muse to a fiery prediction, and by Hymn 54, confidently prophesies against the current political regime:

> If Hosts against me rise,
>> And Men of War shall scare me:
> The Lord of Hosts will send his Hosts,
>> They in their arms shall bear me.
> The Lord will Muster up
>> And send them to the Courts

> Of Tyrant Rulers, who shall down
>   With them, and all their Forts.
> Believe it, there are Thrones,
>   And Nobles sit upon them:
> Above the earthly greatest Ones,
>   And Judgments issue from them
> These, these shall do us right,
>   When we can nothing do;
> With *Herod's* of the World shall fight,
>   And overcome them too.[25]

A trivial verse in Canticles 3:8 ("They all hold swords, being expert in war: every man hath his sword upon his thigh, because of fear of the night") is given remarkable reworking, as Reeve turns from passive victim to active indicter in these lines. Predicting holy war against the persecuting regime, the speaker invokes heavenly justice. Reeve wields his pen in an uncongenial political landscape that threatens his very psyche; his only strength against his melancholy is to summon a super-potent agent of resistance. In the Restoration, Dissenters championed the melancholy stereotype in order to reconstitute lost strength and to bear up for the future. Self-blame could thus quickly shift to blame outwards against persecutors. A mournful affect in the Restoration thus also did political work, as Puritans wore their melancholy as a badge of purity and a mark of solidarity. While many Dissenters refrained from overt political condemnation of their persecutors – whether because of political censorship, shame, or uncertainty about God's ways and means – their self-abasing condemnations and laments may be taken as evidence of protest against the persecuting regime.

When Reeve lances at the pleasure-seeking culture which surrounds and isolates him he embraces a regenerating fury. As his jingly rhyme opposes *melancholy* and *folly*, Reeve challenges the dominant ethos of libertinism, writing to separate his audience of "chast and pure" readers from the rest of society:

> . . . our Loves are still Divine;
> The stinking Dunghils can't put out the Sun:
> While you sing out your shame, we will incline
> To sing the Praise of Gods eternal Son.
> We will in Psalms and Hymns, and Spiritual Song
> Outsing the Mirth obscene, which unto you belongs.[26]

Here melancholy serves as a form of resistance. Writing is taking sides in a world divided into two societies: he does not speak his own love, but "our Loves," as he forges bonds with others of like mind. Reeve's readers must have responded; his volume was reprinted in a second edition in 1693.

Against the ethos of libertine sensuality, this mourning could negate the Restoration policy of joy and make antisociality an alternate basis of community. Baxter, preaching a sermon at St. Paul's before the Lord Mayor and Aldermen of London just two days after the king's legal restoration, 10 May 1660, gave a lightning response to the reckless celebration in the capital. In *Right Rejoycing, or, the Nature and Order of Rational and Warrantable Joy*, he reacted in horror to the air of carnival festivity, and urged moderation: "Alas, Sirs, its a most pitifull sight, to see men frisk about in jollity, with the marks of death and wrath upon them! And to see men so phrantickly merry in their sin, as to forget the misery that will so quickly marre their mirth." Asking his audience to look instead to the heavenly kingdom, Baxter advised that to rejoice in earthly powers was as "*unseemly,* as for a man to glory that his gangren'd foot hath a handsom shoo." To those who were not rejoicing, he comforted, "And though you weep and lament when the world rejoyceth, as their joy shall be turned into sorrow, so your sorrow shall be turned into joy, and your joy shall no man take from you."[27]

LUCY HUTCHINSON AND THE POETICS OF DARKNESS

Although her republican revolution began its failure with the Cromwellian usurpation, Lucy Hutchinson's godly reformation remained alive. Lucy Hutchinson (1620–81) never went to prison herself (though she was born in the Tower of London whilst her father was keeper there), but her husband died in 1664 whilst imprisoned on charges of sedition, and she began composition of his life thereafter in the later 1660s. Lucy Hutchinson, a republican in politics and an Independent in religion, was a formidable, classically trained author, whose literary esteem is revealed in the portrait by Robert Walker, which pictures her holding a poet's wreath of laurels. In the Cromwellian era, she translated Lucretius' *De rerum natura*, and her literary ambition did not stop there; in the Restoration she also composed an epic-length, ten-canto poem, a biblical meditation, *Order and Disorder*, five cantos of which were published anonymously in 1679. She was probably a member of John Owen's Independent congregation in London in the Restoration.[28] In her "Elegies," composed presumably between 1664 and 1668, the republican widow of a regicide offers a series of grieving reflections on the loss of her husband, as well as upon the Revolution's failure. Hers is a backward-looking poetry, remembering the past in order to beseech a witnessing God to act on behalf of the faithful. Just as her history of the

Puritan revolution was fashioned through the story of her husband, so is her response to the Restoration context figured as a personal forfeiture, ever mindful of the conditions of imprisonment in which her husband suffered. Under the rubric of personal elegy, Hutchinson is writing political poetry in a post-Revolutionary climate deeply suspicious of republican, godly politics.[29] In her dark Restoration vision, the world is turned upside down, and there is an interlacing of a grief over civil war atrocity that she would rather keep private, and protest against the relentless theatre that has become the public sphere. The poem "To the Sun Shineing into her Cham[be]r" begins:

> Bright [day] starre looke not in at me
> Thou canst not in Thy Circutt see
> A spectacle of greater woe
> And Those wrongs That haue made me soe
> Ware in Thy guilty p'sence done
> Thou Sawest O Thou alseeing Sun
> The blood of Noble Patriots Shed
> By Those Ingrates for whome They bled
> Thou wartt Their Torch berrer when They
> To Prison and Exile ware led away
> The glory of ye unthankfull Land
> And bound ye Nations Conquering hand
> Thou sawest my Desolation made
> And Comest Thou now my rewin to upbrade
> Let me and my Just greifes alone
> Goe guild ye tyrants bloody Throne
> Cast lustre on The Strumpetts face
> Reveale Their glories in full grace
> And lett The Greate ones by Thy Light
> Act crymes wch Used to black The Night
> But keepe away Thy prying beames
> From lookeing one Those silent Streames
> Which from our Eies in Secrett fall
> Wayling a Publick funerall.   ("Elegies," 489)

In her self-abasement Hutchinson does not take on the blandishments of her enemies; rather, she is led to accusation. The sun may will to see all there is to see, and yet the language depicting that power is that of chastisement. Seeing denotes responsibility, even causality: "Thou Sawest... Thou Sawest" is a phrasing that endows seeing with moral claims. The poem alludes if not to Charles II then to a language that painted him in solar terms; that king whose restoration was hailed as a return of sun after a rain shower, or whose brightness was thought to be increased in lustre due to his previous exile ("More Splendid made by dark Afflictions Night;/ Live ever Monarch in Coelestial Light" crowed a gratulatory poem in 1660[30]). Yet Hutchinson's vision replaces that ordinary meaning of sun with a dark reflection; the world must be turned upside down if that is the sun. Light only illuminates the moral depravity of the contemporary world, and the poem challenges its *lustre* (plying the word *lust*), registering a protest against the sun itself for its moral indifference to public vices. Milton's great ode on light, the proem to Book Three of *Paradise Lost*, likewise sympathizes with that creature of darkness, the nightingale: "Then feed on thoughts, that voluntary move/ Harmonious numbers; as the wakeful Bird/ Sings darkling, and in shadiest Covert hid/ Tunes her nocturnal Note" (*PL*, 3:37–40), evoking the traditional figure of song, but also laying claim to a poetics of darkness. The true source of inspiration is hidden from sight; that the poet is himself barred from seeing is a sign of his elevation. The Dissenting muse is a nocturnal visitor, "who deigns/ Her nightly visitation unimplor'd/ And dictates to me slumb'ring" (*PL*, 9:21–23).

In a perversion of the sun's natural rights, however, Hutchinson chooses not to be seen (indeed her own woe is invisible, noiseless, and secret). Her poem is about looking, making observations on contemporary courtly life, and yet the eye of the all-seeing sun itself is barred from gazing on those griefs which are within. If the sun can see all, Hutchinson herself feels too visible; she wishes to remain in darkness. There is no place for the sun in her inner world of grief, a world that remains, finally, private even though that which it mourns is a "Publick funerall."

"I Thus began to chide Th'im[m]odest Sun," writes Hutchinson in another poem on the sun,

> How Gawdy Masker darst Thou looke on me
> Whose Sable Coverings Thy reproaches be
> Thou to our murtherers Thy taper bearst
> Th'oppressive race of men Thou warmst and Chearst.
> ("Elegies," 492)

If to be in the sun is to partake in murder and oppression, Hutchinson's choosing to remain in the shadows, to insist upon the mode of grief, is a political challenge. Puritanism and melancholy are old partners in the popular imagination; and yet in Hutchinson's elegies we can see that a stubborn resistance to joy is not merely a psychic affect but also conveys political meaning, as she sets her melancholy refusal against those "Who smiling doest on lust & [rapine] shine/ Nor Shrinkst Thy head in at disgorgd wine"

(493). To those currently in the sun she stoutly chides:

> Thou sawst ye league of God himselfe dissolvd
> Wch a whole Nation in one curse Involvd
> Thou Sawst a Thankelesse people slaughtring those
> Whose noble blood redeemd ym from their foes
> Thy staind beames into The Prison came
> But lost their boasts outshind wth vertues flame
> Thou Sawst ye Innocent to exile Led
> And for all This veildest not Thy radiant head
> But comst as a gay courtier to deride
> Reuines we would in Silent Shaddowes hide.
>
>   ("Elegies," 493)

In this lament, Hutchinson reworks the previous poem's material into the more expansive form of iambic pentameter. The anger is given greater amplitude, and the result is a harrowing curse:

> Since yn Thou wilt Thurst into This darke roome
> By Thyne owne light read Thy most certeine doom
> Darkenesse shall shortly quench Thy impure light
> And Thou Shalt Sett in Everlasting Night
> Those whome Thou flattriest shall se ye expire
> And have no light but Thier [owne] funerall fire
> Theire shall They in a dreadfull wild amaze
> At once see all Their glorious Idolls blaze.
>
>   ("Elegies," 493)

The apocalyptic vision will restore the true light, clearing away this pale imposter. To be left to mourn, then, is Hutchinson's only wish; and it is a direct challenge against the forces of mirth released with the return of monarchy in 1660. In the violent fantasy the self-negating impulses of blame and dejection are released outward, against the oppressors.

 The extreme degree of privation was also a sign that radical reversal could be imminent. This logic was the gift of apocalyptic thought. Christopher Ness (1621–1705), an Independent minister who had been excommunicated no fewer than four times, wrote about afflictions in 1679, that "usually sorest is last, as in the bondage of Egypt their bricks were doubled upon them... The last brunt of Affliction before the Church's Moses come will be the sharpest."[31] Extreme suffering was thus a harbinger of radical change. The centrality of the experience of captivity in this apocalyptic scheme of history cannot be overstated; it was both a real experience, and one overlain by the long history of repeated oppressions, a history told in Foxe's *Actes and*

Monuments.[32] The death of Charles I, for instance, had been heralded as a sign of the new order that would come. Preaching on 19 April 1649, within two months of the king's execution, the leading Independent John Owen observed the hand of God in the political travails of the nation: "Now God hath promised saying, Yet Once More, I shake not the earth only, but also heaven. And this word, Yet Once More, signifieth the removing of those things that are shaken, as of things that are made, that those things which cannot be shaken may remain."[33] Owen proclaimed that the reign of Antichristian tyranny was being overturned by the reign of Christ. Reversal at the Restoration was taken by Dissenters as another turn of the wheel. As the Quaker poet Mary Mollineux wrote from prison in 1685, "He'll overturn, and overturn again,/ Until he come, whose Right it is, to reign."[34] Time was servant to God's will. Dissenting chronology was fitted to the irregular paces of long periods of affliction and rapid reversal. Just as suffering could be exchanged for triumph in an instant, so ease could give way to oppression, with an almost inexplicable expedience.

Did not God "now appeare pullinge all downe againe, leadinge our Strength into captivity, and giveing our Glory into his Enemies hands?" asked the republican Robert Overton, languishing in prison on the island of Jersey. But rather than surrender to the belief that God had abandoned "our" cause, Overton rallied, "The Lorde takes speciall notice on w[ch] side we stand, when he is dealieinge wth his owne children for their folly. But his rebuke is not upon his People for their Principle, but for their impious practices, repugnante to [that] principle they held forth, & professed."[35] For Overton, collective sins had led to collective punishment. By believing that national political choices had brought down God's wrath, these religious writers could restore some hope that human reformation of politics mattered.

THE POWER OF LAMENTATIONS

For the prisoner who saw himself in a story larger than his own personal experience, prison was thus a pulpit, a privileged space for expressing disobedience. "Captivity improved into Freedom by the Grace of God," commented Wither in one of his several prison verses.[36] John Bunyan fancies his dream of *The Pilgrim's Progress* whilst sleeping in prison, the frontispiece illustrating the freedom of thought permitted in confinement. A swift turn of mind exchanges the prison for the Holy Land imagined in the biblical Song of Songs, as Mary Mollineux wrote of her imprisonment "only for

Conscience-sake" in Lancaster Castle in 1684:

> And though in Prison's outwardly they be
> Confin'd, the Son of Love doth set them free,
> And leads in verdant Plains of Liberty:
> The fresh fat Valleys, where sweet *Shiloh* flows,
> Upon whose fertile Banks the Lilly grows;
> Where, tho he by some Exercises prove,
> He sollaceth with Flaggons of his Love.[37]

Writing out of the experience of dispossession, and for the real prisoners in his audience, Richard Baxter asks Christ, "What if in Prison I must dwell/ May I not there converse with thee?" continuing:

> No walls or bars can keep thee out:
> None can confine a holy Soul:
> The streets of Heav'n it walks about;
> None can its Liberty controul.[38]

Samuel Butler would mock this nonconformist genre, chiding, "No where, but in a Prison, free."[39] But Butler misses what is important about Baxter's prison: the liberty is not taken, but granted from above. This genre links Puritans to those moving prison songs of the likes of Richard Lovelace ("Stone walls do not a prison make,/ Nor iron bars a cage...If I have freedom in my love/ and in my soul am free"), but Dissenters differ in their expectations from those passively withdrawn Cavaliers by their reaching to God and also a wider audience to effect justice in an apocalyptic scheme.

Writing of liberty whilst in bonds, indeed, any kind of writing, was a potent means for the prisoner to appeal to an unnamed audience, not only to God but to his fellow sufferers. The authorities recognized this when George Wither was sent to prison in March 1662 for writing a libel, when they denied him pen and ink.[40] Irrepressible, Wither wrote in charcoal instead, his writings smuggled out "by a visitant of oppressed prisoners," including a pamphlet examining how "Imprisonment is more safe than Liberty."[41] Incarceration could be made a moral victory, a reversal of the terms of success and defeat. It was also a space for writing and from which publications streamed over the period. Published writings by prisoners indicted oppressors, capitalizing on the familiar image of the long-suffering stoical saint and reversing the narrative construction of "defeat." As Bunyan put it, "the persecution of the godly was, of God, never intended for their destruction, but for their glory, and to make them shine the more when they are beyond this valley of the shadow of death."[42] Neil Keeble has given a rich account of how persecution "is the badge of the saint."[43] Out of this nexus of melancholia and abjection arose an enabling myth, what Jean Delumeau has called a "seige mentality." In describing the early modern theological arousal of fear, Delumeau suggests that "when a seige mentality takes hold of either an individual or a group, there is a risk of feeling more exalted and powerful the more one senses one's growing weakness in a losing battle against the enemy."[44] Restoration nonconformists could find the weapons for rearmament of the self not only by awakening ancient terrors, through apocalyptic thought – with its hopes, its violence, and its paranoia. Exchanging their position of weakness for one of terrifying potency, the disempowered could also transform their alarms of destruction into a heroic struggle between the forces of God and Antichrist. Threats experienced against oneself and one's community could now be turned outward to become threats against enemies, and a language of intimidation and violence could replace that of cowering self-negation. From an experience of dispossession and social exclusion, many nonconformists who gave up on earthly political solutions expressed their radicalism through imaginative writing filled with dreams of apocalyptic revenge.

Psychological survival was not simply personal but social as well, as Dissenters sought known stories which could give meaning to their experiences. The Independent leader John Owen begged his people to be confident that God would indeed remember them: "*Every Circumstance in suffering shall add to the Glory of the Sufferer*; and those who suffer here for Christ without witness, as many have done to Death in Prisons and Dungeons, have yet an *all-seeing witness* to give the Testimony in due Season. *The righteous shall be had in everlasting remembrance*; and nothing that is done or suffered for God shall be lost forever."[45] Owen posits a God who will give the sufferer recognition. What is important is that misery is recognized, given witness, that no one experience pain without record, without meaning. The fear is about the loss of memory that becomes equivalent to the denial of existential meaning. In this circular economy of remembering, Owen and others sought to provide a symbolic network in which to enclose the extended social negations that lay at the heart of Dissent. If nonconformists negated the restored regime and they were negated in turn from social recognition, then God would restitute his beloved people to their rightful place before long.

From biblical history, Dissenters summoned the fall of Jerusalem to Babylon, recalling the Lamentations of Jeremiah as their urtext. Giving meaning to exclusion through the framework of diasporic exile, and finding in the words of the Bible a divine, ongoing purpose, Dissenters could both make sense of recent events and name their place within history. The Lamentations of Jeremiah had long been popular in the Puritan imagination. George Wither (1623) and Francis Quarles (1624) had each composed paraphrases; Wither had noted that they were "as useful as any part of the old *Testament* for these Times (nigh fallen asleepe in securitie)," and that they gave proof that "the overthrow of *Kingdomes*, and *Empires*, followes the abuse and neglect of *Religion*."[46] If suffering was the perpetual mode of Puritan experience, nonetheless it found a match in Restoration circumstances, as if Puritans found confirmation of their place in God's story by taking on misery's mantle. Lamentation as a literary mode recalled a long history of repeated mourning and loss recorded in the Bible. The Bible could help to explain the present, not merely as a decoy for political views that could not be expressed otherwise, but because the present was in fact tightly related to what had happened before. Faith in this connection was a social contract with a God who had promised protection in exchange for obedience.

For the fiery Welsh Baptist Powell, who composed an English version of *The Lamentations of Jeremiah* in 1661 during one of his many incarcerations after the Restoration, the Bible was not simply a parallel to contemporary abasement, but a living source of prophecy and hope. Powell was an unrepentant radical whose poetry breathed the urgency and terrors of the persecuted saint longing to rectify his stature in the world. Powell, who had condemned the Protectorate in a 1654 petition, *A Word for God*, was arrested in April 1660 for alleged plotting against the Restoration. After being held in Shrewsbury gaol for nine weeks, upon his release, and against the orders of the high sheriff of Montgomeryshire, he resumed his preaching, and was arrested again in July along with a number of his allies and supporters. Powell's meetings allegedy attracted 400 listeners, who were seen by the authorities as a militant threat. His tract, *Common-Prayer-Book No Divine Service* (1661), challenged the state religion. He was finally released in November 1667, but rearrested about September 1668. He died at the Fleet prison in London in 1671, still hoping for a Fifth-Monarchist emancipation.[47]

Justice – and violence – were at the heart of his mournful prison poetry. Writing his rendition of Lamentations "in meeter," Powell subjected his foes to the very exclusions and abasement he suffered whilst in prison:

> Render to them a recompence,
>   O Lord, according to
> Their handy works, give them thy curse
>   Yea them hearty sorrow.

> Persecute and destroy them in
> anger from under *Thy*
> *Glorious* heavens, who only art
> The Lord God *Almighty*.[48]

Adding to the original text of Lamentations, Powell characterizes his God: "who only art/ the Lord God Almighty," as if to distinguish his God from that of others, heightening the distinctiveness of his religious choice. Seeking compensation for his pains, the words of Lamentations evoke a vision of justice in which a God of violence will triumph.

With its rough rhyme (Thy/ Almighty), the verse lacks artfulness and certainly fluidity as the lines are forced to fit an English hymn line length, but without regular rhythm. Meaning is severed by conspicuous line breaks. The rendition is halfway between verse and prose, perhaps reflecting uncertainty about the metrical shape of Lamentations that was a subject of debate for Renaissance philologists. Is Powell just a bad poet, or is this roughness a deliberate bid for another kind of protest against smooth rhyme? His Hebraism extends to the abundant use of parallelism, his repetitions of meaning that add force to his vindictive outburst ("give them thy curse/ Yea them hearty sorrow"), but his poetry fails to deploy parallelism to good effect (the various imperatives in this passage – Render to them, give them, persecute and destroy them – stand in no certain relation to each other).

In his Lamentations, rather than poetic affect, Powell serves up a fiery protest, calling for radical action. The poetry is just a vehicle for the expression of sentiment, rather than intricately involved in literariness – there is no aesthetic distance here. As he cries out of prison in echo of Lamentations, "Because I have most grievously/ rebelled this is come," his own affliction gives him assurance that a just God is attentive: "He bent his Bow, and set me as/ a mark for the Arrow." Powell, the sufferer, is God's primary target of wrath. He adds to the words of Lamentations 3:22: "Because his compassions fail not, *we still live in his sight*."[49] Yet that very watchfulness is the condition of his vindication. Admitting sin, abasing himself before the potency of his God, Powell lurches towards a future he is certain will restore right. God's presence in history, even if as punisher, is a reminder that God still has a role to play. His God *will* remember His promise:

> Wherefore dost thou forget us *Lord*,
> *and that* for ever more,
> And us forsake for length of days,
> *This makes our suffering sore.*

> Turn thou us unto thee, O Lord,
> and we shall be turned:
> Renew our days, as *Thou* of old
> *did'st, and hast promised.*[50]

Violence was a sign of God's concern for his suffering people. As Powell adapts Lamentations to suit the needs of the abased Restoration saint he builds on a millenarian hopefulness. Without an interest in the beauty of this poetry, his poetry is meant for action. His own poem finishes with a prod to the saints in the meantime:

> The Lord is good to them that
> wait for him *patiently*,
> And good unto the Soul that doth
> seek him *effectually*.
> It is good that a man should both
> hope, *and* wait quietly:
> For the salvation of the Lord
> *which unto his is nigh.*[51]

This apocalyptic scheme of history makes human virtue and discipline essential to a divine plan.

Maintaining hope that God would indeed rescue his fallen people, Powell prefaced his 1661 prison writings, *The Bird in the Cage*, with an exhortation to his readers not to give up hope:

my Brethren, the hour of temptation being come upon us, let us redeem time, be watchful and sober, keeping our lights burning, our Lamps shining, our Loyns girded, our consciences awakned, & our garments unstained . . . Let us wisely consider Gods works, and wonders (though others should slight them) and maintain Gods Wayes and Cause, though they be despised by most; and let us not carnally comply with, nor superstitiously conform to the world, to save our estates, Liberties or Lives: Nor yet forsake the assembling of your selves together, but edifie, confirm and comfort one another; Encouraging the weak, helping to restor those that are faln, and to establish those that yet stand.[52]

To "redeem time" is an ambiguous statement regarding agency – is it God's or "ours?" – and by evoking traditional biblical images (being watchful, keeping lights burning, lamps shining, loins girded, etc.) Powell recalls ancient actions even as he enjoins his contemporaries to fulfill them in present terms (opposing those who would "superstitiously conform").

To choose the lamenting mode was to identify with the ancient people Israel. The biblical model authorized not only the power to lament, but gave suffering providential meaning and a historical narrative: justifying

God's ways to humans. Jesus "was a Man of Sorrows well (we see)/ Was he with Griefs acquainted? (so are we)" writes a Quaker author in "the Time of his Imprisonment."[53] If Jesus was a model for personal sorrows, Lamentations gave a pattern for collective suffering.

The biblical people Israel provided a model, indeed a national allegory, of collective subjugation and mourning, and gave suffering a meaning beyond the individual. National suffering may have been a sign of failure, but it was also a sign of election, of having a special place within history. In a prefatory poem in his treatise vaunting the superiority of the Hebrew Scriptures to all other claimants to philosophical truth, Theophilus Gale, a debarred Independent minister, moved swiftly from anticeremonial protest to the themes of exile and oppression:

> Pitty! so chaste a Virgin should be forc'd to wear
>   Apparel of an Harlot still,
>   Turne prostitute against her will.
> In Heathen Temples when she would appear,
> Theres nought but Scean, and pageant of her there:
>   They still conceal the Real Saint
>   And shew some Jezabel in paint;
>   This stil has been Religions fate,
> She always in her vaile as Mourning sate;
>   And like the Ancient Jew,
>   Whence her Original she drew
>   Long has her cruel Pharaoh's seen
>   And long in bondage been.
>   Where ere she mov'd,
> The whole World her wide Wilderness hath prov'd;
>   For worse, than that in which
>   The holy men their Tents did pitch:
>   For still she had in sight
>   Much of their Cloud, but little of their Light.[54]

Drawing upon the long-familiar image of the Roman church as a harlot, and merging this with the lamenting woman from Jeremiah, Gale gives cosmic meaning to current suppression of the "True Church." Choosing the English poetic mode of rhymed verse, however, he also carps at Restoration libertine culture, with its theatres, whores, and fascination with pageantry. The irregular line lengths, classical "Pindarics," revivify a Hebraic element, freeing the poet from the confines of regular meter or the prevalent heroic couplet. Resisting Pharaoh's bondage is resisting all bondage, including that of set verse forms. There is a contradictory motif of exile and displacement, however. The fabled "wandering Jew" here becomes a woman, *ecclesia*, a persecuted victim. For the Puritan church at once in bonds and in exile, nowhere is home, "the whole World her wide Wilderness hath prov'd."

The people Israel, as precedent and prototype, sealed obligations to God, as well as created coherence for a community under stress and strain. The Quaker poet Mary Southworth Mollineux (1651–91) is a good case through which to explore how personal anguish and social protest converge in acts of poetic devotion. Mollineux had an unusual pedigree for a Quaker woman. According to her cousin, her weak eyes made her unfit "for the usual Employment of girls," and she was given a grounding in classical education which included Latin, Greek, Arithmetic, and Natural philosophy, by an enlightened father.[55] That classical background is barely evident in the volume of poetry published in 1702, however, since her Poetry revolves around biblical tradition, adopting the stories of notable Israelites, including Elijah and Daniel, and rewritings of Genesis. Colored by an imagination that is intensely architectural, her poems repeatedly imagine open spaces and enclosures, confinements, and the dizzying heights of rocks and towers, perhaps reflecting her prison experiences. Her poetry received enough attention to merit a pamphlet attack by one Francis Bugg, who objected to the poetic and theological content of the Quaker woman's writing, making no issue of the gender of the author.[56] Mollineux met her husband Henry in 1684 whilst both were in prison in Lancaster Castle for attending Quaker meetings. Mary appealed for her husband's release for non-payment of tithes in 1690. Unusually popular, her *Fruits of Retirement* went into six editions through the eighteenth century.

Though she was attacked in print, Mary Mollineux refused to be silenced in public, choosing dramatic confrontation in the name of faith, as did many Quakers.[57] Though her poetry was only published in 1702, it was circulating in manuscript before that time. The first poem in that collection, "Of the Fall of Man," was dated 1663, and it reveals her ambition to rewrite Genesis. The volume also offers a variety of hymns, meditations, and personal epistles to her friends and relatives. Most prominent are the series of reflections on persecution and her quest to find a true relation with God during a time of national disaster.

In "A Meditation" composed in 1668, Mollineux summoned Lamentations to bewail the situation of post-Restoration Dissent, evoking the oral modes of curse and lament by adopting hymn meter:

> Though *Zion* sit in Misery
> And do in Ashes mourn,
> And all her Foes, as they pass by,
> Do her deride and scorn.

> Though like the spotless Turtle Dove,
>   That in the Rock doth dwell,
> 'Wailing the absence of her Love,
>   Whose Grief no Tongue can tell.
> Though for a Season thus she may
>   Sit, like a Widow poor
> And desolate, there is a Day
>   When she shall grieve no more.
> Though yet she mourn, lament and weep,
>   To see her Children dear
> To wander, like poor scatter'd Sheep,
>   Through Desarts far and near;
> Hourly in danger to be torn,
>   By Tyger, Wolf or Bear,
> As they are seeking to return
>   Unto their Mother dear.[58]

The opening verse of Lamentations – "how doth the city sit solitary, that was full of people! how is she become as a widow! she that was great among the nations, and princess among the provinces, how is she become tributary" – evokes the metaphor of the widow for the city of Jerusalem. Yet Mollineux drops the urban, royalist, and geographical figures and develops only the maternal persona, adding her own touches – children lost in the wood, threatened by wild animals – none of which exists in the original. The experience of defeat is an experience of family disunity, but her figures for maternal loss also convey a geographical displacement, a national diaspora. Since the Puritan desires – hopes for true personal and political change through national, godly reform as well as search for inclusion via protest against persecutors – could hardly be acknowledged openly, they could only be ever-lamented, figured through biblical tropes of loss.

That loss was often figured in family terms. "It is not a time for Sions Sons to be Rejoycing, when their Mother is Mourning," gave an adage attributed to the Independent Thomas Goodwin, one of many pious sayings culled from that minister after his death and published in a broadside in 1680.[59] In this scheme, pleasure, joy, and despair, as well as violence, are shared emotions whose degree could all too rapidly shift again. Mollineux's mixed metaphors – the family, the flock – yearn to express a collective body for whom justice is promised. Maternal bereavement marks a social, not strictly domestic, symbolic register. If to Mollineux membership in a whole family or a flock signaled freedom, then separation can only be seen as a tragedy, a diasporic alienation.

Mollineux makes one radical revision to her original in assigning blame. In her poem it was not Jerusalem's own sins that caused the misery. Instead Mollineux rails against others for that fallen condition, "those that would these Sheep annoy," and her "Tyranizing Foes" who will soon receive "just Punishment":

> Yet those that would these Sheep annoy,
>   Let them for certain know,
> They shall not, if such them destroy,
>   Long unrewarded go.
> Ere long this Cloud of Misery
>   Shall vanish quite away;
> She, that sat in Obscurity,
>   Shall see a Glorious Day.
> Then shall her Tyranizing Foes
>   Receive just Punishment,
> Who did her Children dear expose
>   T'Exile and Banishment. (22)

The future is certain to bring down punishment on those who persecute the faithful, and the poem ends with a vision of retributive violence against the unholy:

> But those shall Roar and Howl for pain,
>   And to the Mountains cry,
> Fall on us, hide us from the Wrath
>   Of the Lamb's Anger ... (22)

Those who remained faithful may be mourning now, but they are the ones to be joyful once justice is served. Mollineux's poetry reduces the repetitions offered by the original, and her verse in regular meter and rhyme makes smooth what was irregular. Although her poetic mode is tamer, the violence contained within, however, is anything but contained.

The experience of living under harsh legislation was painful for those now labeled nonconformists, and their reaction, it is important to remember, was not uniform. The very difficult decisions – whether or not to take the sacrament; whether or not to swear the oath of allegiance; whether or not to attend a now-illegal religious meeting; how to live conscientiously under such religious persecution – created daily choices.[60] Resistance to policy was widespread, as we well know from the examples of Quakers and other radicals including John Bunyan. Those who swore primary allegiance to God's rule – the Quakers, Fifth Monarchists, and some Baptists – could only choose to disobey the civil laws. Yet most nonconformists, the

Presbyterians, Independents, and many Baptists inhabited a more complex middle ground between total obedience to the state and total obedience to God: perhaps God was working through the state, they considered. Poetic choices did not simply mirror theological choices. In prison as Dissenters reflected on their condition, many lashed out against persecutors with a fury driven by biblical typology, and found in the Bible models that were poetic as well as political for their suffering. In their mournful laments, Dissenting writers took strength from their communal identification, resisting the dominant ideology of the Restored regimes by recalling the violence of a faithful God. The next chapter deepens this conjunction of despair and violence.

CHAPTER 4

Violence

Barred by imprisonment from preaching, John Bunyan justified his writing in the opening pages of the preface to *Grace Abounding to the Chief of Sinners*, alluding to Samson's riddle from the biblical story in Judges: "I have sent you here enclosed a drop of that honey," he confided, "that I have taken out of the carcass of a lion (Judg. 14:5–8). I have eaten thereof myself also, and am much refreshed thereby."[1] Writing – the honey – is the sweet essence of divine favor, and yet behind Bunyan's biblical story lies an anterior tale of violence. When Samson was attacked by a young lion, he was visited by the Spirit of the Lord, and he killed the lion barehandedly. Later, Samson found a nest of bees making honey in the carcass, a potent and disturbing sight giving rise to his riddle: "Out of the eater came forth meat, and out of the strong came forth sweetness" (Judg. 14:14). Bunyan also serves up a practical lesson, offered in parenthesis: "(Temptations when we meet them at first, are as the lion that roared upon Samson; but if we overcome them, the next time we see them, we shall find a nest of honey within them)" (*Grace Abounding*, 1). Now a moral teaching, the story of honey out of the lion's carcass is a lesson in patience, fortitude, and endurance. An easy exchange puts the honey, rather than the violence, at the center of this story. What then happens to the act of divine destruction that produced the sweetness?

This chapter suggests that the proximity of violence and grace in Bunyan's figure is a common feature of Dissenting writing, and that Dissenting writers deployed violence in order to solicit divine favor as well as to activate readers' desires for sympathy, solidarity, and action. Violence may be a legacy of Reformation apocalyptic and iconoclastic religious writing; of heroic martyrdom and the aftereffects of civil war; of Christianity with its central sacrificial myth: but it is also a consequence of a theology in which the means and reasons by which divine agency coursed through humans remained inexplicable. Dissenters sought means by which to enact relationships with a God whose absence of reciprocity within the realm of representation was a constant source of anxiety. Violence was the means by which the Holy Spirit worked through the bodies of the faithful, and allegories of violence represented that mysterious working even if it could not be explained rationally.

The Bible inspired political action during the English Revolution; indeed, "its centrality made it the battle-ground of several ideologies," as Christopher Hill explains: "It was a huge bran-tub from which anything might be drawn. There are few ideas in whose support a Biblical text cannot be found. Much could be read into and between the lines."[2] Hill's approach is at bottom allegorical, perceiving that for seventeenth-century men and women, biblical citation was a strategic deployment of allegory – it stood in place of another story, whether to justify, query, or to confirm a political ideology – where "real" political ideas lay beneath the allegory, awaiting decoding by the modern interpreter. However, for Dissenters, appeal to the Bible was not solely a means to evade the powerful and disabling condition of Restoration silencing or censorship – where scripture stood in place of contemporary stories that nonconformists dared not express overtly. The Bible was the primary means of explaining existence. Barbara Lewalski's study of the Protestant lyric in the seventeenth century explores how "the Bible became normative for poetic art as well as for spiritual truth," and we might extend her analysis of the private modes of lyric by investigating how typology also fashioned political agency and sustained public affiliation.[3] Indeed, biblical citation was at root an existential mode, a way seventeenth-century Puritans came to know themselves as actors within history and as belonging to a community. Appealing to the Bible was a means of interpreting and explaining circumstances, of giving current suffering meaning beyond the individual.[4]

Even if Dissenters all saw Scripture as the sole bearer of truth, in their literary practice, they disagreed over the purpose of scriptural citation. Dissenters who read typologically insisted upon the memorial functions of the text. But their apocalyptic modes demanded reading not strictly commemoratively. Was the Bible cited in order to remember events that had happened in the past, to seek models for identification that gave coherence to a community? Or was the Bible cited to give prophetic utterance, to testify or to perform God's will as present in the world? In representing the mysterious effects of the Holy Spirit, Dissenting writers often suggested a kind of real presence. Their citations of the Bible were often talismanic rather than allegorical.

As the tension between the immediate and the commemorated was at the heart of the Protestant Reformers' critique of ceremonial ritual, so uncertainty about mediation and temporality was reflected in the Dissenters' memory-practices. I should like to argue in what follows that this sacramental crisis also produced ways of reading that obscured the difference between commemorative and performative action. The typological mode of reading, so central to Protestant poetics, blurred these registers, as the tensions between literal violence and figural violence, as between active and passive disobedience, arose from questions of how the self would mediate God's presence, and how to read God's will. There would be implications for writing history, as will be seen in Richard Baxter's attempt to read the English civil war through a providential framework. Also, there would be heightened self-consciousness about the difficulty of reading the Bible in today's terms, specifically the coded interpretations required by an exemplary figure such as Samson, who is both riddler and divinely inspired destroyer. As we shall see through analyzing Bunyan's writings, the figure of Samson is a shorthand for thinking through such questions of reading, agency, and violent resistance.

FIGURE AND TERROR

Philip Henry is an unlikely candidate for a violent insurgent. Henry, the son of a royalist official, was the ejected Presbyterian minister of Malpas in Cheshire and a reluctant nonconformist, a conservative who occasionally attended Anglican service, although he had not been a supporter of the Restoration. His son later praised not his zeal, but that "long series of an even, regular, prudent, and well-order'd Conversation which he had in the World, and in the ordinary business of it."[5] Mourning the Ejection, Henry feared that his people had been forgotten, as he says, "laid aside, *as if they had not been*," as if the conditions of persecution were utterly annihilating of existence.[6] To restore hope, in his diary he fitted contemporary history to the contours of biblical history, entering on 27 October 1664 four prior instances of ministers' ejections, dating from the primitive church up to current times: "This only I know, hee that hath deliver'd doth deliver & wee trust also hee will yet deliver" (*Diary*, 155–56). Remembering that God delivered in the past was the warrant for future deliverance, and a means of keeping faith in dark times.

Out of a great existential fear comes a call for God to make good on the contract Henry fears has been broken. That commemoration was an annunciation to violence. On the first anniversary of the "Great Ejection," 24 August 1663, Henry describes how he and a cohort of fellow-excluded ministers met to commemorate that "black day." Their prayers evoked biblical passages in which the suffering of Israel was relieved by God's strong, violent action. Yet, significantly, the subject of those prayers was not simply a recollection of God's past actions, but a remembrance of the efficacy of human commemoration. They cited the prophet Zechariah, passages which recalled how the faithful were meant to fast and mourn, as they "have done these so many years" (Zech. 7:3), to commemorate the destruction of the Temple in Jerusalem by Nebuchadnezzar, king of Babylon. Those citations were a kind of shorthand for national remembrance: "Zech. 7.3. comp. Jer.1.3. The Jewes in their captivity fasted in the fifth month, bec. in ye fifth month Jerusalem was carryed away captive, & in ye 7th month, Zech. 7.5. bec. in ye 7th month Gedaliah was slayn – jer.41.1." The Bible here is a handbook for explaining diaspora, and, significantly, it also affirmed the slaughter of a tyrant. By quoting the Bible, Henry and his fellow nonconformists engaged in performative utterance: "Let it be so!" he writes, saluting this history.[7] However in Zechariah, when the Jews' commemorative fast was deemed insufficient (Zech. 7:5), they were once again scattered "with a whirlwind among all the nations whom they knew not" (Zech. 7:14). Henry knows that human remembrance is not always effective.

Was remembering past deeds simply an act of homage? Or was remembering past deeds in some sense to ask for the past to become the present? Was the past truly past, or, because God's spirit was in all times and places, was the past inside and through the present, wholly immanent? An elaborate theological discourse centered on these topics, played out in the question of the meaning of the sacrament. With the Reformation, Protestants negotiated a new relationship to the miracles of the past, and they refuted the doctrine of transubstantiation in order to demystify church ritual by rerouting Divine Presence into commemoration. Rather than to discern "true presence" in the Lord's Supper, Puritans perceived the taking of the sacrament to be a "memorial" of Jesus, a sign of *their faith* rather than of *real presence*. English Puritans followed the Zwinglian tradition of not kneeling at the communion table but choosing instead to stand, or even to receive the sacrament at their pew. Thus they vouched for their beliefs with a resistance to the Roman kinesthetic order by a counter-performance. Their reworking of the sacrament, like the Anglican, was largely Calvinistic, laying emphasis on the heart of the believer rather than on the material presence of the Lord in the wine and bread.[8] It was their resolute anticeremonialism that distinguished Dissenters from Anglicans.

Over a hundred years after the early Reformers attacked the sacrament, the Independent John Owen was still refining the attack. He fought off the papist understanding of the eucharist in a sermon of 1674 by charging that "One of the greatest engines that ever the devil made use of to overthrow the faith of the church was, by forging *such a presence of Christ* as is not truly in this ordinance, to drive us off from looking after that great presence which is *true*. I look upon it as one of the greatest engines that ever hell set on work. It is not a *corporeal* presence; there are innumerable arguments against *that*."[9] Instead of mandating that the Lord's Supper contains a corporeal presence, preached Owen in a 1669 sermon, "The ordinance is *commemorative*: 'Do this in remembrance of me.' And there is no greater joy to the heart of sinners, and a man knows not how to give greater glory to God, than to call the atonement of sin unto remembrance" (527). Richard Baxter, likewise, explained the commemorative function of the Lord's Supper. The sacrament is "the visible representation of the sacrificing of Christ upon the cross to the Father, for the sins of man; to keep up the remembrance of it, and lively affect the church thereby, and to profess our confidence in a crucified Christ."[10] Although in their theologies of the sacrament, there was little difference between these writers and those of Anglican orthodoxy,[11] there were nonetheless different social consequences, since memory served as a focal point for Dissenting identity and community during a time of exclusion.

In their revised ceremonies, taking the Lord's Supper was bearing witness, a commemorative act signaling the *believer's* faith. As John Owen put it, "This bread doth *not contain* the body of Christ, or the flesh of Christ; the cup doth *not contain* the blood of Christ: but they *exhibit* them; both do as really exhibit them to believers as they partake of the outward signs."[12] By stressing the role of "believers as they partake," Owen shifts emphasis away from the divine presence towards human conduct, reproducing an orthodox Calvinist theory of human signification by performance. Christ is not in the signs; but loyalty to him is exhibited by the signs. An act of witness is thus performative of Christian identity. The holiness of the sacrament then is contingent upon reception, the way it is iterated: "The thing we are to aim at, to be carried unto faith in this ordinance, is, that there may be a *near and evident representation* of Christ in his tender unto our souls" (*Sacramental Discourses*, 691). As is traditional in Calvinist belief, Owen resituates the locus of interest to the soul of the believer, prompting a mode of being that would raise self-consciousness to its highest pitch in early modern history.

Not all Dissenters revised belief about the sacrament in the same way. The Independent, Presbyterian, and Baptist reworking of the sacrament all reformed it by a Calvinistic legacy, accounting for human agency as commemorative performance. The Quakers, on the other hand, rejected this interpretation. The Quaker John Perrot targeted the sacramentality of baptism: "For know ye, where God is present, there needs not a representation of him, by any thing; and where the Eternal Fountain of all Virtue is set open, there needs not the digging of another Well for Waters."[13] Perrot wrings polemic from his bad puns, showing that such metaphoric representations as puns or, by analogy, ceremonial ritual, are simply human – and deeply fallible – creations. Perrot swung hard at those practices that forged mediations between humans and God, whether transubstantive *or* commemorative: the bread and wine of the holy sacrament were only shadows which must be cast away: "why shall a *Figure* be as in *the place of Your Formulation?*" he asked those Dissenters closest to him, the Baptists, urging they divest even their rituals of baptism. His pamphlet ends with the performative words of the Song of Songs, the Bridegroom's invitation to "Arise, Arise, and come away . . . come away my beloved" (Perrot, 19), here interpreted as a call to abandon ceremony. The words of the Bible cited are not to be interpreted as figures for the truth, nor as commemorative of a past truth, but as signs of the actual presence of God. The Quakers, repudiating mediation, are those most likely to authorize actions by the Holy Spirit. These accounts of the sacrament bear on the question of human and divine violence.

The cycles of defeat, persecution, and exile so dramatically recorded in the Bible could be assimilated and even ritually commemorated in the Puritan's imaginations. Did biblical history also hold out the promise of relief through violent uprising? Even if the history in the Bible showed the repeated backsliding of the chosen nation, nonetheless God would authorize political rebellion against oppressors. As he and his minister friends recalled the ancient slain king, Philip Henry evoked the Jews' rebellion against a political oppressor: "Then arose Ishmael the son of Nethaniah, and the ten men that were with him, and smote Gedaliah the son of Ahikam the son of Shaphan with the sword, and slew him, whom the king of Babylon had made governor over the land" (Jer. 41:2; cf. 2 Kings 25:25). In their observance of piety on that anniversary of Ejection, then, these ministers coupled the duties of remembrance with insurrection. They announced their fidelity to the scheme of history but also laid claim to their own part in it as they performed their own commemorative acts. In October, Henry was hauled in for interrogation by the authorities for his alleged involvement in a plot.[14]

"Violence is the heart and secret soul of the sacred": so writes René Girard, who sees violence as a compensatory response to fears of overwhelming powerlessness that come from any religious apprehension of the world.[15] How are we to understand then the *particular*, historical formulations of violence? Mythic formulations speak to specific cultural moments, with their attendant political and psychological needs. In psychological terms, the pleasure of imagining violent retribution against enemies corresponds to the degree of self-abasement one feels one has suffered; by indulging in a fantasy of revenge one participates in a dynamic that seeks restitution for that loss of self-esteem.[16] Exploring the emotional affect of an excluded community explains how mourning could be connected to dreams of apocalypse. Yet our mythic explanations should not displace the ways that early modern Dissenters understood their own hopes of violence. In this apocalyptic world view, even grief was taken as part of the divine scheme: violence was a sign of God's care. For several reasons violent emotions were heightened in the Restoration, whether for those campaigning against nonconformity or for those persisting in godly resistance. The aftershocks and memories of civil war, the Anglican royalist brutal revenge against those supporting the "Good Old Cause," the fear of popery fueled by atrocity stories from the Continent, and the Dissenters' own experiences of failed hopes, the lack of social recognition that was the enabling fable of the royalist term "restoration": for these reasons and more, violence featured in the emotional landscape of Restoration writers.

The Old Testament was the master code that authorized the conversion of abjection and fear into violence. Apocalyptic thought in particular offered a model of political disobedience; indeed it continued to fire resistance against the Restored monarchy, as in the case of Thomas Venner, who led a rebellion in 1661 under the slogan "For King Jesus!"[17] Warfare was not only a metaphor for godliness; violence was also the sign of God's involvement in earthly affairs. Dissenters in the Restoration suffered violently under their persecutions. They also feared that another round of Marian oppression was upon them. Daniel Defoe later recalled the terror of the period of the Popish plot frenzy, when he copied out the whole Pentateuch out of fear that the papists would come in and destroy all the Bibles: "how Terrible Apprehensions had we of the Growth of Popery, and its introduction into this Kingdom, Hand in Hand with Slavery... *Fear always puts people upon Extremes.*"[18]

Was there a sharp divide between the weapons of the spirit and those of the flesh? Whilst nonconformists often distinguished between spiritual and carnal weapons, they were also preoccupied with instances and occasions when the divine spirit roused human action, and their writings are colored by the histories of the biblical warriors and prophets: Daniel, Judith, and

Samson. In their substitution of violence for abjection, the saints reworked divine agency as their own. Theological controversy abounded over how to interpret the auguries of the Bible, and publications timing the exact fulfillment of the prophecies of apocalyptic writings were many during this period.[19] Despite the turn of events against them in the Restoration, saints sought a role for human action in a salvational scheme whose ultimate meaning remained a mystery to them. In the meantime, they believed their knowledge about salvation could only be partial, and thus many suffered from fears that there might be no connection between the earthly practice of virtuous self-discipline and ultimate legitimation.

Chiliastic fervor seems to erupt in moments of acute social crisis; at such times, Christopher Hill writes, "millenarian doctrines become equivalent to social revolution." In Hill's tally, the 1640s and 1650s were high water marks in the outpouring of millennialist thought: Grotius was told that eighty such treatises had appeared in England by 1649.[20] After 1660, rather than disappearing, apocalypticism took new forms; indeed the Restoration burst of works concerning end-time continues the biblical apocalypticism of the civil war decades. Out of their experience of dispossession and social terror, nonconformists who wearied of earthly political solutions filled their imaginative writing with dreams of apocalyptic revenge. In their political counsel, even as Restoration Dissenters disavowed disobedience, still they did not reject hopes for apocalyptic change. The recent historical reversals raised serious questions about God's plan in history. Many of the godly, like John Milton in his search to "justify the ways of God to men," wanted to maintain hope in an ultimate recovery. Because of the unpredictability of God's ways, readiness to action was all, and such critical reflection and spiritual reform would prepare the godly for either earthly or heavenly victory. The Quaker Stephen Crisp insisted upon militant readiness in the title of his 1666 pamphlet, *Epistle to Friends... to Stand Armed in the Light of the Lord God.* Even the Presbyterians could admire the uses of violence in God's warfare. Richard Baxter on the title page of his *Christian Directory* pictured the soldier of Christ with his armor and pike, saying, "*Diabolo Resisto,*" I resist the devil (see Figure 4). The ejected Presbyterian Thomas Watson threatened, "The Earth is inherited by the *Meek*... Heaven is inherited by the *violent*. Our life is military; Christ is our Captain... and Heaven is only taken in a forcible way."[21] The Presbyterian Stephen Coven was arrested for allegedly authoring *The Militant Christian; or, the Good Soldier of Jesus Christ* (1668).[22] There were plenty of nonconformist sermons and tracts on Matthew 11:12 ("And from the days of John the Baptist until now the kingdom of heaven suffereth violence, and the violent take it by

Figure 4 Title page to Richard Baxter, *Christian Directory* (1677).

force").[23] In nonconformist imaginative writings well outside the radical fringe, apocalyptic reversal was never far off.

In that scheme, memory would prove to be a complex resource. Dissenters could look to their adopted inheritance of Israelite history to observe how God would remember them and punish their enemies; or they could look to the radical prophecy of Patmos, foretelling an ongoing struggle and a future release through violence. History-writing in Puritanism was absorbed with mapping secular history onto these apocalyptic schemes; even the massive historiographical project of Foxe's *Actes and Monuments* rewrote modern history from this vantage point. In apocalyptic history, to remember was to find correspondences between two stories, narrating the present in the light of past prophecy. But there was a performative element to this hermeneutic. By interpreting the present by prior stories, Dissenters found clues to action, incentive to behavior not only in religious activity, but in all spheres of life. As John Pocock sees this Christian time scheme, "the present, consequently, is a time of remembering past prophecies and expecting the future which they foretell."[24] In this mode, authorship of radical change may be outside of human control, a function of supernatural battles waged between Christ and Antichrist. Indeed, after the failure of godly Revolution, many Dissenters saw a version of history in which their current anguish could be explained, and in which God's presence could be assured – by appeal to the ongoing presence of Antichrist in the world. God's plans may have been inscrutable in recent historical events, but there was meaning to the universe indeed. That meaning, however, did not reside within history, but was an exit from history.

RICHARD BAXTER: THE VIOLENCE OF HISTORY

Given this theology of immediacy, how could current "history" be represented at all? The great pastoral leader Richard Baxter lays claim to being the chief exponent of an ethos of Puritan suffering in the late seventeenth century, viewing the affliction of this world as its defining condition. *The Saints Everlasting Rest* devotes a whole chapter to the explanation of "The Reason of the Saints Afflictions here." In his own justifying of the ways of God to men, Baxter proposes to "give them some Reasons of Gods dealing in their present sufferings, whereby the equity and mercy therein may appear."[25] Though he is best remembered as the author of lasting works of counsel to the afflicted, a prodigiously generous sharer in pain and a forefather of pastoral therapy, Baxter's efforts as a poet have largely gone unnoticed. In literary terms, his are unremarkable affairs. The quality of the verse fails to reach the sublimity of his admired Wither and the mystery and economy of his beloved Herbert. Nonetheless, because he readily involved himself in earthly affairs – in his pastoral innovations, his advocacy of "Comprehension" and Toleration, and in his contacts with the political class – in his poetry, Baxter offers a rich case in which to explore the clash of earthly and unworldly concerns, and specifically to understand the ambivalences of historicist and typological thinking (see Figure 5).

It is little known that Richard Baxter is the author of a poem which includes a history of the outbreak of England's civil war. A colossal autobiographical fragment, fifty pages in quarto, *Love Breathing Thanks and Praise* renders theological concerns and measures his conscience so that its mode of history-writing is difficult to perceive in the same light as Cowley's *Civil War* or Wither's *Speculum Speculativum*. Surprisingly, for one who could write history with ease, this account of his life differs from the autobiographical notices that preface his *Saints Everlasting Rest* and also from that massive prose history, *Reliquiae Baxterianae*, both of which assemble into a providential and chronological order the many momentous events through which Baxter had lived. Instead, *Love Breathing Thanks and Praise* shares themes with Milton's *Paradise Lost*, asking whether obedience is due to earthly or to heavenly authority; what duties inhere in the personal, social, and ethical spheres. By means of the titular "Love," Baxter explores the many obligations that follow from human attachment. The poem closes with a poetic retelling of the divinely charged outbreak of the civil war, and between the lines, offers justification of his own participation on the side of Parliament.

Living in physical pain during most of his adulthood, Baxter had good reason to choose the life of spirit over that of matter. His autobiography recalls gratitude to God that "Pains, though daily and almost continual, did not very much disable [me] from my Duty," even though he did "in Forty years have few hours without pain."[26] Written as a reflection on the harrowing first-hand experience of civil war, Baxter gave testimony of those "sad and heart-piercing spectacles that mine eyes have seen in four years space! In this fight, a dear friend fall down by me; from another, a precious Christian brought home wounded or dead; scarce a moneth, scarce a week without the sight or noise of bloud." Out of his experience in the parliamentary cause, *The Saints Everlasting Rest* outlived its civil war origins to become a classic in spiritual consolation.[27] In Baxter's writings, his minute descriptions of his agonizing physical ailments were always coupled with gratitude for the wonder of divine deliverance from them; even in recounting the life of his wife Margaret, this most beloved of companions,

Figure 5 Frontispiece to Richard Baxter, *Paraphrase to the New Testament* (1695).

he could not resist depicting her physical ailments in their gory detail, along with thanks to God for her deliverance.[28] God's hand is visible in the waxing and waning of one's physical condition, within a metaphysical scheme that gives meaning to pain, assigning causes and consequences to the most mysterious of experiences, the physical experience of one's own unruly body with its fragility and ineffectiveness.

Baxter's political allegiances can only be tracked with difficulty. In 1682 he was still defending himself against the charge that during the civil war he was an outright rebel. "I never went so far against the Power of the King," he asserted wryly, "as R. Hooker whom I have long ago confuted."[29] Hooker, after all, had been cited by Andrew Marvell, in his *Rehearsal Transpros'd*, 2nd part, defending disobedience; Sir Henry Vane during his treason trial in 1662, had cited Hooker and Selden to justify the idea that the law of nature, not the Crown, was the basis of the English legal system; Hooker was for Restoration conformists, however, the defender of the national church against schism.[30] Writing out of this double-edged legacy, Baxter chooses the antimonarchical Hooker. Baxter's self-defense, then, underscores how the meaning of loyalty was never fully clear.

His support of Parliament was deeply ideological; as he recounts in his autobiography: "I freely confess, that being astonished at the *Irish* Massacre, and perswaded both of Parliaments good endeavours for Reformation, and of their real *danger*, my Judgment of the main Cause much swayed my Judgment in the Matter of Wars," resolving that "the *Peoples liberties and Safety could not be forfeited*."[31] During the civil war, he was a chaplain to the Coventry regiment, and later served in Colonel Whalley's New Model Army regiment, ministering to the soldiers during the seige of Worcester in 1646; he resigned his army position around May 1647.[32] Always one to seek accommodation and concord, Baxter stressed godly reform over political reform, yet he went so far as to envision a political rule of the saints in his 1659 tract, *A Holy Commonwealth*, a work he publicly disowned in 1670 (although retaining a private respect for it). All through the 1660s he sought reconciliation and "Comprehension" with the Restoration Anglican regime.[33] Although in *A Christian Directory* Baxter offered his political allegiance to the state, he never came into the state church and was imprisoned for his beliefs from 1684 to 1686. Even in his quietist work, there is a potentially revolutionary antinomianism. Warning against "IDOLIZING MAN," Baxter cites Psalm 118 and Job 32: "*The Lord is on my side; I will not fear what man can do unto me: It is better to trust in the Lord, than to put confidence in man — yea, in Princes*."[34] Baxter hedges however, illuminating the problem of obedience to earthly powers; although "the *Church* is *finally* and *estimatively* to be preferred before the *Common-wealth*; but the *Common-wealth* must first be served in *time*, when it is necessary to the Churches support and welfare: For the Church will else perish with the *Common-Wealth*" (*Christian Directory*, 863).

While on the face of it, *Love Breathing Thanks and Praise* is an account of Baxter's spiritual growth towards enlightenment, a record in general terms of his movement towards love of God and away from selfishness, it is also a meditation on many earthly obligations explored through a matrix of cosmic time. Beginning before the creation of the world – "When Heav'n, & Earth, & Sea, were yet unfram'd/ Angels and men, and all things else unnam'd;/ When there did nothing else exist but Thee,/ Thou wast the same, and still the same wilt be" – it not only praises God's creation and the bountiful gift that is life but does so to insist that the divine power "Canst make and unmake worlds; give life, and kill."[35] If at the start of the poem, Baxter reduces the significance of humans in this divine drama, then this is to serve a larger purpose, that of awaiting the fulfillment of history in the destructive apocalypse.[36] The poem commits to the process of divine destruction and renewal. God's power is "to know ten thousand worlds" (*Love Breathing*, 3), as if to diminish the importance of any single one, especially this one. Baxter's poem calls forth not merely creation, but also destruction as evidence of God's immense power, and of the potential irrelevance of humans to the cosmic scheme: "We make the Events of this day our sorrow,/ Because we know not what will be tomorrow./ Things present, past and future; old and new,/ Thou see'st entirely with one single view" (3). God's majesty commands awe greater than any earthly attachment; paradoxically in the poem, human agency lessens even as the poet increases it by telling his own story.

The rambling, meditative poem is interrupted with passages of power and lucidity by the narration of the outbreak of war. The poet's own voice heats up, as if he is really going to write an epic poem:

> Now *England's* horrid Civil Wars began,
> When God a sinful Nation meant to fan.
> When sin grown high & bold, out-fac'd the Light;
> When Pride and Faction pleaded Divine Right.
> When most their Love, & some their Patience lost;
> When proud malicious men must not be crost:
> When wise men seemed fools, & fools seem'd wise;
> And when the worst were best in their own eyes?
> When Piety with *Lazarus* was loath'd;
> And Sin with Purple and fine Linnen cloath'd:
> And when the sacred Tribe, despising Souls,
> Through love of wealth & honor blow'd the coals.

> When *Demas* for the World deserted *Paul*;
> And their own matters were first sought by all:
> When they that sought their good things in this life
> Had banisht Love, & fill'd the Church with strife!
> Where striving factions Charity defy'd,
> And carnal Counsels did the Church divide!
> When swinish Gadarens did Christ refuse,
> And the prophane his servants did abuse.
> When Holiness the common Foe was deem'd,
> And nothing more intollerable seem'd.
> When holy Truth and Preachers were despis'd;
> And wicked means to cast them out devis'd!
> When sin presum'd to make a mock of grace,
> And folly spit reproaches in Christ's face!
> When vulgar rage had found this common vent;
> And impious scorn on Godliness was spent:
> When sin was not so much oppos'd as God,
> Then were we ready for the bloody Rod.   (47–48)

Where before the poem was filled with self-recriminations and self-abasement, confusing doctrine and pleading with God, here we are thrust into some past tense of heroic action. It is a different past tense, the timelessness of typology, but also, specifically, the time of Christ suffering the depredations of his contemporaries. Baxter took up his ministry as hostilities broke out, and his figuring the civil war actors through Christological parable represents a political struggle as essentially religious. Although Baxter describes the origins of war as a general national sinfulness, it is not hard to see his political leanings, with attacks on the pre civil war ministry ("Piety with *Luzurus* was loath'd;/ And Sin with Purple and fine Linnen cloath'd"; "When Holiness the common Foe was deem'd") and the court ("When Pride and Faction pleaded Divine Right"). If the "Good Old Cause" seems the defender of True Religion, then it was also God's scourge against the sinning nation. The repeated opening, "when," sounds like a tocsin, a reminder and a challenge for those readers in 1681 thinking very much about the origins of civil conflict in 1641, arousing comparisons with the current Exclusion crisis and the common foe, popery.[37]

The poem turns topical, citing particular events culminating in outbreak of the civil war. Baxter is beginning to write a magnificent epic account:

> Then God in Judgment sate to plead his Cause,
> And judge the proud despisers of his Laws.
> The whirlwind in the North did first arise,
> And raise the dust which troubled *English* Eyes.

> And though Heav'ns mercy there prevented blood,
> The *Irish* fury shed a crimson flood.
> And in their preparation to a War,
> Two hundred thousand they surpriz'd and slew,*
> Not that their *Will* so small a measure knew.
>
> (48–49)

Now the poem leaps out of one mode of general reflection and into another – with a footnote starring the numerical figures, "*The Earl of Orery's *Answer to a Petition*," the only asterisk in the poem, and the only cited text other than the Bible. We have entered a new genre altogether – topical history. As if noting the shift in literary mode, Baxter retreats from his narration into an extended epic simile, with which he closes this fifty-page poem, leaving it unfinished:

> But here God checkt their *Power*, & heard the cries
> Of dying Innocents, which pierc'd the Skies:
> *England* affrighted by her neighbours harm,
> Threatned to be the next, takes the Allarm,
> As Citizens that see a raging flame
> Threaten the Neighbours houses with the same,
> Do leave their Trades, and all together run,
> Trying to quench the Fire where it begun;
> And then pull down the houses which adjoyn;
> Some seek to save the goods, some to purloin;
> The well-built Piles, & curious Rooms must down,
> To buy the Safety of the fearful Town,
> A Neighbour's house is used like a Foe's,
> Because the Fire, the Hook, no diff'rence knows,
> Fear pulleth down the next, to save the most,
> And ruines more than needs, lest all be lost.
> Smoak and confused crouds do blind men's eyes,
> All are amaz'd, with hideous flames and cryes;
> So *England*, too combustible before,
> Seeing so great a flame so near her door,
> Was frighted into such Convulsion Fits,
> As first did break her Peace, and next her Wits.
> Dangers breed fears, and fears more dangers bring:
> The Bees to save their Honey use their Sting;
> Rowz'd in an angry Swarm they seek their Foe,
> The next they meet must feel the smarting blow.
>
> (49–50)

The first line here seems to echo the version of history at the conclusion to John Dryden's royalist epic, *Annus Mirabilis*, with a different providential narrative however: the cries heard here bring about civil war rather than

Dryden's Restored vision of peace. In his final passage, the last in the poem, Baxter's narrative adopts a compulsory mode – "must" denotes here necessity rather than choice. What follows from the events described temporally is dictated by a logic no human could stop. Here the account leaves off, as Baxter blames his "painful and spiritless Age . . . now unfit for Poetry." But it is not merely his age, but the subject, "The matter is so large, as would have made the Volume big" (50). But perhaps by summoning necessity, Baxter smoothes over a violence perpetrated by human hands that is too terrible to contemplate, and too difficult to assimilate into a theory of political obligation. For once, then, Richard Baxter is at a loss for words. At page fifty, he breaks off writing his autobiographical poem. Usually not one to be shy whilst composing in an autobiographical mode – his unedited papers which eventually formed the *Reliquiae Baxterianae: Or Mr. Richard Baxter's Narrative of The most Memorable Passages of his Life and Times* (1696) came to 800 folio pages, what Joan Webber has called a Puritan "epic" – Baxter in his incompleteness here requires comment.[38]

The memory of the fire is clearly before the poet: that moment too gives evidence of God's hand in England's history, and in 1681 would have been at the height of excitement about the Popish plot. The causes of the civil war are relevant, again, at a time when many Protestants feared another Catholicizing king. Baxter explained the reasons he had chosen Parliament's cause in the civil war in his *Autobiography*: his shock at the Irish massacre; worry about the endangerment of Reformation; belief in the good aims of Parliament.[39] In his meditative poem, Baxter also reflects upon the moment of his own assumption of political agency, but that recollection is quite different. In poetic memory, that moment is considered less as a conscious choice than as a call to necessity. *Reliquiae Baxterianae*, Matthew Sylvester's compilation of the notes of Richard Baxter, published in 1696, records a history of the mid-century conflict from the vantage point of post-1688 success for Toleration. That backward glance shapes the explanation of the causes of the civil war as a matter of political and religious strife, as Sylvester places Baxter within that context. The *Autobiography* gives a narrative account of Baxter's civil wartime indecision, his refusal to serve as a chaplain to any regiment (*Reliquiae Baxterianae*, Part 1, 43), and then his assumption of a pro-parliamentary role in preaching weekly to soldiers at Coventry. That autobiographical–historical narrative is given an ordering principle by those political events which give the civil war experiences meaning. *Love Breathing* lacks, however, that overarching political intention of justifying nonconformist resistance and supplying explanations about the difficult choices those like Baxter faced. Instead, its audience is God, to whom Baxter's heart is "breathing Love and Thanks." There, an apocalyptic scheme – "the whirlwind in the North" – is what engenders violence.

Baxter's call to arms flowed from an apocalyptic history, resignation unto the inscrutable God whose very creative energies could also awaken destruction at any moment. In his autobiography, Baxter had noted the prevalence of "providences" during the time of the outbreak of the first civil war, those miraculous events whose explanation was thought to be God's hand in history: he notes "the marvellous Preservation of Souldiers by Bibles in their Pockets which have received the Bullets."[40] In his poem, Baxter recounts the call to arms as a response to necessity, the English were putting out the flames of a fire that threatened to destroy all: there is no room for political analysis here, or an account of the assumption of political choice. Baxter's theology has been called Arminian, one that allowed room for human action to matter in the business of salvation; however, when it comes to understanding the civil war past in agential terms, there is little choice in the matter.[41]

Looking back at the civil war, Baxter commented that peace and stability were preferable to that period of internecine bloodshed, "I rather admire at that wisdom and goodness of God, that maintaineth that order and union amongst us, as is: and that he suffereth us not to be still one anothers executioners, and to lay violent hands on our selves, and each other. I dare not think that there is no one gracious that hath laboured to destroy others that were so, in these late dissentions."[42] But the poet can achieve neither historical closure nor narrative mastery over the ongoing trauma of civil war which can only appear as a rent in the fabric of understanding, signaling the higher force of God's power. The civil war is considered as holy war, motivated by God, and ultimately God's doing, whether in punishment of humans for sins or in recuperation of the godly from tyranny. By his use of familiar biblical types, Baxter fudges the question of his own political investiture; as actors in a divine drama, the participants in the conflict performed God's will, re-enacted an eternal story. The poem does not review biblical history to set it firmly in the past, but to lodge it in the unfolding present: type not sacrament. Though the aim of his poem was to find "Love," Baxter instead closes with divine violence: perhaps God's love is violent.

JOHN BUNYAN AND THE HERMENEUTICS OF TERRORISM

What kind of political agency can result from this hermeneutic? Typological reading poses questions about active and passive obedience, and about the nature of interpretation as an active force in the creation and maintenance of political identities. Could reading the Bible not simply explain, but demand resistance to an ungodly regime? The case of John Bunyan is a good one through which to explore the conjunction of biblical hermeneutics, figuration, and political resistance. The answers here are not clear-cut, and yet Bunyan's own interests in parabolic writing, typology, what he called "similitudes" on the title page of his *Pilgrim's Progress*, citing the prophet Hosea 12:10, demand a further investigation of the ways that agency is made to appear as if through the latticework of both human and divine causality.

Little explored in Bunyan's oeuvre is the persistent stain of violence that bleeds through his writings. To be sure, Protestant martyrdom required stoicism in the face of violent assault, as exemplified in John Foxe's *Actes and Monuments*.[43] The life of the Christian was a warfaring life: in *The Pilgrim's Progress*, Christian repeatedly duels with those he meets along the way. Yet that violence is softened by its stylized associations with romance narrative. Much more disturbing is the whole-scale violence of his much-neglected fictional narrative, *The Holy War* (1682), which represents a condition of civil warfare, invasions, and domestic treachery and cruelty in which violence is hard to explain away by generic or allegorical means. Since *The Holy War* is a veiled commentary on the political situation during England's Exclusion crises, it is a good case through which to think about the difference between God's violence and that of human hands. Violence in Bunyan's *Holy War* is not simply that of the patient martyr awaiting the Final Judgment. As in Bunyan's other writing, there runs a stream of terrifying vocations to violence: whether that of Samson, ready to destroy his enemies, or of Christ rendering judgment and punishment on unbelievers and opponents. Violence is a central hermeneutic tool and perhaps a real possibility in the here and now within Bunyan's cosmic scheme of providential history.

Though John Bunyan broke statutory law by addressing a conventicle in November 1660, critics generally agree he did not advocate active resistance or revolution against the restored Stuart monarchy. Bunyan himself disavowed the actions of Thomas Venner and the Fifth Monarchists; rather, against the Restoration Anglican persecuting regime, he preached patience, endurance, and, as Richard Greaves puts it, an "ethic of suffering."[44] Despite the harsh treatment of nonconformists in Bedford, Bunyan refrained from participating in movements for the overthrow of the state.[45] In his long prose tract, *Seasonable Counsel: Or, Advice to Sufferers* (1684), Bunyan commended an ethos of submission in the face of persecution, after the model of Jesus, Paul, Daniel, and Jeremiah, and also after the Marian martyrs chronicled in Foxe.

Still, Bunyan did not relinquish his millenarian views.[46] Was the struggle between the world and the Word to be taken solely in spiritual terms?[47] Bunyan's writings – especially *The Holy War* – do touch upon political contexts, but Bunyan scholarship has generally agreed that the author's attitude toward active political rebellion always subordinated secular to spiritual concerns.[48] Richard Greaves draws our attention to Bunyan's *Seasonable Counsel*, in which the author pursues a path of passive disobedience rather than insurrection. Written in the aftermath of the Popish plot, and, more particularly, following the exposure of the Rye House conspiracy, the tract insisted upon loyalty to earthly powers.[49] In the wake of various political plots against the Crown and church, his words to his congregation were those of consolation under suffering rather than calls for rebellion. Scholars may have retreated from the suggestion of his nineteenth-century editor, George Offor, that Bunyan was a true loyalist and an active supporter of the Stuart regime; but neither was he, according to current consensus, a fire-breathing revolutionary.[50]

To be sure, political content, and radical political content at that, is not far from the center of Bunyan's work. In *The Holy War*, for example, the citizens of Mansoul are repeatedly assaulted by Diabolus and his agents in an allegory about which even the editors admit "it cannot be denied that the struggle for man's soul is seen as emphatically a political transaction," and in their magnificent editorial project, supply the local political and historical contexts that Bunyan draws upon in imagining this spiritual fight, so that modern readers might be able to read between the lines.[51] Bunyan's modern editors, however, absolve their author from the violence of his book, particularly on the crucifixion of the condemned Diabolonians.[52] In Bunyan's *The Holy War*, the Bloodmen are those who persecute the faithful – not hard to see Restoration Dissent here – also, the shuffling of the government of Mansoul reflects reforms in Bunyan's local Bedford municipality. Bunyan's editors have pursued a critical presumption that his allegorical writing may be matched in a one-to-one correspondence to historical contexts.[53] These interpretations assume that Bunyan's allegories provide stable sets of meanings, meanings that are visible once the "key" has unlocked their mystery. Moreover, if the central teaching of *The Holy War* is, as Isabel Rivers puts it, that "the so-called powers of the soul are in themselves powerless; without the help of divine agency – the Spirit of Christ, the Holy Ghost, grace, and faith," then even the human effort of unlocking allegory may contain severe limitations.[54]

Bunyan speaks in the bold colors of emotional affect. In his very act of constructing "similitudes," Bunyan solicits from readers a zeal for an apocalyptic logic, arousing bloodthirsty desires and promising destructive transformation by which the powerless will be restored. Palpable excitement, not calm passivity, is the purpose of his inflaming narratives. For instance, in his allegorical representation of the struggle between Christ and the Devil over man's soul in his fictional *Holy War*, Bunyan takes pleasure in the violent deliverance from enemies. Contrasting the bloody destruction of Mansoul's enemies with the glorification of Emmanuel's forces, Bunyan reveals that from the very heart of Reformation apocalypticism, public humiliation of the enemy functions as a primary means of building community identity. Diabolus is stripped naked, bound, and dragged through the streets. His public harassment not only highlights his function as a trophy of war but serves as a potent rallying point for those previously enslaved by him: "And they said, He hath led captivity captive; he hath spoiled Principalities and Powers." With these words, Bunyan's victorious faithful echo Deborah's song of victory that authorized so many Dissenting hopes for revenge (Judg. 5). The marginal gloss indicates "They sing" these words, making triumph into a victorious hymn to the power of Emmanuel: "Those also that rode *Reformades*, and that came down to see the Battel, they shouted with that greatness of voice, and sung with such melodious notes, that they caused them that dwell in the highest Orbs to open their windows, put out their heads, and look down to see the cause of that Glory."[55] As in *Pilgrim's Progress*, delight in the destruction of one's enemies was the occasion of song (see Figure 6).

Violence is to be celebrated after the biblical paradigm of triumphant jubilation; so too is the destruction of enemies. Bunyan reports simply, "they crucified the *Diabolonians*, that had been a plague, a grief, and an offence, to the Town of *Mansoul*" (*Holy War*, 135). These executions find favor from the Prince, "and he said to them, that by this act of theirs he had proved them, and found them to be lovers of his person, observers of his Laws, and such as had also respect to his honour" (135). Written in the climate of Popish plot fury, Bunyan gives this message a local political resonance. Divine approval will not just command, but will applaud, earthly violence.[56] In *The Holy War*, this triumph against the enemy is short-lived however. The inhabitants of Mansoul soon succumb again to temptations and, backsliding, find themselves once again enslaved, this time to the Puritan's Restoration bogeys, "Lord *Fornication*, the Lord *Adultery*, the Lord *Murder*, the Lord *Anger*, the Lord *Lasciviousness*, the Lord *Deceit*, and Lord *Evileye*, the Lord *Blasphemy*, and that horrible Villain the old and

Tho doubting Caſtle be demoliſhed,
And the Gyant diſpair hath loſt his head:
Sin can rebuild the Caſtle, make't remaine;
And make deſpair the Gyant live againe.

Figure 6 John Bunyan, *The Pilgrim's Progress... Second Part* (1684), p. 182.

dangerous Lord *Covetousness*" (161). These dangerous incendiaries, it should be noted, are all titled aristocrats, as Bunyan serves up his class warfare. In typical anti-Catholic fare, their existence is described as aristocratic and pestilential at the same time. Again, the savior Emmanuel beseeches the citizens of Mansoul to keep their loyalty. In the final lines of the story, he invokes the contract whereby violence is the guarantor of protection:

Remember, therefore, O my Mansoul! *that thou are beloved of me; as I have therefore taught thee to watch, to fight, to pray, and to make war against my foes, so now I command thee to believe that my love is constant to thee. O my* Mansoul, *how I have set my heart, my love upon thee, watch.* Behold, I lay none other burden upon thee than what thou hast already, hold fast till I come. (*Holy War*, 250)

In an echo of the closing lines of the Song of Songs, Emmanuel promises a true love: this time allegorical representation includes violent reprisal. With allegiance to an apocalyptic hermeneutic, reading is not merely allegorical but sets history in motion.

Is that imagined violence a safety valve through which can be expressed the abundant rage at injustice in the present? Or is the violence itself a real threat? Either way, imagined violence is part of the process of forging individual agency and reincorporating a community of the excommunicate. For Bunyan, God's remembrance of his faithful was signified by violence. In his unfinished *Exposition on the Ten First Chapters of Genesis*, a work published posthumously in the 1692 *Works*, Bunyan explained the biblical phrase, "And God remembered Noah." Defining "remembered," Bunyan opines, "This word *remembered* is usual in Scripture, both when God is about to deliver his people out of Affliction, and to grant them the petition which they ask of him. It is said, *God remembred Abraham*; and sent *Lot* out of *Sodom*, that He *remembred Rachel*, and hearkened to her; that He also *remembred his Covenant with Abraham*, when he went to bring *Israel* out of their Bondage."[57]

Because the moment of God's arrival was utterly unpredictable, the saints needed in the meantime to cultivate self-discipline, living in a perpetual state of readiness for action. In *Pilgrim's Progress*, Bunyan's Christian comes face to face with the emblem of Despair when he and Hopeful are caught and imprisoned by the eponymous giant, who after giving them a bloody beating and imprisoning them, suggests that they make an end of themselves rather than continue to suffer further tortures; "'For why,' said he, 'should you choose life, seeing it is attended with so much bitterness?'" Hopeful in this case counsels, "Let's be patient, and endure a while; the time may come that may give us a happy release."[58] Likewise, the Son in

Milton's *Paradise Regain'd* also resists action but perhaps only at this time. There will come another time, another season, when action is called for: "Know therefore when my season comes to sit/ On *David's* Throne, it shall be like a tree/ Spreading and overshadowing all the Earth" (*PR*, 4:146–48). Apocalyptic history demanded that saints live in the present only *contingently*; they should be ever-ready for the abolition of history, time, and earthly attachment.

Bunyan counseled his readers to "labour to be patient" in their suffering: quoting the Bible, he avows, "The Artillery of a Christian, is the *word*, *faith*, and *prayer*: and in our *patience we must possess our Souls*."[59] But neither did Bunyan rule out a violence that was to come: the Bible had promised so much, and had given plenty of examples from the past.[60] The title of his tract, *Seasonable Counsel*, denotes the contingency of the present conditions: "The times then, and the seasons, even for the sufferings of the people of God, are not in the hands of their enemies, but in the hand of God" (*Seasonable Counsel*, 67). The implication is that there would be another season, and, once again, the figure for God's annunciation to violence is Samson: "For as surely as ever the Spirit of God moved *Samson* at times in the camp of *Dan*, when he lay against the *Philistines*; so will the Spirit of God move in and upon thee to comfort and to strengthen thee, whilst thou sufferest for his name in the world" (92). As we shall see, Samson repeatedly becomes the sign for that violent promise.

THE SAMSONIAN MOMENT

Living under persecution offered many temptations for the suffering saint, and the temptation to forget was but one of many. As Bunyan advised, "They that suffer have other kind of temptations upon this account than other Christians have. The liberty of others while they are in bonds, is a temptation to them; . . . And this temptation, were it not that we have to do with a God that is faithful, would assuredly be a great snare unto them. *But God is faithful, and will not suffer you to be tempted*" (*Seasonable Counsel*, 89). In urging his readers to consider the story of Samson as a story of overcoming temptation, Bunyan writes that there is a reward to come, a "drop of honey." His own writing, as that drop of honey, serves as a taste of such a reward. The Samson story thus holds out several possibilities for the Restoration writer, several points of identification between biblical type and the living writer. Deliverance is possible after suffering and overcoming temptation; the honey itself a sign and seal of this grace.

But, in *Grace Abounding*, Bunyan adds a parenthetical note on the topic of this "drop" of honey: "The Philistines understand me not."[61] In the biblical source, the Philistines were unable to solve the riddle of the sweetness, and Samson's strength against them held until he betrayed his secret to his wife, the woman of Timnah, who in turn betrayed the secret to her people. Bunyan's use of the "riddle" of Samson, however, stops the story before the secret is betrayed. Frozen at that point in the narrative, Samson's secret is safe, and the Philistines are not only without knowledge, but also without power over him. The riddle, then, protects Samson from those who do not understand. In the larger allegory, the riddle typologically divides the chosen nation Israel from the outsider Philistine nation. Significantly, the Philistines' lack of understanding takes place in the present tense: "The Philistines understand me not." Bunyan writes allegory here about his own potentially hostile Restoration readers. As a model of reading then, Samson's riddle offers a second meaning, a moment of exclusion of outsiders. The text implicitly asks readers not to break their seal of silence, to resist in a manner the loose-lipped Samson had not.

What are we to make of this recurrent motif in Bunyan's writing, this pointed use of the figure of Samson as a practitioner of allegory, sign of typology and violence? This moment signals interpretive choice for faithful readers, a chance to swerve from the literal, and possibly to evoke – even if only through desire – the politics of violent reprisal. If rage threatens to erupt at any moment, Bunyan's use of "similitudes" provides a means by which that rage can both be known, put into a logical or cosmic frame, and also be directed towards a community, through shared texts and stories which sharpen group solidarity. Reading Bunyan thus becomes a form of action, a collective identification through the shared myth of Samson, where readers are asked to signify loyalty to their community of those who understand by assenting to the typological structure.

Bunyan ends his introduction to *The Holy War* by taking on the persona of Samson, both predicting violent triumph and, at the same time, hiding that prediction in sublime mystery:

> Nor do thou go to work without my key
> (In mysteries men soon do lose their way);
> And also turn it right, if thou wouldst know
> My riddle, and wouldst with my heifer plough.[62]

The Bible story tells that Samson condemns the Philistine men for encroaching on his own rights as a husband, on discovering that his wife has revealed his secret: "if ye had not ploughed with my heifer, ye had not found out my riddle" (Judg. 15:18). Bunyan, unlike Samson, offers his readers help to understand his own riddle with the assistance of the marginal gloss. Bunyan's final anagram in the poem that is appended after the end of *Holy War* also forces the reader to read between the lines to discover the author's name: "Witness my name, if Anagram'd to thee,/ The Letters make, *Nu hony in a B*" (*Holy War*, 251): author merges with subject through the efficacy of language both to conceal and to reveal his true identity. Neither strictly passively obedient nor obviously actively resistant, then, Bunyan's reader participates in an economy of typological identification.

Samson and his riddles became the sign for Bunyan of this double action of typology to invoke the past and construct the present. His hornbook, *A Book for Boys and Girls* (1686), explained the educational mission that undergirded his practice of parabolic writing:

> *May I by them* [the poems] *bring some good thing to pass*
> As Sampson, *with the jawbone of an ass;*
> ...
> *I have my end, though I myself expose*
> *To scorn; God will have glory in the close.* (*MW*, x, 192)

In these lines, Bunyan couples the violence of the deliverer Samson with the practice of writing and reading riddles. The Samsonian mode thus accomplishes several tasks. Bunyan takes on the mantle of Samson himself by creating riddles that others do not understand, and thus divides those in the know from those who are outsiders. However many gaps there were between representation and reality, Bunyan himself *believed* these could be bridged by the partnership of humans and God. Bunyan aimed to educate Christians in proper habits of reading, so that they could practice proper habits of living.[63] Bunyan's readers were to become active and engaged, bonded to each other and to the writer through these practices. Though Bunyan eschewed active political resistance to civil authorities, he was aware he offered textual resistance in the form of his preference for the figural over the literal. That figuration was yet another means to restate the ongoing truths of God's presence in the world, a hermeneutics of immediacy demanded by typology.

In a powerful moment of his late, posthumously published, apocalyptic tract, *Of Antichrist, and his Ruine* (1692), Bunyan shows the figure of Samson as a fault line on which can be read the clash of the literal and the figurative realms of being, and the problems of understanding political agency through divine inspiration. In his account Bunyan holds that the era of the Antichrist is nearing an end, a fact that can be read by observing signs in the world. However, those signs are extraordinarily difficult to interpret; "If *Samson's* Riddle was so puzzling," Bunyan muses, "what shall we think of this?"[64] In a feat of imaginative hermeneutics, Bunyan offers that reversal of the worldly that marks the oppositional poetics of post-Puritan Dissent. Rather than the typical "Annus Mirabilis" signs, where bad weather, road accidents, and the like are seen as auguries of God's wrath, Bunyan holds that the world needs to be read backwards.[65] The apparent victory of the forces of evil is a sign of their spiritual emptiness, and of their imminent ruin. Drawing upon Revelation 11:10, Bunyan finds that joy and merriment are signs by which Antichrist's ruin is to be announced, and very soon. One instance is "When the *Philistines* had, as they thought, for ever overcome *Samson*, that *Nazarite* of God, how joyful were they of their victory!" That joy should herald their gloom and the ultimate victory of the True God is a sign of Antichrist's imminent downfall, the sign of which is Samson, unwitting agent and sufferer of supreme debasement:

Poor *Samson*! While thou haddest thy Locks, thy Liberty, and thine Eyes, thou didst shake the Pillar that did bear up their Kingdom! But now they have conquered thee, how great is their joy! How Great is their Joy, and how Near their Downfall! This therefore is a Joy that we have under Consideration, to wit, the Joy of them that dwell on Earth; for that the Witnesses that did bear up the Name of God in the World, were *overcome* and *killed*.[66]

The way of reading joy is to invert the royalist interpretation that their victory was a sign of God's favor. Samson, now in chains, will be yet free again.

Is there such a bright line between literary or spiritual resistance and political resistance, as Bunyan scholarship has drawn? The locus of Bunyan's anti-resistance teachings, according to Greaves, is *Seasonable Counsel*. Written in the darkest period for nonconformists, in the time of the "ultra-Tory" Anglican backlash against the Whig and nonconformist bid for exclusion of James from the throne, *Seasonable Counsel* offers that those who wish to remain loyal to God should do so with patience and submit to the suffering brought upon them by secular authority.[67] Bunyan transforms the persecution of the godly into a testament of their faith, adopting the pattern of Christian martyrs.[68] Instead of resisting, the faithful demonstrate their chosen status by their suffering:

Let us therefore covet to imitate Christ and the Scripture Saints. Let us shew out of a good conversation, our works with meekness of wisdom. Let us take heed of admitting the least thought in our minds of evil, against God, the King, all men, and things are in the hand of God...we are with patience to bear what God by man shall lay upon us. (36)

Active resistance is condemned in the strongest terms: "speak evil of no man, reproach not the Governour, nor his actions: as he is set over thee, *all his ways are Gods*, either for thy help or the tryal of thy graces. Wherefore he needs thy prayers, not thy revilings; thy peaceable deportment, and not a troublesome life... To wish the destruction of your enemies doth not become you" (99). Revenge and violence are not to be used against persecutors (100). Among the examples against resistance Bunyan cites is Absalom, a common allusion in the Restoration period, most recently figured by John Dryden in his brilliant satire against the Earl of Shaftesbury, *Absalom and Achitophel* (1681), written in the same Exclusion-crisis context as *Seasonable Counsel*. Such an example, along with the figure of Abishai in 1 Samuel 26:7–8, was meant to warn Bunyan's readers that civil response to political oppression was not acceptable; only God would punish evil kings. Bunyan's use of the figure of Absalom, moreover, seems to provide clear evidence that he even shared the Tory Dryden's condemnation of the politics of active resistance.

Nonconformists, however, did not all agree upon this point. Dissenters did play a major role in plotting against the Stuart regimes, both in the Rye House plot and in support for Monmouth. Bunyan's printer, Francis Smith, was frequently associated with resistance plots, and was a member of the Baptist and republican Salutation Tavern group, heavily tied in to activist London radicalism.[69] Yet Greaves, after sifting evidence of Bunyan's association with radicals, including several Rye House plotters, concludes that "no evidence connects Bunyan with active resistance to the Stuart regime."[70]

In a closer look at the text of *Seasonable Counsel*, we can see that Bunyan's treatment of biblical civil insurrection did not take the form of simple condemnation however. Dissenting hermeneutics allowed for reading otherwise, and this would have relevance in current English history. In citing Abishai's plans to commit regicide, Bunyan reflects that *"Abishai*, tho' a good man, would have kill'd the King, and that of conscience to God, and love to his Master. 1 *Sam* 26.7,8. and had *David* delivered *him* up to *Saul* for the attempt, he had in all likelihood died as a Traitor" (*Seasonable Counsel*, 32). David however, did *not* bring Abishai forward to the king as a traitor; he let the plotter be. A second case is brought forward, that of Peter: "*Peter* drew his Sword, and would have fought therewith, a thing for which he was blamed of his Master, and bid with a threatning, to put it up again. *Mat.*26.52. Besides, Oppression makes a wise man mad; and when a man is mad what evils will he not do?" (32). With these two scenes from the Bible, Bunyan expresses sympathy towards those who are driven to take up arms against persecutors or tyrants. In the first case, Abishai sought to relieve David of Saul's persecution – Saul had repeatedly broken David's trust – and yet David forbids Abishai from killing Saul, thus approving resistance to the temptation to take violent action. David refused to let Abishai commit the murder when the occasion arose: "Destroy him not: for who can stretch forth his hand against the LORD's anointed, and be guiltless?" (1 Sam. 26:9). The lesson against king-killing is clear; and yet in his redaction Bunyan does not only seize on the lesson, but also on David's ensuing compassion towards Abishai. Bunyan emphasizes that David did not deliver up Abishai to Saul for the attempt on his life; rather, David continued to rely upon Abishai to help him. David lets the would-be regicide live and flourish. In the second story, Peter is the would-be political activist; this time it is Jesus who prevents him from acting; Peter's impulse is made understandable in Bunyan's interpretation: "Oppression makes a wise man mad." There is sympathy here for those who wish to take revenge on their persecutors. Revenge becomes an understandable, if misguided, response to persecution. Bunyan allows that impulses to violent revenge are permissible, although action is not. There might also be a message to the Dissenting community – that of compassionate treatment of rebels.

According to Bunyan, violent action against persecutors was a temptation to be avoided. "Doth not God, oft-times, even take occasions by the hardest of things that come upon us, to visit our Souls with the comforts of his Spirit, to lead us into the glory of his word, and to cause us to savour that love that he has had for us, even from before the world began, till now." Bunyan ends this consoling passage with an italicized allusion, and this time, he unites past and present mysteries of God's grace with the violence that wrought such a conclusion: "*A Nest of Bees and honey did Sampson find, even in the belly of that Lion that roared upon him*" (*Seasonable Counsel*, 35). The figure of Samson stands as a figure for the solitary sufferer, the lone believer to whom God will return and for whom God will provide. Bunyan continues in his consolation, "let us learn like Christians to kiss the Rod, and love it" (35). As the one specially chosen by God as an instrument through which deliverance will come, Samson figures later in the tract again as an example of God's promise not to depart from the suffering Israel. However, seventeenth-century readers could not forget that Samson was a bloody warrior, the figure through whom God worked violent revenge upon the enemies of Israel.

Samson is a curious figure to praise for resisting temptation. For radical Protestants from the beginning to the end of the seventeenth century, Samson served as a token of God's providential workings, and also, more powerfully, as a symbol of physical strength. During the interregnum, the figure of Samson was adopted as a symbol for the "Good Old Cause"; even one of Cromwell's warships was named *Samson*, unfortunately sunk by the Dutch in 1653. Samson was an emblem for the New Model Army, in its prayer book touted as the exemplary soldier doing the Lord's battles; he was frequently alluded to in Cromwell's circle, and was used by radicals such as Lilburne as a model to imitate.[71] Milton's *Areopagitica* likens the reforming nation of England to the figure of Samson, as Milton imagines "a noble and puissant Nation rousing herself like a strong man after sleep, and shaking her invincible locks."[72] Edward Sexby, defending violent resistance in *Killing Noe Murder*, asked, "Now that which was lawful for *Samson* to do against many Oppressours, why is it unlawful for us to do against one? Are our Injuries less?"[73] Samson was a figure in Revolutionary England who raised the question of violence, of divine inspiration, and specifically the question of political resistance to secular authority.

In the Restoration period, the figure of the iconoclastic Samson took on a powerful resonance, both as a frightening specter of the violence of the civil war years, and as a threat to stable political order. Andrew Marvell acknowledges the fear that Milton would still be attached to the works of violence he had defended in his regicidal years, when he glossed Milton's *Paradise Lost* with an introductory poem in 1674 which likened Milton to Samson: "So *Sampson* grop'd the Temple's Posts in spite."[74] Milton's poem *Samson Agonistes* can indeed be read as a brutally revolutionary fantasy. Bunyan himself imagined Samson along these lines. Evoking the power and violence of Samson in his *Holy War*, the "true lovers of the town of Mansoul" rise up against the plotting Diabolonians in their midst, "like so many *Sampsons*, they shake themselves, and come together to consult and contrive how to defeat those bold and hellish contrivances."[75]

Bunyan's Samson is both the "riddling" Samson and the promised violent deliverer. As riddler, he exemplifies how Christians must become special readers, but as deliverer he embodies divine presence. These two components are the entangled strands of commemorative and sacramental logic at the heart of Reformed theology and hermeneutics. Baxter and Bunyan, it must be remembered, sat at quite a distance from each other on a Dissenting spectrum with regard to learning and attitudes toward Scripture.[76] Nonetheless they shared a historical outlook of providential hermeneutics, which in the Restoration yielded potentially incendiary results. The promise of typological reading was to explain the gaps between sign and signified, and this was also to open up a space for enthusiasm, that is, zealous religious action. Not in human laws, nor in political order, but in persistent loyalty to God's plan – even if inscrutable to humans – would meaning reside. Neither Baxter nor Bunyan actively participated in insurrection, but nor did the Restoration tame their violent hopes. Rather, the period of persecution offered ever more ambiguous forms through which those hopes could be expressed. By coupling interpretation and violent deliverance Bunyan offers a community of readers a mode of action, perhaps itself a performance of revelation mirroring the arrival of God's deliverance through violence. For both Bunyan and Baxter, the legacy of violence is a complex reminder of the inscrutability of God's ways in history. The saints' understanding of holy war could justify what is known today as terrorism. How would such a divine imperative square with a politics of toleration? In the next chapter John Milton tries to find out.

CHAPTER 5

Milton

In his account of the life of John Milton, the eighteenth-century commentator Jonathan Richardson noted Milton was a Protestant, though admitting, "of what Denomination of all the Several Sub-divisions of These, or if of Any, Known and Profess'd, is not Clear." One thing was sure: "but he Ever was a Dissenter from Our Church as by Law Established."[1] What does it mean to say Milton was a Dissenter in the Restoration? Milton's Restoration activities are shadowy, his political invisibility well warranted as the king's initial offers of forgiveness upon his return to England were broken by a retributive Anglican Tory Parliament and ministry.[2] Milton did write on the subject of religious liberty, publishing a tract defending a broad toleration of Protestants in 1673. Yet there remains a biographical gap in understanding Milton's precise relation to Dissenting culture.

In contrast, the portrait of Milton in the English Revolution has been drawn much more robustly. *Paradise Lost* has been taken as a testament to the Revolution's failure, where the fallen are consoled for their loss of Eden by the promise of "a paradise within thee, happier far" (*PL*, 12:587). This turn inward, it has been argued, represents Milton's withdrawal from Revolutionary politics, with his turn to poetry in the Restoration taken as an admission of defeat. The premises of this study are that the English Revolution was not a complete failure; that radical energies released there continued to fire politics and religious controversy in the Restoration; and that the literary activities of the radical sectarians merit attention for their complex engagement with political and otherworldly concerns. I shall argue here that we can consider Milton's ongoing commitment to religious radicalism as his response to the agonies of the present, and that he explored those agonies through a complex theological engagement with questions of human volition, prophecy, and toleration. This chapter views Milton's late writings in the context of Dissent, suggesting that we can see his political commitments by means of, not apart from, his theology.

Milton was intimately familiar with the conditions of Dissenters in the Restoration. His own neighborhood, the parish of St. Giles Cripplegate, was an area of London noted for its nonconformist concentration and there was controversy about its local ministry through the early 1660s. In 1662 Cripplegate's Presbyterian preacher, Samuel Annesley, aroused opposition and was legally ejected from the parish and an Anglican royalist installed in his place.[3] Cripplegate boasted a famous Puritan past: John Foxe, John Speed, and the radical Protestant printer and poet Robert Crowley, the parish's first recorded rector, had each lived in Cripplegate. Daniel Defoe was born there in 1660. During the Restoration period, Cripplegate ward was known for the poverty of its inhabitants, its breweries, and for its lively Dissenting community. A haven for Huguenots, those persecuted French Protestant dissenters who had long affiliated with Puritans, Cripplegate boasted the highest number of ejected ministers in the younger Edmund Calamy's account. Jewin Street, where Milton lived, was crammed with Dissenting meeting houses.[4] Milton lived just by Grub Street, which had already attracted a derogatory meaning in the 1640s due to its association with Puritan pamphleteering and radical divinity.[5] The name of that street – with an unexpected irony – has now been changed to Milton Street. Close by was Bunhill Fields, in 1666 converted from a plague pit into the burial ground for nonconformist worthies: in 1731, the will of one Neil Ward quipped: "Oh! Bury not my peaceful corpse/ In Cripplegate, where discord dwells/ And wrangling parties jangle worse/ Than alley scolds or laundry bells."[6] In 1663 Milton moved into a house down the road from the cemetery, and he may have heard the trains of mourners in procession pass on their way there.[7] Milton's neighbors and friends were sectaries, including the Penningtons and Thomas Ellwood. This neighborhood remained Milton's for the rest of his life, and it was there he penned his last great poems. Milton's wife Elizabeth was a Baptist, remaining so in her widowhood of fifty-three years.

Even at the time of his flight from London during the plague in the summer of 1665, Milton preferred to live near other Dissenters, residing in the Buckinghamshire village of Chalfont St. Giles, a known Quaker stronghold, close to the home of the Penningtons and soon the location of their meeting house at Jordans. While Milton lived close by, Isaac Pennington was arrested in September 1665 and his family turned out of their house; Mary Pennington took lodgings very near Milton while her husband was in prison. The Chalfont house in which he lived belonged to Anne Fleetwood, daughter of the regicide George Fleetwood, and Presbyterian meetings were reported as taking place there in 1669.[8]

For all Milton's literal proximity to Dissent, the truth is that we have no written record of his attendance at any known church or meeting house. There has recently come to light a tantalizing clue: in 1659 Milton had interceded on behalf of a French church in London, one supported by Bulstrode Whitelocke and others of a radical and Independent religious cast, by writing a letter to a prospective minister. Geoffrey Nuttall has shown that "in 1659 Milton was closely involved with the congregation."[9] This would corroborate John Toland's estimation that "In his middle years he was best pleas'd with the *Independents* and *Anabaptists*, as allowing of more Liberty than others, and coming nearest in his opinion to the primitive practice."[10] Whether Milton remained associated with this church in the Restoration, when it conformed, is unknown. Toland continues, "but in the latter part of his Life, he was not a profest Member of any particular Sect among Christians, he frequented none of their Assemblies, nor made use of their peculiar Rites in his Family" (195).

As to his church loyalties, we do know, however, that his body was interred in Cripplegate parish church, leaving us wondering if he made his peace with the Anglican ministry. Why was Milton buried in the church at Cripplegate? Contemporary comment has it that Milton was laid to rest there because that was where he had put his father.[11] We do not know if that was John Milton's intention; his will was orally dictated to his brother. But even if it was his wish to lie there, Milton's burial at this church rather than in the Dissenters' burial ground at Bunhill Fields need not be seen as his reconciliation with the Anglican Restored church in 1674. The church at Cripplegate at that time can hardly be called orthodox; indeed, all through the Revolution and Restoration periods, Cripplegate endured controversies ecclesiological and political, fluctuating from Independent to Presbyterian, low Anglican, and higher Anglican. Though reclaimed as orthodox with the coming of Uniformity, at the time of Milton's death the church seems to have been run by a nonconformist curate, since the appointed orthodox minister had permanently, though not officially, fled the area at the time of the plague.[12]

Even if Milton's precise religious affiliations are unknown, there are his great works of poetry to give us his imaginative responses to persecution and orthodoxy, his testaments to godly fortitude and political radicalism. In the Restoration Milton published his poetry, challenging the ancients in his epic *Paradise Lost*, published in 1667, and, in 1671, retelling the temptation of Christ in a chaste epic, *Paradise Regain'd*, and the plight of the fallen Samson in a searing classical–biblical drama, *Samson Agonistes*. As Theophilus Gale would urge in explaining the divine origins of literature, as we shall see in Chapter Seven, Milton proffered an inspired, biblical mode, wedding this to pagan literary forms. He also threaded his Restoration works with themes and situations arising out of the conditions of nonconformity.

This chapter falls into two parts: the first surveys dissenting themes in Milton's late poetry, examining them as his case(s) for tolerance, exploring Milton's conception of true ministry and his attacks on priestcraft and compulsion. Milton's Restoration prose tract, *Of True Religion* (1673), offers his clear liberal defense of toleration; but his last works also show investments in apocalypticism that drew him in a different direction from Locke on questions of toleration and persecution. Thinking about Milton's apocalypticism will mean exploring some tensions between voluntarist and determinist accounts of human action. The second part of the chapter takes the 1671 poems to address Dissenters' troubling questions: what were saints to do in the meantime? How could one remain loyal amidst troubling doubts and temptations? By what means would God's wishes be made known? In the meantime of cosmic history, after the vocation of Christ but before his return, Milton and the saints were feeling bereft, having experienced great loss: they wondered if God had abandoned them. Staging dramatically moments where God's disappearance and reappearance had already taken place in the past could help to master that painful situation, to offer hope in the form of a reminder. For those Dissenters patiently awaiting God's vindication, as we have seen, doubt was a chief temptation; Milton represents the disciples in *Paradise Regain'd*, who "begain to doubt, and doubted many days,/ And as the days increas'd, increas'd thir doubt" (*PR*, 2:11–12). In *Paradise Regain'd* and *Samson Agonistes* Milton explores how God is ultimately revealed through inexplicable divine action on and through the person. The ending of both poems confirms an identity (the Son) and a name ("Samson hath quit himself like Samson"), but that confirmation is made only in retrospect, "in the close." As Bunyan in his *Holy War* made violence a kind of confirmation, Milton also saw violence as God's assurance, a certainty that promises would be made good. I hope to show the complex interplay of voluntarist and irrational modes of human agency in this great writer's last poems, as well as to highlight the ways his poetry was ever drenched with philosophical as well as political questions arising from his experience of history.

MILTON AND RESTORATION POLEMICS

Milton's first publication in the Restoration was a small affair, a sonnet, unsigned and inserted in a seditious volume. Appearing in a biography of Sir Henry Vane, who had been executed for treason in January 1662 in a very public show of governmental strength, Milton's poem was allegedly written in 1652. When it was published in George Sikes' biography it was a speech act, as David Norbrook reminds us, "that was strongly opposi-tional."[13] That biography did not simply commemorate a zealous martyr but sharply lanced at government and monarch by suggesting the world had been turned upside down if the likes of Vane were considered traitors: "The case then is this; when the World is in a mad, bruitish, disordered hurly burly, they that attempt to bring righteousness a-floate, are accused of turning it up side down. Setting all to rights, is reckoned the greatest Confusion. The Rights of the Kingdom, are reckoned the Wrongs of the King."[14] In strong terms Sikes attacked the current regime, predicting its violent overthrow in passages culled from the Bible, asking: "Do you imag-ine that the Mass, or a barren Episcopal Ministry with an Organ and a Common-prayer Book will down with a Nation that has such light stir-ring in it, as not only the Presbyterian, but in a manner all the variety of Congregational Churches, yes the rest Fift-Monarchy-men (so called) will hardly bear?" Writing as if all the English were like the biblical Samson, Sikes closes this extraordinary passage, asking, "Will you pull out all our eyes?"[15] Milton's sonnet assisted in drawing this portrait, with its praise for Vane's distinguishing the realms of spiritual and civil power: "to know/ Both spiritual power, and civil, what each meanes/ What severs each, thou hast learn't, which few have done." Vane's specifically religious leadership – his robust Independency – was exemplary: "Therefore on thy firm hand Religion leanes/ In peace, and reckons thee her eldest Son."[16] Sikes cer-tainly read Milton's poem with that emphasis, as he explains: "The latter part of this Sufferers Elogy in the 'bove-mentioned Verses, concerns his skill in distinguishing the two Swords or Powers, Civil and Spiritual, and the setting right bounds to each. He held that the Magistrate ought to keep within the proper sphere of Civil Jurisdiction, and not inter-meddle with mens Consciences by way of Imposition and Force, in matters of Religion and divine Worship."[17] Though we don't know the extent of Milton's involvement in the production of this volume, we can make certain inferences from the nature of Sikes' readership: the ideas in the poem were mightily relevant to the political situation of the early Restoration as it concerned charges of sedition and freedom of religious worship.

Milton's next Restoration representation of Dissent may be found in *Paradise Lost*, written between 1658 and 1663, and complete by 1665 when he gave it to his friend Thomas Ellwood.[18] When read for its politics, the great epic is much more than a backward glance to the issues (and failures) of godly revolution and republican political theory.[19] Its publication in 1667 coincided with a shift in political affairs after the fall of Clarendon, when a lessening of hardship for dissenters appeared possible.[20] Yet the poem only rarely topically engages with contemporary politics and polemics. Instead, with Adam and Eve's temptation, it is centrally concerned with how to maintain obedience to God, despite the very human propensity to surrender will to compulsions, whether external or internal.

The term "dissent" in the text of *Paradise Lost* turns up three times, linking three different characters: a fallen angel, a repentant angel, and a fallen man. Milton is neither drawing an allegory of Restoration Dissenters nor is he commenting directly on the persecuting regime. Nonetheless, the language of "dissent" in each case approves a right course of action, in sharp distinction to Milton's terms associated with rebel – "rebel Angels" (1:38), "rebel King" (1:484) – most often in relation to Satan and his crew. The first instance of "dissent" in the poem is relatively trivial, a joke. After the anointment of the Son, Satan is unable to sleep. His comrade Beelzebub, by sleeping, is coyly figured by Satan as a dissenter from their friendship: "Both waking we were one; how then can now/ Thy sleep dissent?" (5:668–69). Although Satan's use of the term is teasing, still dissent is very much a political action, signifying loyalty to the Almighty.

The second occurrence of the term is more significant, denoting Abdiel, whose name means "servant of God." Interrupting Satan's speech to his troops, the lone angel stands up to resist the rebellion, "and in a flame of zeal severe/ The current of his fury thus opposed" (5:807–08). Challenging Satan's specious logic as blasphemous, Abdiel urges Satan to relent, to make peace with God, but his arguments do not sway Satan from his course (8:809–95). That better angel, "though alone/ Encompass'd round with foes" (5:875–76), stands in for Milton, also "with dangers compast round/ And solitude" (7:27–28): the situation of both resonates with Restoration Dissent.[21] It may be that Milton added the Abdiel material as a later interpolation.[22] His Abdiel is not reducible to topical allegory, however. Abdiel represents the dissenting type, in every age burning fiercely against the evil ones, speaking out boldly against the atheist, the doubter, the conformist: those who refuse to see God's truth. The moving portrait of this valiant angel reveals the familiar Miltonic themes – absolute loyalty to God, persistence in the face of public rebuke, solitary resistance, bold speech acts, and most powerfully, a desire to convince through argument. Milton's *Paradise Lost* is one such argument.

Read typologically, Abdiel was a figure of Christ, and of righteous belief more generally. For Restoration Dissenters, his was a story reassuring them that their own experiences of public humiliation were being witnessed by God and would be vindicated. In resisting Satan, Abdiel does not refer to his "conscience," that inner knowledge of God's ways. Indeed, Milton seems to have avoided that language altogether, as if staying far clear of contemporary debates over toleration in which the term conscience was the sounding call. Abdiel's ark, rather, is that of "faith," as Milton allows no room for the charge that his conscience is erroneous; nor does he open the door to charges of antinomian enthusiasm. Nor does Abdiel speak against persecution or tyranny, but rather against the faithlessness which gives rise to both institutional means of compulsion. The charge is more radical than a blast against persecution; instead it unsettles the merely moral and material beliefs of Satan and his followers, and resembles the charge of the Congregationalist George Sikes, who lambasted the "Episcopal Ministry, whose Divinity amounts not to so much as sound and well managed moral Philosophy. Their words have no power to awaken Consciences," or Marvell's satirical titling of Samuel Parker as "his morality" rather than "his grace."[23] In *Paradise Lost*, Abdiel does not protest persecution as among Satan's crimes. The Restored church was evil not *because* it persecuted, but it persecuted because it was a false church.

Abdiel's dissent from Satan is judged "out of season" (5:850: perhaps alluding to "To every thing there is a season," Eccl. 3:1). But Milton shows it is very much the season for God to vindicate his faithful. Milton's closing words in a 1659 tract rejecting a national ministry attested that "If I be not heard nor beleevd, the event will bear me witnes to have spoken truth: and I in the mean time while have borne my witnes not out of season to the church and to my countrey."[24] Finding the right season was a great matter of concern for Dissenters in the Restoration, as they contemplated past and present political action. Suggesting that God would soon reverse the course of history, a number of pamphlets actively opposing the Restoration of monarchy in 1660 were titled *A Word in Season*.[25]

"Though Worlds/ Judg'd thee perverse" (*PL*, 6:36–37): Abdiel's powerful act of dissent is soon approved by God, who praises this most difficult battle: "single hast maintain'd/ Against revolted multitudes the Cause/ Of Truth" (6:30–32). In a final confrontation, Abdiel rebukes the rebel angel for having failed to see rightly. Here the term dissent finally appears, as Abdiel defends his "sect," that minority who dared challenge the majority:

> ... there be who Faith
> Prefer, and Piety to God, though then
> To thee not visible, when I alone
> Seem'd in thy World erroneous to dissent
> From all: my Sect thou seest, now learn too late
> How few sometimes may know, when thousands err.
>
> (6:143–8)

The seeming dissenter is indeed God's beloved. This sense of the visible world as an inversion of the True World was common to Dissenters. As George Sikes put it in his biography of Vane, "'Tis a sign Monarchy is notoriously degenerated, that persons of *Joseph's* and *Daniels* spirit are for that very reason hated and slain... The enemies of this *English Joseph* and deliverer, were of the right Satanick spirit; hated him only for following the thing that good is."[26] If only Milton's England could see, too, that Dissenters were truly faithful, the minority virtuous, the majority worthy of contempt; yet, in the meantime, "so shall the World go on,/ To good malignant, to bad men benign" (12:537–38). Nowhere in the poem is faith set more clearly against the world than in the encomium for the solitary angel with which Milton closes Book Five:

> So spake the Seraph *Abdiel* faithful found,
> Among the faithless, faithful only hee;
> Unshak'n, unseduc'd, unterrifi'd
> His Loyalty he kept, his Love, his Zeal;
> Nor number, nor example of him wrought
> To swerve from truth, or change his constant mind
> Though single. From amidst them forth he pass'd
> Long way through hostile scorn, which he sustain'd
> Superior, nor of violence fear'd aught
> And with retorted scorn his back he turn'd
> On those proud Tow'rs to swift destruction doom'd.
>   (5:896–906)

As a string of negatives ("Unshak'n, unseduc'd, unterrifi'd"), encloses the choices that Abdiel, and others like him, must face, Milton models the Restoration Dissenter who must say "no" to the most difficult temptations of social, political, and psychological surrender. With abrupt enjambment and broken line endings, Milton lays emphasis on the processual difficulty of taking a stand. Grammatically, Milton requires a jump from verb to the modifers "though single/ long way/ superior" in each of three consecutive lines, leaps of faith, as it were. This moving portrait of Abdiel, the dissenter, prompts the cowering persecuted to bear up bravely and perform their unshaken beliefs.

The third dissenter in *Paradise Lost* is Adam. In Book Nine, he has permitted Eve to part from him for a morning of work in the garden, though he had initially, and rightly, been reluctant to let her go. With obstinacy, Eve had prevailed. While alone, she was approached by Satan. After the Fall, Eve blames Adam for not having prevented her separation: "Hadst thou been firm and fixt in thy dissent," she chides, "Neither had

I transgress'd, nor thou with me" (9:1160–61). Although her reasoning is unreliable in many places in the poem, I think she is right here in the sense that if Adam had been firmer, she would not have left him. By characterizing his opinion as "dissent," she also correctly asserts that hers was taken as the prevailing authority. We know that's not the way it was supposed to be: the Son later reprimands Adam for failing to know "thyself aright" (10:156):

> Was shee thy God, that her thou didst obey
> Before his voice, or was shee made thy guide,
> Superior, or but equal, that to her
> Thou didst resign thy Manhood, and the Place
> Wherein God set thee above her made of thee.
>   (10:145–49)

Adam's "dissent," it turns out, should have been the superior guide: another instance of how labels could be inverted or misapplied. Though this suggests that, in working for the Lord, separation is not good, Milton does not draw an allegory to the church, condemning schism or ratifying compulsive uniformity.[27] If there is any ecclesiological allegory, it is to suggest, as the Puritans did, that the current state church was indeed a falling off, a separation, from a truer mode of worship.

For Milton to defend dissent in his great poem puts him in relation to contemporary debates over tolerance. Indeed, Adam answers Eve with tolerance. Though he dissented from her, he did not embrace coersion. He had used all rational means to restrain Eve from her error, "I warn'd thee, I admonish'd thee, foretold/ The danger" (9:1171–72), but anything more "had been force,/ And force upon free Will hath here no place" (1173–74). Adam's views accord with those of Milton, who ever defended liberty of conscience, but, as Joan Bennett has argued, in Eve's case, perhaps Adam had been a little too tolerant, too quick to be permissive.[28]

Compulsion, specifically as it thwarted freedom of the will, had long been Milton's bugbear, from his earliest prose polemic to his last poems. Compulsion was the fault of Antichristian powers, whatever their guise, whether Roman Catholic, pre-civil war episcopacy, Presbyterian prelacy, or Restored Anglican. A history of the corruption of the church is offered in the final book of *Paradise Lost* in Michael's teaching, in what C. S. Lewis has criticized as an "untransmuted lump of futurity."[29] Its apocalyptic mode and anti-priestly themes accord with Milton's earlier writings:

> Wolves shall succeed for teachers, grievous Wolves,
> Who all the sacred mysteries of Heav'n
> To thir own vile advantages shall turn . . .

> Then they shall seek to avail themselves of names,
> Places and titles, and with these to join
> Secular power, though feigning still to act
> By spiritual, to themselves appropriating
> The Spirit of God, promis'd alike and giv'n
> To all Believers; and from that pretense,
> Spiritual Laws by carnal power shall force
> On every conscience; Laws which none shall find
> Left them inroll'd, or what the Spirit within
> Shall on the heart engrave...   (12:508–24)

The false pastor as wolf is an image Milton had used in *Lycidas*, foretelling "the ruin of our corrupted clergy then in their height." There the grim wolf was threatening destruction of the sheep, who are hungry and unfed.[30] The Laudian episcopacy was backsliding to the idolatries of Rome, with a "Tyrannical crew and Corporation of Imposters, that have blinded and abus'd the World." In his tracts from the early 1640s, Milton lanced more at ceremonialism than at persecution, with the bishops as "Egyptian taskmasters of Ceremonies thrust purposely upon the groaning Church to the affliction, and vexation of God's people."[31] In his Restoration poem, however, that false church is specifically a persecuting church:

> Whence heavy persecution shall arise
> On all who in the worship persevere
> Of Spirit and Truth; the rest, far greater part,
> Will deem in outward Rites and specious forms
> Religion satisfi'd.   (*PL*, 12:531–35)

Persecution is the effect of Antichristian powers. *Paradise Lost* is not an argument for toleration; rather, the poem offers reassurance that the victims of spiritual tyranny will find ultimate vindication in a cosmic scheme. The very last vision in the entire poem reveals a violent apocalyptic judgment: "till the day/ Appear of respiration to the just/ And vengeance to the wicked, at return/ Of him so lately promis'd to thy aid" (12:539–42). The sum of Adam's knowledge is that "suffering for Truth's sake/ Is fortitude to highest victory" (569–70).[32]

What kind of toleration can emerge from this approach? It is difficult to say, especially since in the Dissenters' apocalyptic scheme persecution was a sign of God's punishment for sin. The remedy against it was repentance. If God heard the sinner's cry, he would lift the sentence. Writers opposing religious persecution in the 1660s confronted the situation of coercive state authority and religious persecution by calling it slavery. For John Locke, such slavery was an external condition, the unjust abrogation of rights belonging to citizens. Arguing for toleration for Protestant Dissenters in 1667, Locke wrote that persecution will "bring this island to the condition of a galley where the greater part shall be reduced to the condition of slaves, be forced with blows to row the vessel, but share in none of the lading, nor have any privilege or protection."[33] The origins of slavery, in this liberal account, were not inward, but external.

In Milton's *Paradise Lost*, however, the internal enslavement preceded the external sentence of the Fall, in Adam's self-surrender to Eve. Likewise, in *Samson Agonistes* the blind hero suffers several kinds of slavery, and the internal also precedes the external condition. Before being enslaved to Dalila and to the Philistines, Samson was self-enslaved: "foul effeminacy held me yok't (*SA*, 411). Internal slavery is more disgraceful than the other kinds, as Samson explains early on in the drama when he laments his condition:

> The base degree to which I now am fall'n,
> These rags, this grinding, is not yet so base
> As was my former servitude, ignoble,
> Unmanly, ignominious, infamous,
> True slavery.   (*SA*, 414–18)

True slavery, as these remarks show, is to be complicit in one's own slavery, freely and willingly to contribute to surrender of one's own freedom, a republican concept of dependence. Yet Samson's personal enslavement is not simply internal but connected to his outward, political condition. As Samson himself remarks, again sounding a republican note:

> But what more oft in Nations grown corrupt,
> And by thir vices brought to servitude,
> Than to love Bondage more than Liberty,
> Bondage with ease than strenuous liberty.
>   (268–71)

The theme of self-enslavement was often used in the Restoration to describe English citizens' complicity in their loss of liberty under the Restored Stuart monarch. By welcoming the Stuart regime, English citizens were reducing themselves to the condition of slaves, as the republican Algernon Sidney wrote in the mid 1660s: "God hath deliver'd us from slavery, and shewd us that he would be our King; and we recall from exile one of that detested race."[34] Milton, too, in the last lines of his eleventh-hour appeal to his nation before the return of monarchy, evoked the parallel in the closing sentences of his tract. He challenged his audience in *The Ready and Easy Way*, "to become children of reviving libertie; and may reclaim, though they seem now chusing them a captain back for *Egypt*" (*CPW*, VII, 463).

In a republican view, failures of virtue cause a people's decline of liberty.[35] "Tyranny must be,/ Though to the Tyrant thereby no excuse" (*PL*, 12:95–96): thus Milton explains the reign of Nimrod. To this republican view of ethical lapse, Milton's *Paradise Lost* adds an apocalyptic component. With the biblical example of the debauched Ham, Milton comments:

> Thus will this latter, as the former World,
> Still tend from bad to worse, till God at last
> Wearied from their iniquities, withdraw
> His presence from among them, and avert
> His holy Eyes; resolving from thenceforth
> To leave them to thir own polluted ways.
>
> (12:105–10)

If God had withdrawn, as it seemed very like it in the Restoration if one was a Dissenter, when would He return? Note the subjunctive mood here: "till God...withdraw" – a parallel to the opening promise of the whole of *Paradise Lost*, "till one greater Man/ Restore us" (1:4–5). That syntax sets the action not in the past tense of Ham but in the ongoing, processual present and future. Milton writes not of old, but of now.

In Milton's view, persecution and slavery were part of the greater story of providence. What, then, of toleration? The emergence of ideologies of toleration is crucial to the liberal tradition, and the literature concerning its rise is vast, much of it focused on John Locke's stunning contributions. Dissenters and others on the radical left, including Locke, formulated a panoply of tolerationist positions unleashed by the mid-century wars of religion and the Revolution.[36] Milton participated in an analysis of toleration, combining seemingly contradictory liberal and apocalyptic premises.

OF TRUE RELIGION: MILTON ON TOLERATION

Milton was ever an advocate of a broad Protestant toleration. Even if his great poems promised God would ultimately settle the score between the just and unjust, Milton did not stop writing for the here and now; indeed, his last published work was a tract defending toleration of Protestant sects. Though not specifically referring to the proposals being weighed in that session of Parliament, Milton published *Of True Religion, Haeresie, Schism, Toleration* in the spring of 1673, while or just after Parliament met to cancel Charles' Declaration of Indulgence and to pass a Test Act for Catholics. Milton strongly opposed Charles' gesture of toleration for Catholics.[37] Nicholas von Maltzahn sees his last tracts pushing toward Whiggery in their advocacy of Protestant toleration and elective kingship.[38] Like Locke, Milton defined "True Religion" as revealed religion only: "learnt and believed from the Word of God only. No Man or Angel can know how God would be worshipt and serv'd unless God reveal it" (*Of True Religion*, in *CPW*, VIII, 419). And because that faith must not be an implicit faith, but rather directly coming from Scripture, "no true Protestant can persecute, or not tolerate his fellow Protestant, though dissenting from him in som opinions" (421). The language of "True Religion" attempted to reach beyond sectarian dispute, and thus Milton took scope to register an attack encompassing England's persecuting church, its Romanizing king, and the papacy.

As the tract called for a universal Protestant toleration, it also characterized other elements of a liberal society, including freedom of the press: "If it be asked how far they [sectarians] should be tolerated? I answer doubtless equally, as being all Protestants; that is on all occasions to give account of their Faith, either by Arguing, Preaching in their several Assemblies, Publick writing, and the freedom of Printing" (426). The Bible authorized believers "who agree in the main, are every where exhorted to mutual forbearance and charity one towards the other, though dissenting in some opinions" (435). Protestants should unify against evil: "To save our selves therefore, and resist the common enemy, it concerns us mainly to agree within our selves... The Gospel commands us to tolerate one another, though of various opinions" (436). Building on the commitments of *Areopagitica* (1644), where he urged Parliament to lift pre-publication censorship, Milton saw the existence of sects as no threat to truth: "It is written that the Coat of our Saviour was without seame: whence some would infer that there should be no division in the Church of Christ. It should be so indeed; Yet seams in the same cloath, neither hurt the garment, nor misbecome it; and not only seams, but Schisms will be while men are fallible" (435–36). With a tip of the hat to the latitudinarians who emphasized the fallibility of knowledge of God, Milton contends that sifting all ideas would be a never-ending process because of humans' incomplete knowledge on earth. Open communication was therefore vital to national reformation. Milton turns to the biblical passages he had cited in *Areopagitica*:

And we are bid, 1 *Thess.* 5.21. *Prove all things, hold fast that which is good*. St. *Paul* judg'd that not only to tolerate, but to examine and prove all things, was no danger to our holding fast of that which is good. How shall we prove all things, which includes all opinions at least founded on Scripture, unless we not only tolerate them, but patiently hear them, and seriously read them? (*Of True Religion*, 436; cf. *Areopagitica*, *CPW*, II, 511–12)

Controversy would only sharpen a person's faith. The daring of these views may be seen when one takes into account that this was a period when the state church was preventing just that kind of open controversy. Richard Baxter was thrown into prison for arguing along similar lines to Milton, interpreting Jesus' words "Forbid him not" (Mark 9:39) as support for toleration: "Men that Preach in Christ's Name therefore, are not to be silenced, though faulty; if they do more good than harm." But Baxter goes further in condemning the silencers: "Dreadful then is the Case of them, that Silence Christ's faithful ministers." This was one of the passages highlighted by Sir Roger L'Estrange in charging Baxter with sedition, for which the Dissenter sat in prison for two years.[39]

Milton bases his toleration on the principle that "In Religion nothing is indifferent" to God (428). Like Locke, Milton insists that "neither he can impose, nor the other believe or obey ought in Religion, but from the Word of God only" (428). In contrast to those strands of rational religion – whether Anglican or latitudinarian – which accepted a division between necessary and unnecessary things, both of which were consistent with state demands for uniformity of religious belief and practice, Milton turns to revelation. Milton, of course, values reason: "reason is but choosing" (*Areopagitica*, in *CPW*, 11, 527). From his earliest writings on religion, Milton emphasized the importance of reason and grace, and reading with assistance of the Holy Spirit. In *Of Reformation* (1641), he was critical of people who "scan the *Scriptures*, by the Letter, and in the Covenant of our Redemption, magnifi'd the external signs more than the quickning power of the *Spirit*" (*CPW*, 1, 522); his argument for reason-as-choosing in *Areopagitica* is an emendation of the earlier emphasis on the workings of the Spirit. Echoing 1 Corinthians 12, where Paul had enumerated "diversities of gifts, but the same Spirit," in *Of Reformation*, Milton insisted on the democratic possibilities of the Spirit, to engender great works in any person, regardless of sex, education, or social position:

The very essence of Truth is plainnesse, and brightnes; the darknes and crooked-nesse is our own . . . If we will but purge with sovrain eyesalve that intellectual ray which *God* hath planted in us, then we would beleeve the Scriptures protesting their own plannes, and *learned*, but the *simple*, the *poor*, the *babes* foretelling an extraordinary effusion of *Gods* Spirit upon every age, and sexe, attributing to all men, and requiring from them the ability of searching, trying, examining all things, and by the Spirit discerning that which is good. (*CPW*, 1, 566)

In his last writing on tolerance, Milton once again shattered social hierarchy: "an ordinary Protestant, well read in the Bible, may turn and wind their

Doctors" (*Of True Religion*, 432). It was popery to monopolize authority over Scripture: "Our Church on the contrary hath proposd it to all men, and to this end translated it into English . . . that all sorts and degrees of men, not understanding the Original, may read it in their Mother Tongue" (434). Milton pairs his defense of what would become liberal icons – education, freedom of the press – with an illiberal account of the cosmic clash between the forces of evil and those of good, a struggle beyond and through time between God and Antichrist. That scheme would demand holy warfare.

Not all tolerationist roads lead to Locke. Gary De Krey has categorized four separate, but overlapping strands of tolerationist thought in the Restoration that claimed conscience as a ground, not all Lockean. Some Dissenters based their claims upon the principles of natural law (Independents such as John Owen and Philip Nye), and from this strand emerges an account of the rights of the subject. Other defenses of conscience stood upon interest theory (Slingsby Bethel and Presbyterian John Humfrey); separation of church and state (Quaker William Penn and Independent Sir Charles Wolseley); and some rested upon apocalyptic visions (sectarian Dissenters, including Fifth Monarchists).[40]

Milton's thought is a hodge-podge of these approaches, but his Restoration poetry belongs in this last strand, proffering an apocalyptic theology rooted in the efficacy and immediacy of divine impulsion. The troubling, anti-rationalist side of Milton and the Dissenters invokes a theology of violence and an otherworldly reliance on unaccountable agency. We must take care not to over-secularize Owen's (and other Calvinists') commitments to "rights of individuals." By rooting our analysis of dissenting political thought in defenses of conscience in which it is seen as wholly a human affair, we miss the larger possible consequences of the dissenting position. The notion of the "individual" as such in some Dissenters' writings is quite different from the starting point taken by liberal authors. The resistance of Owen and others on the grounds of conscience was not because conscience was an inalienable right; it was that conscience did not belong to any person, but to God. While in practice an argument about conscience as an inalienable right may have functioned in the exact same way as an argument about conscience belonging to God, this is a conceptual distinction that has several notable consequences. If the conscience belongs to God, the idea of self-as-property will be different; the possibility of severing the "public" from the "private" will have no force; and the separation of spheres between "religion" and "politics" will be impossible.

In basing his arguments for liberty of conscience and freedom of the will upon an account of divine agency in cooperation with human reason,

Milton approached politics differently from those making proto-liberal, natural law, or prudential arguments. Milton saw the purpose of politics not, as it would be for the Whigs and early liberals, to guarantee property relations and order in the civil realm. Rather, it was to provide an indifferent form through which an appropriate, that is, *immediate*, relation to God might be maintained. Most early modern theorists agreed with Milton that the aim of the state was to serve God. But in Milton's view, the being who served God was not the autonomous agent in the classic liberal or even the Whig sense. For Milton, conscience could function as a radical brace preserving individual liberty against coercive state authority, but it was also radically open to the workings of divine impulse.

THE 1671 VOLUME

With boldness and a sense of political timing, Milton produced his slim volume, *Paradise Regain'd. A Poem... To which is added Samson Agonistes* (1671). Across the winter and early spring of 1670, both Houses of Parliament had discussed the merits of a bill against conventicles, an act that did tighten persecution of Dissenters when it went into effect.[41] Following its passage in April, and the adjournment of Parliament, there was a great crackdown on Dissenters, as well as civil unrest in London.[42] That summer, during which Charles was pursuing his secret treaty with France, the *Paradise Regain'd* volume went to the licenser, its publication virtually coinciding with the reconvening of parliament in the fall. That Parliament early set as its task the reconsideration of the Second Conventicle Act.[43] 1670 also saw the publication of Samuel Parker's anti-tolerationist *Discourse of Ecclesiastical Politie* (followed of course by Marvell's parody, *The Rehearsal Transpros'd*, in 1672), as well as other important rebuttals.

While this political context calls out for an ideological reading, Milton's poems resist any easy engagement in polemics over toleration. Both poems evoke circumstances of political and religious disorder; and topical references have been found in each. Milton like Samson found himself blind, in prisons both literal and metaphoric during the Restoration; he, like Samson, was questioning his divine gifts: "What is strength, without a double share/ Of wisdom" (*SA*, 53–54). Samson has been seen to represent the New Model Army, or the crushed "Good Old Cause," and the Son a repudiation of worldly politics, as critics have debated the relation between the seemingly contradictory implications of these two poems on the question of political activism.[44] Critics have asked whether Samson can be considered a Christian hero, questioning the nature of Samson's inspiration and regeneration.[45] We are right to examine the play's emphasis on human thought, reflection, and choice.[46] In my reading, the 1671 poems are not just backward-looking reflections, however, but active comments on the Restoration context of religious persecution and especially on the pubic requirements – proofs – demanded by Anglican orthodoxy.[47] The two poems explore the nature of conscientious performance and harken back to the biblical circumstances for its flourishing, to Samson in the Philistine Temple, and to the disciples awaiting the return of Christ from the wilderness. Milton presents Jesus, the disciples, Samson, and the Israelite Chorus as moral agents who undertake their actions under the dubious and terrifying human condition of serving as God's instruments.[48]

Reversing biblical history in his 1671 volume, Milton puts his Old Testament hero *last*. We do not know Milton's reasons for choosing this sequence, though in general he was concerned with the order of his poems in his several publications.[49] Though *Samson Agonistes* was probably substantially composed first, Milton placed it finally, as if the first led up to it, or as if it was his culminating word. On the title page, however, *Paradise Regain'd* is the main focus – "A Poem" – and *Samson Agonistes* (unidentified as to genre) follows as if an afterthought, in smaller type (see Figure 7). Milton may have feared political repercussions in overemphasizing his Samson on the title page of the volume by a known advocate of king-killing, and in highlighting *Paradise Regain'd*, the volume advertises itself as a sequel to *Paradise Lost*. To add more mystery, in the first edition of the volume *Samson Agonistes* received a wholly new title page, following "THE END" of *Paradise Regain'd*, and new pagination begins afresh with the second poem, as if attesting to the separate, and equal, worth of the work in relation to the previous poem. The register, however, is continuous, with *Samson Agonistes* beginning with gathering "I." This second title page was probably printed first.[50] The second edition of 1680, produced by the same publisher, runs the pagination (as well as the register) in sequence through the whole volume, even though it keeps the second title page. Critics have wondered about the thematic connections between these two works, asking whether they were intended as companion or contrastive pieces.[51] By putting the Son before Samson, Milton challenges his readers to consider the relations between liberation, faith, and violence.

I read *Paradise Regain'd* first, as I believe Milton meant us to, exploring a Dissenting dilemma perhaps less obvious, but no less searing, than that in *Samson Agonistes*: that of the loyal witnesses awaiting the return of their guide. What should they do in the meantime? How could their impatience

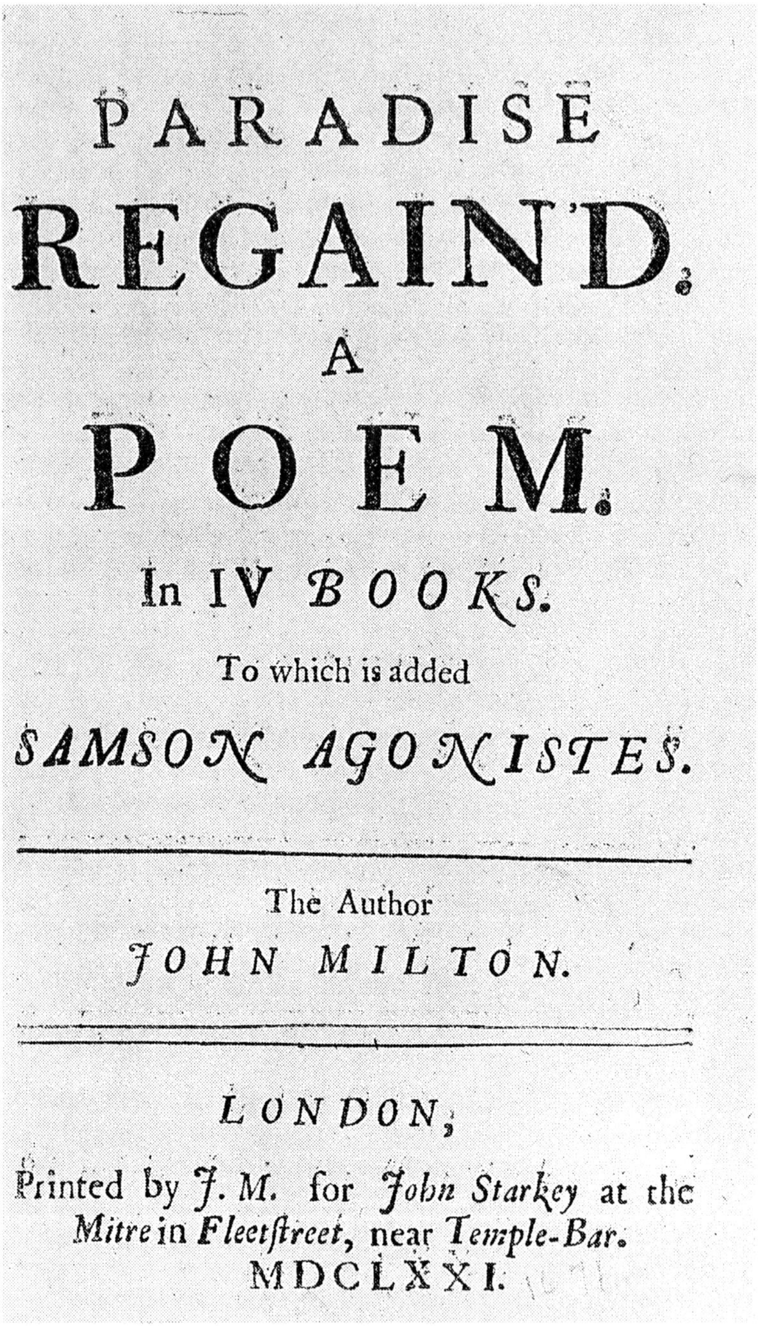

PARADISE
REGAIN'D,
A
POEM.
In IV BOOKS.

To which is added

SAMSON AGONISTES.

The Author

JOHN MILTON.

LONDON,

Printed by *J. M.* for *John Starkey* at the
Mitre in *Fleetstreet,* near *Temple-Bar.*
MDCLXXI.

Figure 7 Title page of John Milton, *Paradise Regain'd* (1671).

also be a temptation? As Satan charges the Son to make himself known, the demon's hurry reveals a mistrust of divine wisdom, just what Dissenters were tempted to feel in their impatience and despair. Indeed *Paradise Regain'd* helps readers learn to recognize Satan, and to combat his allure, specifically the danger of priestcraft. *Samson Agonistes* more obviously intersects with Milton's Dissenting context.[52] There Milton also presents a series of temptations, Dissenting dilemmas, among which is whether to offer obedience to an unjust regime. At the same time as the hero recovers his independence of will, he becomes the savage instrument of his deity. What would be the meaning, then, of political obedience, whether active or passive, in an age where "true experience" was difficult to attain, and where its culmination yielded bloody fruit?

PARADISE REGAIN'D AND THE AGONIES OF THE PRESENT

Through his appealing temptations and guiles, Satan is revealed in *Paradise Regain'd*. Although much critical scholarship has chosen to focus on how the Son makes himself known, it is a very great task of *Paradise Regain'd* to understand the ways in which Satan appears in history. Paying attention to Satan's identity, not taking it for granted, I see Milton forcefully engaging with the questions of ministry, toleration, and virtue I have been chasing. Answering Satan is ultimately the burden of the drama, as the poem can be read as something of a handbook for talking back to the ungodly, specifically against false priests, those who might appear harmless in their pastoral guise, "an aged man in Rural weeds" (*PR*, 1, 314). In presenting Satan's first assault on the Son, for instance, Milton evokes the Puritan reformers' attack on the sacrament: "Think'st thou such force in Bread? is it not written ... Man lives not by Bread only, but each Word/ Proceeding from the mouth of God" (1:347–50). Echoing the Dissenting critique of a state ministry, the Son offers up an attack on Satan's priestcraft:

> The other service was thy chosen task,
> To be a liar in four hundred mouths;
> For lying is thy sustenance, thy food.
> Yet thou pretend'st to truth; all Oracles
> By thee are giv'n, and what confest more true
> Among the Nations? That hath been thy craft,
> By mixing somewhat true to vent more lies.
> (*PR*, 1:427–33)

The four hundred mouths, perhaps a reference to the "lying spirits" of Ahab's prelacy (1 Kings 22:23), link the charge against Satan with the

Dissenters' common use of the figure Ahab to describe the tyrannous church of their own day.[53] Milton himself drew upon the lying four hundred mouths in his theological treatise, distinguishing these from the Holy Spirit: "If that lying spirit, 1 Kings xxii.22. were able to fill four hundred prophets at once, how many thousands ought we not to think the Holy Spirit capable of pervading."[54] Further, the word "Craft" was beginning in Milton's time to refer to the priestly monopoly on power, and was the basis of the emergent Whig discourse, as Mark Goldie has argued.[55] And though the language suggests an attack on Romanism, Milton's charge against Satan, of "mixing somwhat true to vent more lies" (1:433), could just as easily refer to that incompletely reformed protestantism currently ruling in Milton's England. That idolatry was soon to end, however, as the Son prophesies Satan's downfall, in language resonant with charges against the state church. When God's "purpose is/ Among them to declare his Providence" (1:444–45), then those worthy ones who "themselves disdaining/ To approach thy Temples" (1:448–49) will be rectified. Then "this thy glory shall be soon retrench'd;/ No more shalt thou by oracling abuse/ The Gentiles" (1:454–56),

> And thou no more with Pomp and Sacrifice
> Shalt be inquir'd at *Delphos* or elsewhere,
> At least in vain, for they shall find thee mute.
> God hath now sent his living Oracle
> Into the World to teach his final will,
> And sends his Spirit of Truth henceforth to dwell
> In pious Hearts, an inward Oracle
> To all truth requisite for men to know. (1:457–64)

Satan as the false shepherd, the head of an idolatrous church, is posited against the true spirit within.

This first temptation sets up the most important theme, that of proper ministry. For the Son himself to opine on the question of ministry denies the authority of the visible church *tout court*. Other temptations are revealed as Satanic, erudition being one of them. It has surprised readers to see the Son rejecting the knowledge of Greece and Rome, given Milton's own depth of classical learning. But there Milton reminds us that even such learning may be a ruse to lead one away from the centrality of divine utterance, Scripture. With empire, glory, sensual appetite, and statesmanship, Satan brings to view the current attractions of worldly advancement and pleasure; the Son must stake his plight against these. Like the Dissenter, he risks all to gain all. Returning to Jesus and to the first disciples' experiences, as so many resisting the state church in the 1660s and 1670s did, Milton offers forceful poetic engagement, casting doubt on the legitimacy of the state institution in his own day. As the opening sentence of his *On Christian Doctrine* proclaimed, Milton sought to restore "religion to its pure state after 1300 years."[56]

What were the saints, then, to do in the meantime, a meantime that was so clearly a time of profound defeat? In *Paradise Regain'd*, Christ's disciples wander from city to city in search of their lost leader, "Thir unexpected loss and plaints outbreath'd":

> Alas, from what high hope to what relapse
> Unlook'd for are we fall'n! Our eyes beheld
> Messiah certainly now come, so long
> Expected of our Fathers; we have heard
> His words, his wisdom full of grace and truth;
> Now, now, for sure, deliverance is at hand,
> The Kingdom shall to *Israel* be restor'd:
> Thus we rejoic'd, but soon our joy is turn'd
> Into perplexity and new amaze:
> For whither is he gone, what accident
> Hath rapt him from us? will he now retire
> After appearance, and again prolong
> Our expectation? God of *Israel*,
> Send thy Messiah forth, the time is come;
> Behold the Kings of th'Earth how they oppress
> Thy chosen, to what height thir pow'r unjust
> They have exalted, and behind them cast
> All fear of thee; arise and vindicate
> Thy Glory, free thy people from thir yoke!
> (*PR*, 2:30–48)

Simon and Andrew are the first witnesses, those fishers of men who changed the course of human history. Why does Milton include such characters? Though they echo the Israelites' fear about Moses' delay in returning from the mountain in Exodus 32:1, Milton's poem also introduces characters and an incident which do not appear in the source account from Luke. Critics have neglected this doubting moment, choosing to focus on the reformed epic combat between Satan and the Son. Yet the predicament of these witnesses is an important aspect of the poem's theology. As Edward Tayler has noted, "The lesson is that of delay, deferment of hopes and aspirations," and Barbara Lewalski's brilliant study of the genres of this poem reveals Milton's engagement with "the myth of human process, of human striving toward ideals of comprehension and order."[57] The theme of waiting also offers a powerful engagement with the Dissenting climate of the poem's composition.

In the disciples' heartfelt plea, Simon and Andrew spur divine vindication, prod end-time into the present, insist on "now, now, for *sure*," plying a language of certainty that only reveals their own uncertainty. Their helplessness, and their vigor in prompting divine action, mirror the condition of Restoration Dissenters, whose harrowing cry of "How Long?" from Psalm 6 and Revelation 6:10 we have seen etched into their very tombstones.[58] To Restoration nonconformists and political radicals, patience would be a lesson requiring self-mastery; that ethical control would be the aim of the saint in the meantime, a stoicism borne not out of philosophic idealism alone, but through hard-fought battles in this world. John Bunyan's *Holy War* closes with words which exhort patience in awaiting salvation, as the savior Emmanuel commands his fold: "Watch. Behold, I lay none other burden upon thee than what thou hast already. Hold fast till I come."[59] Milton's *Paradise Regain'd* echoes and deepens these concerns, probing the meaning of patience. Even Jesus, like the many tempted by impatience during the Restoration, needs to repeat the lesson of fortitude, of resisting temptation to hurry the work of the Lord: "All things are best fulfull'd in their due time, / And time there is for all things, Truth hath said" (*PR*, 3:182–83).

In *Paradise Regain'd*, the disciples' impatience is relieved only by their faith, as they look not simply toward end-time, but to the past:

> But let us wait; thus far he hath perform'd,
> Sent his Anointed, and to us reveal'd him,
> By his great Prophet, pointed at and shown,
> In public, and with him we have convers'd;
> Let us be glad of this, and all our fears
> Lay on his Providence; he will not fail
> Nor will withdraw him now, nor will recall,
> Mock us with his blest sight, then snatch him hence;
> Soon we shall see our hope, our joy return. (2:49–57)

It is a speech voicing belief in the efficacy of a promise, a category of action expressing desire. "Thus far he hath perform'd": the logic of the perfect active tense, phrased with a past participle so that the iambic long beat sounds on the "*hath*," so emphasis falls on the doing: a finite, completed action in a temporality that assuages fears about the future, projected abandonment. As the Independent minister James Livesey put it, "Elijah's prayer fetcht fire from Heaven, because it carried fire to Heaven."[60] For the worried fishermen in *Paradise Regain'd*, God will not renege on his vow, because he did not do so formerly. The structure of recollection becomes thus primary to the work of faith: reminders from the past not only serve as confirmation for the future; they are ratifications, albeit after the fact, of the belief in that assurance. Milton boldly puts the word "soon" into their mouths: what is promised will be granted shortly as they convert the imprecise temporality of the promise into a certain future tense.

In *Paradise Regain'd*, recollection substitutes for certainty. The Son, like the poet himself, performs the ritual utterances of commemoration that prompt the future but do not complete that future. When the Son rejects the Imperial throne, he invokes the structure of once/now that informs the human condition of incompleteness regarding history.

> Yet he [God] at length, time to himself best known,
> Rememb'ring *Abraham*, by some wond'rous call
> May bring them back repentant and sincere,
> And at their passing cleave the *Assyrian* flood,
> While to their native land with joy they haste,
> As the Red Sea and *Jordan* once he cleft,
> When to the promis'd land thir Fathers pass'd;
> To his due time and providence I leave them.
>
> (*PR*, 3:433–40)

The Son here insists God's time is best, but in these brief lines also are compressed several powerful murderous instances that serve as biblical precedent for God's violent, but confirmed, action in history: Abraham's call, and the victory of the Israelites and destruction of enemies on the shores of the Red Sea. Indeed, Milton's passage is almost a *mise-en-abîme* since the allusion to the *Assyrian* flood refers to Isaiah's reminder to the people of Israel to remember the parting of the Red Sea (Isaiah 11:16). The first poetry in the Bible was that sung on the banks of that sea (Exodus 15), praises sung for a God whose proof was violent deliverance. These were not singular events. Rather, around these moments – Abraham's call and the deliverance at the Red Sea – was structured a whole practice of ritual remembering commanded by the Bible; the text of Deuteronomy 6:6–15 enjoins their ritual recitation. Jesus' allusions, then, do the work of prayer, recalling the past and reaching into the uncertain future, rendered however not as finite, but potential; the operative verbs are predicated by "may": "*may bring* them back . . . And at their passing *cleave* . . . to their native land with joy *they haste*": the *may* preceding these verbs indicates they are not to be taken in the future tense, but rather, in the optative. The repetition of the language of *cleaving* of waters – "*cleave* the Assyrian flood"; "the Red Sea and Jordan once he *cleft*" – may also function as the figure of that which is a rupture, a cut in the logic of cause-and-effect.

The mechanism of the promise, with its temporality of then-and-now, may be taken as an ordering structure for Milton's account of divine agency. A rhetoric of promises, further, helps us understand the ambiguous agencies – voluntarist, compelled, indeterminate, otherworldly, terrorist, disavowed – that comprise radical action for a Dissenter. The biblical past was known for certain, and the messianic future was guaranteed. In the meantime, however, it was impossible to know how that promise would be made good, by what means, at what time. James Livesey urged his congregation to be patient: "Man is for the shortest time; and God is for the fittest time; And if we wait long and have not so quick an answer, yet we shall have a fuller answer; and when the mercy comes it will be sweeter."[61] Yet Dissenters often seemed to whistle in the dark. As the signs of the times might or might not yield knowledge about God's plan, so Dissenters worked over what they knew with certainty to be God's doing by citing instances from the Bible: Samson, Daniel, and Deborah. It was faith, then, and communication with the divine, that would supply what inference alone could warrant. In evoking the contractual structure of commemoration – if we remember God, God will remember us – Dissenters invoked a logic of inference that was not a logic of certainty. That was the function of prayer: to tender, in the subjunctive mood, the relations between past, present, and future.

With *Paradise Regain'd*, Milton pitches his countrymen into the early times of Christ's ministry, where the Word was not yet fully revealed. As he had done on the eve of Restoration, when considering the nature of a righteous ministry, he asks his readers to have "the same faith which those disciples had to trust in God and the promise of Christ for thir maintenance as they did." Milton wonders, "Why are ye so distrustful both of your own doctrin and of Gods promises, fulfilld in the experience of the disciples first sent... But he who is Lord of all things, hath so ordaind: trust him then; he doubtles will command the people to make good his promises of maintenance."[62]

SAMSON AGONISTES

In *Samson Agonistes*, Milton deepens the questions of righteous ministry and temporal fulfillment that he raised in *Paradise Regain'd*. From the very beginning of the play, we know that the time of action will be a time of idol-worship: "This day a solemn Feast the people hold/ To *Dagon* thir Sea-Idol" (*SA*, 12–13) – "feast" also being a synonym for the sacrament of Holy Communion, that matter of extreme theological controversy.

Samson, temporarily permitted a rest, retreats from that profanity as far as is possible. So when the Public Officer, Samson's very last visitor, comes to demand Samson's attendance at a public festival, it is a moment of opposition that is formal and thematic:

> This day to *Dagon* is a solemn Feast,
> With Sacrifices, Triumph, Pomp, and Games;
> Thy strength they know surpassing human rate,
> And now some public proof thereof require
> To honor this great Feast, and great Assembly;
> Rise therefore with all speed and come along.
>
> (*SA*, 1311–16)

Rites, Triumph, Pomp: all these recall the familiar language of idolatry in Milton, with a distinct whiff of anti-royalism.[63] Yet the feast commanded in *Samson Agonistes* is not merely a topical allusion, a cheap aside attacking the Restored Stuart monarch. This description of what goes on at the Philistine festival, and the invitation, especially with its language of "public proof," recall the specific context of Restoration Anglicanism and its demands not merely for passive obedience, but for active participation in public ritual. Much of the Clarendon code enjoined compelling "public proof" of conformity, as authorities enforced allegiance by significant public performances. The Act of Uniformity required all ministers and teachers to adopt the new prayer book, and to mark their "unfeigned assent and consent to the use of all things contained and prescribed in and by...the Book of Common Prayer" by St. Bartholomew's Day or face ejection from their posts.[64] The act pertained not only to ministers, but to all manner of public speakers, including college students and schoolmasters.

According to the act, it was not enough that ministers adopt the revised prayer book in their services; they also had to *perform*, as the words of the law require: to "openly and publicly before the congregation there assembled declare his unfeigned assent and consent" with words prescribed by the statute.[65] The minister was required to use "these words and no other." Failure to perform this public action, that of reading a set script, would lead to stripping of his office. Not only were the ministers obliged to perform these acts, they also had to make a verbal sign of their subscription through an oath.[66] Thus accordance to the get-tough religious regime required not only passive obedience, the adoption of liturgical conformity by using the new prayer book, but also active obedience: public, active assent. All English citizens were required to attend Anglican service, to use the Anglican prayer book, and to make a public performance of loyalty by the compulsory requirements of physical comportment (taking the sacrament), utterance (oaths and prayer), and gesture (kneeling). In their justifications of religious compulsion, Anglican church spokesmen appealed to civil order, fear of sedition, and the threat of yet another civil war; and Anglican divines found scriptural precedent for their rigor. As Benjamin Laney, Bishop of Lincoln, put it, in defending the Act of Uniformity in a sermon preached before Charles in April 1663: "*That our Liturgie or Common Prayer is a true Sacrifice to God*...And to this I shall not *beg* the assent of those that like it not, but *require* it."[67] The key text authorizing such compulsion was the parable of Jesus' calling all to the feast (Luke 14:16–23).

Samson's invitation to the feast honoring Dagon resonates with this situation. In Luke 14, a lord bids a servant to invite others to come in for a supper, and when they do not come freely, Jesus recounts that the lord says to the servant : "Go out into the highways and the hedges, and compel them to come in, that my house may be filled." Luke 14 was thus a powerful symbol for those defending the policy of persecution. The archconservative Laney used this text in a sermon preached before Charles in March 1664, "For our Saviour in the *Parable*, when the guests came not to the *banquet* at his invitation, commanded his servants to *compel them to come in*" (*Sermons*, 85), and he glosses Luke 14:23 in the margin.

Defenders of toleration also wrestled with this text. Hugo Grotius, attacking religious compulsion, put his finger on that hot biblical passage, Luke 14: "as in that Parable the word *compel* argues nothing else but a vehement sollicitation."[68] As the great ally of toleration, the politician Sir Charles Wolseley (1630?–1714), a one-time Cromwellian and member of Cromwell's Councils of State, who was arrested in Monmouth's rebellion, put it, "force upon men will never beget, or change Principles or Opinions...When I have used rational su[i]table means to inform another, I ought to acquiesce...he that forceth me to a Religion, makes me hate it, and makes me think, there wants reason, and other evidence to evince it. Nature abhors compulsion in Religious things, as a spiritual rape upon the Conscience."[69] Richard Baxter interpreted this verse as Jesus' command to "Go to the most barbarous remote Nations, and call them into the Church": remote signifying *not* local.[70]

Milton also reflected on the meaning of this very passage, Luke 14, in his *Treatise of Civil Power* (1659): "We read not that Christ ever exercis'd force but once; and that was to drive prophane ones out of his temple, not to force them in" (*CPW*, VII, 268). In his examination of this text, moreover, Milton evokes a discourse of the divine Spirit that is absent in Grotius and Locke. Milton's civil discourses seem subordinate to his theology:

Yet some are so eager in thir zeal of forcing, that they refuse not to descend at length to the utmost shift of that parabolical proof *Luke* 14.16, &c. *compell them to come in.* therefore magistrates may compell in religion. As if a parable were not to be straind through every word or phrase, and not expounded by the general scope therof: which is no other here then the earnest expression of Gods displeasure on those recusant Jewes, and his purpose to preferre the gentiles on any terms before them; expressed here by the word *compell*. But how compells he? doubtless no otherwise then he draws, without which no man can come to him, *Joh.* 6.44: and that is by the inward perswasive motions of his spirit and by his ministers; not by the outward compulsions of a magistrate or his officers. (*CPW*, vii, 260–61)

The compulsion, Milton avers, was meant historically, directed at those recalcitrant Jews who refused the truth. For Christians, persuasion would suffice, "the inward perswasive motions of his spirit": dialogue, discussion, and argument, but also something more than autonomous human communicative norms. Milton was troubled by the idea of man without free will, he saw him as a puppet, "a meer artificiall *Adam*, such an *Adam* as he is in the motions" (*Areopagitica*, *CPW*, iii, 527). The language of "inward perswasive motions" in his passage explaining Luke 14 resembles the "rousing motions" felt by Samson in his dramatic performance in *Samson Agonistes* (*SA*, 1382), as well as those experienced by the Son, spurred to visit the desert for his revelation (*PR*, 1:290–91: "by some strong motion I am led/ Into this Wilderness"): they are in *Christian Doctrine* the very signs of the divine spirit.

In the scene with the Public Officer in *Samson Agonistes*, then, Milton examines the meanings of compulsive state power from the starting point of a discourse of civil liberty, though, as we shall see, Milton also considers how divine injunctions thwart certainty in the civil realm. Divine compulsion to attend the "feast" is a scriptural precedent that Milton must address. The Public Officer threatens to compel Samson to come to the feast; if Samson resists: "we shall find such Engines to assail/ And hamper thee, as thou shalt come of force" (1396–97). Is there a possible free answer to this question? Dissenters pondered it long and hard. As Sir Charles Wolseley saw it, "Men are to be ruled over as Creatures, that have immortal souls to be chiefly cared for, and they are to be ruled over as such who have a special relation to God, and a homage to pay him, above all the rest of the world; a rule over men without some respect to this, would denominate Mankind into Brutes."[71] The difference between man and beasts is not just human rationality, but also that "special relation to God." Samson also refuses to be reduced to the moral status of a beast: "they shall not trail me through thir streets/ Like a wild Beast" (1402–03). When he ponders the topic of "absolute subjection": "Masters' commands come with a power resistless/ To such as owe them absolute subjection" (1404–05), Samson weighs not only what he "owes" civil masters, but also the moral conditions under which obligation is exacted. The masters, by enslaving Samson, have taken away his freedom to consent.

Despite all this discourse of civil liberty, however, the bare fact is that Samson does *not* owe them obedience in spiritual matters; absolute subjection in matters of the soul can never be proffered to humans, but only to God. Thus in his tricky way, Samson speaks the doublespeak that is the sign of the meantime, before God's end is known, in the time where obligation and faith may be challenged at every turn. When Samson assents, "I am content to go" (1403), he signals his acceptance of responsibility for his actions to the Public Officer and his friends, and confirms that he will perform as a morally free agent and not as a beast; he does not assert, however, that he wants to go.

Dissent was a performance, a drama, because preserving the inner realm of conscience alone was not enough to define human freedom; the state's compulsory regime made actions matter.[72] The Independent leader John Owen remarked that liberty of conscience was not only an inner freedom but that it obliged one to act: "if conscience to God be confined to thoughts, and opinions, and speculation about the general notions... [of] true and false... the whole nature and being of conscience, and that to the reason, sense, and experience of every man is utterly overthrown... Conscience... obligeth men to act or forbear accordingly."[73] Against the imposition of liturgies in 1662, Owen argued, "It is not about stinted forms of prayer in the worship and service of God, by those who, *of their own accord*, do make use of that kind of assistance, judging that course to be better than any thing they can do themselves in the discharge of the work of the ministry, but of the imposition of forms on others [italics mine]."[74] Occasional conformity – the practice of performing Anglican ritual yet withholding conscience's assent from the performance thereof – would not do in this scheme. Religious observance is freely consensual performance, reflecting internal assent, "of their own accord." The word, *accord*, has at its root the word "heart": "joining heart with."

In his biblical drama, Milton has the Chorus proposing that Samson ignore these problems concerning the conditions of consent, urging Samson to comply externally to the state – occasional conformity. He could do this, it suggests, without surrendering inner belief: "where the heart joins not, outward acts defile not" (*SA*, 1368). But Samson rejects the idea that inner and outer performances are so distinct: "where outward force constrains," he replies, "the sentence holds" (1369). This contradicts the antinomian doctrine of inner purity. It also reverses Milton's earlier positions: his line in *Areopagitica* ("to the pure all things are pure"), and the Lady's defense against compulsion in the masque *Comus*: "thou canst not touch the freedom of my minde" (663). Samson rejects the Chorus' plea for passive obedience, its occasional conformity, insisting that external action, how one "performs" in the world, matters. Samson's final action then is taken in this spirit of the only freedom left to him – willing compliance to God's laws, "Of mine own accord."

As the Restored regime queried the nature of public performance, Milton in *Samson Agonistes* comes to the position that inner belief must be matched by outward action. This is dramatized when the Chorus asks Samson why he resists attending the feast when he does not mind performing physical labor for his oppressors. Samson answers the Chorus that to refuse to attend the feast of Dagon is not to contradict his compliance to perform other acts for the state. He simply upholds a distinction between civil and religious spheres of obligation: "Not in thir Idol-Worship, but by labor/ Honest and lawful to deserve my food/ Of those who have me in thir civil power" (*SA*, 1365–67). In some sense, Samson's slave-labor is consensual (it earns his food), and in submitting to conquest, Samson exchanges obedience for protection. Idol-worship (or any religious worship) is different however, as there are no reciprocal obligations owed to the state.

When Samson finally consents to go to the feast, then, he owns his obedience to civil authority: it will not do dishonor to "our God, our Law, my Nation, or myself" (1425). This list stands as a kind of declaration of political obligation, in which each element establishes a realm of responsibility and a context for liberty. And these lines – the last Samson utters – establish an order, even a hierarchy, starting from the most general to the most specific.[75] Authentic action ideally encompasses all these spheres of moral obligation: Samson finally "owns" his actions, as he has owned up to his full morally free nature.

And yet that ownership is incomplete. Samson's final act is his, but also not his. Linguistically represented in a bounty of metaphor and symbol, the thunderstorm, the evening Dragon, the Eagle, the Phoenix (1691–1706), the action bears all the marks of divine presence. Samson's final work is "as with the force of winds and waters pent/ When Mountains tremble" (1647–48), strengthened by the force of the divine impulse working through the human body. Samson's "inward perswasive motions" are not the workings of reason alone. Critics' uncertainty over whether Samson has "decided" to go or what "motivates" his actions touches precisely on the zone of obscurity about the inner processes. In Milton, however, that which is "inside" is not merely rational decision, the actions of the will, but also the cooperation with the divine. This is not to say Milton's theological commitments are clouded by indeterminacy.[76] Violence, above all for Dissenters, offered certainty, the sure mark of God's care, the aftereffect by which divine agency and intention become visible. As Dissenters practiced biblical typology, they built upon these irrational modes in radical Protestant thought, and their embrace of holy war was a residue of the unassimilable violence and ruptured history offered by their typology.

REMEMBRANCE AND PETITION

Milton stands on the cusp of divergent approaches towards predetermination, grace, regeneration, and the interpretation of the Fall, matters of relevance to political ideology as they undergird an account of human autonomy and agency.[77] Milton's voluntarist economy of salvation, as Stephen Fallon has demonstrated, paralleled his politics in several respects: as earnable grace emphasized human merit and active virtue, not an inborn disposition, so could it fire a republican assault on hereditary aristocracy. Arminianism was not strictly an ecclesiological doctrine – a prop of the Laudian church – but a theology with powerful political consequences.[78] But Milton's trouble over matching divine acts from the past with those of the present and future also reflects a Calvinist uncertainty about the efficacy of autonomous human action. Worldly politics and an otherworldliness are in tension in Milton's interplay of Arminian and Calvinist approaches to grace, represented in a drama whose end is known but whose means are not.

In *Samson Agonistes* the hero's vocation is confirmed by the "true experience" of his witness (1756). Barbara Lewalski has explored how "The thematics of true political experience in this work offer readers no definitive answers, but instead present a process for making such choices in such circumstances."[79] In the Milton I am sketching here, with the cosmic uncertainty of the links between past, present, and future, that process is incomplete in the here and now of mere morality. The presence of divine impulsion disrupts, and perhaps fulfills, the political analysis of the subject's obligations. Samson begins "to feel/ Some rousing motions" (1381–82), an immediate presence so longed for by the Dissenting writers. As Samson admits in his final words to his persecutors, his action crosses the boundary from reason to another kind of sway:

> Hitherto, Lords, what your commands impos'd
> I have perform'd, as reason was, obeying,
> Not without wonder or delight beheld.
> Now of my own accord such other trial
> I mean to show you of my strength, yet greater;
> As with amaze shall strike all who behold.
> (1640–45)

A striking deletion from the biblical account is the omission of Samson's prayer to God (Judg. 16:28–30). Milton had previously in his career evoked the praying Samson. Admiring the heroic Samson in 1651 whilst defending the regicide, Milton wrote: "The heroic Samson ... whether prompted by God or by his own valor, slew at one stroke not one but a host of his country's tyrants, having first made prayer to God for his aid. Samson therefore thought it not impious but pious to kill those masters who were tyrants over his country" (*First Defense* [1658], *CPW*, IV, 402). In *Samson Agonistes*, however, Milton leaves out the prayer, but includes Samson's words of warning to the Philistine crowd, thus leaving open the question of divine participation in Samson's bloody work. The outward posture of the performer reveals nothing about the operations of agency: "eyes fast fixt he stood, as one who prayed/ Or some great matter in his mind revolv'd" (1637–38). Rather than representing the violence as a consequence of Samson's petition, Milton leaves the connection between uttered desire and fulfillment mysterious.

Milton's Christianity has been understood as a rational Christianity, and his theology tending towards Arminian; yet Milton is just as commited to a dependency upon that which is beyond human capacity, upon the affective experience of the regenerative power of divine grace.[80] Milton's emphasis on works and faith have led many to align him with a voluntarist theology, but, in the matter of faith, "works" for Milton are not autonomous; that is, they cannot be fully "owned" by their doers. To believe otherwise would be to eliminate the need for Christ's sacrifice. Milton in *Christian Doctrine* asserts that "both faith itself and the works of faith are works of the Spirit, not our own." Here Milton is interpreting Ephesians 2:8–10: "*by grace you are saved through faith: and this is not something which comes from you, it is the gift of God. Not by works, in case anyone should boast; for we are his work, created by Jesus Christ for good works, which God has prepared that we may perform them.*" Milton continues to distinguish these God-sourced works from those we may properly call "our own": "Here the works about which a man might boast are distinguished from those works which do not give rise to boasting" (*On Christian Doctrine*, CPW, VI, 491). Grace may therefore not be reduced to mere morality.

In Milton's last poems, remembrance is one mode that bridges the certain past with the unknowable present and future. Samson, wondering about his current status – so debased, so low – almost accuses God of reneging on his word:

> Promise was that I
> Should *Israel* from *Philistian* yoke deliver;
> Ask for this great Deliverer now, and find him
> Eyeless in *Gaza* at the Mill with slaves,
> Himself in bonds under *Philistian* yoke;
> Yet stay, let me not rashly call in doubt
> Divine Prediction...   (38–44)

The time of that fulfillment is vague; all that can console are the words of a promise whose terms are, unfortunately, rendered grammatically incomplete – Samson "*Should...deliver*" – not a linguistic mode offering certainty, but one of hope. In his doubt, Samson wonders about the gap between past and present:

> I was his nursling once and choice delight,
> His destin'd from the womb,
> Promis'd by Heavenly message twice descending...
> But now hath cast me off as never known,
> And to those cruel enemies,
> Whom I by his appointment had provok't,
> Left me all helpless with th'irreparable loss
> Of sight, reserv'd alive to be repeated
> The subject of thir cruelty, or scorn.   (633–46)

Evoking the past, it is hoped, however, will bear consequences and solicit divine response.

Samson puts into narrative a life that has not yet been completed, very much like those Dissenters in the meantime, but unlike Samson, for the Restoration Dissenters, the ending *was* certain, a Christian Judgment victorious, known as truly as the faith that upheld them in times of despair. Bridging the past with the future, the Chorus offers prayers during most of the drama, in a final prayer responding to Samson's change of heart about attending the idolatrous Philistine feast. To God, it solicits, "Be efficacious in thee now at need" (1437). As an envoy and a blessing, but also as an appeal for divine action, the Chorus evokes a structure of commemoration as well as a projection into the future:

Go, and the Holy One
Of *Israel* be thy guide
To what may serve his glory best, and spread his name
Great among the Heathen round:
Send thee the Angel of thy Birth, to stand
Fast by thy side, who from thy Father's field
Rode up in flames after his message told
Of thy conception, and be now a shield
Of fire; that Spirit that first rusht on thee
In the camp of *Dan*
Be efficacious in thee now at need.   (1427–37)

A command to Samson – "Go," an imperative – is also a bidding farewell, and a surrender to the higher will that is God's plan. That surrender is represented in a recollection of Samson's former call. In the phrases "be thy guide" and "Be efficacious in thee now," the Chorus utters a "let it be" not as a performative utterance (without effecting the action it enjoins), nor as a command (without power over what it wills), but rather, as a prayer, that optative class of speech that is the language of unearthly desire, without autonomy to complete the action it enjoins.

The genre for divine solicitation is prayer. Petition was a vehicle for the expression of communication to, and from, the divine, not to be constrained by set forms, according to Restoration nonconformists who attacked the set prayer book. Most importantly, set prayers, they believed, stopped communication from the Holy Spirit.[81] Prayer was to be transactional, dependent upon something from without, spontaneously emanating from the depths of the individual's soul, and unintelligible to the external observer. Whether they believed prayers were definitively answered, or whether they sought through prayer a relation with the unknowable divine, prayer represented a creative type of speech that was unaccountable in the worldly sense of human institutions and governance. It could thus be a space for the expression of emancipatory hopes; and was politically dangerous.

Could prayer be effective? How could one know if one's prayer had been heard? Was prayer sufficient as human utterance to achieve its aims; or, as in the Calvinist approach, was prayer to signify the subordination of the saint to a higher power, a mark of obedience?[82] It is precisely in the gap between these two positions that we find Milton invoking divine impulse. Publishing his translation of the Psalms in his 1673 volume of poetry, Milton reveals he was thinking about this question in August 1653. Psalm 6 is a remarkable, self-reflexive poem. It is both a prayer to God from a man in distress as well as a confirmation of God's responsiveness to prayer. A petition for God's deliverance, it also exults that David's prayer was heard.

> And thou, O Lord, how long? turn Lord, restore
>   My soul, O save me for thy goodness' sake,
> For in death no remembrance is of thee;
>   Who in the grave can celebrate thy praise?
> Wearied I am with sighing out my days,
>   Nightly my Couch I make a kind of Sea;
> My Bed I water with my tears: mine Eye
>   Through grief consumes, is waxen old and dark
> I'th' mid'st of all mine enemies that mark.
>   Depart all ye that work iniquity.
> Depart from me, for the voice of my weeping
>   The Lord hath heard, the Lord hath heard my pray'r,
> My supplication with acceptance fair
>   The Lord will own, and have me in his keeping.
> Mine enemies shall all be blank and dash't
>   With much confusion; then grow red with shame;
> They shall return in haste the way they came
>   And in a moment shall be quite abash't.[83]

Psalm 6 is both appeal and proof, robust evidence from the Bible that God answers prayers and punishes enemies.[84] In the biblical original, and in the Authorized Version, the retribution against enemies is put in the optative: "Let all mine enemies be ashamed." In Milton's words, on the other hand, God's action is decisive and set in the definite future tense: "Mine enemies *shall* all be blank... they *shal* return..." No longer a plea, Milton speaks a prophecy.

Milton redoubles the confident call for assurance – his own voice merges with the words of David, even as his poem is a remarkable display of prosodic experimentation. Unlike his psalm translations of 1648, here Milton injects his own poetic innovations, rendering the Bible in iambic pentameter quatrains, using a rhyme scheme of *abba*, as if to suggest that the sentiments of the "mean time" will be ultimately contained and resolved by rhyme. His lines, however, are not smooth, but instead break at key words: "restore" leads on to "My soul," the proper object of restoration. The run-on lines give urgency, a breathless quality, and make the utterance seem like spoken words, spontaneous. The result is a rhetoric of certainty overlaying a poetics of fear.

Could human prayer impel God? A tract written by the Independent minister John Goodwin on the Holy Spirit, published posthumously by Ralph Venning, answered *yes* to this question. Goodwin, whose republican past suffered his book *The Obstructours of Justice* (1649) to be burned along-side Milton's *Pro Populo Anglicano Defensio* and *Eikonoklastes* in the summer of 1660, like Milton went into hiding as he was initially excepted out of the Act of General Pardon, though it was later granted to him. Goodwin's ideas on the operational efficacy of prayer may explain why he may have been a supporter of Venner's rising and possibly the author of the radical pamphlet, *Mene Tekel: Or the Downfal of Tyranny* (1663).[85] His posthumous publication, *On Being Filled with the Spirit* (1670), reflects his longstanding theological Arminianism, and it posits the efficacy of prayer: "such persons who excell in righteousness, and that are wont to lay themselves out freely for God, he is wont to express himself with an *answerable freedom* and bounty to them; and consequently, to give them the power at the Throne of Grace, and interest there [italics mine]."[86] Goodwin cites Psalm 18:3 and the very psalm translated by Milton, Psalm 6. Thus Milton's position on the feats of prayer shades towards the Arminian theology; prayers, heard, may be answered. This, perhaps, is that "answerable style" he seeks in *Paradise Lost*.

Though Milton sided with the Arminian position in favor of free will, nonetheless, he also evoked the more radical Calvinist doctrines of divine impulsion. Indeed, as Milton's language about prayer promulgates a model of the mutual dependence of human and divine agency, he ascribes to the divine Spirit an authorizing function.[87] The second book of *Christian Doctrine*, Milton's culminating theological treatise, is concerned with matters of worship, setting prayer in a doctrine of immediate presence: "Petition is the act by which, at the instigation of the Holy Spirit and through faith in Christ we ask God reverently for lawful things, both for ourselves and for other people" (*CPW*, vi, 699). The Latin original helps us see what kind of role is performed by the Holy Spirit: *Petitio est qua res quasvis licitas auctore sancto spiritu reverentur a Deo ex fide in Christo* (Columbia Milton, xvii, 80). John Carey's English translation in the Yale University Press prose works leaves out the important – and ambiguous – word, *auctore*, that which authorizes, originates, and ultimately owns the petition, and that is the Holy Spirit. Milton rejected set prayers because he sought to be open to divine impulse. Milton holds that the Lord's Prayer is only a "pattern or model, rather than a formula to be repeated verbatim either by the apostles or by the churches today. So it is clear that the church has no need of a liturgy: those who prompt and assist our prayers are divine helpers, not human" (this is an adaptation of Rom. 8:26). The Latin makes clearer the authorizing role of divine impulse: *cum auctores adiutoresque precum nostratum divines, non humanos habeamus*...(Columbia Milton,

XVII, 84). Underlying his anticeremonialism is an account of divine agency. In *Eikonoklastes*, Milton had condemned the king's theft of material from Sidney's *Arcadia*, as well as his appropriation of David's psalms: "It is not hard for any man, who hath a Bible in his hands, to borrow good words and holy sayings in abundance; but to make them his own, is a work of grace onely from above," he writes (*CPW*, III, 553), emphasizing the insufficient human component that is prayer.[88] In *Paradise Lost*, Milton's readers see that Adam's prayers find audition because they witness the Son's appeal to God to answer the human plea (*PL*, II:142–58; cf. II:22–47). Would Restoration Dissenters' prayers be answered so?

Samson's were. The Messenger, breathlessly relating his last actions in *Samson Agonistes*, likens the hero–martyr's condition to that of a man at prayer (*SA*, 1637–38), and the Semi-Chorus describes the final moments of the hero, in which he prepared his inspired revenge, "with inward eyes illuminated/ His fiery virtue rous'd" (1688–90). Milton left out the precise words of the prayer that is in Judges (Judg. 16:28: "O Lord GOD, remember me"), words in which Samson calls upon God to wreak vengeance on his enemies. Perhaps they would have been too dangerous to write in 1670. The implication is clear enough. Milton's Samson speaks to the assembly, warning them of a demonstration that is to come: "such other trial/ I mean to show you for my strength" (1643–44). The only way to represent the Spirit's instantiation is in an efflux of metaphor: crashing together are a blinding pastiche of biblical images for Spirit: Dragon, Eagle, Phoenix.[89]

As the waiting disciples in *Paradise Regain'd* had asked whether God would "again prolong/ Our expectation," (*PR*, 2:41–42) the Chorus, in that last moment before Samson's murderous performance in *Samson Agonistes*, wonders, "Yet God hath wrought things as incredible/ For his people of old; what hinders now?" (*SA*, 1532–33). Curiously, these lines were appended to Milton's text in a special "Omissa" in the publication of the 1671 volume. This appears not to have been a compositor's or printer's error, but a Miltonic addition.[90] Were the lines added later, after licensing, thought by Milton to be too precarious, too outspoken, too resonant of those Vennerite calls for insurrection in the name of Jesus? This late addition seems to augment the activist, apocalyptic impulse in the poem. In later editions of the poem, these verses were assimilated seamlessly into the Chorus' speech, but I think in this 1671 edition they call attention to themselves (see Figure 8). Milton's page of correction dramatically points to these lines as if to a separate, truncated, nine-line sonnet, with the ominous and multivalent, goading word, "restore." Cut off from the context, these added lines of the poem

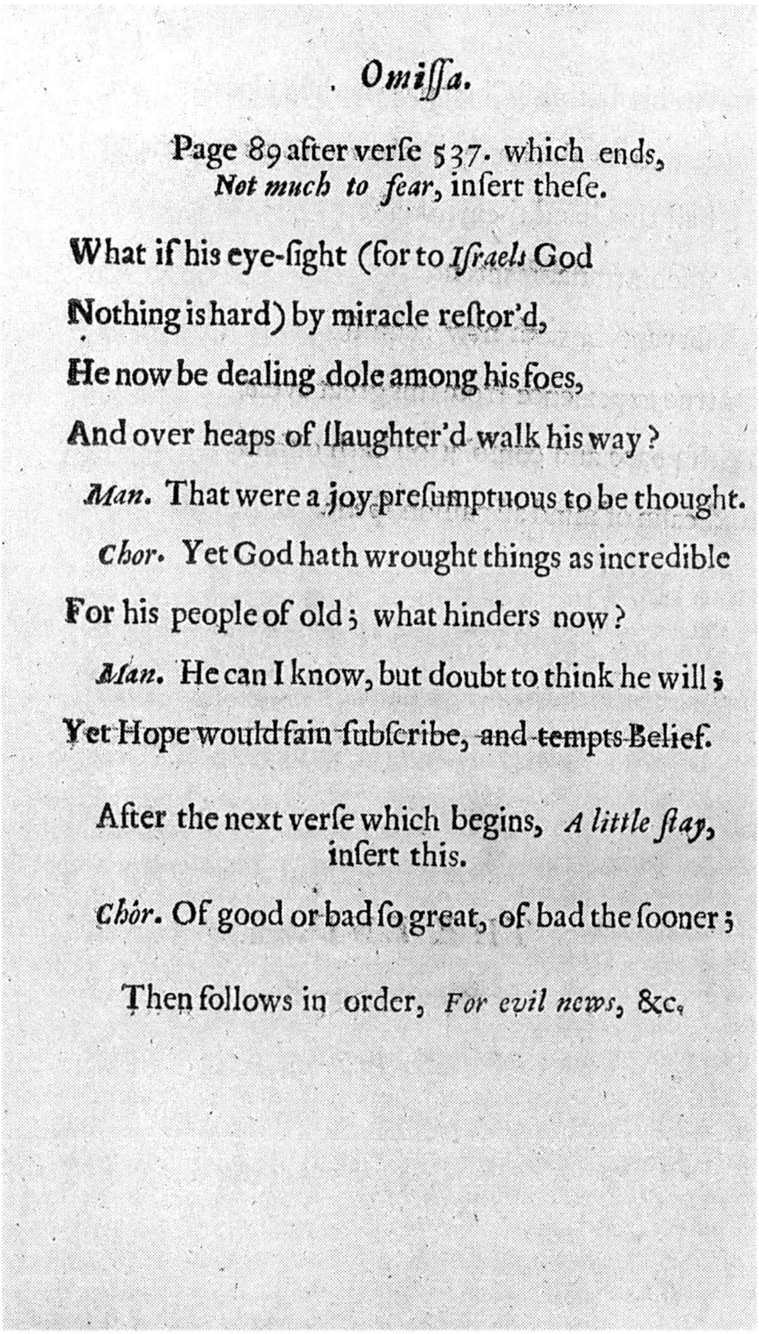

Page 89 after verſe 537. which ends,
Not much to fear, inſert theſe.

What if his eye-ſight (for to *Iſraels* God

Nothing is hard) by miracle reſtor'd,

He now be dealing dole among his foes,

And over heaps of ſlaughter'd walk his way?

Man. That were a joy preſumptuous to be thought.

Chor. Yet God hath wrought things as incredible

For his people of old; what hinders now?

Man. He can I know, but doubt to think he will;

Yet Hope would fain ſubſcribe, and tempts Belief.

After the next verſe which begins, *A little ſtay,*
inſert this.

Chôr. Of good or bad ſo great, of bad the ſooner;

Then follows in order, *For evil news,* &c.

Figure 8 "The Omissa," John Milton, *Paradise Regain'd* (1671).

speak undeniably to the present: "What hinders now?" a rallying cry to spur divine vengeance, and a testimony of belief that miracles were not simply in the past. This would summon the radical energies of militant prophecy, and invoke the angry God to answer the call of Dissenters.

The order of poems in the volume, set by Milton, leaves us with an unsettling, violent ending. Yet violence and Redemption are conjoined in Milton's thinking; Samson is not strictly to be relegated to the past, superseded by a New Covenant. Rather, that fiery ancient rage instills meaning for the present and future, spending a passion that will yet be spent in a final moment of revealed truth. Milton's drama posts a letter to the future, prompting divine energies in its recollection of the past. Both *Samson Agonistes* and *Paradise Regain'd* compass the temporal and moral condition of the period "in the mean time," that is, in the time without full knowledge of how God will act. The ordering of the poems, then, reflects the uncertain temporality after the promise and before the fulfillment – very much like the time of Milton's dissent. Both poems look into a radical otherworldliness that is at the heart of divine action; and both poems meditate on the temptations of worldliness that accompany that condition of absence of knowledge. Thus Milton's last poems may be said to work on that often-repeated Dissenting question, "How Long?" In his last works, Milton offers more than a political critique of persecution and coersion. His question was not solely how to live under oppressive conditions – those which many nonconformists, and especially Quakers, faced in prison – but also how to maintain readiness to serve God's command, a mandate that could rouse a saint from sleep at any moment and summon actions by a directive whose authority was undeniable and immediate. Thus the central philosophical issues in Milton's writing life: what was it to act in the service of God? How to ground human choice upon God's indeterminate means? In order to speak of the immediately particular yet ultimately unspeakable nature of divine experience, Milton turns to biblical history, summoning the past to rekindle faith for the present. Was the age of immediate apprehension over? Or was the surprising and immediate presence of the spirit still at work in the world? Milton's testimony in art argues for the latter, as he turns to figures who clearly *were* moved by the spirit. The stories of the Son and Samson are alike in that both figures come to assume a place held for them by repute or by annunciation: the plots, if there are any, tell of the assumption of their names. As Milton draws upon traditions of typological writing to voice his religico-political anguish and hopes, there is yet another political dimension to his rhetorical use of catachresis, a forward thrusting into the future. In his evocation of the sacrificial figures, he shows how divine agency inheres in the spaces opened up by temporal disjunction and biblical poetics, nowhere more evident than in that hazy grammatical mode of prayer. With commemoration as well as prophecy, Milton appeals to the past to solicit future divine deeds. At the heart of Milton's late writings, then, is a struggle to join the *once* with the *once more*.

CHAPTER 6

Enthusiasm

Nathaniel Lee spelled out the contrast between Dryden and Milton in his preface to *The State of Innocence*, Dryden's operatic reworking of *Paradise Lost*:

> For *Milton* did the Wealthy Mine disclose
> And rudely cast what you could well dispose:
> He roughly drew, on an old-fashioned ground,
> A Chaos, for no perfect World was found.

Though *Paradise Lost* was still in print when this laud was published in 1677, Lee wanted readers to view Milton's poem as "old-fashioned," a relic of a former, rougher age, already out of date, a natural ore which Dryden mines and refines. As Lee continued his praise for Dryden, he explained what needed polishing:

> So when your Sense his mystic reason clear'd,
> The melancholy Scene all gay appear'd;
> New Light leapt up, and a new glory smil'd,
> And all throughout was mighty, all was mild.[1]

While Milton, like the creator of the Old Testament, made a chaos, Dryden brought form to that primordial anarchy. Like Jesus, he fetched "new light" out of darkness. A new day was dawning after a mysterious night, as the grace of Christ followed and corrected the rough judgment of the Old Testament God, as the Restoration followed the Revolution, as Enlightenment followed Enthusiasm.

The shadow of the English Revolution hung long and dark across the last decades of the seventeenth century, emerging in different shapes at times of political crisis, and the figure of Milton was often synecdoche for that radical upheaval. As literary form or style mediated religious or political ideologies in the Restoration period, Milton's enthusiastic poetics were seen to serve a radical political agenda.[2] Milton's *Paradise Lost* raised important Restoration questions, and became a field upon which opposing parties clashed. Whether it begged readers to discover concealed political meanings, or whether it invited later authors to fashion a literary tradition, Milton's work also highlighted Dissent's paradoxical aesthetic program in its critique of representation, its ambivalence towards human agency in history, and its positing the uncertainty of earthly knowledge.

Lee drew upon a rhetoric common to those opposing religious Dissent after the Restoration of monarchy. High church Anglicans shared with the Puritans a portrait of the nonconformist as suffering from melancholy, an orientation that was antisocial and heterodox. While for the godly that mournful affect was a sign of penitence, a token of self-abasing otherworldliness, for the Anglican satirists, on the other hand, it was the sign of mental disorder, a melancholia and morosity bordering on insanity. Like Lee's charges against "melancholy" and "mystic reasoning," the conservative Anglican apologist Samuel Parker wrote, " 'tis no wonder if Non-sense run so lamely, when Truth and Reason tread so close upon its heels; and the babble of a Fool never appears so fulsom, as when he discourses with a Philosopher."[3] Even the Dissenter Daniel Defoe, stung by the poor reception to his satire, *The Shortest Way with Dissenters*, accused his fellow nonconformists of a shortage of sense: "That's a further testimony of your being a Dissenter…I say, God Almighty would have seemed unkind to you, if he had not given you a great deal of grace; for he has given you but little wit."[4]

A critique of inspired prophecy could be productive of various discourses of social control. Defenders of Uniformity construed a binary opposition between rationality and zeal; but, as we shall see through analysis of the writings of Andrew Marvell, the discourse of charismatic authority, and its opposite, the self-disciplined political subject, registered an important engagement with the complex political consequences of religious radicalism. In this chapter, I shall also investigate the theological ground of inspired prophecy, the Calvinist doctrine of the Holy Spirit. However much the image of Dissenter as fanatic served the interests of the Restoration persecuting state, that image also became a problem for those defending toleration of Dissent. Indeed it led some, including John Locke, to rethink the nature of rationality, authority, and community. Here I shall explore the ways in which the charismatic authority of spiritual prophecy was tempered, in part due to the Stuart state church's legitimation strategies, but also from within a tolerationist tradition.

MILTON'S SPECTER

Milton's name was still a ready weapon in the debates over the religious settlement in the early 1670s, a bludgeon used against Andrew Marvell's defense of toleration, *The Rehearsal Transpros'd* (1672). In the Restoration, it is clear, Milton's name was still synonymous with rebellion, Milton and his books a shrill reminder of all the fury and chaos of the previous twenty years. On 13 August 1660, an official proclamation of the Restored King had condemned the author for "treasons and offenses."[5] No matter that his objectionable books had appeared a decade earlier: to the shaky new regime they seemed very much alive. To eradicate the Revolution's literary legacy, authorities removed books from the Bodleian Library and listed condemned titles. Milton did escape the death penalty, but his books burned in bonfires in the summer and autumn of 1660, part of the exhilaration and vehemence of the festivities greeting the new king, and one among the many rituals undergone to consign the previous period to oblivion. Their author judiciously went into hiding, where he lay perhaps, "In darkness, and with dangers compast round,/ And solitude." He was finally sent to prison in October.[6] Throughout the 1660s Milton lived in fear of assassination and even in the 1670s his political pamphlets were burned at regular intervals. Two of his printers, Peter Parker of his 1667 *Paradise Lost*, and Samuel Simmons of his 1674 edition, had already had at least one run-in with the government, having been arrested in 1667 for their association with a Quaker tract.

For Anglican royalists, Milton's name was a rallying cry of abuse, but its meaning in the 1670s was different from that in the immediate post-Restoration moment. After the Declaration of Indulgence of 1672, nonconformists gained some measure of public acceptance, although the performance of Dissent was sharply circumscribed and keenly surveilled. Although the republican experiment and the Cromwellian regimes had suffered defeat, and Milton no longer defended the killing of kings, still the author's spirit posed a threat, especially in the minds of those like Parker who backed Uniformity and worried that Indulgence might open the floodgates to anarchy. In 1673, the author of *The Transproser Rehears'd* accused Marvell of writing "nothing but *iconoclastes* drawn in Little, and *Defensio Populi Anglicana* in Miniature," taunting, "there are many *Miltons* in this one Man." Marvell was a "*Martin-Mar-Prelate*, a *Milton*... Every day produces not such Wonders."[7] Samuel Parker wrote in *A Reproof to the Rehearsal Transpros'd* (1673) that, "Once perhaps in a century of years there may arise a Martin Marprelate, a Milton," likening Marvell to both.[8] By pointing to the Marprelates, these authors sharpened the identification of Marvell and Milton with a radical and rebellious tradition that stretched back to the sixteenth century. Parker dismissed Marvell with an allusion to Milton: "your Collection will afford as good Precedents for Rebellion and King-killing, as any we meet with in the writings of J. M. in defence of the Rebellion and the Murther of the King."[9] The afterlife of Milton and his *Paradise Lost* thus became the occasion for a discussion of how an oppositional literary mode, no less than revolutionary ideas, might coexist with an orderly state. At stake were the antinomian claims of inspired poetry and politics, what was called enthusiasm.

Historians have argued that there was a "cooling down" of religious enthusiasm towards the end of the seventeenth century.[10] J. G. A. Pocock has seen the phenomenon of enthusiasm as "the essential characteristic of Puritanism: the claim to personal inspiration by an indwelling spirit, with all its chiliastic and antinomian capacity to turn the social as well as the metaphysical world upside down."[11] Enthusiasm, the belief in a direct apprehension of divine impulsion, was closely related to the doctrine of immediate efficacy of the Holy Spirit. These were not strictly theological matters, but touched on the question of human voluntarism and the scope and prerogatives of human reason. Over the course of the seventeenth century, tensions between Arminians and Calvinists focused precisely on these matters; by century's end, Socinianism and rational religion offered further challenges to the antinomian implications in the doctrines of the Holy Spirit. As was made clear by those who attacked Milton's style, enthusiasm in literature and enthusiasm in radical action often went hand in hand. There was thus a political agenda in the "cooling down" of enthusiasm, and that was to eradicate some grounds of individual authority. In their different responses to *Paradise Lost*, Marvell and Dryden shared political anxieties over the role of Dissent, which was causing a sizeable rent in the Restoration polity. In their treatment of Milton, both authors came to terms with the scope allowed to literary inspiration. In struggling with Milton, these authors came to formulate protocols for alternative Restoration literary cultures: Marvell's, in which Dissent – both religious and literary – is tolerated, and Dryden's, in which it is not.

Marvell's prefatory poem to the twelve-book edition of *Paradise Lost* (1674) is best remembered for its response – in rhyme no less – to Milton's blank verse.[12] Having just survived the firestorm of his pro-toleration pamphlets, Marvell may have sought to render Milton fit for further deployment in the "Good Old Cause," even though the later poet admitted that "the

Cause was too good to have been fought for."[13] If "On *Paradise Lost*" is a covert defense of Milton's revolutionary politics, censorship may have kept Marvell coy.[14] Marvell, like Milton, had already missed several close brushes with the censor's lash. In 1671 his printer, Thomas Palmer of Westminster, was fined 40 marks and pilloried for two days for selling a satirical "Painter" poem, most likely his "Directions to a Painter."[15] Conscious of the dangers of Restoration punitive press restrictions, Marvell scorched censors in *The Rehearsal Transpros'd* for their treatment of "ugly Printing-Letters, that look but like so many rotten-Teeth, How oft have they been pull'd out by B. and L. the Public-Tooth-drawers!"[16] The Licensing Act of 1662 had required all manuscripts to be presented for approval to the official censor, who, after requiring emendations, had to testify that nothing in the book was "contrary to Christian faith or the doctrine or discipline of the Church of England or against the state or government of this realme or contrary to good life or good manners."[17] In debates over religious toleration, "doctrine and discipline" were precisely the unsettled issues, so there were quite a few items which fell under that heading. Choosing a biblical theme, as Milton did, was hardly a neutral choice under the Anglican imposition of Uniformity. For printing a radical biblical analogy in 1663, the printer John Twyn was executed.[18] A slight loosening of censorship in 1670–73, due to policies of greater toleration for Dissenters, came right before the publication of Milton's twelve-book edition which included Marvell's prefatory poem, even though books such as Marvell's *Rehearsal Transpros'd* still had to undergo cuts.

Milton himself had included a political allegory in his justification of his blank verse in the 1674 edition of *Paradise Lost*, claiming, in the language of the "Good Old Cause," "it rather is to be esteem'd an example set, the first in *English*, of ancient liberty recover'd to heroic Poem from the troublesome and modern bondage of Riming."[19] Milton's Restoration enemies knew precisely what political allegory was being expressed by this, namely the revival of doctrines of "ancient liberty" that had infused English revolutionary rhetoric.[20] Theodore Haak, Milton's old friend and fellow translator, upon hearing the poem's title, had feared "it would be a lament for the loss of England's happiness with the downfall of the revolutionary regime."[21] Perhaps his friend, like Samson, chose revenge rather than acquiescence; perhaps reading *Paradise Lost* invited a reader to discover the coded Revolutionary message hidden beneath the surface. Since *Paradise Lost* was written under censorship, argues Christopher Hill, "references to England, [Milton's] analysis of the failure of the Revolution, could not be direct."[22]

And as one of that privileged audience who can read between the lines, it would be Marvell's job to make sure those messages were kept well hidden from others.[23] Rhyme, for Milton, served in a covert battle against modern tyranny, and by using rhyme to commend the lack of rhyme, Marvell sets Milton's poetic achievement apart from his own, presenting Milton as a "one just man" figure who remains loyal to his principles in the face of powerful opposition.

Although writing between the lines was crucial in a time of suppression, that may not have been the only reason for elliptical writing. The radical obscurity found in inspired writing may appear to be a strategy of concealment, yet may not actually hide anything specifically subversive except to point to an otherworldliness that is beyond representation. From their theological starting points of an inscrutable God and their critique of human forms, Dissenters wove together political and aesthetic agendas in their complicated attitudes towards figuration. This is not to suggest that strategies of encoded writing were irrelevant to Restoration writers; on the contrary, the nature of writing under persecution demands the skills of encrypting and decoding shared secret languages. It is to suggest, however, that encryption was not the only reason for writing cryptically in the Restoration. A poetics of obscurity was part of an otherworldly orientation.

In strife over religious toleration, an obscure literary mode – an excess of language, where words could point in many directions at once (whether to communicate an enthusiastic rapture, to apprehend the divine essence, or to delve into the abyss of the soul) – was also the mark of a theology of immediate presence. So argued Robert Ferguson, the radical Whig writer and ejected minister, writing in defense of obscurity and toleration. With the uneasy interest of a Calvinist who wishes to explain that human reason has a significant role to play, Ferguson offers a connection between obscurity and a space for individual understanding, part of a great debate in the 1670s between flanks of Calvinists over the Arminian presuppositions regarding human rationality and grace. A theology of rationality and grace is important for understanding an orientation towards radical action: was God or were humans the instigators of political action? A chief actor in the Rye House plot in 1683, and a key player in the Monmouth rebellion of 1685, drawing up a significant Whig constitutional document, Ferguson later fled to the Netherlands in the aftermath of the political failure.[24] For Ferguson, obscurity was one of God's ways, and was a significant kind of illumination:

The Sun doth not more overpower and dazle the eye, than those things of the Gospel from which all our pardon and peace flow's, do overmatch our understandings... It is enough that we are perswaded of the infallibility of the Testimony, we must not hope to comprehend the things testified... The obscurity of the Mysterious truths of the New Covenant is not to be reflected on the darkness of the Declaration, but is to be ascribed to the Majesty of the things declared.

Quoting the French Calvinist theologian Moses Amyraut (1596–1664), whom Marvell had visited in Saumur in 1656, and whose modification of Calvinism had been opposed by Calvinist orthodoxy, Ferguson goes on to talk about the nature of God's mystery: "The things are in themselves so sublime, that were our understandings pure and unspotted they could not be grasped or comprehended; our finite capacities bearing no proportion to them."[25] Dark meaning may be the truer meaning since human reason is incapable of perceiving the full truth. Ferguson opposed the doctrine of *recto Ratio* in Pelagianism, lamenting, "But Alas! Reason is now so darkened by sin, and misled by prejudice, passion and self-interest; that it frequently stiles Evil Good and Good Evil" (*A Sober Enquiry*, 80). Calling the "immediate powerful operation" of the Holy Spirit a "secret" (157), nonetheless, Ferguson lays emphasis on the faculty of human reason only to confirm, not produce, the truths of Revelation.[26] As church leaders sought to compel conformity in religious practice, those defending toleration sought to protect religious liberty on the grounds of inner conscience, a space where meaning could remain undisclosed.

For Anglican opponents of radical prophecy, Milton was associated with a dissenting tradition not only because of his ideas; he represented what I call *literary enthusiasm*, that powerful force that embodied the most dangerous aspects of revolutionary energy: the conviction that one's ideas were immediate from God. With the Holy Spirit working within one in ways that could be barely comprehended, there could be a vocation to political violence in the name of that Spirit. Milton's *Samson Agonistes*, with its blasting force of the Holy Spirit as visited upon enemies through the instrument of the willing human body, offers a powerful vision of that antinomian possibility. Milton's literary mode in *Paradise Lost* may have been an allegory for king-killing politics, but was also ideologically meaningful in itself as a marker of a devotion like Samson's, a belief in an irresistible divine impulsion: "Immediate are the Acts of God, more swift/ Than time or motion" (*PL*, 7:176–77). The enemies of enthusiasm claimed that this mode of immediate compulsion was dangerous not only because of its rhetorical power – its reliance on ambiguity or dense language through which subversive political opinions might be encoded – but also, and more importantly, because those who used it appeared to make unverifiable, and unstoppable, claims for their own private authority. They recognized its critique of representation was in both aesthetic and political registers.

Protestants in the later seventeenth century disputed the question of immediate divine impulsion, specifically focusing their attention on the actions of the Holy Spirit.[27] The matter of divine impulsion was no dusty biblical exegetical exercise; men and women in the Restoration pondered the very nature and scope of God's purpose in their daily lives; and it was a particular question in the matter of religiously motivated violence. Enthusiasm, with its antinomian consequences, was a very great worry to those supporting toleration. But higher claims for authority were also grounds for the challenge to earthly social and political order. I will spend a moment on the discourse of the Holy Spirit to investigate the ways that its otherworldly orientation could prompt violence.

The humanist methods of critical reflection, rhetorical analysis, and philology, when trained on the culture's classical and biblical key texts, may have contributed to a secularization of Western culture.[28] But when some Dissenters read, as their enemies feared, they asked the Bible to speak directly to and through them. George Fox, the Quaker leader, went farthest: "I have that spirit dwellinge in mee of ye father which speakes to you"; "hee...askt mee...whether I had ye same spiritt as ye Apostles had & I tolde him yes."[29] In this radical hermeneutics, Fox's spirit was one and the same as that of the prophets. Uttering the words of the Bible was therefore performing the work of God. This took to the extreme the Protestant premise that the Holy Spirit should guide the reading of Scripture, and gave scope to a new valuing of individual experience. Indirectly assaulting the humanizing tendencies of biblical hermeneutics and holding out against rationalization and secularism, the radicals read this way as an outcome of despair. Theirs was a rearguard action to re-ignite the truths of the Bible as self-evident, available through individual experience, different from the claims of reason, tradition, and empirical proof (and the rising dominance of rationalism, hierarchy, and materialism in the Restoration). It is no surprise that the orthodox Restoration divines turned to a historical approach to biblical texts, and, with their theologies of voluntarism and Arminianism, attempted to stall such a radical, immediate theology.[30] Post-Reformation theology was falling into an epistemological morass regarding proof and providence, and writers such as Locke in his *Essay Concerning Human Understanding* and the Latitudinarians were attempting to map the contours of validity – to rescue certainty, now conceived as probability, from the Scylla of religious antinomianism or the Charybdis of infallibility arguments.[31] It was in reaction to the Dissenters' belief in an ongoing process of divine revelation that many developments in Enlightenment thought were motivated. Indeed, John Pocock calls Enthusiasm the "Antiself of Enlightenment," arguing that in developments within Protestant thought, the shift from Calvinism to Arminianism, lie one of the origins of the Enlightenment.[32] Rather than seeking to rationalize religion, many Dissenters instead sought to articulate with more care the precise nature of the *irrationalism* of religion, to reawaken faith against the incursions of a reason- or history-centered religion that many feared would lead to atheism. Thus Dissenters contributed to the dialogue, asserting proofs of ongoing revelation, weighing the meaning of predetermination and grace, and giving anatomies of doctrines of the Holy Spirit.

The Independent divine John Owen may be the most comprehensive chronicler of the doctrine of the Holy Spirit in the period. The Calvinist Owen's massive study, *Pneumatologia, or, A Discourse Concerning the Holy Spirit* (1674), claimed to be the first of its kind.[33] In it Owen writes from the awkward position of defending a middle ground between orthodox Anglicanism on the far right and Quaker antinomianism on the far left; he also disputes the rationalist Socinians who would deny Christ's divine nature; opposes Baxter's Arminian doctrines of works; and refuses to go as far as Quakers in eschewing the Word for the Spirit alone. The first of five volumes of the work was published in 1674.[34] Owen's topic was regeneration, the process by which the Spirit exerts both moral and physical influence, leading the saint to conversion and sanctification. This work of the Spirit of God, writes Owen

is an especial and immediate work, wherein he acts suitably unto his nature as a spirit, the spirit or breath of God, and suitably unto his peculiar, personal properties of meekness, gentleness, and peace. So his acting is inspiration, whereby he came within the faculties of the souls of men, acting them with a power that was not their own.[35]

In figuring the Holy Spirit as the authorizing source of human action, Owen gives an ontological and a phenomenological account of Old Testament prophecy. Such analysis is of particular interest in the Restoration because of its antinomianism implications, as professed by the Quakers for example. Owen wants to distinguish such modern, false prophets from the true prophets of Old Testament times; but in his account of the Holy Spirit, it is almost impossible to render a difference.

It is hard to say where divine agency ends and human agency begins: this is the heart of the question of religious enthusiasm. When the Holy

Spirit is upon the prophet, Owen avers, it elicits "a power that was not their own." The prophet himself is not the owner of his prophecy; indeed, he utters words he himself may not understand. Writing of the biblical prophet Daniel, for instance, Owen shows how one may be an instrument of God's will: "Nor did Daniel, who had those express representations and glorious visions concerning the monarchies of the world, and the providential alterations which should be wrought in them, understand what and how things would be in their accomplishment" (*Holy Spirit*, 132). Despite the radical unintelligibility of the message to the messenger, Daniel's prophecy was effective, proof enough for Owen that it came from a divine and not a Satanic source (133). The place of rupture, even violence, in this divine economy is central. Over and over in Dissenting writing, as we have seen, and as it is in Owen's examples, proof of true witness is offered through narrative recounting of God's violent hand in history.

As Owen describes various effects of the Holy Spirit, the biblical Samson is taken as a chief example. "*Adding unto the gifts of the mind*, whereby he qualified persons for their duties, even *bodily strength*, when that also was needful for the work whereunto he called them. Such was his gift unto Samson. His bodily strength was supernatural, a mere effect of the power of the Spirit of God" (150): under the influence of the Holy Spirit, then, humans are not autonomous actors, but instruments of God whose agency is only visible through command performance. As Owen writes:

the persons by whom [the miracles] were wrought were never the real subjects of the power whereby they were wrought, as though it should be inherent and residing in them as a quality, Acts iii.12,16; only, they were infallibly directed by the Holy Ghost by word or action to pre-signify their operation. So was it with Joshua when he commanded the sun and moon to stand still, chap. x.12. There was no power in Joshua, no, not [even] extraordinarily communicated to him ... (146)

What happens in the moment of inspiration is that "the parts of the bodies of men were made instrumental of the miracle itself, as in the gift of tongues. They who had that gift did not so speak from any skill or ability residing in them, but they were merely organs of the Holy Ghost, which he moved at his pleasure" (146). These fundamentally religious conceptions of evacuated personal agency do not simply oppose a secular, political framework, though the disentangling of political and religious selfhood is difficult. Owen does not recommend giving up on worldly politics. "Our duty is to apply ourselves unto his commands," Owen insists, "according to the conviction of our minds; and his work it is to enable us to perform them" (204). Indeed, Owen was ever persistent in striving for political solutions to religious disagreements, working with a number of parliamentary leaders after the Restoration to further programs for toleration.

This is a truly radical theory of action. Not simply in their appeals to the Holy Spirit were Dissenters able to justify their acts of resistance to the state, but in their theology – with its logic of investiture via the Holy Spirit as one basis of prophecy – they understood earthly politics as secondary to the real action which was taking place elsewhere and for other ends. As one critic of Owen noted, this doctrine seemed to readmit the Eucharistic concept of Real Presence.[36] The violent possibility that the Holy Spirit could now act through chosen figures was, of course, truly threatening to state order. The Anglican divine William Clagett noted its political ramifications by objecting that Owen's account made the mind or will into "merely a passive instrument in its Conversion," where "the Minde is unperswadable by any Reason and Argument."[37] Others denounced the doctrine of the Holy Spirit for its antinomian, and thus democratic, possibilities. George Hickes condemned those who "pretend that the Holy Ghost now comes down upon their Assemblies, as it did in the Apostles time, and moves them to preach and pray by inspiration without any regard to condition, or sex," in a sermon preached to the University of Oxford on 11 July 1680.[38] Oblivious of rank or gender, the Holy Spirit threatened the social hierarchy, and not only that of the Anglican church. Further, those who carried the Spirit's mantle used it to justify seditious speech, as Hickes put it: "They have called Protestant Princes *Persecutors*, *Idolaters*, and *Jeroboams* to their faces, and told them that God would destroy them and their house" (*Spirit*, 43).

Opponents of the doctrine of the Holy Spirit's ongoing work insisted that the time of God's immediate apprehension in the world was long past. The Anglican Clagett is typical in arguing that no immediate inspiration or new revelation was needed beyond that already given in the Gospels: the Holy Spirit reveals "not to us as he did to the Apostles; to *them*, by Inspiration; to *us*, by their Writings; whereby we may be fully instructed in all necessary Truth."[39] As writing is superior to prophetic testimony, as representation over immanence, Clagett's is also an argument about the pastness of the past:

There is not any one promise in the Scripture, that I can finde, that God will give us any further testimony of the Holy Ghost to the truth of the Gospel, after that which was given to it by the Holy Ghost at first. Wherefore we have no warrant to look for any private Illumination and conviction of the Holy Spirit, to assure us of the truth of that Doctrine, which hath been abundantly confirmed to our hands by so many divine Testimonies already. (*Discourse*, 162)

In these thorny theological issues, by analyzing (and in Clagett's case, circumscribing) the immanent efficacy of God in the world, early modern thinkers were getting to the heart of defining human action. This debate signifies the decline of providence, a disenchantment of the world: those key Enlightenment stories. Clagett, though eager to engage in schoolboy one-upmanship and obviously partisan in his politics, nonetheless touches upon the way that the doctrine of the Holy Spirit had implications for understanding not only human knowledge and the relation between the written and the immediate, but also human agency. To Clagett, the strict Calvinist portrait of the Holy Spirit left humans devoid of authority for their actions, and more importantly, it excluded reason. Accusing Owen of demoting human moral capacity and reducing conversion to an "irresistible Operation" Clagett attacked the Calvinists, asking whether in that view of conversion, "*Violence and Compulsion is in the highest manner offered to the Will?*"[40] Since in the Calvinist account, humans surrendered reason and will to God's authority, then what was left to the human, asks Clagett? The answer is, nothing: the human has become an automaton, a pure piece of mechanical action: "So that you may as well say that a Clock strikes, and the Clapper makes the Bell sound...the soul is then moved, just as if it were a senseless *Machine*, which *Obeys* indeed (if you will so call it) the necessary Laws of Motion."[41]

Not only to Anglican detractors, but to fellow nonconformists, the Calvinists' emphasis on the authority of the Spirit seemed a principle that undermined human autonomy. For Richard Baxter, this extreme position would diminish people's plans to do good works here on earth. Baxter based his practical theology on the efficacy of the Holy Spirit in daily life, but he differed from Owen on the question of how much authority people had over their actions. While the Spirit works within, Baxter held, it does so with the assistance of, not over and against, the human powers of the subject:

Doth the Spirit work on a man as on a beast or a stone? and cause you to speak as a clock that striketh it knoweth not what; or play on man's soul, as on an instrument of music that hath neither knowledge of the melody, nor any pleasure in it? No, the Spirit of God supposeth nature, and worketh on man as man; by exciting your own understanding and will to do their parts.[42]

Baxter allied Spirit with reason, in what would become a position closer to Locke's: "The Holy Spirit assisteth us in our hearing, reading, and studying the Scriptures, that we may come, by diligence, to the true understanding of it; but it doth not give us that understanding, without hearing, reading or study."[43] With an "enhanced opinion of the value of man," many Dissenters like Baxter headed towards Arminianism, holding that the elect had some share in their justification. Orthodox Calvinists held the line by insisting on the operation of the Holy Spirit in bridging the gap between decree and act.[44] The question of divine impulsion, whether driven by the Holy Spirit or God, came about in discussions of predetermination more generally. Writing against a Calvinist interpretation, the Presbyterian John Howe also enlarged the role for human volition: "it seems infinitely to detract from the Perfection of the ever Blessed God, to affirm he was not able to make a Creature, of such a nature…capable of acting; unless whatsoever he thus *enables*, he *determine* (that is, for it can mean no less thing, *impel*) it to do also."[45] Andrew Marvell wrote approvingly of this anti-Calvinist argument in his defense of John Howe in 1678.[46]

The political thinker John Locke would later write in *An Essay Concerning Human Understanding*,

> I am far from denying, that GOD can, or doth sometimes enlighten Mens Minds in the apprehending of certain Truths, or excite them to God Actions by the immediate influence and assistance of the Holy Spirit, without any extraordinary Signs accompanying it. But in such Cases too we have Reason and the Scripture, unerring Rules to know whether it be from GOD or no.[47]

Locke limits the possibly radical antinomianism of the Spirit by grounding it in an external measure, reason. Baxter's tendencies toward Arminianism also allow for human reason and agency to work in the world, even as he differs from Locke in empowering the will over reason.[48] These early thinkers were all coming to terms with how to admit toleration for a variety of religious practices and beliefs while hedging against their antinomian implications.

Andrew Marvell, as we shall see in the next section, is a figure crossing two worlds, generationally and temperamentally. Marvell, during the English Revolution, served as assistant to Milton, Cromwell's Secretary for Foreign Tongues. The author of a brazenly apocalyptic panegyric to the Commonwealth conqueror, Marvell was to become in the Restoration a key polemicist, an MP in whose writings blossom the Whig principles of constitutional liberty and toleration. The Restoration Marvell encompasses a variety of discordant voices, refusing to reduce these to a rigorous religious and literary uniformity.

REHEARSING INTOLERANCE

Andrew Marvell's place in debates over religious liberty was made by his response to the pro-tolerationist Duke of Buckingham's farce drama, *The Rehearsal* (1671), which had struck at enemies, including Henry Bennet, the Earl of Arlington, one of Charles II's chief ministers, also viciously satirizing the poet Dryden in the figure of Mr. Bayes.[49] The play suggested that Charles' regime had been glorified by pompous, but empty, heroic poetry (that of Dryden) and that it was promoting pompous and empty ministers (Arlington). Buckingham's drama had ended its epilogue with a plea for a time "When we may hear some Reason, not all Rhyme."[50] Inspired by Buckingham's mock-heroic attacks, Marvell in *The Rehearsal Transpros'd* attacked the "Irrefragable Doctor of School-Divinity" Samuel Parker, taking the political satire one step further.[51] In alluding to Buckingham's *Rehearsal*, Marvell made the conceptual link between literary and political positions clearer than Buckingham had done, appealing to court and town against church. Writing of Dryden and Parker, Marvell left no doubt about his message: "Mr. Bayes and he do very much Symbolize; in their understandings, in their expressions, in their humour, in their contempt and quarrelling of all others... both their Talents do particularly lie in exposing and personating Nonconformists" (*RT*, 9–10). Maintaining the offensive against Dryden in his prefatory poem to *Paradise Lost*, Marvell mocked the "*Town-Bayes*" who, "like a Pack-horse," "writes all the while and spells."[52] By equating Parker and Dryden in *The Rehearsal Transpros'd*, Marvell related the political agenda of toleration to the literary agenda of preserving freedom from rhyme.

The Anglican response helps us see how the charge of enthusiasm contained literary as well as political critique. In *The Transproser Rehears'd*, a pro-Uniformity pamphlet written against him, Marvell was trounced for his poetical and political proximity to that "libeller" Milton who was a "Schismatick in Poetry" and "nonconformable in point of Rhyme."[53] In the outrage over Marvell's *The Rehearsal Transpros'd*, critics taxed him not only for giving an "Apology for the Rebellion."[54] They also carped at his bad literary style ("play-book style") as a means to attack his political views. As the author of *The Transproser Rehears'd* noted, nonconformity went with three things: the "doctrine of killing kings," "the People's Propriety in Language (a new *Privilege of Subject* for which our Author contends)," and a "play book" – i.e. popular – style.[55] A good Anglican royalist opposed all three.

If those promoting Uniformity tarred nonconformity with the charge of populism, this was an accurate assessment of the Dissenters' effective use of the press.[56] Marvell's style was deemed to cater to the "rabble."[57] Dryden, a popular playwright himself, admitted that prose drama would appeal to the vulgar, but that the "better sort" preferred a drama in which strict verse forms were maintained.[58] Distinctions in social rank inhered in literary as well as in religious style. Questioning the political and social authority of the people, Richard Leigh alludes to their new, and inappropriate, uses of language – "the People's Propriety in Language" now mockingly considered "a new *Privilege* of *Subject*." In 1663, when Roger L'Estrange made proposals for licensing the press, his targets were "the great masters of the popular style," those who "speak plain and strike home to the capacity and humours of the multitude."[59] At root was the recognition that the medium of the press was an effective political tool for an ever-wider audience.

Discrediting a political ideology by accusing its fomenters of a popular or vulgar style betrays the social anxieties and authoritarian fears at the heart of this mission against nonconformity. Dryden for one attacked his Whig enemies in his preface to his poem "The Medall" (1681–82) by numbering among their party such lowly folk as "Footmen," remarking that "A Dissenter in Poetry from Sense and *English*, will make as good a Protestant Rhymer, as a Dissenter from the Church of *England* a Protestant Parson": a literal impossibility. Dissenting poets could only be poor rhymers, immediately to be recognized by stylistic tics: "if you encourage a young Beginner, who knows but he may elevate his stile a little, above the vulgar Epithets of prophane, and sawcy Jack, and Atheistick Scribler… when the fit of Enthusiasm is strong upon him: by which well-mannered and charitable Expressions, I was certain of his Sect, before I knew his name."[60] Dissenting style, vulgar style, unrhyming while at the same time enthusiastic ("a fit of Enthusiasm") and sublime ("elevate his stile"): these dangers were all linked to the wide dissemination of unorthodox ideas through the medium of print.

With their repeated parallels between religious and literary freedom; their attacks on press circulation of unauthorized opinions; and in salvos against popular style and populist politics, these Restoration authors expressed political as well as poetical desires. Dryden did reject Milton's unrhyming verse in his opera, *The State of Innocence* (completed before 1673–74), perhaps concerned over the political valence of literary form. But the relationship between rhyme and political order was more complex than a simple allegory of polarized ideologies; indeed what was at stake was the ground of authority within a state, how the civil was to constrain the spiritual.

The problem with inspiration was not only that it spoke from within the interior of the individual, but that it often challenged the existing social and political hierarchies. The Anglican attack framed the debate as the false "light" of inspiration as against socially accountable norms, as we saw in Chapter One. Anglican propagandists not only attacked nonconformists for their spiritual cozening and vulgar appeal; paradoxically, they also blamed them for using an obscure style. The author of the 1673 *Transproser Rehears'd* jeered at Milton's "absurdity of his inventive Divinity," selecting passages from *Paradise Lost* which baffled him: "What dark meaning he may have...I am not able to say."[61] Dark meaning is that which is inscrutable, and at root, incommunicable. The author hits upon the essence of charismatic authority, its resistance to communicative rational norms. In their various attacks on Dissenters, the Anglican Tories returned with vehemence to the central metaphor of light and darkness, comparing the Dissenters' spurious claims of true inspiration to a dark obscurity, an opposite not only to the royalist tropes of monarchy as sun-bringing, but also to their metaphor of the "light" of reason: Enthusiasm versus Enlightenment.

Enthusiasm was not merely heterodox; it eclipsed reason itself. Parker narrated its progress: "Zeal is a fire in the Soul, which...doth not only prey upon the mind, and devour its intellectual Powers, and enflame all the Passions, but its rage breaks forth, and sets whole States and Kingdoms into a combustion, and reduces the whole World to Ashes; the greatest Zealots always proving the greatest Incendiaries."[62] With "ashes" and "incendiaries," Parker recalls the recent Fire of London, blamed by Tory propagandists on Dissenters and papists. In this line of thinking, calls for freedom of conscience were really calls for a dangerous sort of individualism. Liberty of conscience would, in this view, lead to rebellion: "of all Villains the well-meaning Zealot is the most dangerous: Such men have no checks of Conscience, nor fears of miscarriage to damp their industry, but their Godliness makes them bold and furious."[63] Church uniformity was needed to help rein in such bold fury. Because Dissenters denied the claims of reason, so went the defense of Anglican church authority, persecution and force were the only means of controlling them. Refusal to accord to social norms of language and religious behavior would justify the state or the church imposing forms upon them. According to Parker, "to think to argue rude and boysterous Zealots out of their folly meerly by the strength of calm and sober Reason, is as likely a matter as to endeavour by fair words to perswade the Northern Wind into a Southern Point. If you will ever silence them, you must be as vehement as they: nothing but Zeal can encounter Zeal."[64]

Restored church propagandists commonly exposed the religious Dissenter as irrational, often caricatured for his rabid imagination. For his energy and persistence in sketching this grotesque, none could outdo Dryden. In his immensely popular satirical play, *Sir Martin Mar-All, or the Feigned Innocence* (1668), for example, Dryden presents the titular character as a buffoon, always "plotting" to gain his mistress. He boasts, "I have play'd such a Prize, without thy help, of my own Mother-wit ('tis true I am hasty sometimes, and so do harm; but when I have a mind to shew myself, there's no man in *England*, though I say't, comes near to me as to point of imagination) I'le make thee acknowledge I have laid a Plot that has a soul in't." Mar-All's imagination and misguided wit are to blame for his disruptive and comic behavior.[65] His hero's name reminds the audience of a cultural lineage of religious activism stretching back to Martin Marprelate, the satirical creation of the 1590s that had been revived by Richard Overton during the civil war years. Dryden's Mar-All is praised for his "rare invention" (IV:i, 127), but later reviled as "a confounded busie-brain, with an eternal Wind-mill in it; this in short, Sir, is the Contents of your Panegyrick" (IV:i, 155–59). Radical, inspired religion is the disease of this brain-crazed Don Quixote who suffers due to his mistakes in reading.

Dryden's mocking caricature echoes the fears of Samuel Parker, who represented nonconformists as dangerous to society because of their power over the imaginations of their audiences:

Now the unavoidable consequence of this way of trifling is to betray the People into Enthusiastick and giddy conceits of Religion: it fills their heads full of something, they know not what; and this heats their Fancies, and sets their Brains awork, and makes them talkative and impertinent; and then they abound and overflow with Mystery and Non-sense, and the whole neighborhood is annoyed with the Rattle of their Phrases, and canting Noise. But that which is worst of all is, that if once men fall into this Crazedness of mind, as there is little hopes of their recovery, so there is no end of their Frenzy. Non-sense and Enthusiasm are unbounded things, and they seldom stop till they run stark mad with zeal and reformation.[66]

Parker and Dryden, though they may have differed in many respects theologically, nonetheless join forces in seeing religious enthusiasts as dangerous to social order because of their "mystery" or "non-sense." *The Transproser Rehears'd* had represented Milton as this type of excessively imaginative plotter, and uses the contrast between light and dark so common to this assault: "No doubt but the thoughts of this *Vital Lamp* lighted a *Christmas Candle* in his brain." Milton was accused of suffering from "chimerical conceits," being "struck blind with his own *Idea* of the *Sun*, and admiring those *imaginary* heights which his fancy has rais'd."[67] Though the terms of this attack were formed before the Restoration, informing a poetic theory of William Davenant in the Cromwellian period, for example, they became official state policy after the Restoration.[68]

Milton was thus linked to dangerous religious enthusiasm, not solely for his radical regicidal past, but for his prime literary method, inspired poetry: what would later be called the sublime. Annabel Patterson has argued that the sublime could be used as a veil for disguising subversive political intention.[69] Both Dryden and Marvell were aware of the political freight of this powerful kind of writing. However, if the sublime could hide possibly dangerous political meanings, it could also signal a register intended to remain outside human adjudication. Perhaps obscurity did not hide an interior or veiled meaning, but, as in a Calvinist account such as John Owen's, could stand for the obscurity of inspiration itself, a very otherworldliness that was irrational and a potential threat to civil society or state.

When Dryden inaugurates a program of literary reform, then, insisting upon the earthliness of literary creation, where the critic is supreme, he attempts to codify and mediate literary creation so that its excellences are subject to the human eye and ear.[70] In his adaptation of *Paradise Lost*, Dryden's opera, *The State of Innocence*, limits such "license" by wrapping Milton's rough language in rhyme, condensing the plot and narrative structures of *Paradise Lost* to a more ruly order.[71] Dryden gives a straightforward chronological progression, formally inscribing the principle of temporal uniformity on his drama. Not simply a "tagging" of Milton's lines, Dryden's work thoughtfully condenses and tightens his language.[72] Mediation by the rules of poetry would do the work of containing an irrational, and irrepressibly uncivil, mode.

Dryden aimed to neutralize the potentially incendiary equation between uncontrollable art and uncontrollable religious expression. His campaign against Dissent is intimately bound up with his interest in constructing an English society, whether in literature or politics, that is earthbound, mediated through critical norms and sociable modes. In his "An Essay of Dramatick Poesie" (1667), Dryden reiterates the idea that poetic form could control what was a dangerous energy. Verse, he argues, properly puts "bounds to a wilde over-flowing Fancy," and is both "a great help to a luxuriant Fancy," and a "Rule and line by which he [the Poet] keeps his building compact and even, which otherwise lawless imagination would raise either irregularly or loosly."[73] Parker, writing of Dissenting preachers, follows the same logic, though with sexual, not architectural, language: "Thus their wanton & luxuriant fancies climbing up into the Bed of Reason, do not only defile it by unchast and illegitimate Embraces, but instead of real conceptions and notices of Things, impregnate the mind with nothing but Ayerie and Subventaneous Phantasmes."[74] Dryden, in opposition, offers something he calls "judgment," which is what good rhyme expresses, that of "maturest digestion," and "second thoughts."[75]

A discourse of reason is thus cast against that of enthusiasm. Champions of a state church thus posited compelled uniformity against the violence of prophecy and the inner callings of conscience. Yet it is not simply a matter of saying defenders of Anglican Uniformity were *right* in their analysis of the prophetic mode of a Milton or the otherworldliness of a radical saint. The Dissenters themselves posited their own communicative norms, as we have seen. My point is that the Dissenting modes of forging solidarity were countered by a language of civility and sociality. The Anglican royalist diagnosis of radical prophecy thus engaged in a war of impressions, with political and philosophical consequence, as they took up a radical opposition between earthly/otherworldly and transformed it into a neater, civil/uncivil, binary pair.

MARVELL'S TOLERATION

Though sympathetic to Dissent, Andrew Marvell did not present himself as a Dissenter. On the contrary, in *The Rehearsal Transpros'd* he created a distance from nonconformists, asserting, "Not on the other part to impute any errors or weakness of mine to the Nonconformists, nor mistake me for one of them, (not that I fly it as a reproach, but rather honour the more scrupulous:) for I write only what I think befits all men in Humanity, Christianity and Prudence" (*RT*, 186). Voicing his loyalty to the king, Marvell insisted that toleration for Dissenters was not a revival of the old antimonarchical, revolutionary energy.

Whig tradition hails Andrew Marvell as a champion of religious toleration, even though his precise religious beliefs are hard to pin down. Departing from strict Calvinism on prescience, Marvell insisted on the difference between a human sphere of action and a divine sphere; as he put it, "Religion hath parts which belong to eternity, and parts which pertain to time." To time belonged the duty of "humane reason."[76] In the transition from Calvinism to Arminian tendencies within left-Protestantism, Marvell found himself allied with Arminians. Entering a pamphlet debate between two Presbyterian ministers in a 1678 tract on divine prescience, Marvell defended John Howe against the orthodox Calvinism of Thomas

Danson. Even though he denied the label of Arminian, nonetheless the tract represents a shift long taking place within Presbyterian thought, a slide towards Arminian belief in voluntarism and an emphasis on the capability of human reason.[77] More an attack on Danson's logical inconsistencies than it is a full justification of Howe's position, Marvell's book pledges to "intermeddle not as an Opinionist either way."[78] In the process, Marvell points out the absurdities of Danson's ideas and supports those of the voluntarist Arminian.

The tract engages seriously with the question of God's efficacious influence over human actions, specifically addressing the question of whether God is the instigator of evil actions, and, uncharacteristically in his Restoration religious polemic, Marvell refrains from satire, calling instead for civility between the quarreling men (*Remarks*, 173). Maintaining the difference between divine power and human freedom, "concurring, though never so immediately, by an influence which doth but enable to an action, and by that which doth determine to it, or impell" (196), Marvell cuts to the heart of the matter. God's prescience, he insists, is not a compulsion, but rather an enabling of human action. Just as William Clagett had objected that John Owen's emphasis on the power of the Holy Spirit rendered humans mere automatons, Marvell challenges the orthodox interpretation of predetermination so as to grant more potency to human participation in intentions originating from God. Allowing more scope for human action, Marvell's theology girds his voluntarist ideas regarding liberty of conscience, toleration, and individual civil liberty. John Locke was also thinking about the properties of reason, will, and understanding in the 1670s, during a period of intense scrutiny of the capacities of human freedom. It was then Locke began writing the work that would become his *Essay Concerning Human Understanding*.[79] The political protection of private judgment was one accomplishment of these nascent Whig bids for toleration in the early modern period, after private judgment was leeched of its dangerous, antinomian possibilities by a new theological rendering of the meaning of grace and the Fall.

Marvell was bruised by his confrontation with Samuel Parker, writing to Sir Edward Harley that his was "the rudest book, one or other, that ever was published – I may say since the first invention of printing." In thinking about how to answer it, Marvell commented that he would consult friends, and betake himself "some five miles off to enjoy the spring and my privacy."[80] In his prefatory poem, added to the second printing of *Paradise Lost* in 1674, Marvell had a chance to reply in another vein. Believing that

Parker was making "Conscience fit for the nonce,"[81] Marvell addressed the problem of individual inspiration, and in a completely different way than did Parker and Dryden. For Marvell, Milton may indeed be inspired and, further, whether that inspiration is authentic is left up to readers to judge, not the state or church authorities. Marvell offers an account of *reading* Milton's poem, one in which he works out the awkward relations between interpretation, text, and the public display of inspiration, holding to the premise of individual liberty.

Marvell's introductory verse from 1674, "On *Paradise Lost*," belongs in the context of the political controversies over tolerance of Dissent, amongst tolerationist efforts to consider the scope in latitude for individual conscience in freedom of worship, and the theological reconsideration of human action. It is easy to overlook the opening forty lines of the poem and jump to its raucous conclusion, those prongs attacking Dryden and his rhyme. In the first forty lines, however, Marvell fends off charges of Milton's alleged false inspiration. By emphasizing his own processual reactions to the text, Marvell gives a pattern or protocol for literary evaluation (1–44). Marvell emphasizes his personal response because defending a process of personal and private judgment was a chief task of those pleading for the rights of Dissenters to practice their religion.

Marvell's views on theology, usually elusive, become clear on this point in the second part of his answer to Parker. An apology for conscience was theologically proper, argues Marvell, since only through divinely assisted conscience could the Holy Spirit do its work. By calling upon a theological understanding of the Holy Spirit, Marvell links support for toleration with an account of the cooperation of humans with the transcendent. Marvell charged that Parker, in his mechanical account of enthusiasm, was "debasing the operation of the Holy Ghost."[82] "This Hypothesis of yours," chides Marvell, referring to Parker's allusions to a physiological explanation of enthusiasm, "confounding the extraordinary influx of Gods Spirit for the power of Nature, seems to arise from your being ill principled, and not well read in the Doctrine of the Church of *England* concerning Original sin" (*RT*, 2nd. part, 267). Continues Marvell, using the personal voice, "For my own part I have, I confess, some reason, perhaps particular to my self, to be diffident of mine own *Moral Accomplishments*, & therefore may be the more inclinable to think I have a necessity of some extraordinary assistance to sway the weakness of my belief, and to strengthen me in good duties" (*RT*, 2nd. part, 268). Parker, by reducing Dissenters' claims of divine assistance to mere physical aberrations, threatens

Christianity's core teaching on the Fall, indeed, challenges the very need for saving Grace.

In writing on Milton, Marvell rehabilitates inspiration while not ceding reason. The first lines of his homage record a reader's changing reactions. At first, Marvell admits, he beheld the book, "misdoubting his Intent."[83] The doubting reader is a literary trope in prefatory poetry.[84] As Marvell praises Milton in the context of the Restoration settlement of religion, he gives those doubts a political valence. Indeed, an anxious response to *Paradise Lost* was to be found among Milton's friends – we recall Haak – who expected a revival of the Revolutionary Milton. Those friends may have found reassurance that Milton was not using the story of the fall of Adam to represent England's current political situation; to write that kind of political allegory might be to lay himself open to the kind of charges of sedition for which Algernon Sidney had lost his life. Marvell seems worried, however, not simply about a secular political allegory, Milton's possible revival of classical republican energies, but rather about the theological or prophetic aspects of his literary endeavor, the "sacred Truths" of Milton's subject matter.

In the poem on Milton, Marvell considers the relationship between political and spiritual obligation. Worried that Milton "would ruin (for I saw him strong)/ The sacred Truths to Fable and old Song," Marvell vaunts his own particular act of witnessing, admitting that the poem did make him "fear" and be "jealous" – Restoration slogans hurled by both sides over the causes of civil war. Butler wrote of the "jealousies and fears" in the opening lines of *Hudibras* as the causes of the English civil wars; Dryden's rebellious Achitophel "fills the ears/ Of list'ning crowds with jealousies and fears."[85] By using these terms – code words for the false inspiration that led to the rebellion – to describe his misgivings, Marvell signals that he, too, is concerned about false inspiration that could lead to political turmoil.

Marvell's "jealousies" and "fears," however, do not stifle his curiosity. With suspicion, then, he goes on to investigate Milton's epic task of rendering God's totality: "*Messiah* Crown'd, God's Reconcil'd Decree,/ Rebelling Angels, the Forbidden Tree,/ Heav'n, Hell, Earth, Chaos, All." Milton's mode – perhaps his "Mar-All" – indeed dares to compete with God for the title of supreme being. Such ambition was remembered as chiefly belonging to the prophetic radicals of civil war politics, and was made into a target by those defending Restoration orthodoxy. As Dryden put it, "They, for God's Cause, their Monarchs dare dethrone;/ And they'll be sure to make his Cause their own."[86]

Marvell is also vexed that Milton's claims to prophecy might be contagious:

> Jealous I was that some less skilful hand
> (Such as disquiet always what is well,
> And by ill imitating would excel)
> Might hence presume the whole Creation's day
> To change in Scenes, and show it in a Play.
> ("On *Paradise Lost*," 17–22)

These lines have rightly been understood as a swipe at Dryden for "tagging" Milton's verse, for turning *Paradise Lost* into a drama, for copying it at the expense of the original. But Marvell picks up on the several risks of imitation: a plagiarist author's failed imitation of a secondary poetic talent, as well as the false imitation of the work of that primary author – God. In *Paradise Lost*, "Ill imitation" is the work of Satan, who committed the sin of pride in his "God-like imitated State" (Milton, *PL*, 2:511). The matter of imitation contained another register in the attack on enthusiastic religion as high Anglican ministers accused those with false inspiration of passing their evil to a gullible populace. A susceptible audience would "imitate" dangerous leaders whose power was outside the control of the state. Benjamin Laney had preached to Charles in 1661 that those vaunting liberty of conscience could easily corrupt others – the familiar antipopulist trope: "If a man should be so unreasonable as to say, his conscience may be bound by himself, but not by any else…though the truth is, they bind none but themselves, and that to repent for corrupting Gods word, and misleading the people into Faction, Sedition and Disobedience, to say no worse."[87] The danger of imitation is that there are social and not just literary or theological consequences.

If the poem introducing *Paradise Lost* is an autobiographical account of a reader's intellectual progress from doubt to certainty ("As I read," Marvell recounts, "soon growing less severe,/ I lik'd his Project"), then it is also an account of individual judgment as the basis of authority. Judgment would not inhere in legislated forms but emerged, rather, from human response. Marvell thus nullifies the fears of the political opposition – that the work's context may have a socially dangerous impact – within a framework of private judgment.

The question remains, however: does Milton's topic hold out the potential for violence? Marvell suggests as much in his comparison of Milton to Samson: "So *Sampson* grop'd the Temple's Posts in spite." The figure of the iconoclastic Samson seems doubly powerful in the Restoration, a menacing reminder of the violence of the past, as well as the dangerous enthusiast of the present; as we have seen, *Samson Agonistes* portends both possibilities. Royalists had asserted that Milton's blindness was God's punishment to Milton for his interregnum acts, and Marvell, though not endorsing this interpretation, needs to confront this myth. If Milton was still possessed with Samson's revolutionary irrationality, he was liable to break forms, to tear down the "Temple's Posts." After all, Milton himself sought to break free from the "bondage" of rhyme. In "fearing" the project's success, Marvell wonders,

> . . . how he his way should find
> O'er which lame Faith leads Understanding blind;
> Lest he perplex'd the things he would explain,
> And what was easy he should render vain.
> ("On *Paradise Lost*," 13–16)

The word *perplex* in his dedicatory poem posits that Milton might offer a radical kind of obscurity, like that mocked by high Anglican preachers; the very presence of *Paradise Lost* itself induces a state of perplexity in its potential readers even before they read, as, for example, Marvell notes in announcing his own initial "misdoubting." In the minds of Anglican Tories, the attitude of perplexity or of "amazement" – attributed to Samson, Mar-All, and Milton – is a sign for potentially dangerous enthusiasm itself. Yet, in Marvell's tolerant Anglicanism, it is also the stance of a reader who wonders, who seeks for himself to understand what is in the world, or in a text. What makes such inspiration possibly threatening to Marvell is not its very presence, but rather its potential for violence. Over the course of the prefatory poem, Marvell breaks the comparison between Milton and the dangerous enthusiast, converting Samson into Tiresias, that impotent soothsayer: "Just Heav'n thee like *Tiresias* to requite/ Rewards with Prophecy thy loss of sight." This is not a violent, frenzied, masculine inspiration, but submissive, hermaphroditic truth-telling.

In the choice between spite and truth, Marvell refers perhaps to his own exchange with the bitter Samuel Parker, who finally gave up on reason and chose instead spite. Commenting on their vitriolic exchange, the Independent minister Robert Ferguson also noted the keenness of Parker's savagery: "something might be pleaded for [Parker's] keenness against A[ndrew] M[arvell] being a sacrifice to Revenge rather than Truth."[88] Parker had made good on his program to fight zeal with zeal.[89] Marvell takes his authority as a reader to judge that the poem is indeed imitative of true divine order, finally insisting that Milton's poem, "In number, weight and measure, needs not rhyme," an echo of a Renaissance trope which typifies God's order of creation. Choosing Tiresias over Samson, Marvell sides with inspired truth-telling rather than revenge.

Having decided that the meanings of *Paradise Lost* are indeed godly – that which "Draws the Devout, deterring the Profane" – Marvell asks for forgiveness for his previous hostile treatment. He addresses Milton directly, now a "thou," insisting that Milton belongs in the Restoration world of letters. Though Marvell welcomes him into that world asking for his blessing: "Pardon me, Mighty Poet, nor despise/ My causeless, yet not impious surmise," Marvell rebukes himself then for the false "surmise" of thinking divine truth would be "ruined" to "Fable and old Song" in Milton's literary genre. Marvell's surmise was "impious," because he formerly doubted what now turns out to be a truly inspired poem.

Marvell's surmise, however, could be taken as "causeless" in another sense – quite literally – since Milton is presently without his (political) cause. At this point in the poem, such a literal meaning becomes only an idle pun. Or is it? Though he addresses overtly only the problem of authentic inspiration, Marvell does invite secondary political meanings, leaving these to the individual judgment of his readers. Marvell judges that Milton had adhered to the essence of "sacred truth":

> That Majesty which through thy Work doth Reign
> Draws the Devout, deterring the Profane.
> And things divine thou treat'st of in such state
> As them preserves, and thee, inviolate.   (31–34)

In successfully adapting biblical truth to poetic genre, Milton succeeds in "preserving" the "things divine" in an "inviolate" state. Other meanings will of course be found in the double language of Marvell's praise: "Majesty" refers to England's ruler, under whose complaisance Milton publishes his poem, but it also refers to God's rule, perhaps at odds with the former. Marvell reassures his readers that in Milton's poem, "Majesty" does "reign," and he thus makes an ambiguous or obscure equation between biblical decorum and political submission, one that requires interpretation. Doubting and perplexity are necessary risks in Marvell's poem.

The literary style of obscurity, then, could protect an interior space: the space of conscience, of interpretation, of individual rational action and agency – realms of freedom apart from legislation by the state. If Milton's is a "theme sublime," then perhaps it is just private, and not dangerous. Marvell works towards the political end of defending Dissenters by his insistence on freedom for personal reflection, a space apart from control. Setting out to make Milton's poem palatable to Restoration literary culture, not simply veiling revolutionary political intent, but also respecting obscurity and his inspiration as prophetic, Marvell vouches it is not a danger to civility. Marvell's politics here are those of the emergent tolerationist Whig position in the Restoration, not those of the radical Revolution.

MILTON A LA MODE

Marvell knew that literary form was no idle thing (we think of the complexity of his praise of Cromwell in his "Horatian Ode," for example), yet with his closing section on rhyme, Marvell firmly anchors Milton's poem in Restoration literary practice, one in which Milton's writing could be made safe. In the close of the poem ("On *Paradise Lost*," 45–54), Marvell's tone shifts abruptly. Though still addressing himself to the "Mighty poet," Marvell turns satirical, writing a jaunty, snaky piece of poetry more closely resembling his own Restoration squibs than the first forty-four lines of this poem:

> While the *Town-Bayes* writes all the while and spells,
> And like a Pack-horse tires without his Bells:
> Their Fancies like our Bushy-points appear,
> The Poets tag them, we for fashion wear.
> ("On *Paradise Lost*," 46–49)

All of a sudden, we are in the urbane world of Restoration satire; the language is rife with contemporary, "fashionable" content – the streets of London with their pack-horses, the hack poets of Grub Street, the ornaments of couture, "bushy-points," and fashion – a far cry from the "sacred truths," "gravity and ease," and the inspired bird from Paradise of the earlier lines (8, 36, 39). If Dryden is a "pack-horse" for his rhyming, however, he lacks the agency of a freely rational being. His adherence to rhyme is slavish, even beastly. Marvell, in figuring Dryden as a literal beast of burden, suggests that unthinking allegiance to a literary form denies the free exercise of choice and rational agency.

Despite the rhyming couplets in his opening section, Marvell gives rhymes a fallen, topical, mode: rhyme, he demonstrates, can accommodate both extremes. In this final section of the poem, Marvell still warrants individual judgment, as he vaunts the importance of the "mode" – the importance of individual style – here, in literary form. For Marvell, fashion is not mere ornament; rather fashion denotes an opportunity for an individual to make choices. His *Mr Smirke: Or the Divine in Mode* (1676) lanced at the Church of England hack writer, "because his wit consisting wholly in his dress... being huff'd up in all his ecclesiastical flusster, he might appear more formidable... the Divine in Mode might have vyed with Sir Fopling Flutter."[90] John Locke, in his 1685 *Letter Concerning Toleration*, also referred to religious differences as those of "mode." In writing of "frivolous things" which "breed implacable Enmities amongst Christian Brethren," Locke turns satirist, mocking those who wish to regulate, and punish, private taste: "perhaps I wear not Buskins; because my Hair is not of the right Cut; because perhaps I have not been dip't in the right Fashion."[91] In this rare satirical moment, Locke relegates such personal preferences – along with those concerning religious worship – to a private sphere. Marvell, in offering a response to Milton's *Paradise Lost*, differs from Dryden in promoting a tolerationist stance in the realm of letters, siding with John Locke, who had argued that differences in religious protocols, though significant, were not inherently dangerous to social order.

We are left with an enthusiastic Marvell, however, "transported" by the "mode" of rhyme. His "transport," it is clear, is not that of a dangerous religious radical, but rather that of the fashionable wit, who merely "commends" the poem to his audience, coyly refusing to "praise" it. In his response to *Paradise Lost*, Marvell agreed with Milton's potential critics that the poem proposed a sort of inspiration. Yet Marvell suggests a solution other than legislated forms such as censorship or the imposition of regulatory verse. Rather, the effects of poetry can be effectively managed by individual readers' judgments. Marvell does raise the specter of the political and social stakes of literary genres, reminding readers that poetic form might carry more than one message. But form itself does not convey information about essential inner meaning. In taking up rhyme as against Milton's blank verse, Marvell signals that he has made a conscious personal choice. This move may reflect Marvell's desire to keep safely what was hidden between the lines. He thus preserves the power of the individual reader to make judgments, and of the poet to remain obscure.

Paradise Lost indeed summoned current radical energies for its literary enthusiasm which was associated with radical religion. Marvell's poem has been read as a defense of the "Good Old Cause" in *Paradise Lost*, as if content were the kernel in the poetical nut. Marvell's enemies certainly read in this ideological vein, threatened by the oppositional intent of Marvell's writing. John Dryden, in consequence, made literary form serve the business of state regulation, seeking by literary and religious protocols to inhibit an extravagant imagination, thus curbing religious enthusiasm. But Marvell's poem carves out a third position, as he guards Milton's freedom to create an inspired poetry. If Milton, to some Restoration writers, represented dangerous enthusiasm, Marvell comes to his rescue by a literary toleration that parallels a political theory of toleration for Dissent. For Restoration readers, Milton's obscurity might just stand for the importance of guarding private opinion, or inspired poetry. Marvell's is a Whig solution to a Dissenting problem.

In 1667, John Locke had defined religious worship, "being that homage which I pay to that God I adore in a way I judge acceptable to him, and so being an action or commerce passing only between God and myself."[92] Uncharacteristic for Locke here is his use of the first-person voice. Even in his rhetoric, Locke is wary of speaking for anyone other than himself: matters of worship are to be left to the individual. Locke construes an arena where human and divine commerce is a private realm, invincible to government or church authority. To defend religious diversity, authors along the Dissenting spectrum hailed this personal "I" as against the claims of the state. Marvell's defense of conscience, too, professes an individualistic logic, a challenge to the Tory program of public conformity. In his defense of Milton's "Theme sublime," he admits his own "transport," safely shielded by rhyme.

CHAPTER 7

Poetics

Inspiration had long found a safe harbor in the realm of art, as Protestant poetics accented the fit between religious and poetic inspiration. The power of the poet was "the inspired gift of God rarely bestow'd," pleaded John Milton in 1642.[1] Edmund Spenser's *The Shepheardes Calender* conjoined the functions of spiritual and poetic leadership in his pastoral ethos, and inaugurated the first use of the term enthusiasm cited by the *Oxford English Dictionary*, celebrating the "perfecte paterne of a Poete" as partaking in "indede so worthy and commendable an arte: or rather no arte, but a divine gift and heavenly instinct not to bee gotten by laboure and learning, but adorned with both: and poured into the witte by a certain ENTHUSIASMOS and celestiall inspiration..."[2]

Although Marvell may have coyly welcomed Milton's literary enthusiasm, some Dissenters on the other hand were uneasy about the status of their own works as art. This chapter turns from the politico-religious critique of enthusiasm to attitudes within the Dissenting tradition towards literary creation. How did Dissenters reflect on their own human artifacts as works of imaginative creation? From inside Dissent, this was a vexed matter, given the long-familiar attack against art in the history of Puritanism. Richard Baxter's warning against literature may be taken as exemplary: "Play-books, and History-Fables and Romances, and such like, are the very poison of Youth, the prevention of Grace, the fuel of Wantonness and Lust, and the food and work of empty, vicious, graceless Persons." Baxter thunders against the "trash": "it dangerously bewitcheth and corrupteth the minds of young and empty People, to read these books. Nature doth so close with them, and delight in them, that they presently breed an inordinary of Affection, and steal away the heart from God, and his holy Word, and Ways." Always at war with natural man, Baxter does not condemn all literature, just that which detracts from godliness. He finishes his diatribe with a platonic flourish: "and it's great pity that they be not banished out of the Common-wealth...I beseech you throw away these Pestilent Vanities, and take them not in your hands, nor suffer them in the hands of your Children, or in your Houses, but burn them as you would do a conjuring-Book."[3] With the censure of the Reformation iconoclast, Baxter recognizes that books indeed are everywhere, in the hands of children, in every house.

Out of Baxter's condemnation, out of this war against formal art and its dissemination, what literature can emerge? Surely it should not surprise us that edification was the Puritan's goal; what interests me in this chapter is how, along with this Puritan attack on art, nonconformists also defended a poetics of sensuous feeling: "Sure there is somewhat of heaven in Holy poetry," muses Richard Baxter, who lists admired poets in the preface to his own verse collection: Abraham Cowley, Katherine Philips, George Wither, Francis Quarles, Joshua Sylvester, Fulke Greville, John Davies, George Sandys, and, above all, George Herbert.[4] Others were even less constrained in defining the pleasures of divine poetry. As the Independent minister Theophilus Gale asked:

Alas! who so dul or flegmatic, but can, upon some more than ordinary experiments of Divine Providence, find some poetic strains, to vent his more warme and melted Affections in and by? Thus much Experience learnes us, that where any extraordinary occasion happens, for the moving the Affections, specially Admiration, Love, Joy, or Sorrow, there this Poetic vein is most pregnant and ripe.[5]

Richard Baxter, in a worldly note, advised, "Lay by all the passionate part of Love and Joy, and it will be hard to have any pleasant thoughts of Heaven."[6] Arousing spiritual desires was a chief end of Dissenters' writing.

Given their opposition to set forms in religious worship, then, how could Dissenters embrace formal poetry? Dissenting authors understood the paradox: a Baptist called the Quakers hypocrites for condemning set prayers but admiring the Quaker author Mary Mollineux: "how much soever they condemn *David's* Psalms in Meeter; yet herein there is about a hundred and fifty Pages in English and Latin Meetre."[7] The Dissenting war against secular and purely formal literature had profound political, theological, as well as social causes and consequences. These are the subject of this chapter, which unearths Dissenters' poetics, specifically the many defenses of pleasure in poetry. The first part of the chapter explores Dissenters' ideas of literary and divine inspiration, of which the primary example is the biblical Song of Songs and whose primary target is a neoclassical libertine literature. The second part of the chapter deepens the problem of human art by investigating the influence of George Herbert on many Dissenting writers who took up his name in a divine, inspired poetics. The Dissenters' practice of imitating, and even copying, Herbert verbatim, may help us understand the values of a literary economy in which derivativeness need not be scorned.

Re-creation, I suggest, is a better model than originality to deploy when thinking about much Dissenting writing. By valuing the source of poetry as divine, many devotional authors subscribe to a scriptural model of composition, rather than an authorship model. This is not the competitive model of authorial imitation whereby later poets stand in hostile relation to those earlier poets whose works they admire but whose very prior existence threatens the very integrity and worth of their own. Rather, in the scriptural model of imitation, the goal is fulfillment of, rather than competition with the original, paralleling the Christian paradigm of an unfolding, progressive revelation in history.

HEBRAISM: A DISSENTING DEFENSE OF POESY

The Bible offered the clearest instance of inspired poetry. In Milton's *Paradise Regain'd* Jesus reflects, "All our Law and Story strew'd/ With Hymns, our Psalms with artful terms inscrib'd/ Our Hebrew Songs and Harps in *Babylon,/* That pleas'd so well our Victors' ear, declare/ That rather *Greece* from us these Arts deriv'd" (*PR*, 4:334–38). These later arts, Jesus goes on to argue, "Will far be found unworthy to compare/ With *Sion's* songs, to all true tastes excelling,/ Where God is prais'd aright, and Godlike men,/ The Holiest of Holies, and his Saints" (346–49). Hebrew poetry is superior to the arts of Greece, and the source of that better art is divine: "Such are from God inspir'd, not such from thee" (350), declares Jesus, denouncing the Tempter's suggestion otherwise. Insisting on the divine origins of inspiration, however, Milton hedges a bit, "Unless where moral virtue is express'd/ By light of Nature, not in all quite lost" (351–52). *Is* the light of Nature lost with the Fall; or is there a remnant of it in some virtuous few, whose actions might therefore be virtuous? This question of how the Fall affected human virtue and reason holds consequences for Milton's faith in autonomous human action, and autonomous human art. In *Paradise Regain'd*, Milton includes the orthodox Calvinist position by claiming art originates in divine inspiration. But he also raises – through the conditional "unless" – the Arminian possibility that human efforts can participate in God's work, as well as that more radical principle, that reason or virtue may be unblemished despite the Fall.

Theophilus Gale (1628–78) attempted to shore up Calvinist orthodoxy against just such questions. The Independent minister was a pupil of Thomas Goodwin at Magdalen College, Oxford, from where he was ejected from his fellowship in 1662. Gale exemplifies the fate of ousted ministers under Uniformity; he served as tutor to the sons of the great patron of Dissent, Philip, fourth Baron Wharton (and was reported to have kept a land tortoise in his garden).[8] While he monitored the education of the Wharton children on the Continent in the 1660s and reported in daily letters back to their father, he was also at work researching and writing his magnum opus, an orthodox Calvinist defense of divine predestination especially as against Arminians, his four-part *The Court of the Gentiles* (1669–78). In that work, Gale sought to re-establish God's primary influence over human action, and by studying the origins of all learning in revelation, considered the complex relation of the divine to human reason. In line with his Calvinist understanding of the inadequacy of human art, Gale sought to reinstall divine power.[9] The doctrine of the Holy Spirit has been aligned to sectarian mysticism, but Gale's defense of enthusiasm emerges rather out of conflicts within mainstream interpretations of English Reformation theology about the nature of the sacrament, of grace, of the meaning of the Fall, and of the scope of the elements in the Trinity, particularly of the Holy Spirit.[10]

Musing on "the genuine and original ground or occasion of al poesie, specially sacred," Gale gives a primer in Dissenting aesthetics, of which I want to examine parts in some detail. Challenging the pagan focus of Europe's humanist Renaissance, Gale used his humanist skills of philology, comparative ethnology, and history to trace all knowledge back beyond the Greeks and Romans to the biblical Hebrews. An interest in the divine origins of human art was a preoccupation of Calvinist theologians in the mid- and later seventeenth century; the Independent (and Calvinist) John Owen also composed a Latin treatise much to the same effect. As for Milton's Jesus, for Gale, poetry began in the human response to God's miracles, and he evokes the doctrines of the Holy Spirit:

> The sense and apprehension of such wondrous issues of Providence, could not but make a deep impresse, on the tender and soft Affections of his own People, in whose behalf these signal providences were vouchsafed. Now the Church in this her Childish state, (like Children who are much affected with wonders) being struck with the sense of these prodigious Apparances of Divine power in her behalf; and having her Affections much stirred and moved hereby, was not able to contain herself within bounds, (for Affections melted are very diffusive) without venting her self in Poetic Hymnes and Raptures.[11]

In this account of poetic origin, God's presence – and with it the miraculous – is still at work in the universe (a subject under dispute by Latitudinarians, skeptics, and John Locke). Passions, apprehensions, and affections all precede notions humans might have of them, and poetry is the record of these. Outside of language, there exists God. With this epistemology, Gale overturns the conventional language of wit: "For Affections are the greatest Wits that may be, and delight to vent themselves in Poesie, which is a Witty Art, or rather passion; and therefore the most expressive of extraordinarie and choicer Affections" (*Court*, 8). Emotions, not mental conceptions, are wit's spring. Gale's poetics contains a political corollary. Because poetry originates outside of language, that is, in the admiration for divine effects, it is potentially a democratic art, open to any person who can experience the bounty and divine effects of nature.

In his Dissenting poetic manifesto, Gale defends enthusiasm in poetry:

> We know that the Forme or Mode, wherein the First Divine Poesie was deliverd, was Enthusiastic . . . [those persons] . . . were transported, beyond the ordinarie capacitie of their natural Fancies, into a Rapture, for the composing of such Hymnes, as might most conduce to the celebrating the Name and the Honor of God. Such also were the Songs of Deborah and Barak, of Esaias, Simeon, and Anna, Luke 2.25,36. (*Court*, 12–13)

Miriam's anthem of the deliverance of the Israelites from the Egyptians is the pattern for all poetry, as we shall see in Chapter Eight. The other biblical passages Gale cites are those violent, impassioned, and glorious moments of divine action, when figures are transported by the Holy Spirit whether to poetry or violence. In what we might call a "Defense of Hebrew Poesie," Gale theorizes what had become Dissenting literary practice, as he weds a campaign to shore up Calvinist orthodoxy with a literary corollary, that of admitting the presence of the Holy Spirit in human affairs.

True inspiration of the Holy Spirit can compete with the pagan muses: this is a clear engagement with the literary values of "The Age of Dryden," the neoclassical pursuit of order through aesthetic means, for instance, the balanced couplet and the formally perfect drama. The Dissenting poetic offered an alternate set of values. For instance, a laudatory poem by the ejected Congregational minister, Thomas Gilbert, on John Owen's "Book of the Holy Spirit" opens with a glance towards contemporary materialist poetics. In an age of neoclassicism, this affront retained its zealous and radical charge; in an age of libertine poetry, the Dissenter defends a chaster poetics:

> Hence ye Pierian Mountain Sisters, hence,
> This noble Work does scorn your Influence.
> It's the Third Person of the sacred Trine
> I shall alone invoke, before you Nine.

Thou Holy Ghost that Owen didst inspire,
To write thy mighty Arts with sacred fire
Some Heavenly wisdome into me infuse;
So shalt thou be my Subject & my Muse.[12]

In their poetic practice, and warring against the worldliness of neoclassical
art, then, Dissenters welcomed inspiration. Poetry proceeds from strong,
rapturous emotions, and is an expression of admiration for, and response
to, the divine. "And look," Gale wrote, "by how much the more stupendous
and amazing the Objects of Admiration are, by so much to more violent
wil its impulsion on the Soul be" (*Court*, 10). Rather than seeing the condition of enthusiasm as disabled or erroneous, as did Meric Casaubon, in
A Treatise Concerning Enthusiasm (1656) and Henry More in *Enthusiasmus
Triumphatus* (1662), the tumultuous experience is rather the sign of true
receptivity to the divine power.

For many Dissenting writers along a wide theological spectrum, poetry
emerges likewise from the quest for the divine presence, that search often
rendering ordinary language useless. This phenomenon may be observed
in a Quaker pamphlet whose prose surface is suddenly broken up by unan-
nounced eruptions of verse. The Quaker Dorothy White exhorts her readers
to heed God's word: "Arise, shake off the dust of the Earth, and Christ shall
give you Life. And this is the Day of God's Visitation, and of free Love and
everlasting Consolation, wherein Salvation is founded unto the Inhabitants
of the Earth," but prose is too frail a medium to convey her message. The
text melts, mid-sentence, into poetry:

Great is the Sea, whose blessed bounds are Love,
Whose Compassions her own doth move.
Great is his Love that now hath led us home,
To sit again upon our Father's Throne.
Great is the Light by which now we do see
The Glory of our Father Abrah'ms day:
Great is the Love by which we overcome;
Our Vict'ry stands in the beloved Son.
And in the Love and Fulness of his Power
In us, is shining in this glorious hour.
And all must come within unto the Light,
T'live in that Pow'r, which gives the blind their sight.[13]

Interrupted by the spirit of victory, White echoes the biblical song of Miriam
on the shores of the Red Sea, her poetry jubilant with a vitality her prose
cannot compass. Rude though it is, the phrases offer a jangly beat, where
the repeated opening rhythms of "Great is the Sea/ his Love/ the Light"

introduce each next line with the bumpy, even syncopated, measure of trochee and iamb pushed up close together. Her desire is to "live in that Pow'r": the closest this speaker can come is through poetry, whose forceful effusions *become* a sign of God's power to move the spirit.

There is, however, the worry that by writing poetry, the poet may erroneously prize the external forms rather than the inner meaning. With the fervent anticeremonialism that is at his theological core, the Dissenting poet faces a complicated, and perhaps morally dubious task. Because poetry is a formal creation, one anonymous poet fears, it offers an opportunity for hypocrisy:

> External Forms may seem devout,
>   Yet no Acceptance find;
> Nor all the Pomp of Words, without
>   A correspondent Mind.[14]

Ever defensive about writing poetry in the first place, the Quaker promises not to abuse the power of words, and this goes some way towards explaining a turn to a plain style.[15]

The Quaker friend to John Milton, Thomas Ellwood, knows inspiration is under attack in his own day, aware his poetry will fall upon hostile ears:

> Should there be of that scoffing Stock,
> Who are so destitute of GRACE
>   They at the SPIRIT's *Infl'ence* mock;
> To such my Muse no Pleasure brings,
> Who scorn the Power by which she sings.[16]

Those "destitute of Grace" will only offer scoffing, mockery, and scorn, and the poem sets up an acoustic contrast between the vowel sounds of "o" (scoffing Stock, mock, scorn) and "i" (SPIRIT, *Infl'ence*, brings, sings), along with a rivalry between the harsh consonantal "k" sounds and the soothing "ng" (*In'flence*, brings, sings). The aural link between "destitute" and "SPIRIT" perhaps hints that the distance between the two is not so great, if only the poetry can smooth the kinks out of language. Edgy about the attitudes of a Butler or a Swift, Ellwood suggests that pleasure in his poetry requires readers to remain humble to that "Power" which inspires it; this is not simply a religious view, it is an aesthetic program.

Quaker writers often show how the spirit's motivation bore literary consequences. Katharine Evans and Sarah Chevers' simple hymn, composed during their imprisonment on Malta, insists upon it:

> How gracious is our God,
>   and kind to Israel,
> With us he doth make his Abode
>   his presence doth us fill.[17]

These lines of heartbreaking plainness betray the Quaker's enmity towards set forms, and raise questions about how art may suffice to mediate God's presence. Likewise, the Quaker John Kelsall epitomizes worries about the proper *use* of his faculties by a pledge to God:

> Let not my Fancy wander to mis-use
> That understanding which thou shalt infuse
> Nor 'ere my thoughts so far divided be
> But they may meet again and enter still in thee.[18]

As these lines express the Quaker mystical unity between human and God, they also show the aspiring poet daring to command his deity: "thou shalt infuse." The worry is about right use of the faculties; God has granted them to humans as a tenure, not as a possession. What pleasure they may bring is not for the individual, but to be returned to God.

The Baptist Benjamin Keach (1640–1704) moves towards heaven in his hymn, echoing Exodus 19:4:

> My Soul mounts up with Eagles wings
> And unto thee dear God, she sings;
>   Since thou art on my side,
> My Enemies are forc'd to fly,
> As soon as they do thee espy;
>   *Thy Name be glorify'd.*[19]

Violent, impulsive, and stupendous, Dissenting poetry originates with God. The poetics of Dissent maintains a gap between human art and God's power in order to sustain a theology of prescience, justification by faith, and regeneration through grace. The paradoxes of an art that hides its artifice are evident. To believe that the divine could make an immediate presence in human language is also to defend an inspired poetics. With a source in the divine, raptures, hymns, and other ejaculations are represented as produced almost involuntarily.

One model of the divine poet was David, and Psalms again and again figure in Dissenting poetry.[20] In his poem "On David's Psalms," Richard Baxter cringes, as one who deems himself undeserving of God's attention; but at the same time, the Psalms serve as means for his spiritual arousal. His heart "panteth for that Grace/ Which may exalt it," but Baxter however finds it is "dull and heavy." David's psalms mockingly spur the poet to question his own ability to muster "coelestial fire":

> Here are the sacred words: Here's *David's* Lyre:
> But where's the quickening coelestial fire?
> I know the Eye of Heav'n is on my *Heart*:
> God looks my Soul should bear the chiefest part.
> It's winged Faith, and flaming Love within,
> That must the pleasant Melody begin:
> The holy Spirit must tune and touch each string;
> Else smoothest Verse will be a harsh dull thing;
> Display thy Love; shoot down thy vital Raies!
> Teach this cold heart the works of Love & Praise.
> O then, what Life and Joy these Psalms will bring,
> When it's thy Spirit, and my Soul that sing!
> And though low streins with stops, are here my best,
> Yet Perfect Love and Praise shall be my REST.[21]

Mourning the separation between *res* and *verba*, that difference which at once provokes both his anger and his desire, Baxter reaches for an unmediated union with the Holy Spirit. Wanting to be touched directly, the poet is transformed by the musical figures into David's humble instrument, the lyre. Baxter imagines himself as the component parts of the stringed assembly, and he longs to be *tuned*, so that he can *bear* the *melody*, the *chiefest part*. In a rejection of his humility, however, Baxter loosens his frustrations, charging the Holy Spirit with his commands: "Display thy Love; shoot down thy vital Raies!/ Teach this cold heart the works of Love & Praise." The energy of the Holy Spirit breaks up two sets of repeated rhymes surrounding this couplet, as if Baxter is calling attention to the attempt at liberation from the bondage of poetic form; the constraints of poetic form are perhaps an emblem for his dejected human condition of cold corporeality. The end of the poem, however, leaves us holding a musical "rest," a pause, and this is an ambiguous conclusion. Has the poet earned his song? Or has he just given up?

Baxter's poem is all the more unsettling because of its recognition that the divine gaze is for ever observing the poet's heart, along with his paltry attempts at verse. Thus there is a circular round of theatricality inherent to this poetic creation: Baxter performs for his maker by making a work of art. But he also asks that God perform for him on demand ("Display thy Love"): there is an apparent impasse about subject and object. This ontological problem is fudged when the poet resolves he's done his *best* and ceases his creation. Perhaps, too, this is why he moves to the acoustic register in his figures. This work of art, like David's psalms and like the glory of creation, is ultimately meant to be beheld, but God's gaze is positively unnerving for the struggling artist. Sole authorship is denied, but the work of art exists uneasily in the space between two objects, the psalms and the heart of the poet. Beyond that is silence. Pushed to its limit, a poetics of immediate presence was a reaction not against pleasure, nor against sense; it was, rather, part of the early modern experience of transforming pleasure to reconcile it with materiality.

THE SONG OF SONGS AND HEBRAIC POETICS

Nowhere is the dialectical relation between worldly desires and spiritual longing more clearly seen than in the Dissenting renditions of the biblical book, the Song of Songs. Over the course of the seventeenth century, this biblical poem became almost the exclusive property of the nonconformists. I have found thirty-two commentaries and works of poetry uniquely dedicated to the Song of Songs published during the period 1640 to 1700, twenty-four of which are Puritan and just four Anglican; among these are sixteen different titles of volumes of poetry written in imitation or paraphrase of the book – and of these, only four are Anglican texts.[22] The Anglican vicar John Lloyd, hoping to wrest the poem from Dissenting hands, denounced those translators and adapters who had "exposed her, and that Fairest of Ten Thousand to people of the world in the vilest of Pilgrims weeds." Writing a dedicatory poem to Lloyd's volume, John Speed condemned those readers, patently nonconformist, who might object to its fine style: "... they hate to see/ Our Words, and Lines in Couplings to agree/ It looks too like abhorr'd Conformity."[23] Dissenting renditions of the Song of Songs also did political work against a libertine ethos and aesthetic practice.

The Song of Songs was the instance of "Sion's Songs" that offered the greatest challenge for the English Puritan exegete precisely because it was the most mysterious; through it was rendered the complex relation between God and his people in terms that were patently erotic. It was also a primary model of otherworldly creativity. John Milton praised the Song of Songs, writing that "The Scripture also affords us a divine pastoral Drama in the Song of *Salomon*, consisting of two persons, and a double *Chorus*, as *Origen* rightly judges."[24] The obscurity of the book paralleled much of the incertitude regarding God's ways, but that unclarity opened up the space for human intervention and interpretation. Because of its "enigmatical phrases and dark speeches," wrote the Congregational minister John Robotham, it "admitteth more variety of interpretation" than any other book of the Bible.[25] Commentators quarreled over whether or not the book was to be taken as a prophecy, and if it was, then at what date it would be fulfilled.[26]

In defending an affective relation to the divine, Dissenters turned to the Song of Songs for its strong emotional impact. "Oh who can chouse, but long to look, & pry,/ Into this blessed, glorious mistery," wrote the Presbyterian Julia Palmer in echoing the Song of Songs to describe her relationship with Christ. The Presbyterian John Collinges writes: "Can a reasonable Soul read of him who is the eternal Son of God, bringing the Soul of his Creature into his *Banqueting-house*, and making his *Banner over it Love*; and not find it self melted into his embraces, and cry out as the Spouse, in this Chap. *Stay me with Flaggons, comfort me with Apples, for I am Sick of Love?*"[27] The "as" blurs two meanings here: the Soul might cry out *in performing the role of* the spouse; or the Soul might cry out *in imitation of* the Spouse's *actions*. As a performance, the Christian inhabits the role, lives the allegory, and makes a possible gender translation to female; as an imitation, the Christian wills some distance between *res* and *verba*, and there is no need for gender translation. By evoking both positions, Collinges leaves room for the reader to select a stance, and leaves open the possibility of gender exchange. This is a crucial theological point in debates over the sacrament, reiterating the conflict about whether the sacrament was a memorial of the Last Supper or its re-enactment. Translating the mystery of the sacrament onto the very act of reading, the religious interpreter would perform both rituals, that of re-enactment as well as remembering. Reading itself could become sacramental.

Pleasure is both to be experienced and yet it must be the right sort of pleasure: "Oh the unspeakable pleasure that a due understanding of this sacred Song must needs affect every Spiritual Christian with!" Collinges rhapsodizes.[28] Against the abuse of the flesh, the Presbyterian William Guild hoped to direct the physical response into a proper course: "The serious and sanctified meditation whereof as it requireth an elevated and heavenly disposed mind," he cautioned, "so it cannot likewise but ravish such a soul with spirituall joy and comfort, and inflame the same with a holy fervour of heavenly affection"; more simply, James Durham effused, "so few can read this Song, but they must fall in love with it."[29] The text may licitly exert physical effects on the body. As reading is intended to produce bodily affect, erotic passion may even have a place in the Puritan imaginary. Richard Turner, who would be ejected from his vicarage in Preston in 1662, hopes "that such fire should raise/ Some sparks within thy soul, and make it blaze/ With flames of love." In the conclusion of his verse adaptation, he hopes that his readers "Thaw thy frozen, chill desires/ At these warm, and melting fires," the body giving evidence of the spiritual devotion of the saint.[30]

The Dissenters' fascination with the Song of Songs is a curious one, however, since part of their interest was in denying precisely those qualities that to many readers make it great: the physical love between two bodies that is depicted in an exquisite variety of images, textures, colors, tastes, and odors. Especially in the Restoration, with the flourishing industry in libertine writing, Dissenters chose the Song of Songs to do ideological service, reforming sexual desire and reshaping earthly relations, insisting on a chastened body and a chastened poetics, reinventing pleasure by directing it toward the otherworldly.[31] Devotional writers in the Restoration fought a holy war against libertine ideologies, just as the newly exuberant sexual culture was a backlash against a perceived repression in the Cromwellian era, as James Turner puts it, "frenetic hedonism became a badge of anti-Puritan loyalty."[32] While all around them, the discourses of libertinism were investigating and amplifying carnal desires of the here and now, the Dissenters' discipline of desire and their cultivation of an alternative poetics worked in two contrary directions: it hoped to shore up monogamous heterosexual relations within the realm of the family; and it also projected desire forward into the future towards communion with God.

Spiritual longing and sexual longing have often intersected in discourses of devotion. Christian texts dealing with the love of humans for their God, or with the love of God for humans, often evoke sexually charged language; they often blur or reverse gender roles in figuring that relation.[33] In the Song of Songs, "the Earnest desire of the Church is set down under the similitude of a love," wrote the Congregational Dover divine John Robotham, who curbs desire to reconcile it with earnestness. Robotham, a former "teacher" in Colonel Sydenham's regiment, who was called a "wheelwright and Anabaptist...a mere tradesman," launches a defense, classic since Origen, of the epistemology of erotic signification in the Bible.[34] For eroticism to be rendered spiritual, and for spirituality to be rendered erotic, there must be some resignification of the body, both as a material object and as substance to be registered through signification. Opening his verse adaptation, Richard Turner warded off the erotic reading at the same time as he called attention to it: "All you that cast your eies upon this Book/ Remember it is holy; Do not look/ To satiate your carnal palat here,/ This fountain's pure, and all the streames are clear."[35] The Song of Songs gives not the odor of the body but the perfume of the spirit.

The Baptist hymn writer John Reeve, in rewriting the Song of Songs 1:2 in Hymn 4, gives no personae to his speakers. Instead, he transforms the drama into a personal plea:

> Love me, my dearest Jesus, love me,
>> And shed that Love, and let me see
>> A Letter written full of Love,
>> And superscribed unto me.[36]

In its plainness and vulnerability, this represents the essence of Dissenting poetry. In an unorthodox, punning movement, Reeve makes the spirit become the letter, a reversal of the letter killing and the spirit giving life. The interpretations transform kisses into words, and dematerialize the relation altogether. Likewise, Benjamin Keach dispenses with the physical kiss altogether, opening his Hymn 91, "He is altogethr Lovely," thus:

> The gracious Words that drop
>> From Christ's sweet Mouth so free,
> Are sweeter than the sweetest Myrrh,
>> To all that do Love Thee.[37]

Kisses have become words. Further, there is no personal "I," no speaker in the hymn, as the impersonal "all that do Love Thee" replaces the first person of the original text.

Voiding a carnal reading, John Reeve voiced the twin possibilities signified by the Song of Songs in his subtitle, *Spiritual Hymns upon Solomon's Song: Or, Love in the Right Channel* (1684), pointing to a "wrong" channel for love. Reeve laid bare the contrast in his prefatory poem:

> Hands off you venemous Creatures; you that draw
> The rankest Poyson from the sweetest flow'rs:
> Yea, that by Rigor of a lustful Law,
> Would force Divine love to conform to yours.
> I fear, if you should light upon this Book;
> You'd force it from it self, and like a love-song look.[38]

Figuring misreading as a kind of rape ("force it from it self"), Reeve also evokes the language of conformity and compulsion common in Anglican and nonconformist Restoration discourse. To read with purity is to resist conformity; like resisting other ceremonial behaviors, it is to render one vulnerable to persecution. Reeve points to those "lustful" readers who are driven by private passion to a singular law ("yours"), rather than those who subscribe to the universal love, that of God. Likewise, Christopher Jelinger, the radical separatist, chastised those who preferred pleasures of the flesh to those spiritual delights offered by Christ. Evoking the language of the Song of Songs, Jelinger did war against contemporary libertine culture: "Christ, who should lye even all Night betwixt your brests lieth a farr off in the bosomes of his reall Saints, and some wanton Dames and Carnall Companions must be neere to you, because the love of Christ is not in you."[39]

Pleasure is admitted, but the full enjoyment of it delayed. John Bunyan's *Book for Boys and Girls* (1686) offered to its little readers a poem "Of the Spouse of Christ," promising sensual pleasure as the reward for fending off lust in this world. Anticipating the experience of heaven, the poem represents the transformation of unholy to holy: "Instead of Filth, she now has her Perfumes,/ Instead of Ignominy, her Chains of gold:/ Instead of what the Beauty most consumes,/ Her Beauty's perfect, lovely to behold."[40] The young reader here is permitted to indulge in fantasies of scent and texture, consumable sight and pleasure, but the look is forward in, and out of, time.

Nonetheless, reading *A Book for Boys and Girls* was not to be without its pleasures. In the meantime, the godly should behave, as Benjamin Keach advised, as the waiting lover of Canticles. They should prepare to "come, haste away without delay/ With all speed and endeavor" with the beloved.[41] This apocalyptic scheme was another interpretive tool with which to wrest the poem from literal meaning.[42] The great hymn writer Keach frequently evoked Canticles in his prolific writings, entwining his theological lessons with worldly desires. The leading Calvinistic Baptist divine was punished for seditious writings in 1664, but he nonetheless preached from the pillory. In the waning years of Puritanism in the seventeenth century, he attempted to hold the Calvinist predestinarian line against assaults on theology from moderate nonconformists. The enormous success of his writing spread his backward-looking views widely, however; his *War with the Devil* ran through twelve editions between 1673 and 1702.[43] Keach's bookseller John Dunton later remembered the author's popularity, confessing that his "*War with the Devil* and *Travels of True Godliness*, (of which I printed ten thousand) will sell to the end of time."[44] With dramatic detail and a good sense of pace, Keach translated the theology of romance into a narrative, aiming to reform youth in his epic poem *The Glorious Lover* (1678). While elsewhere, Keach could locate his narrative with precision in the human history of his own time, in *Distressed Sion Relieved* (1689) for instance, which chronicles the years of persecution of Dissenters in England during the Exclusion crises, particularly from 1680 to 1688; or in *Sion in Distress* (1681), lamenting present persecution, here he chose sacred history as his time frame, and avoided topical allusion to English history. This evacuation of historical referent parallels the evacuation of sexuality and corporeality: the true was outside time, or in a time scheme so vast that particularities mattered little: indeed, as the millenarians could remark with Solomon, "There was nothing new under the sun."[45]

The pleasures of pagan and carnal literature were contrasted to purer pleasures in Keach's *The Glorious Lover*, written for the young. This work was an early modern bestseller, running to four editions in twenty years. The book was directed towards youths of both sexes. With romance as his narrative genre, the goal of the story was "conversion," and there would also lurk the opposite possibility: that instead of arriving at heaven, the hero would go to hell. The frontispiece illustration of the 1679 edition shows a two-part story of a young woman who has gone bad (see Figure 9).[46] In the upper image, she is finely dressed, in "gallantry," and she yet possesses inward beauty. At the beginning of the reader's journey into *The Glorious Lover*, the virgin elicits sympathetic identification from readers. Her present existence is shown to be precarious however: the physical image in the book poses a threat from the beginning. If it is desire that is offered by the title of the work, so it is fear that compels readers forward: conversion begins with the arousal of terror. She sits in a landscape surrounded by the beauties – perhaps the follies – of earthly pleasure here represented by the cultivated rows of tulips and other flowers; tulipmania becomes an emblem for worldliness. Like Eve, she peers up at a serpent threatening from a tree. In the second panel, gone is the garden scene: she has fallen. Pursued by angry angels, the lass is driven towards the fiery depths of hell, where the devil himself awaits her embrace. In contrast to the virginal Little Miss Muffett among the tulips, this young woman has been stripped of her clothes. Was there erotic pleasure in observing her naked body, with the exposed nipple, the long, unbound hair, and the firm thigh? By his image, Keach spells out what literature his book is staked against: the "cursed products of a *wanton Muse*," and "trifling *Fables… Romances*" seen as "poisoned froth,"

> Which only tend to nourish Rampant Vice,
> And to Prophaneness easie youth entice;
> Gild o'er with Wit, black Venom in they take,
> And 'midst gay Flowers hug the lurking Snake.[47]

Secular literature may indeed be enticing; it may seduce young readers much as Eve was seduced in the garden, as depicted on the printed frontispiece. Yet, above the image of the gallant young woman, the fable suggests that fine clothing and the joys of tulip gardening are not in themselves sinful; she still possesses her "inward beauty." That finery and comfortable habitat

The Virgin drest up in her Gallantry
The glorious state o'th' soul doth signify
Before the Fall. Her outward Robes decl...
Her inward Beauty was beyond compar...
But naked stript, when satan did deceive her
And Hells wide jaws stood ready to receive h...

to front y' title.   I. Oliver. Scul...

Figure 9 Frontispiece to Benjamin Keach, *The Glorious Lover* (1679).

are not the *cause* of her great loss; although their disappearance registers the pain she is suffering as she enters hell. As the romance plot works to wrest this young woman from earthly desires towards a Glorious Lover, at the same time this opening image suggests that one may be godly and live in this world as well, even wear nice clothes.

Keach is the great fabulist of romance genre as spiritual erotics. Justifying his fictional approach, he echoes Herbert's dictum in his preface: "A Verse may catch a wandring Soul, that flies/ Profounder Tracts, and by a blest surprize –/ Convert delight into a Sacrifice –." Keach's own epic itself belongs to the genre of romance, tells the story of the travails of the soul as she is confronted by one or another assailant, and finally reaches her destination in the Court of the Divine Lover:

> Here's no such danger, but all pure and chast;
> A Love most fit by Saints to be imbrac'd:
> A *Love 'bove Women: Beauty*
> As none can be enamour'd on too much.
> Read then, and learn to love truly by this,
> Until thy Soul can sing (Raptur'd in Bliss)
> *My Well-beloved's mine, and I am his.*[48]

A reformation of romance serves a divine purpose, and tells the story of True Romance: the love of God for his people.

The drive to unearthly sensuality did strange things to the assignment of gender, moreover: "A Love 'bove Women," as Keach puts it, aimed at the male reader who must undergo a gender exchange in order to read in the position of the female soul. Thomas Ager also claimed the Song of Songs was a poem of love, "wonderful, and passing the Love of Women."[49] In reading a book that wishes to turn young men and women away from the seductions of amorous literature towards a divine love, however, Keach's male reader would also have to forego traditional heroic masculinity and surrender, as the soul does, to the male Glorious Lover. The Song of Songs sanctions Keach's whole work, so much so that he closes his proem referring to it, "*My well-belov'd's mine, and I am his.*" Through imitation of the Song of Songs, Keach translates gender from male to female, but he also shows sexual desire to be part of a human condition that points to what is essentially beyond gender. The appeal to the Beloved asserts an apocalyptic framework, a redemptive scheme outside history that matches the structure of waiting and longing of those persecuted in the present.

If Keach hoped to inflame "A Love 'bove Women" in *The Glorious Lover*, that fantasy would be open for the female as well as the male saint. Keach's epic relates the affairs of the soul as she is persecuted and then eventually finds (and, important theologically, *chooses*) her true love (259–61). With heaving "ravishments," Keach repeats conventional terms for lover's sighs (later the soul herself exhales: "this Celestial Fire/ That's kindled in my breast, comes from above./ And sets my Soul into this flame of Love" [260]), a love properly transvalued away from any earthly objects. Sexual eroticism may be deployed in the service of evangelical Christianity. But in that final encounter between soul and lover, a remarkable gender change happens. When the soul at last reaches "her" destination and unites with her Lover, "she" bursts out in song:

> He is my All,
> My soul's to him united,
> As *Jonathan*'s to *David*, who delighted
> So much in him that in his greatest trouble
> Dear *Jonathan* did his affections double;
> When *David* was in great distress and fear,
> Then did his love and loyalty appear.
> (*Glorious Lover*, 261)

Here the allegory no longer identifies the soul as female.[50] To become "all" is to divest of a particular gender marking and to assume another.

In Dissenting renditions of the Song of Songs, sultry kisses were transformed into chaste letters or words, lovers translated into friends, a relation of equality. During the interregnum, the Westminster Assembly interpreted the love relation in the Song of Songs as "Friend, companion next to me, or whatever else that can express kindnesse and love, is compassed in this word."[51] Friendship – the equal relationship among men and women – is the image taken for the denomination of the sect of Quakers as "Friends." It is the best way to transcend the limitations of rank, sexuality, and embodied hierarchy, as Quaker Thomas Ellwood writes in "An Epistle to a Friend": "Who in true Friendship are combin'd,/ Have in two Bodies but one Mind"; or as the Quaker Mary Mollineux puts it, "to communicate/ Pure Streams of Love."[52] Dissenting women also took up the Song of Songs, reworking the terms of gender hierarchy to fashion more egalitarian relations or autonomous relations to their communities through God than were possible in the traditional family hierarchy.[53] The translation of gender in the Song of Songs also opened up utopian possibilities for equality of relation. The discourse of friendship, like Levellerism, was one of the most significant modes for figuring the relation of equals in the early modern period. The discourse of friendship, however, leapt over differences of matter, rank, gender, position, or age. Though it began as an aristocratic male genre, with a lineage from classical Roman stoicism, nonetheless in Puritan fantasy, friendship was identity without borders, without particularity, without gender: it was a space of freedom. The discourse of friendship was the one way to neutralize gender difference and ultimately relieve the pressures of bodily difference and bodily attraction; but it also served to replace an earthly economy of material interest and exchange with a wholly spiritual economy. In a political reading, moreover, the notion of a spiritual relationship could offer protest against the dominant relations of the here-and-now, providing a powerful image of equality in an age fascinated by external marks of hierarchy, whether gender, rank, or nationality. Figuring a relationship of equals, this fantasy could point to an opening up of a radically democratic space for free exchange. Reworking the erotic relations in the traditional biblical texts thus allowed for experiments in social revolution.

READING AND WRITING HERBERT

Just as the Bible was made a common treasury, so, too, were the devotional poems of George Herbert. These set the gold standard for spiritual lyric for several generations after the posthumous publication of *The Temple* in 1633, a volume that went into eleven editions by the end of the century. Only the low church Francis Quarles offered competition with both his *Barnabus and Boanerges* (1644) and his *Divine Poems: Sions Sonnets* (1630) totalling ten by century's end. Quarles provided a means for ordinary readers to attempt a spiritual relationship through poetry, as well as presenting a daring anti-Laudian muse. To Restoration Dissenters, Herbert offered not merely the timelessness of a great poet, the man speaking across time to men. Aiming for those qualities of "transparency or self-effacement," as Helen Vendler has characterized them, Herbert's poems present a fiction of an authorless, timeless, impersonal abstraction, but, to the early modern godly, Herbert revealed the most intimate of self-scrutinizing reflections by his purifying impulse, a personal devotion.[54] Dissenters, long used to the practice of biblical allusion and an inspired poetics of purifying language and form, exercised these habits on George Herbert's poetry, seen as a powerful artistic model of the authentic utterances of souls striving for spiritual truth and a proper sacrifice to God. The poems in *The Temple* breathed life into a new generation of poets in the Restoration period. Herbert's poetry seemed to invite all – low, high, women, poorly educated, and humble – to come in by its aesthetic plainness and abstraction.

Nonconformist allusions to Herbert were many and varied in the later seventeenth century as the poet became the standard for an astonishing range of literary and theological activity, from many points along the theological spectrum. On their frontispieces and title pages (Samuel Crossman, John Bunyan, Samuel Bury); in educating children (Thomas White); in their theological controversy (Peter Sterry, John Bryan, John Reynolds), and especially in their poetry, citing Herbert became all but orthodox for the Dissenters, for whom the poet stood for sacred authenticity in a corrupt age. Richard Baxter recommends Herbert's riddle "A Poor mans Rod when thou dost ride, is both a Weapon and a Guide," in defending a doctrine of earthly poverty in *Saints Everlasting Rest*.[55] Baptist Thomas Vincent counseled godliness to the suffering victims of the fire and plague by citing Herbert; the nonconformist publisher John Dunton advised readers of *The Athenian Mercury* that Herbert was especially appropriate to women readers.[56] Richard Baxter signed off his massive tome, *Saints Everlasting Rest*, with a verbatim transcription of Herbert's "Home," as if that poem summed up the whole of his preceding work.[57] Indeed, several editions of Herbert's *Temple* that preceded Walton's *Life* were published by the known nonconformist London bookseller Philemon Stephens, whose long association with Herbert was passed on to his publisher son, and then his wife, Dorothy Stephens, who licensed Herbert's poems after the death of her husband in 1670.[58] Philemon Stephens was a mainstay in Dissenting publishing; it was Stephens, for instance, who brought out twelve editions of the works of the divine John Owen after 1643. As Kathleen Lynch has argued, "*The Temple* proves to be promiscuously available to multivalent readings and competing genealogical claims of church disciplines."[59]

Nonconformists found in Herbert much to justify their resistance to state-sponsored outward practices.[60] They also made Herbert's poetics a paradigm for their poetry of devotion, laying claim through him to an alternate set of literary values to those of Restoration public poetry. In the defense of their nonconformity, then, Herbert served in both an ecclesiological and a literary struggle to forge identities outside orthodoxy. Robert H. Ray has concluded that roughly seventy percent of allusions and adaptations of Herbert in the later seventeenth century were Anglican–royalist.[61] This is however a misplaced emphasis; as we recover the Dissenting literary legacy and look beyond works of established literary value we will find a plethora of allusions found in low-church, sectarian, and Dissenting productions of lesser literary merit. Although Herbert was transformed in the Restoration into an Anglican icon, that transformation was part of a contest; and it was not definitive.[62] Eighteenth-century Dissent kept Herbert in high visibility: John Wesley was a sure apprentice; he included no fewer than forty-seven poems from *The Temple* in his many collections of hymns and devotional poems, and brought out *Select Parts of Mr. Herbert's Sacred Poems* in 1773.

For nonconformists, Herbert was the most personal of poets, expressing a multitude of inner states with agonizing precision. Herbert's works were a mother lode for imitators in the divine mode. One modern reader bemoans the "unscrupulous" thefts from Herbert "in an age of indiscriminate psalm-phrase borrowing without acknowledgment"; another derides the way a later author "shamelessly appropriates" the poet.[63] Robert Ray and Helen Wilcox have tracked the voluminous literature of these would-be Herberts, and Helen Vendler devotes a chapter of her study of Herbert to his successors, many of whom come in for near contempt.[64] Yet by attending to their adaptations of Herbert, we can learn much about the literary values grounding dissenting poetry: Dissenters appealed to Herbert in creating their own literary tradition. They were aroused by his poetics of immediacy, a simplicity that inspired them to take up pens and open hearts. They vaunted an alternate literary economy in which ownership of literature was open to all and to none, since all human creativity properly came from, and belonged to, God.

Herbert saturates the Dissenting spectrum. As the Quaker John Perrot works with Herbert's materials in "To the Children of the Day," the imitator reduces himself to silence as the poem itself shrinks down to a single point:

> This *thing* may many *prove*,
> behold, *stretcht wings* of Sion's Turtle *Dove*,
> in swiftest *course* of *flight* do *move*,
> with *weight* of *wooings* unto *love*;
> A little simple *Wren*,
> waits with the *Pen*,
> in *clear* sight
> to write,
> *Amen.*

A truncated version of Herbert's "Easter-wings," this pattern poem is perhaps less ambitious than its predecessor.[65] It is not that Herbert's stylistic intentions did not succeed, but that they need to be constantly invoked, made present, in order to express anew the heartfelt passions. Citation is performance, where iteration seeks a renewed experience of the holy, but where the visible signs of that experience yield little that is new; indeed they are meant to be a sign of the same. The poem is concerned with a theme of proof, promising to prove "this thing," that which is left unsaid in the poem – a matter for the heart, invisible to the human eye. But what needs proving is indeed audible, heard in the repetition of sounds of the dove's wings, the whooshings of "s"s and "w"s, and the vowels of the long "o" in prove/rove/move/love/wooings: all these give the poem movement, the rustlings of the Holy Spirit, felt upon the body. As the poem reaches its end, however, the windy sounds recede, and we are in the quieter, stiller scene of waiting, of writing. Yearning for authenticity, the Dissenter nonetheless indulges in imitation; but he has lopped off the second half of the pattern, as if he writes with clipped wing. Or is the shape of the poem rather that of the nib of a pen? More fitting the humility of the Quaker author, the poem does not build up again and end with a long line, but instead closes with a single word – then silence, the space for prayer.

Perrot had courted censure from the Quaker leader George Fox for his poetry. Perrot, however, saw poetry not as formalism, but as an authentic expression of the inner self: however, the contradictions are visible in the degree to which Perrot dabbled with Herbertian patterning and form. Perrot had traveled abroad to evangelize – he even sought a meeting with the Pope – and was imprisoned and tortured by the Inquisition for eighteen weeks, remaining in prison in Rome between 1658 and 1661; upon his return to England he visited Isaac Pennington in 1662, and then traveled to Ireland and the New World. Against the Quaker leader George Fox's objections, whose disapproval he responded to whilst in prison in Rome, Perrot defended his practice of versifying. As Perrot was reported writing to the Quaker Francis Howgill, "Touching Verses, I told him [Howgill] that if they offended any Friend in *England*, when I sent them from *Rome*, if any had (Brother-lie) turned the sense of them into Prose, to have taken off the offence from any; I believe that I should have taken it dearly – well."[66] Because of his strife with Fox and within the Quaker community, Perrot sought voluntary exile in the New World, traveling through Barbados, Maryland, Jamaica, and Virginia, and dying in Barbados in 1665, although the schism he ignited lasted into the 1670s when the Quaker leadership confronted the issue of standards for worship.

Nonconformist poets, choosing freedom outside the church rather than constraint within it, fashioned their poetic tradition upon a devotional model of authorship. The Presbyterian Nicholas Billingsley, an ejected minister working out of the Forest of Dean, was a self-styled "Private Chaplain to the Illustrious and Renounced Lady Urania The Divine and Heavenly Muse." With his allusion to Urania as a patron, Billingsley marks his participation in a literary economy that was an alternative to that of courtly literary or ecclesiastical patronage. Billingsley too drew inspiration from

Herbert's pattern poetry, prefacing his *Treasury of Divine Raptures* (1667) with a poem entitled "The Invocation," which inscribes the double wings of Herbert's Easter poem in a like act of annunciation that is also an announcement of a poetic career:

I.

O Lord,

Who only art

The Greatest and the Best,

An ever-flowing Fount

Whence Grace & Glory, & all Goodness springs:

Afford

Thy Spirit; Impart

Thy gracious aid; devest

My soul of sin, that she may mount

To thee, and live above terrestrial things.

II.

O Thou,

Who didst inspire

The Prophets, that did use

In sacred Canto's heretofore

To celebrate thy great and glorious Name,

Fill now

With sprightly fire

My Heav'n-descended Muse,

And grant that she may evermore

Thy deathless praises to the World proclaim.[67]

The poem's two parts pull in contrary movements, and they represent the tension between heaven and earth. Inspiration functions something like a contract between two parties: in the first part, the soul mounts upward, and the strong, long end-rhymes (springs/things) evoke a silent third, the "wings" of Herbert's poem, or those of the Holy Spirit. In the second part, the muse is to descend, to answer the call of the poet, whose plea for assistance follows the logic of then-and-now: "heretofore... Fill now." That spirit which came to the prophets, illuminating those who spoke in sacred cantos, is asked to descend upon this poet, completing an invocation that is at once a citation and a prayer. To match the strong, long end-rhymes (Name/Proclaim), the hidden rhyme for this second part is "fame," a word that is banished, but barely repressed from this divine economy. Rhyme in this poem serves to enclose, but also to reveal: by rhyme, "*Lord*" is linked with "*afford*"; the "*Muse*" with "*use*": these are actions, valued for their own sakes, existing to enact a divine transaction.

In contrast to Herbert's poem, Billingsley's lines begin at the minimum and swell towards the capacious grace of the spread wing; his poem grows from a small trochaic beginning into a regular, ten-beat line. Each short line addresses God and begs, offering the simple request of a prayer, a single focus widening to a grand conspectus. Whilst Herbert's poem shrinks from an opening long line to admit the inadequacy of the human subject, Billingsley's swells to accommodate the effects of the spirit. The poet implores to be filled, and the lines that follow his request do just that, become filled with words and praises. Imitation of Herbert then might be not a secondary, lesser act of poetic creation, but instead a stance of humility, a proper disavowal of sole authorship and acknowledgment of indebtedness. After all, God is the author of all things, and to imitate Him is no shame. Imitation could be emendation, recitation with a difference; it could also be the evocation of a familiar past in order to prompt some future action.

Richard Baxter was a famous admirer of Herbert, recommending him in the introduction to his own collection of poetry in 1681: Herbert "speaks *to God* like one that *really believeth a God*, and whose business in the world is most *with God. Heart-work* and *Heaven-work* make up his Books."[68] If Baxter seems haunted by the possibility that one might *not* "really believeth a God," it is because Herbert's labors are summoned to serve as a talisman in an age in which hypocrisy or atheism were distinct dangers. As a prompt to do his own "heart-work," Herbert's books of poetry are themselves not "works," but rather, works are what they promote, works of heaven, heart, and worship. Baxter is no Quaker however. The labor of contact with the divine would involve the visible church: like Herbert, Baxter believed in an active and liturgically coordinated ministry. Herbert's poetry, like David's psalms, offers reminders and promptings to action, work taking place spontaneously in the heart of the reader or the poet.

Baxter's "Divine Love's Rest" summons its predecessor with its subtitle, "Written on *Herbert's* Poems," and yet this information offers only a provocation.[69] No lines in the poem are recognizable as Herbert's. Instead, Baxter seeks a state of being, a posture of mind and heart – "Divine Love's Rest" – which is beyond mediation, beyond language. The relationship between the two poets and the meaning of Herbert for Baxter, are private matters, although the relation prods fresh composition, a renewed spiritual yearning. Herbert's poetry ignites desires of animation and serves as the fetish to provoke and embody desires: but it cannot replace the work of the saint to achieve his own relationship with God in the meantime. All that "heart-work and heaven-work" are means to an end of "Divine Love's Rest," a favorite theme of the suffering Baxter, whose *Saints Everlasting*

Rest pointed toward that heavenly country where there was no work to be done. Herbert's poetry can serve as an aid and a travel guide, but not as a substitute for personal reflection and aspiration. Herbert is for Baxter, then, something to aid him in his spiritual ejaculations, a prompt to stir his soul towards God. Baxter's Herbert leads the reader to God, not to Herbert. "Herbert" becomes the sign of that sincere process.

Though Baxter's theology is miles from that of the Quakers, nonetheless in poetic practice, there are similarities in his attitudes towards predecessors and the original of poetry. The Quaker pupil of John Milton, Thomas Ellwood, erupts into Herbertian lines even without acknowledging them; it is as if Herbert has become so much a part of a rhetoric of devotion that his authorizing name is not necessary. Ellwood, the first editor of the *Journal* of the great Quaker leader George Fox, and an aspiring poet in his own right, who brought out a life of David in verse in 1712, like other Quakers, however, refused formal prayers and formal preaching, seeking instead to speak to one another with the spirit's prompting. Nonetheless Ellwood found a use for the literary, reconceived as for the people; as he put it in his preface to the reader of *Davideis*, "I write for common Readers." There is a literary imagination and aspiration in Ellwood as he contrasts his epic with Cowley's, even as he insists, "I don't affect the Title of Poet."[70] For Ellwood, Herbert speaks what is a general or collective mind. In "Love's Caveat," vice is dangerously disguised as virtue, and the speaker succumbs to temptation,

> And then too late,
> Cry O! my Fate!
> Was ever Grief like mine?
> I thought my Love
> Sprung from above,
> And that it was divine.[71]

Echoes of Herbert's "The Sacrifice" emerge as inadvertent emission from the oppressed Ellwood's groaning heart. Christ's dramatic monologue is translated into an autobiographical account and warning against the temptations of vice. Ellwood takes over Herbert's voice just as Herbert has taken over the voice of Christ on the cross observing his mocking persecutors. In Ellwood's poem, however, the speaker has become both persecutor and sufferer; he has absorbed Herbert's Christ's "mine" into a personal possessive pronoun, bringing Herbert's poem into a private application. Just as Christ's "mine" then becomes available for any reader, so does citing Herbert's language. Herbert becomes the sign authorizing the move from bodily sensation to otherworldly bodilessness. Herbert becomes a common resource, a most prized interpreter of the Bible; he becomes, like the Bible, a text open to resignification. His name sanctions others to use or rewrite the Bible, and his poetical practice authorizes others to engage in formal experiments in language and verse. The origin is at the same time always in view: God. Herbert becomes the sign but not the signature of authentic speech.

If Herbert became an open text, like Scripture, then he also became instantly accessible to, and even the property of, all. A wide range of readers, both Dissenters and orthodox, used Herbert for their own very personal, and different, purposes; Herbert's "The Altar" was adapted to commemorate the "martyrdom" of Charles I.[72] Found in commonplace books from a range of theological, political, and poetic vantage points, Herbert's poetry attracted many different readers in many different contexts. His poetry is found in compilations of love-lyrics as well as in the commonplace book of the republican Major-General Robert Overton, whose 360-page work was compiled in prison to honor his deceased wife, Ann (née Gardiner) who died in January 1665.[73] The transcriptions become a personal memorial, and the act of appropriation can be seen not only as a religious duty, "heart-work," but also as a democratic opening up of literary activity to include non-original acts of creation. The value of the work of art, as in Renaissance poetics more generally, was the use that could be made of it for spiritual or ethical reform.[74]

Usable in private moral reform, the poems found their way into nonconformist religious worship as well. Herbert's line lengths and meter were regularized in a 1697 adaptation of his verse into hymns, a collection which at times challenged Herbert's theology, and at others merely sought to make plain what was obscure in the original, and made the poems possible to be sung. To be sure, nonconformist authors in the Restoration needed to bring Herbert into line and up to date with their changed theology. For instance, the 1697 rendition rewrote the opening line of "Aaron," where Herbert's original reads, "Holinesse on the head." The altered version reads, "Holiness *written* on the Head." This minor clarification dispels an ambiguity in Herbert's original, settling the question of whether holiness inheres in the priest or is put upon him. The later version gives the nonconformist attack on priestly mediation by emphasizing that holiness is not *in* the priest, but is instead an aspect conferred by his office.[75] In its rendition of "Home," the hymn redactor omitted misogynistic sentiments ("what is this woman-kinde, which I can wink/ Into a blacknesse and distaste"[76]); and on the whole the volume reduced the degree of self-centeredness of

Herbert's spiritual quest and lyric persona. Herbert's legacy, then, was open to adapt to new circumstances.

The preface to the 1697 nonconformist hymnal based on Herbert's poetry honors the currency of its original: "*Mr. Herbert's* Poems *have met with so general and deserv'd Acceptance, that they have undergone Eleven Impressions near Twenty Years ago: He hath obtain'd by way of Eminency, the Name of* Our Divine Poet, *and his Verses have been frequently quoted in Sermons and other Discourses.*" Defending a wholesale emendation, the 1697 redactor explains why there is need for still one more version: "*yet, I fear, few of them have been Sung since his Death, the Tunes not being at the Command of ordinary Readers.*" An appeal to "ordinary readers" marks much of the discourse of borrowing and emendation that undergirds hymn writing; as we shall see, a language of justification for a Dissenting poetics of accessibility. The hymnodist continues, "*The attempt therefore, (such as it is) is to bring so many of them as I well could, which I judg'd suited to the Capacity and Devotion of Private Christians, into the* Common Metre *to be Sung in their Closets or Families.*"[77] By a new rendition, Herbert's poems will be put to use and will be made available to a wide group of readers, to circulate now in the private spaces of the bedroom and the public spaces of the godly home.

The author of *Select Hymns, Taken out of Mr. Herbert's Temple* does not disguise the theft: "I hope I shall not be counted a Plagiary seeing I claim nothing here as my own, but what they [i.e. Herbert and others] allow me, viz. a Liberty to Sing and use their Hymns, which I was no more able to do in their Metre and Tunes, than I was able to compose them as they did."[78] Herbert and other divine poets belong as much to all as one could say that "meter and tunes" or hymns belong to anyone. All that belongs to the creator of this volume is a right, a "liberty to sing": but this is a significant property of the subject. The Dissenters' appropriation of Herbert is thus a special case of a more general paradigm of devotional literary production involving reading and rewriting, citation and reiteration. In translating Herbert's writings, the 1697 hymnal served the "ordinary reader," and promised to speak to an experience that could be made unique to the individual. Hymns would be the means by which humans could partake in communal action, and singing could assist in the transformation of the home into the primary site of fellowship.

These transactions between poet and precursor, poet and public, and poet and God, point us towards several topics of vital importance in an account of Dissenting poetics. The literary artifact serves as a record and offers evidence for the existence of a realm of freedom and action; that realm may be self-enclosed, sealed off from the world of external action, or it may open out into the public sphere, as a work-in-progress. It is not dependent upon human creativity understood as individual innovation or self-mastery; instead the creativity is that of rearrangement, spontaneity, organization, appropriation: or it is a profoundly and mysteriously inspired work. In these creative acts are found the awareness that human productivity is contingent, liable to error, and that the products of human labor are open to emendation and addition. Dissenting writers, living in a world where a reconception of political activism led to an extraordinary flowering of poetry, recorded their inner travails in finding and maintaining a connection with God. During the English Revolution, such immediacy bore explosive political consequences, with the evolution of a new type of citizen, the radical saint, who saw God's handiwork in every action. After the Restoration, Dissenters continued to seek God's immediate presence, and the literary consequences make for omnivorous poetry. Along with revolutionizing the world through divinely prompted action, they revolutionize language and poetic tradition itself. All styles, devices, tropes, and genres seem insufficient to express a sincere connection between God and human, and so they are refashioned, as if only continual emendation can accomplish the arduous task of maintaining spontaneity.

Elizabeth Rowe sums it up: "Our maker thou, our great original/ We own thy right, and thee our father call."[79] Dissenters insisted that the origin of all poetry – indeed of all creation – be divine. The implications of a theocentric model of artistic originality and of authorial propriety have yet to be fully explored for the early modern period. In this theocentric scheme of creation, *all* human artifacts are copies. So much of Dissenters' writing can be dismissed as unoriginal, but their penchant for imitation is an engagement with the terms of ownership within a culture in which property relations, indeed the conception of private property, were undergoing change and formulation. Dissenters pledge a demotic, easily accessible poetry. The devotional poets, in offering a radical critique of human innovation in religious worship, also deny ownership of their works, their habits of borrowing refusing a closed notion of authorship. This is especially true for their composition of hymns, as we shall see in the next chapter.

CHAPTER 8

Hymn

Recalling the institution of a new psalm book, the ejected Presbyterian minister Henry Newcome (1627–95) tells an anecdote: "Some old people were offended that the old Tunes which served their Forefathers wold not content us," he recalls. "This a child about 7 years old, a great lover of singing, hearing asked what the old woman meant by four-fathers, for says he, I never heard that I had more than one."[1] This anecdote – yes, a Puritan joke! – raises the issues I shall be discussing in this chapter; how ancestry becomes freighted with ideological controversy; how the transformation of religious aesthetic form, here psalmody, over this turbulent period, aroused conflict and confusion; and how men, women, and children in Dissenting congregations loved singing. The genealogy of the literary genre of the hymn, psalmody's rough offspring, gives a superb example of the multiple possibilities for creating ancestry and enshrining a legacy.

The hymn, refined in the English Revolution in the fires of sectarian religion, achieved an ecumenical status unprecedented for a radical literature once the genre was stripped of its oppositional colors. Most of the great Augustan poets composed hymns. The multi-author, multi-sectarian collection, *A Collection of Divine Hymns and Poems*, shows the degree of depoliticization by the time of its publication in 1709 by its inclusion of hymns by John Dryden, John Dennis, John Norris, Katherine Philips, the Earl of Roscommon, Elizabeth Singer Rowe, and others. Whilst the political orientation of the eighteenth-century hymn writers reflects the adoption of the genre into the mainstream, nonetheless, the origin of the hymn was decidedly not orthodox, and its radicalism spoke an aesthetic ideology not of rare literary value but of accessibility, freshness, openness to revision; it was a vehicle for expressing links between divine and human action and for justifying politics by providence.

In ignoring the radical roots of this genre, scholars have underestimated the social function of the hymn for Dissenters across the early modern period.[2] While it is true that the absence of overt radical content in hymns in the early modern period largely accords with a depoliticized account, this underestimates the purpose of hymn singing in a broader culture of persecution, its role in building community and securing religious commitment in forms of worship and expression. The hymn, as we shall see, produced broad social meaning.

This chapter has two ends in mind: first, to trace the history of the hymn across the later seventeenth century as a story of depoliticization; and second, to articulate further what I call a Dissenting poetics. The hymn presents in microcosm a history of the taming of Puritan zeal over the turbulent politics and ecclesiology of the period; but it also mediates those shifts by its program of aesthetic values. With the hymn, we come to the genre that poses the most difficulty for a traditional literary analysis. Hymn writers do not aim, for the most part, to make works of art; they disdain esotericism, opacity, density of language, erudition, and courtliness. Instead, they propose an alternate set of literary values: openness, transparency, familiarity, and accessibility. For the Dissenter, hymns were meant to be sung by as many people as possible, in the privacy of the home as well as in communal worship. The traditional markers of literary value pose a special challenge for the hymn, since hymn writers disdain rhythmic individuality or irregularity as that would impede smooth singing. All aesthetic components become subordinate to issues of dissemination in performance. The authors of new hymns felt that previous hymns and psalms were too elaborate, and vaunted their own work as easier to sing.[3] The emphasis was both on the audience of God as well as on the communicability and access to the widest possible audience.

Further, hymns participated in the cultural war against worldliness. Hymn writers saw themselves in competition with secular art, and there are intriguing overlaps. The great Baptist hymnodist Benjamin Keach, the so-called father of the hymn, hoped to wean children, "who generally are taken with Verse, and are much addicted," from those "Songs and Ballads which generally tend to corrupt Youth."[4] The Scottish Presbyterian divine William Geddes, who was forced to resign from his post after refusing to take the Test Act in 1682, engaged in a transvaluation of pleasure in the title of his collection of hymns, *The Saints Recreation*, where his aim was "reclaiming (if possible) our profane vulgar from obscene, bawdy Songs (which are most scandalous to our profession) to more Christian-like divertisements."[5] Their alternative tradition sought to lead readers and singers to godliness, recreating pleasure as discipline. "They cannot chuse but sing," writes Elias Keach, of a hymn-writing dynasty; "being ravish'd with joy,/ In th'Presence of th'glorious King."[6]

Song is an especially powerful artistic medium; it depends on performance in time, oral and physical transmission, the aesthetic frames of melody, rhythm, and lyric, and also the kinesthetic modes of bodily expression and shared performance. Early modern England was a culture infused with song, from the street-sung popular ballads that memorialized bloody deeds, to the cries of the vendors and tradesmen, to communal singing in religious worship, and lullabies for children. Song is a kinesthetic art, and attention to the words of a lyric alone only gives us part of its meaning; as a physical action experienced by separated individuals, hymns brought people together to partake in their community – its memories, hopes, longings – through song. Hymns, like prayers, are performative utterances; they are also performances of the body: as George Wither put it, "Hither bring one consent/ Heart, and Voice, and Instrument."[7] Through hymns, Dissenters performed acts of recitation, commemoration, and ritual. Even if using set words or tunes, song expressed a heartfelt sincerity and fashioned individual experiences into a united one. The hymn was a distinctive Dissenting legacy, one bequeathed to the Anglican church and also to poetry in general.

The poetics of the hymn may be taken not solely in theological terms, but in terms of a mode of labor and action. The Baptist Joseph Stennett, calling upon that cliché of reluctant publication, claimed he brought out his volume of songs because members of his congregation had already made copies of the songs sung in his church, copies that had circulated with errors.[8] And yet, his disavowal was not to highlight his proprietorship over the fruits of his labor; instead, he wanted to be sure that the copies were accurate so that the hymns could be sung in unison with no mistakes. The human labor involved in creating the hymn was always to be secondary to its relation to the divine, and to a social economy. These relational qualities make for a theory of originality, composition, authorship, and aesthetic form that runs opposite to many modern assumptions about literary value and ownership.

With their attachment to spontaneity, sincerity, and freedom of action, Restoration period hymn writers and singers also made a political gesture: by writing and performing their own hymns, singers announced their resistance to the mandated forms of the state church. The radicalism I hope to trace then, is not strictly in the stated content of the hymns; it is in the way hymns organized social relations; how they consolidated a horizontal culture and a vertical tradition through performance and citation; and, not least, how they fashioned children and families into a coherent culture centered in the home.

In this chapter, we shall see how hymns were leeched of the overt political content of Revolutionary Puritanism but nonetheless maintained a radical course by other means. By their writing and singing hymns, Dissenters performed acts of opposition to the official state church. Further, hymns functioned in a cultural campaign, an aesthetic battle against neoclassical decorum that was also an ecclesiological battle against ceremony. Other radicalisms emerge: hymns are shown to contribute to a reformation of the family. And on the aesthetic front, the hymn is involved in a counter-tradition of antiproprietary aesthetics, contributing to a stream in the current of English literature whose values were not those of originality or uniqueness, but of accessibility, commonality, and spontaneity.

FROM REFORMATION TO REVOLUTION:
ENGENDERING VIOLENCE

The hymn was a child of the Protestant Reformation, its history in England mirroring theological and ecclesiastical conflicts over the early modern period.[9] Psalm singing had been legitimized by the Calvinistic wing of the Reformation that could brook no innovation nor addition to Scripture; so for most of the century, adaptations and translations of psalms formed a literary industry that included John Milton among others. The English Psalter (Sternhold and Hopkins) was first produced by John Day in 1562, and though it was rejected during the period of the English Revolution, it remained in use until the Tate and Brady version (1700) replaced it at the century's end.

The Psalms took on new political colors during the English Revolution. Cromwell himself is reported to have broken off the chase of royalist troops after the Battle of Dunbar to sing Psalm 117.[10] The hoary Sternhold and Hopkins, deemed too closely associated with the pre-civil war episcopacy, proved unsatisfactory for the radical elements now in power, and the 1640s saw the production of new paraphrases of the Psalms, with a new version meant to replace Sternhold and Hopkins commissioned by the General Assembly in 1647.[11] Milton may have worked with the committee established in April 1648 to translate the Psalms and replace Sternhold and Hopkins.[12] It was during this turbulent period that the genre of the hymn came of age. Publication of godly ballads may have declined over the course of the late sixteenth century, but in their place arose the hymn. In the period 1560–88, Tessa Watt has found that godly ballads comprised as much as thirty-five percent of all ballads produced; by the period 1625–40, they were only nine percent of the total.[13] This decline may have been due to

Puritan mistrust of the vagrant ballad-seller, their division of culture into sacred and profane.[14] The origins of the hymn in the godly ballad in publishing history show an intersection between secular and sacred topics and modes. Psalm versifiers had adopted secular ballad tunes, and hymn writers continued this practice.

The hymn, however was a radical departure from the scriptural literalism of the psalm. It promoted a greater range of creativity and innovation; indeed a neo-Latin tradition of hymn writing had long flourished in Scotland and on the Continent, where the Polish Jesuit Casmire Sarbiewski earned his epithet the "Christian Horace."[15] George Herbert's "A True Hymne" followed Paul's exhortation to use "psalms and hymns and spiritual songs" (Eph. 5:19; Col. 3:16), citing texts that were to become orthodox in defending the public singing of hymns in congregation, but during Herbert's time hymns were not sung in the Anglican service.[16] George Wither's *Hymnes and Songs of the Church* (1623) produced a high literary standard for this new genre. The ceremonial use of hymns was of interest to Wither, who recommended they be sung in congregation: "not for that I would have it thought Part of the Churches *Liturgie*: but because they are made in the Person of all the Faithfull."[17] Wither evokes the concept of communion rather than ritual.

Although psalms had been sung as part of religious worship since the Reformation, the hymn represents a departure. In deviating from the precise text of the Bible, hymn writers seized a free space for creativity of worship in which to develop their distinctive voices. Under the Commonwealth, hymns came into their own. New words were created to the tunes of Sternhold and Hopkins by the radical fringe group, the Ranters.[18] Hymns were composed to celebrate the victories on the civil war battlefield by John Goodwin, Vavasor Powell, and a Mr. Appletree; these were sung publicly in their congregations to commemorate the victory against the Scots on 8 October 1650, and were later published for wider consumption.[19] John Goodwin's hymn celebrating the victory at Worcester also included a rebuke against those ministers who disdained the bloodthirsty, vengeful theme.[20] Parliament is the addressee of William Barton's 1651 collection of hymns:

> How great a crown of glory
> Hath God set on your Head!
> And brought you into Story
> Of all men to be read!
> A thousand thousand Pages
> Your Chronicle shall write,
> And all ensuing ages
> Shall read it with delight.[21]

This hymn announces its political and commemorative work: to tell the divine and glorious story of Parliament and the nation's deeds as driven and rewarded by providence; and further, to *become* that story once prophesied. Deborah, the "mother of Israel" whose victory against the Canaanites on Mount Tabor was recounted in Judges 4–5, is the model for this victory song.[22]

The Revolutionary Milton in the peroration to his *Of Reformation*, when he commended new deeds, also called for new hymns to match those of old: "amidst the *Hymns* and *Haleluiahs* of *Saints* some one may perhaps bee heard offering at high *strains* in new and lofty *Measures* to sing and celebrate thy *divine Mercies*, and *marvelous Judgements* in this Land throughout all AGES" (*CPW*, 1, 616). With "new and lofty" means, song will accompany those deeds that are unprecedented but which will become precedents to others. For Milton, hymns represented poetry in its purest form, and his defense of hymns in the chapter entitled "Of External Worship" in his *Christian Doctrine* points to the very texts favored by those promoting hymn singing in the Restoration period.[23]

The biblical figures of Miriam and Deborah, long evoked in defenses of female preaching across the early modern period, were also famous and often-quoted singers. Women's hymns and songs were thus gendered "sound-tracks" for radical action, whether metonymic icons justifying a poetics of warrior song or metaphoric figures for later women to rally to in seeking to speak and to sing in public. The biblical verse Exodus 15 in particular served as justification for song in praise of violence, and indeed in justification of song altogether, a conjoining of violence and hymnody that would make later authors such as Isaac Watts squirm. Exodus 15 is the source for two rousing protest hymns appended to the Song of Songs commentary by the famous Elizabethan Puritan Arthur Hildersham and published in 1672. Found at the conclusion of the volume, they are based on the key radical texts: Exodus 15, rejoicing in Pharaoh's army's defeat; Deuteronomy 32, interpreted as vengeance summoned opposing a false ruler; and Judges 5, where praise is offered for vengeance against foes in the story of Jael, the heroine who slew Sisera. Deborah's song is powerfully marked as feminine: "The Land uncultivated lay,/ In *Israel* men became a prey,/ Till I arose, I *Deborah*,/ Till I their Matron bore the sway."[24] Miriam's song, too, was a summons to righteous action, pledged on the title page of the key tract in Venner's uprising, *A Door of Hope* (1660), calling for violent resistance. Its title page demanded, "We must begin with this Song: *Great and Marvellous are thy Works*," citing Revelation 15:3, itself an echo and allusion to the Song of the Sea, Miriam's Song, in Exodus 15. Praise for deliverance from enemies as well as calls for vengeance were thus authorized under the sign

of the feminine. Miriam's song at the Red Sea was cited over and over as
the key text justifying the composition and singing of songs, authorizing
Mary Mollineux' collection of poetry, for instance: "And *Miriam* answered
them,/ Sing ye to the Lord, for he hath/ Triumphed Gloriously."[25]

If Miriam at the Red Sea authorized later writers to create hymns, the
figure of Deborah became the warring muse. Deborah is the muse of
William Barton's 1651 volume, *Halelujah*. A hymn which "Celebrates
Nazeby, and other great Victories of the Church," gives a free paraphrase
of Judges 5, which it cites in the margins. Its final verse is a straightforward
application to English history:

> Awake awake, O {Parliament,/Deborah,}
>   rise {Barak/ Conqu'rors Fairfax/ Cromwell} sing a Song.
> Lead captive {thy/your} captivity,
>   come lead them all along:
> So perish those that are thy foes...[26]

Barton equates England to Israel, Barak to the victorious generals Cromwell
and Fairfax, and implicitly himself to the republican Judge Deborah, who
authorizes the song. If the muses were traditionally gendered female, then
the prominence of Deborah or Miriam offers a counter-poetics, evoking
schemes of providential intervention and violent justice for a heroic people.

The figure of Deborah had been a radical Christian heroine since Lollard
times, and during the Revolution period, she took on the political colors
within a struggle over power in the church and state that left bloody bodies
on the battlefields in county after county. In *Two Hymns*, Goodwin cites
both Miriam and Deborah in his defense of singing hymns of vengeance,
availing himself of this authority to justify the violence of civil war.
Deborah's song (Judg. 5) was the inspiration for Stephen Marshall's radical
tract *Meroz Cursed* (1641), an attack on tyrants. We might see this political,
warring background as the reason for Milton's naming his youngest daughter Deborah in 1652. Lucy Hutchinson's *Order and Disorder* cites Judges 5
in the margins, evoking Deborah's song in an outburst against tyrants:
"The Lord his glittering hosts thus send/ To execute the just threats they
portend."[27]

In the Restoration, Deborah's song echoed in the suffering protests of
Quakers Sarah Chevers and Katharine Evans, whose prison writings also
include a number of hymns. Out of the darkness of their cells, their words
repeat the call of Jael, in an apocalyptic framework of vengeance upon
their assailants: "Arise oh Lord, arise in haste,/ and punish for these things,/
These men that have sought thy disgrace,/ that they might reign as kings."[28]

Thomas Ellwood deplored that "cruel law," the 1662 Act of Uniformity, with its supplements over the next few years that had targeted particularly Quakers. These were acts which made him "cry earnestly to the Lord that he would arise and set up His righteous judgment in the earth for the deliverance of His people from all their enemies" and his response was to compose a vengeful hymn, as he puts it "and in these terms I uttered it":

> Awake, awake, O arm of th'Lord, awake,
> Thy sword uptake;
> Cast what would Thine forgetful of Thee make
> Into the lake.
> Awake, I pray, O mighty Jah [sic], awake
> Make all the world before Thy presence quake,
> Not only earth, but heaven also shake.
> Arise, arise, O Jacob's God, arise.[29]

Rustic, even clumsy, the repetitive monotonous rhyming sound "ake" reveals a heartache but also the key sound gives name to Ellwood's identity as a Qua*k*er. Even though Quakers ajured violence, these words utter an ominous threat. Reluctant to rely upon book-worship, biblical language nonetheless saturates these utterances, under the sign of the female heroic action of Jael in Deborah's song, soliciting divine violence.

THE DEPOLITICIZATION OF THE HYMN

After the Revolution's demise, the hymn underwent transformation and development. John Playford, a music publisher of considerable importance during the mid century, and who had served as clerk to the Temple church, produced his *Psalms and Hymns* (1671) for the restoring English church, a Psalter that continued in print until the last part of the eighteenth century, with the twentieth edition coming out in 1757. Playford's hymnal reflects the inroads that sectarian hymn creation had made even among the orthodox, since the volume included seventeen original hymns, several canticles, and two versions of *Veni Creator*, along with its rendition of the psalms. His hymns included at least fourteen by John Austin (as Edna Parks has found, these taken from Austin's *Devotions in the Antient Way of Offices* [1668]); Playford also lifted texts by George Herbert and Francis Quarles. In 1677, his second Psalter defended the singing of psalms and hymns in the church service, lamented the condition of psalm singing in congregations, and urged reforms to train clerks, organist, and congregation in the proper ways of making music.[30]

With its proliferation into all the nonconformist sects, the hymn also underwent a wholesale whitewashing, indeed, a radical depoliticization, with the removal of topical reference. The fate of the publication of William Barton's hymn collection tells a story of the transition from Revolutionary Puritanism to Restoration Dissent. It is a story of the end of one kind of radical politics and the development of another. When an alternative to the Sternhold and Hopkins Psalter was sought by Parliament, Barton competed against Francis Rous, who was favored by the House of Commons. Barton's version, preferred by the House of Lords, was accepted by Parliament and licensed for printing in 1644; the Protector maintained Barton's copyright for the psalms in 1654.[31] The life of this great hymnodist exemplifies the shifts of Puritanism through the Revolution. Barton began his ministry as a Presbyterian, turned Congregationalist in the 1650s, and after the Restoration at first resisted conformity, and then finally settled into the Anglican church as a conforming Puritan in 1663; he died in 1678. A prodigious hymn writer, his posthumously published collection of 600 hymns in *Six Centuries of Select Hymns* (1688), dedicated to Sir Matthew Hale, was in use by nonconformists until it was replaced by Watts' *Hymns and Spiritual Songs* (1707).

Barton's collections of hymns reproduced earlier hymns and added new ones; from the seed of his *Halelujah* (1651) were sprouted 100 in *A Century of Select Hymns* (1659); from this came the 400 of *Four Centuries of Select Hymns* (1668), and then the 600 in *Six Centuries*, published posthumously by his son in 1688.

The fate of the hymn in the Restoration may be told in little by attending to the fortunes of Barton's 1650 hymn "Celebrating Naseby," his adaptation of Deborah's song from Judges 5. Though it had initially appeared in 1650 with precise notation referring to Revolutionary England (see above p. 216), when it was reprinted in 1659, that song was stripped of its political allusions, and topical English Revolutionary history deleted from its title. It was now simply, "Deborahs Song." This unannotated and untopical version was reprinted in the 1668 *Four Centuries*, and in all the later editions of his hymns. Historical memory is erased in favor of a timeless typology.

Would the radical past inhere in the very words of the Bible that had inspired the Revolutionary violence of the previous twenty years? The debates over hymns in the later seventeenth century show unease about such bloody retributive fantasies, and represent another facet of the contest over historical memory. Richard Baxter for one, in defending hymn singing, noted that "Some are stumbled that David's Psalms have so little about the Life to come, and speak with so great concernedness about prosperity and Adversity here, and especially that he saith so much through almost all the Book against his Enemies, and the Oppression and Cruelties of wicked men, and his great danger of them, and sufferings by them, even cursing them and their Posterity."[32] Baxter's worries were not without warrant. For example, authorities had reported in November 1668 that a group of 500 persons calling themselves the "Congregation of saints" were found singing Psalm 149 with militant overtones – a psalm that appealed to God, "To execute vengeance upon the heathen, and punishments upon the people; To bind their kings with chains, and their nobles with fetters of iron."[33] To Baxter that kind of appeal to Old Testament violence summoned memories of the civil war radical uses of the Bible. By rethinking his relation to a Hebraic past, Baxter also rewrote the identity of contemporary Puritanism. His was a revision in historical memory, as biblical Israel proves to be too complex and disturbing a figure for identification, inseparable from the violence implicit in its heroic providentialism.

In his answer to the question about the violence of the psalms, Baxter walks the thin line between radical poetry and political obedience. He also expresses the deep ambivalence over the practices of citation and commemoration that on the one hand provided shapes for mourning and identification, but on the other could not end the violence upon which they were premised. "And though Christ teach us to love our enemies, and bless them that curse us, and pray for them that hate and persecute us," Baxter comments, "yet he forbids us not to desire deliverance from them, nor to hate their Diabolical Lying, Malignity and Cruelty, and Enmity to the Gospel."[34] Baxter explains that the kind of violence and prayers for vengeance found in the psalms are rooted in a historical experience of persecution and corrupt governance, writing, "they that live in an Age and Land where these prevail and are in power, will have a sensible Commentary of David's Psalms: And in Prisons, and in Wars and Fields of Blood and Torments, many have confessed, that now they understood the Psalms of David, which they never soundly understood before" (preface to *Baxter's Paraphrase*, fol. A7v).

Baxter helped to tone down the vengefulness of religious radicalism in the Restoration. His hymn book closes with a postscript, "Directions for the Use and Tuning of the Psalms, &c." which specifically opposes the politically radical use of psalms, noting that

times of Calamity, Danger, Oppression, and Persecution, will render men capable of a sensible understanding of the greatest part of the Psalms, otherwise hardly understood; which aggravate the furious Rage, Malignity, Violence, Bloodiness, and Diabolical Nature, Designs, and Attempts of the wicked enemies of Truth, Piety, and Holy Peace; and teach us to fly to God only for help from these wicked and unreasonable men.

Instead of vengeance, however, Baxter recommends obedience: "if we consider that it is not their eternal damnation that [David] prayeth for but publick Justice by God" (275–76). As these words close his volume, Baxter recognizes that to summon the spirit of holy song was also to summon the ethics of vengeance and violence, perhaps to sanction radical resistance to political authority, as had happened during the Revolutionary years and in the repeated plots against the Stuart regimes. Baxter wished to tame such passion by a "sensible" understanding, that is, to promote the felt experience of suffering, a rage which must then be properly directed towards the relation with God, not against human rulers no matter how cruel. Thus he pulled the hymn away from its possible earthly political solutions, even as he summoned the feelings of rage and violence aroused by the psalms. Despite its whitewashing, however, the genre of the hymn still bore a radical mark well into the Restoration period. A satiric attack on Whig politicians probably dating from the Exclusion period was entitled "A Whig Psalm." The refrain of the psalm joins sedition and communal singing: "Let us pray & plot, & plot & pray, these Bills may be rejected."[35]

DOMESTIC ACTIONS

During the Restoration, hymns may have avoided topical reference, but in prizing moral reform they did not veil criticism of contemporaries. A cultural war against unholiness was a political campaign launched in the heart of the family. When Richard Baxter sought to combat the forces of wantonness, he turned to hymn singing:

Godly families have still been defferenced from the ungodly by open singing the Praises of God, when the other sing wanton and idle Songs. Good Christians will not (among Christians at least) be ashamed, that such Psalms of Praise be heard by their Neighbours into the Streets, when Players, or Ballad-singers are not ashamed, more openly to sing amorous, foolish, ungodly, or abusive Songs. Our Psalms in Metre were set forth by Authority, to be used both in Church and House, laying apart all ungodly Songs and Ballad, &c.[36]

Despite its ideological purging of the topical, radical intent of the fires of the English Revolution, there was thus a new political purpose to the hymn. Through hymn singing the godly were to perform religious worship as a group, constituted not in a congregation but in a public space within the household that was to be the site of indoctrination as well as community, a replacement for the church that could not assemble by law. Through the family, children would be brought to distinguish between worldly and godly concerns. The hymn was a prime arena for this education.

Children were a primary focus of Dissenters' attention, and a focus on the intimate family was a legacy of Puritanism in early modern England.[37] Within the sphere of the domestic, the hymn was to bind family members together to fend off the dangers of worldly pleasure. Hymns were also to be the medium for the indoctrination of children (see Figure 10). The Baptist Benjamin Keach hoped to slip in doctrine by means of this sweet song: "Now these *Hymns* being short," he advised, "Children will soon get them by heart, as also full of varieties, and if instructed to sing, they maybe the more affected with the matter, and receive the greater advantage."[38] The Presbyterian minister Samuel Bury suggested the setting in which the book might be used in his title, *A Collection of Psalms and Hymns, and Spiritual Songs, Fitted for Morning and Evening Worship in a Private Family* (1707). Baxter urged the private benefit of his psalm paraphrase: "And as I did it for my own use under my constant dying pains, and solitude, so I leave it for the secret or Family-use of those with whose Condition and spirits it best suiteth, without disparaging the more excellent Labours of any others. That is best for some (in private) that is not so for others."[39] Benjamin Keach recommends his collection of hymns for "*Parents* and *Masters of Families*," urging that his book "may prove of great advantage in their Children, who generally are taken with Verse, and are much addicted to learn such Songs and Ballads which generally tend to corrupt youth."[40] His son, Elias, must have learnt these lessons well, as his volume of hymns was published, "That you may have such Hymns and Spiritual Songs by you for your publick use in your Families."[41] This did not construe the family as relegated to a private sphere; singing at home was a "public" use.

Hymns could help to spiritualize the household, translating domestic space into a prime site of godliness. George Wither's collection, *Halleluiah*, indicated in its title that it was "to be Sung in Families." A reformation of the household was chief among the aims of the Presbyterian Matthew Henry, who sought to "promote the Singing of Psalms in Families, as a part of their Daily Worship." In *Family-Hymns* he professes the domestic purpose, emphasizing hymns' use in educating children into piety: "It is the Wisdom of Masters of Families, so to manage their Family Worship,

Figure 10 Frontispiece to Samuel Crossman, *The Young Man's Calling* (1725).

that they may make it as much as possible a Pleasure, and not a Task, to their Children and Servants. Nor let want of Skill be an Excuse; there may be much of acceptable Affection, where there appears but little of Art. Plain Songs best befits plain Israelites."[42] Henry paints a portrait of the hymning discipline: "an Exercise which (however it be now with other Instances of the warmest Devotion sadly disus'd, yet) was antiently practised by the generality of serious Christians, who thus turn'd their Houses into Churches" (*Family-Hymns*, fol. A3). Seeking to revive this ancient duty, Henry imagines the family as the "Nurseries and Seminaries of Piety" (fol. A3v). He also recommends families purchase multiple copies of his hymn-books (fol. A5). In his own family worship, Henry lived what he preached. Writes his biographer William Tong: "After Exposition, some Part of a Psalm was constantly sung in the Morning as well as the Evening . . . every one had a Book, and so neither the Sense nor the Melody suffered that Interruption, which can scarcely be avoided where it is read Line by Line."[43]

The Puritan Revolution may have been most successful in transforming the home. Especially when their public roles were denied them, Dissenters created their resistance within the space of the family.[44] The meaning of "public" and "private," indeed, underwent change during a time when nonconformist "public" worship was outlawed; the domestic spaces of the family home took up the roles previously performed by the church. Bunyan emphasizes the family as a little religious community in diaspora in the second part of his *Pilgrim's Progress*, where Christiana travels with her children toward the Celestial City (see Figure 11). Like the houses of many other Dissenters, that of Matthew Henry was described as "a little Sanctuary to the Silenced Ministers and those that adhered to them."[45] Not simply because of their family-centered affective bonds, but for political and religious reasons – using their domestic spaces for illegal conventicles, or for the daily habits of family prayer – nonconformists cultivated an ethos of retirement and domesticity.

The interest in reforming not simply the state but their children was a powerful tradition developed by these godly households. Baptists Benjamin Keach, John Bunyan, and Samuel Crossman were among the first to create a literature specifically directed to children. Crossman stressed the importance of training children to virtue in the preface to his *The Young Man's Calling* (1678), appealing to their future legacy.[46] The hymn was considered to be an apt device for bringing children to sacred truths, for joining them to the social and domestic order, and for transmitting a pious inheritance.

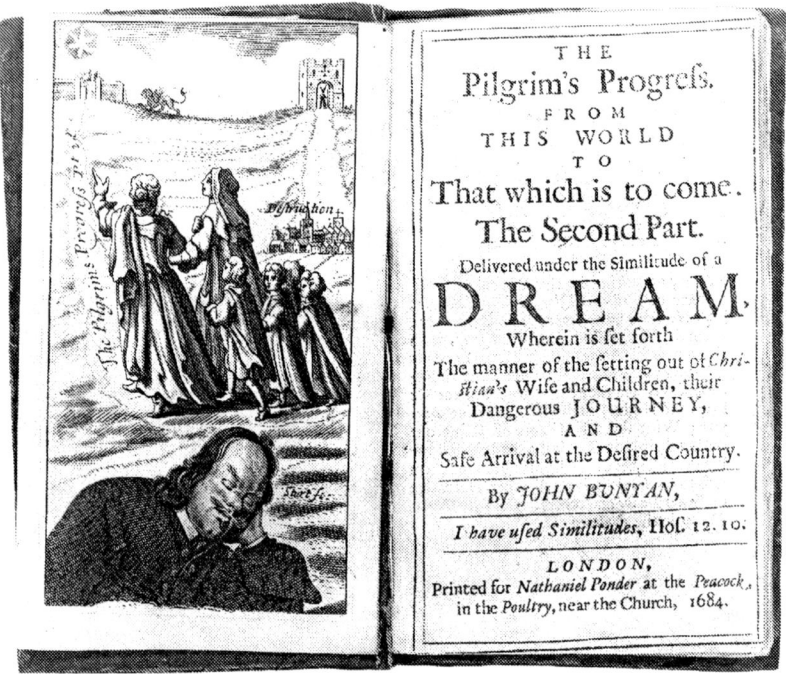

Figure 11 Frontispiece and title page to John Bunyan, *The Pilgrim's Progress . . .
Second Part* (1684).

PERFORMING RADICALISM

Even if radical intent was not visible in the words of the published hymns,
nonetheless hymn authors were often religious or political radicals. The
self-educated Benjamin Keach (1640–1704), a tailor by trade, who became
a minister to the General Baptist Church at Winslow, Buckinghamshire,
composed over 400 hymns. When he published hymns in *Instructions for
Children* in 1664, the whole edition was seized and destroyed, Keach fined
and imprisoned and put in the pillory for expressing views contrary to the
prayer book, specifically his references to baptism and his interpretation of
the Book of Revelation. He subsequently rewrote the book from memory,
and in 1673, introduced the singing of hymns in public congregational
worship, first inserting a hymn after the sacrament of the Lord's Supper, and
then extending the practice to allow a hymn every Sunday. His 1676 hymn
book became his *Spiritual Melody*, published in 1691 by John Hancock, who
specialized in nonconformist divinity.[47] Keach was a defender of women's

right to speak in the churches, and was a participant in the controversy over women singing hymns in the 1690s.[48]

The hymns voiced their radical meaning not strictly through topical political content – although that was never very far from the surface – but because they eschewed the forms of set worship. Not all Dissenters resisted as far as the Quakers, for whom set texts smacked of idolatry. The Quaker Mary Pennington rejected the singing of set songs as she rejected the Book of Common Prayer, commenting that "We tore out of our Bibles the common prayer, the form of prayer, and also the singing psalms, as being the inventions of vain poets, not being written for that use. We found that the songs of praise must spring from the same source as prayers did; so we could not use any one's songs or prayers."[49] Quakers, above all nonconformists, avoided set liturgy: set songs, like set prayers, violated the freedom of the spirit to move as it wished. But Pennington carefully does not reject singing altogether; the songs must emerge from the self, spontaneous and free. The Quaker leader George Fox recounts a powerful moment of Quaker song, when a company of foot gathered in Scotland to expel Fox and an associate, James Lancaster, from the place in 1657:

So when they were guarding us out of the town we got on our horses and James Lancaster was moved to sound and sing the way of the Lord and the glorious everlasting gospel: and all the streets was up and filled with people and the soldiers were so ashamed that they cried and said they had rather have gone to Jamaica than to guard us so.[50]

Song and sound: both were vocal opportunities to express faith and move listeners to sympathy.

The Quakers' singing whilst under persecution was an act of resistance even if the words of the songs did not utter topical *political* content. Katharine Evans and Sarah Chevers, imprisoned on the island of Malta, composed "victorious Hymns, songs, Praises, all in Verse," keeping up their spirits in a time of painful deprivation, at the same time reassuring readers that their words emerged "from the Seed of life, its perfect Righteousness."[51] The Baptist John Bunyan in *Pilgrim's Progress* shows how hymn singing was a powerful mode of utterance, as his characters often make song to express faith in times of duress; to celebrate their deliverance; or to signify resistance to often painful physical force. Bunyan reacted to the rise of hymn singing in his own day, and between the publication of the first part of *Pilgrim's Progress* in 1678 and the second part, in 1684, seems to have accepted hymns as a distinct genre. In the second part, the many songs in Bunyan's work have evolved into the stricter formulae of the hymn. In the first part, all songs were presented in iambic pentameter, with rhymed couplets. In the second part, all songs are now hymns in the traditional meter of 8/6. This transformation mirrors the acceptance of hymns among some Baptist worshipers. Bunyan advocated hymn singing in his Bedford Congregation, and he illustrates the singing of a hymn in the celebration of the downfall of the Giant Despair (see Figure 6, p. 105 above).[52]

Richard Baxter, at the opposite end of the spectrum from the radical Quakers, danced carefully around the subject of singing hymns, eschewing the charge that he might be too liberal in adding his own innovations to biblical song. His advocacy of song is thus not to render it more spontaneous, but in some ways less so. Baxter claimed to have avoided innovations to Scripture in his adaptation of psalms: "I feared adding to God's Word, and making my own to pass for God's."[53] In his *Poor Man's Family Book* (1672), Baxter did however publish an original hymn, "Ye holy Angels Bright," to be sung to the tune of Psalm 197. His psalm paraphrase championed literary originality, citing the familiar biblical precedents authorizing hymns:

I confess my Metre, and Tunes, and Apocryphal Hymns are not in words found in the Scriptures, nor are the words of my ordinary Preaching and Prayers there. But they are commanded by the general Precepts of the Scripture: Let all be done to Edification, and Exhort one another in Psalms, and Hymns, and Spiritual Songs, singing with grace in your hearts to the Lord, Col. 3.16. What sweeter foretaste of the Heavenly Everlasting Praises? There is no Exercise that I had rather live and dye in, than singing Praises to our Redeemer and Jehovah.[54]

Human invention was not to be shunned, but neither need it lead to strictly reiterated formalism. In performative terms, then, not simply in ideological ones, Dissenters along a spectrum from Quaker to Presbyterian made song one means of the production and dissemination of Dissenting experience.

DEMOCRATIC AESTHETICS

Despite their evasion of political applications in the Restoration, then, the hymn writers may be understood as adopting a radical genre. Not only did hymnodists reject artifice in favor of spontaneity; the hymn also carried with it a revolutionary legacy of popular action. Restoration nonconformist hymn writers self-consciously shaped a tradition of a popular literature, making their works accessible in the public sphere of publishing and in the public spaces of collective worship, as well as at home. Their broad appeal led to the hymn's castigation as a literary mode, however. When George

Wither was remembered in the Restoration as a strong poetic father, it was as a divine poet, not as a fiery revolutionary. His populism was inextricable from the divinity of his poetry. Richard Baxter praises "Honest *George Withers*" as he heads up his list of holy poets worthy of emulation. Baxter is aware of the poor aesthetic reputation of this poet in his own day, but reveres Wither for a different kind of estimation: "Honest *George Withers*, though a Rustick Poet, hath been very acceptable as to some for his Prophecies, so to others for his plain Country-honesty: The Vulgar were the more pleased with him for being so little Courtly."[55] For his anticourtliness, his rough verse, rather than for his defense of the violent Revolution, then, Wither was to be remembered. Baxter chooses a rough model of poetry for his canon, a demotic aesthetics suitable for ordinary readers.

The hymn was to be the chief demotic form of poetry. Foremost in the aims of the hymn writers was accessibility to the common reader or singer. To assist his presumably unlearned audience, Joseph Boyse appended to his volume of hymns a two-page glossary: "Lest any unskilful Reader should be at a loss about the meaning of the following words, I have added the Signification of 'em." The following list includes the terms "Benignity," "Transcendent," "Inviolable," "Indemnity," and "Emblem."[56] Through hymns, the Presbyterian Boyse introduced readers and singers to points of doctrine, making them accessible through the medium of song. As Elias Keach, Baptist minister son of the famous hymn writer Benjamin Keach, explained, "I have not need (neither do I pretend to) [of] Rhetorical Flourishes, and Guilded Flights, but have accommodated my self to your Temper and Capacity, even the meanest and weakest among you." His aim was usefulness, not complexity, and his dedication spoke directly to his congregation at Carriers' Hall, London: "And if I had used a higher Style, it may be many of you could not have sung with that Understanding that is required: A plain Preacher and Author suits best a plain Hearer and Reader; and I designed these Hymns only for your Use, not for any others, either Learned or Unlearned, and if you kindly accept and make use of them, I have attain'd my End."[57]

Even the great hymn writer Isaac Watts excised those works from his 1707 hymnal that he deemed beyond the abilities of ordinary readers or singers: "The Metaphors are generally sunk to the Level of vulgar Capacities. I have aimed at ease of Numbers and Smoothness of Sound, and endeavour'd to make the Sense plain and obvious." Aware that his hymns work against the values of proper literature, Watts nonetheless defends his demotic aesthetics, not simply on the grounds of ease of singing, but for the goal of reaching a wide audience in a spontaneous manner. "If the Verse appears so gentle and flowing as to incur the Censure of Feebleness," he continues, "I may honestly affirm, that sometimes it cost me labour to make it so: Some of the Beauties of Poesy are neglected, and some wilfully defaced: I have thrown out the Lines that were too onorous, and giv'n an Allay to the Verse, lest a more exalted Turn of Thought or language should darken or disturb the Devotion of the plainest Souls."[58] Defending his reputation as a poet, Watts registers some unease, aware that those of taste and discernment may find them too rude, too easy; he reassures readers that his simple lines came out of intense labor, an artful artlessness.

The aim of usefulness also invited writers to seek a different register than high literary value. Hymns were meant to be lovely, but their loveliness consisted of their acceptance by God and their ability to express the breathings of divine spirit. Hymns were thus to be the means by which the saints could find "recreation." Theodosia Alleine reported that her minister husband would sing hymns daily whilst sitting in his bath: "Having his Curtains drawn close, he spent his time in Holy Meditation, and Prayer, and Singing," whilst taking his cure in the waters at Bath.[59] Richard Baxter expressed his joy in hymn singing: "What sweeter foretaste of the Heavenly Everlasting Praises? There is no Exercise that I had rather live and dye in, than singing Praises to our Redeemer and Jehovah, while I might in the Holy Assemblies, and now when I may not, as Paul and Silas in my Bonds, and my dying pains, which are far heavier than my Bonds."[60] Rather than expressing originality, the singer strives for divine communication. "Recreation" is the key term, meaning re-creation of prior affective or spiritual states. William Barton defends reiteration and the principle of re-creation in his first collection, where "I have here composed an hundred Hymns out of express Scriptures, not injured I hope in their conjunction."[61]

Hymns were patchwork affairs. Barton's hymns are in fact a mish-mash of biblical tidbits. Richard Baxter himself had incorporated others' works in his book, and he noted that borrowing. Yet this did not mean barren repetition. For Psalm 136, for instance, he included two different versions, "The Scots Version" and William Barton's. When we compare Baxter and Barton, however, we see Baxter has made real changes upon his originals.[62] Joseph Stennett's hymns, too, strung biblical phrases together to compose hymns, with the originals cited in the margins. Samuel Bury, also published by the major hymn publisher Thomas Parkhurst, went further in incorporating former hymnodists in new ways. His hymn book indicates in the margins from whom he lifted lines. For his Psalm 15:1, 2, for instance, individual lines derive from Tate and Brady, Richard Baxter, and the Scottish psalm book. Barton and Herbert topped his list of cited sources; Boise, Burgess, Crashaw,

Foxton, Vincent, and "Woodroof" (Woodford) are also cited. Herbert's "Home," interlaced with the words of others, comes in for adaptation for a "Spiritual Song, for Saturday Morn."[63]

Composing the hymns was by no means to be considered artistically adventurous work. Divine poets expected their audiences would take pleasure in recognizing the threads of biblical verse or divine poetry woven into the fabric of their new creations. Their exaggerated allusion and citation also covered over ambivalence about the very act of poetical creativity. They worried about adding to Scripture, claiming for themselves what was not their own. Matthew Henry admits that what he has done in his hymns might be considered plagiarism:

> I have taken that out of each, which I judg'd the best and most suitable to my purpose, acting herein not as a Censor, but as a Gleaner. Books are known to have their Fate, *Ad captum Lectoris*, and therefore I hope my Pardon for making this use of the Labours of others will be easily granted, and this general Acknowledgment will suffice to acquit me from the Charge of Plagiarism.

As a gleaner, Henry hides his innovation under a crust of legitimating names. But Henry also wants to improve on the old, "in many Places to build anew (especially where I was willing to contract) according to the best of my skill. The Performance indeed is but very small, yet the Design is honest."[64] The Presbyterian Joseph Boyse echoes the humanist paradigm of imitation by admitting in his copying: "For the Publication of this Little Book, I may not make use of the Instance of the Painter, that took and Eye from one, a Limb from another, and a Complexion from a third, &c." Boyse's compilation of hymns is a magpie affair, silently snatching lines from other hymn writers, most notably John Mason, and acknowledging their debt. Psalm 95 is marginally glossed, "Dr. W," and similar figures (Dr. H; Dr. M; B; M) dot the margins of this work, allusions to a known body of hymnodists whose names are so familiar they may be understood in abbreviation, whose signs legitimize the arrangement, and who also perhaps exonerate the real crime of literary originality.[65]

The alleged unoriginality of the hymn, its willed derivative and secondary nature, were to be selling-points, but that unoriginality was a disguise for the very real innovation at the heart of the hymn project. When Joseph Boyse included Herbert's "Twenty-Third Psalm" in his 1704 collection of hymns, he noted that "the three following *Hymns* being excellently done to my hands by Mr. *Herbert* and Mr. *Patrick*, I took the liberty to Subjoyn 'em," considering the works of these two authors to be common property.[66] The adoption of Patrick shows the traffic between nonconformist and orthodox writings late in the century, even though Boyse was based in Ireland because he refused to conform in England. John Patrick's psalms also had the blessing of Richard Baxter. The hymn theft, however, is understood as a "liberty," still an unorthodox, and uncontrollable assertion of this individual over the past inheritance.

That innovation was at the heart of the hymn project. For recreation meant the renewal and refreshment of previous authors and forms, not a slavish dependence upon fixed words. When John Milton castigated Charles I in *Eikonoklastes* for pilfering psalms to his own purposes, he chided the king not so much for theft as for hypocrisy. Charles lacked the spiritual qualities required of one who would use David's words to forge a spontaneous relation to God: "He borrows *Davids* Psalms . . . Had he borrow'd *Davids* heart, it had bin much the holier theft. For such kind of borrowing as this, if it be not better'd by the borrower, among good Authors is accounted *Plagiarie*" (*CPW*, iii, 547). Plagiarism, then, was not merely copying words; it was taking only the letter, and not the spirit, of another. For Milton, as for the other Dissenters, imitation and appropriation were not in themselves evil; the question of the morality of literary theft could not be adjudicated on external evidence alone. What mattered were the spontaneous, intimate, and, above all, *genuine* workings of the heart. Re-creation was a mode open to one whose heart was pure, and appeal to former authors was also an appeal to the divine source of inspiration and true author of poetry.

If the hymn was to be spontaneous and efficacious, moreover, the ethos of allusion, theft, and counterplay insisted that poetry was never fixed, but always open to revision by re-creation. There was a danger that hymns would slip into becoming poetry, would become frozen in static form, Milton's satanic "Forc't Halleluiahs" (*PL*, 2:243). Boyse debates the merits of hymn composition and raises the worry that hymns might resemble too closely the set prayers and strict formalisms rejected by his brand of Protestantism. "For all Psalmody," and here Boyse includes hymns, "falling under the Rules of Art, and confin'd to Sounds, there is not that freedom of the Soul to express the present Conceptions of our Mind and Spirit as in Prose." However formally constraining set forms might be, there is still an advantage to be had in using them:

There is a necesity of betaking our selves to well Composed Forms in Hymns and Psalms; for I know of no Ministers or Christians that pretend to any Accuracy in sudden Extempory [sic] Hymns, or putting a Psalm of David into Verse, so well suddenly, as they can by Study, Premeditation, and Composure; especially for the use and Benefit of others.[67]

Premeditation and spontaneity can coexist.

Thus hymns may be seen as recreation in several senses of the word; they re-create the majesty of the Bible, re-work prior authors' creations, and they serve as proper objects for the soul's entertainment. Recreation is a kind of labor, not a diversion nor a pleasure, but a work of spiritual affirmation. Baxter plies the modesty trope in presenting his paraphrase on the psalms: "I am not so vain as to expect that my Version should be of publick Church-use...I wrote for my own use, not intending any Publication." But he supplies his own particular motive for composition, to ease the burdens during his imprisonment: "in my Restraint, when my soul's great Concerns made it my chief and necessary Employment: When it was my interest and daily work to speak to God. And I found the Psalms so fitted to my use, as if they had been purposely made for me. When I used not to sleep one minute in many Nights, through pain and disturbance, these Psalms were my recreation."[68] Matthew Sylvester, who helped to put Baxter's psalms into print, also echoed this language: "Singing of Psalms he called, and used, *his Recreation*. When his sleep was intermitted or removed in the Night, he then sang much, and relished this course and practice greatly well."[69] Pleasure is thus wrought from the creative power to reorder language, voice, body: the hymn provides the shape in which pleasure can be produced, ever enjoyed, and made serviceable.

The aim of the hymn was to incite to performance, not to create a finished artifact; indeed, hymn writers believed in the value of spontaneity so that they built in obsolescence; ever new hymns were needed to keep the spiritual life fresh. Enoch Watts wrote to Isaac in 1700 praising his vigor: "[John] Mason now reduces this kind of writing to a sort of yawning indifference," he wrote, "and honest [William] Barton chimes us asleep. There is, therefore, great need of a piece, vigorous and lively as your, to quicken and revive the dying devotion of the age."[70] Isaac Watts interpreted Isaiah 42:10 ("Sing unto the Lord a new Song") as an injunction to make new hymns in an incessant scheme of production that mirrors the ongoing work of God's presence in the world. Of those hymns and psalms in the Bible, he suggested,

It can never be imagin'd that these are a compleat Collection of Psalms to suit all the Cases of a Christian Church; They are rather given to us as small Originals, by Imitation whereof the Churches should be furnished with Matter for Psalmody, by those who are capable of composing spiritual Songs, according to the various or special Occasions of Saints or Churches.[71]

Despite this affirmation of the new, it is the case that hymns are among the most derivative and unoriginal of art forms. Originality, then, is not in the text but in the spirit.

Why are hymns so bad? From the point of view of literary values that prize exceptionality, innovative use of imagery, language, and form, one might take the hymn as an impoverished genre. Richard Baxter, invoking divine assistance in his meditative poem, comments on his literary inadequacy within a cosmic scheme: "Angels must sing thy Highest praise, not we:/ But if thy warming beams cause Worms to speak,/ Their baser part will not the Consort break."[72] There were practical and ideological reasons for the choice of bad poetry: hymns were not to be difficult nor especially artful because they were to be sung by a wide audience; hymns also shunned ceremonialism and artificiality. Over and over, hymn writers excused their artlessness on grounds of accessibility. Joseph Boyse confessed he was no poet, "as I never had a Genius that way, so I am so far from thinking it necessary for composing such Divine Hymns for Public use, that those follies of Wit in 'em that would be Entertaining to the refined Judges of Poetry, would render them wholly unserviceable to the common People."[73] Further, he promoted a poetics of the plain style, not on formalist grounds but on those of spiritual need: "the things themselves shine the brightest in their native simplicity, without any borrow'd colours, and need nothing more to raise our Affections than to be clothed in clear and intelligible Expressions."[74] His pursuit of "native simplicity" squares with the rejection of ritual objects, a familiar Puritan iconoclasm. Boyse pointed out the difference between those engaging in collective public prayer and those singing hymns: "He that Prays is the Mouth of all the rest, and it's their great Duty that join with him to labour affectionately. But in Psalms and Hymns they are all Mouths, all Vocally Praise God."[75]

Furthermore, in this demotic, inelegant performance, earthly simplicity could better lead to purified feeling. William Geddes used familiar Reformation iconophobic rhetoric to present the chastened poetic mode of his hymns: "I supposed, that neither the whorish dress of human eloquence, or high flowing notions, nor yet the sluttish Garb of rustick expressions, were suteable for the chast Lady of Divinity; but the grave Matronal habite of Godly, pertinent and Spiritual simplicity." Geddes' mission is to reclaim song for holiness, and his collection snatches secular ballad tunes to accompany his hymns.[76] For many composers, hymns as a genre were themselves not original compositions, but were adaptations from secular song; the compiler's job was merely to aid in restoring poetry to its proper object. The hymnodist who translated Herbert to hymn form in 1697 asserted that "I do not find it hath been made a Pattern of scruple to turn the Temples built for Idols into Churches."[77] The work of divine poetry involved an ongoing task of purification.

Hymns were thus the medium through which Dissenters expressed an abundant creativity, but not in ways to which we traditionally assign literary value. The hymnodists' rejection of set forms of prayer created space for unconventional authors to enter into literary production. The Quaker Elizabeth Hincks of Cornwall offered a defense of her poetic mode, admitting, "Poet I'm not nor *Poets Son* at all that I should *rhime*," but she adamantly charged onward in defense of her song,

> That they that do not like the Verse may read the same in Prose.
> And yet the *Sacred solid Truth*, will be the self-same thing,
> Tho *Joyes* surround did make me sound *Praises to Sions King*.
> And though I clap my hands for *Joy*, O who will angry be,
> *Raptures of Love doth my Soul move, Oh 'tis my Love, 'tis he!*
> *That doth redeem poor Souls from Death, their Feet from falling to,*
> *And makes the Desolate to sing, Praises* to him as due.
> And why may'nt I sing that *New Song*, as *David* formerly.[78]

David's example authorizes this poet's own "new" song, where the soul can physically express its enthusiasms, be moved by "raptures of Love," and voice its fervent spark. Like prose, hymns can also communicate doctrine.

To answer Quakers' scruples against forms, Hincks suggests that the spirit moves through song, and in a manner acceptable to the claims of liberality. The whole body is freely involved – the hands clap, the soul moves – just as the voice is produced in song. Inadequacies of poetic training (*nor poets son*) are made up for by the authenticity and spontaneity of the human expressiveness. Her own situation within a persecuted minority provides the context for this astonishing exuberance in verse. Defending the poetic form of her forty-seven-page explanation of Quaker beliefs in rhyming couplets, Hincks alludes to her time of persecution: "printed for the use and benefit of such *Bees* as suck their *Hony* from the *Flowers* and *Blossoms* that God makes to spring; that they may have to keep *themselves alive* in the *dark stormy Winter*, 1671" (*Poor Widow's Mite*, t.p.).

Promoting the hymn often meant implicitly or explicitly attacking the conventions of Restoration Augustanism, its neoclassicism or courtliness, and polemically rejecting an aesthetic mode that had become artificial, libertine, or self-serving. The Baptist Joseph Stennett eschewed "those very bold Flights and those Heathenish Phrases which some have indulg'd even in Divine Poesy; for I cannot think 'em consistent with the gravity, Purity and Perspecuity which ought to be preserv'd in Hymns calculated for the immediate Service of God."[79] This is not merely a matter of purification of doctrine: it was to do war against "Heathenish" forms of literature whose chief end was pleasure, not spiritual profit. The threat of the secular hovered behind much of this Restoration hymn writing: "For it was not my desire," Joseph Boyse concluded, contrasting his aesthetics with that of secular poetry, "to please a wanton Ear, but to suit and improve a devout Temper."[80] Moral improvement, not pleasure, was the aim of this aesthetic. The point, aesthetic and ecclesiological intertwined, was to clear away impediments to direct experience.

In this poetic contest and cultural campaign against the worldliness of art, John Milton was a champion. When he heroically sought to liberate poetry from the "bondage" of rhyme in his 1674 preface to *Paradise Lost* he did battle in aesthetic form. For Milton, the hymn, too, was to be deployed in this campaign against ungodliness. Milton turns to the first sources of poetry in *Paradise Regain'd*, where Jesus reclaims poetic honor from the Greeks. There he insists (as did Theophilus Gale in the *Court of the Gentiles*) on the biblical origin of all song, and reinstates the priority of sacred creation. Jesus' combat contains much resonance to debates over contemporary poetry. *Paradise Regain'd* is not a work that calls attention to itself as "A Defense of English Poesy," but it should be seen in relation to current theses about the role, forms, and function of poetry, in an era in which John Dryden professed an alternate set of literary values. Milton's Jesus gives an *Ars Poetica* rebuke to Satan in vaunting "profit" and "delight" of divine hymns:

> All our Law and Story strew'd
> With Hymns, our Psalms with artful terms inscrib'd
> Our Hebrew Songs and Harps in *Babylon*,
> That pleas'd so well our Victors' ear, declare
> That rather *Greece* from us these Arts deriv'd;
> Ill imitated, while they loudest sing
> The vices of thir Deities, and thir own
> In Fable, Hymn, or Song, so personating
> Thir Gods ridiculous, and themselves past shame.
> Remove their swelling Epithets thick laid
> As varnish on a Harlot's cheek, the rest,
> Thin sown with aught of profit or delight,

Will far be found unworthy to compare
With *Sion's* songs, to all true tastes excelling,
Where God is prais'd aright, and Godlike men,
The Holiest of Holies and his Saints;
Such are from God inspir'd, not such from thee;
Unless where moral virtue is express'd
By light of Nature, not in all quite lost.

(Milton, PR, 4:334–52)

Setting profane Greek civilization against Hebraic godly inspiration, Milton's charge reflects the terms of his cultural war against a Restoration infatuation with pagan literary culture, its atheism, libertinism, courtliness, and decadence. Interweaving an attack on the ornaments of the church as well as on the artifice of poetry, Milton condemns "the vices of thir Deities, and thir own," claiming that their work is merely "ill imitated," that is, reflective of a prior, purer tradition: that of the Hebrews. There could, however, be a good imitation. In *Paradise Regain'd*, Milton transforms this theological point into the realm of poetics, promoting an aesthetic evacuated of worldliness, restored to its proper relation to the divine. Authentic, inspired, and primary, Sion's songs reverberate throughout Milton's poetry. Indeed, among the creative acts prized in *Paradise Lost* is hymn singing (e.g. *PL* 3:345–49; 3:369–417; 4:679–88; 7:592–633).

In this Restoration culture-war against worldliness, debates about poetic form, simplicity against ornament, could serve allegorically in the ecclesiological contest over forms of worship, although it oversimplifies the story of the rise of competing aesthetics to take one as an allegory for the other. For the extreme anticeremonialists, however, there could be a tight fit between rejection of literary as well as ecclesiological artifice. The Quaker author of *The Book of the Song of Solomon in Meeter* disdained "high flourishes" and "affecting strains," asking, "What can it be the less Sacred for that? Such eloquence but feedeth the outward ear."[81] The Quaker Thomas Ellwood rejected arid ceremonialism in favor of the spontaneity of the hymn:

> Not chanting, in a formal Note,
>   *States* touch'd in ancient Song,
> Perverting what the *Psalmist* wrote,
>   Whose Case cannot to all belong;
> 'Tis who their own Exper'ence bring,
> With *Spirit* and with *Judgment* sing.
>
> Instead of Incense to perfume
>   The Altar, from the Soul arise

> In Flames (that warm but not consume)
>   Sighs, Supplications, Groans, and Cries,
> Which tho' but weak, do never fail,
> At MERCY'S Fountain to prevail.[82]

Ellwood emphasizes kinesthetic experience: both heart and tongue are involved in singing, as the body confirms the soul's holy commitment.

Hymnody as a genre, then, actively produced Dissenting religious experience. To sing the hymn was to resist the conforming strictures of the Anglican church, and to reinvent a pure relation to God. It was not enough to know one's devotion to God; through hymn singing, one made that evident by bodily performance. A hymn becomes most true when it is sung, and this opens up an approach to this literary form in which performance, duration in time, and personal interpretation (in the sense of a performer's interpretation of tone, pace, and color), may be valued. In contrast to analysis of other kinds of literature, what matters is the situation of singing more than the actual text of the song. Hymns represent a mode of practice, not static art. Though its goals were unworldly, hymns provoked many actions that were decidedly earthly: resistance to set forms, communal gathering, and democratic participation in worship in the home and in public.

The religious hymn, born in the Lutheran Reformation and honed into a political weapon in the Revolution, survived in the Restoration only to face new controversies among sectaries, and these controversies revealed the ways that radical agency had shifted for Dissenters. Disagreement was to erupt over the question of set forms, and over the role of women in the churches. The Baptist Benjamin Keach is posited as the first to introduce hymn singing in the course of normal worship in 1673–75, and this was deemed controversial within the nonconformist gatherings because organized hymn singing could merely seem to replace old formalism with new.[83] There was also renewed dispute over the role of women speaking – or rather, singing – in Dissenting congregations, and though the terms of debate may seem to echo those of the earlier *Querelle des Femmes*, the Renaissance dialogues on the capabilities and moral worth of women. Indeed these controversies signal that the hymn as a social practice had been accepted and could ratify or query other concerns such as gender discipline. The hymn had thus become a part of the Puritan campaign to order signs, and to challenge mediation, a space in which to negotiate what had been central issues within Puritanism for a century. The hymn had finally been domesticated as the central Puritan genre.

A RADICAL PRESS

Even as radical politics was sapped from the hymn, nonetheless the production of hymns rested upon a material base of book publishers, printers, and sellers who comprised an oppositional sphere of cultural activity. For Dissenting printers and publishers, hymns may well have been their financial bread-and-butter business. Hymn books, despite the period's intense theological and ecclesiological disagreement, were only rarely the objects of governmental censure. Hymn collections often ran into several editions, revealing the lucrative side of the enterprise. Hymn authors urged their public to purchase multiple copies, so as to assist in proper uniform singing. The most eminent Presbyterian bookseller, Thomas Parkhurst, was first in hymn publication, and his stable included hymnodists William Barton, Richard Baxter, Joseph Boyse, Matthew Henry, and John Mason. Very much in the mainstream of nonconformist publishing, Parkhurst achieved eminence in the printing industry, rising to be elected Master of the Stationers' Company in 1707. He published the *Select Hymns Taken Out of Mr. Herbert's Temple* in 1697. The publishers of Dissenting hymns were also publishers of other works by Dissenters, many of them with long records of run-ins with the authorities, and leading members of the underground radical press of the Restoration.

However, on the fringes of hymn publishing, there were a number of printers, publishers, and booksellers who were also major players in the Restoration radical book world. John Darby, the London printer whose plant was in Bartholomew Close between the years 1662 and 1704, printed many books for Milton's publisher Brabazon Aylmer, and was repeatedly in trouble with the authorities in the Restoration, being an unstoppable producer of satires and lampoons. Darby printed Marvell's *Rehearsal Transpros'd*, and it was Darby (who had been convicted and fined in 1684 for printing the libellous *Lord Russell's Speech*), or his son John who continued in his father's spirit, who produced the Baptist hymns of Joseph Stennett in 1697. Stennett's *Hymns* would run to six editions in the next twenty years. John Dunton called Darby a "religious printer. He goes to Heaven with the Anabaptists but is a man of general charity. He printed that excellent speech of my Lord Russell and several speeches of Col. Sydney, and is a true assertor of English Liberties."[84]

The publishers and booksellers of Benjamin Keach were well traveled in Dissenting literature and they repeatedly faced the law for their dangerous publication or bookselling. Keach frequently acted as his own publisher. His printer was often William Marshall, who also published the Independent hymnodist Richard Davis. Marshall also sold books by Joseph Caryl and was known as a Dissenting printer, who had risked danger by publishing in 1662 the High Commission's examination of the Elizabethan separatists Henry Barrow, John Greenwood, and John Penry, evoking the image of a historical parallel of persecution. Marshall was associated with Yorkshire dissidents in 1664–65, and though he dealt chiefly in divinity, he was involved in the printing and publication of several Protestant pamphlets during the Popish plot.[85] John Hancock, another publisher of Benjamin Keach and also of the Baptist hymnodist John Reeve, was committed in March 1677 for selling copies of a seditious pamphlet, *The Long Parliament Dissolved*.[86] Elias Keach was published by Benjamin Harris, the producer of the famous New England primer, and who had published Benjamin Keach's *War with the Devil*. An ardent Protestant, Harris had been put on trial for his 1679 publication of *An Appeal from the Country to the City*, and in 1681 he was also prosecuted, fined, and pilloried; soon after his arrival in America, he ran into trouble with the authorities there.[87] The Independent hymnodist Richard Davis was co-published with Henry Bernard, also a nonconformist printer, who brought out the work of Tobias Crisp, *Christ Alone Exalted*, in 1693, the spark of the Socinian crisis.

Contemporary historians of bookselling and publishing have warned that it is difficult to determine the publisher or printer's ideological leanings from the books he or she printed or published.[88] Still, the London bookshop could become a significant space for shaping a community. In Restoration England, bookshops served as places for meeting and conversation; they generated sociability and served as places for political exchange. Some booksellers provided daily newsbooks for customers, imitating the burgeoning coffeehouses that arose in the Restoration period. Publishing and bookselling went along with political discussion.[89] In the case of those publishers of Dissenting literature, their livelihood was at stake in publishing works of a certain cast; the hymns, while not always overtly bursting with radical doctrine, nonetheless belong to the same frame of reference as that radical printing world.

ISAAC WATTS AND THE END OF THE RADICAL HYMN

In 1721 a Dissenter said of John Bunyan's poetry, "That the burning of it wou'd be no Damage, if People might, by that means, come better to relish such as Mr. Watts."[90] This admirer of Watts reveals a major shift in Dissenting poetics from the age of Bunyan to that of Watts. Isaac Watts' career spans the transition from Old to New Dissent, and his rejection of the backward-looking modes of Revolutionary Puritanism is evident in his aesthetic program, epitomized in his hymn project. The great Dissenting hymn writer heralds a decisive shift in the political economy of the hymn, as he assiduously eradicated its political past, also rejecting its origins in Calvinist-dominated theology. Watts inaugurated a campaign to clear the hymn of its radical forebears in the preface to his first collection of hymns in 1707.

Though he derided his predecessors on artistic grounds – William Barton "chimes us asleep" – Watts' complaint against contemporary hymns was at root an ideological one.[91] "I have been long convinc'd," he writes in the preface, "that one great Occasion of this Evil arises from the Matter and Words [in] which we confine all our Songs. Some of 'em are almost opposite to the Spirit of the Gospel: Many of them foreign to the State of the New-Testament, and widely different from the present Circumstances of Christians."[92] Watts criticizes what he calls the "Jewishness" of contemporary hymns, that is, their emphatic use and application of Old Testament sources, and their application to a particular history:

While we are kindling into divine Love by the Meditations of the *loving Kindness of God, and the Multitude of his tender Mercies,* within a few Verses some dreadful Curse against Men is propos'd to our Lips; That *God would add Iniquity to their Iniquity, not let 'em come into his Righteousness, but blot 'em out of the Book of the Living*, Psal. 69.16,27,28. which is so contrary to the New Commandment, *of loving our Enemies.*[93]

Shunning the violence of the English Revolutionary hymns, Watts' campaign was a reformation of the hymn. Watts' form of Dissent, V. De Sola Pinto with no little scorn writes, "had little in common with the democratic Puritanism of Bunyan with its intense bibliolatry, its intolerance, and its Philistinism," instead vaunting the rationalist mode of Enlightenment.[94] Watts' rejection of that radical past takes the form of anti-Judaism, as he severs the history of the Israelite people from that of his own day: "the Application of many Verses of *David* to our State and Circumstances was never design'd, and is utterly impossible; and even where it is possible, yet 'tis so exceeding difficult that very few Persons of an Assembly are capable of it."[95] This is nothing short of a rejection of typological thinking, that hoary resource of apocalypticism and immediate revelation.

Watts had been raised as an orthodox Calvinist, succeeding to minister John Owen's congregation in Mark Lane, London, but he belongs to a new generation of Dissenters, moving away from high Calvinist orthodoxy. With Watts we observe a reconsideration of a radical past, and indeed a different approach towards temporality than the ever-present "now" of God's imminent appearance. This accompanied a generational shift in Dissent, but also the political shift as Whiggism turned from opposition to mainstream with the Revolution of 1688, and as Dissent reconsolidated over the politics of Queen Anne. As the martyrs of 1662 were fading far into memory, Dissent was in decline, particularly among the gentry.[96] Toleration and occasional conformity had produced splits among Dissenting groups even though they offered new opportunities for moderate conciliation. New latitudinarian and Socinian theologies were calling a God-centered approach into question. And the "heart-religion" of the early Methodists was claiming Dissent for the lower classes. Although the high church legislation of Queen Anne's reign had produced persecuting laws such as the Occasional Conformity Act (1711) which prevented Dissenters from qualifying for public office, as well as the Schism Act (1714), these were ineffective, and repealed. What could Dissent still offer its adherents? The future, to many Dissenting leaders, seemed to lie in the principles of Rational Dissent, liberty of conscience, and rejection of ritual impositions, rather than in the doctrines of violent apocalypticism and the Holy Spirit.

Because reason has its limits, however, Watts' poetry expressed the importance of the affections in spiritual exercise. As he suggests in a work disputing Locke's account of innate ideas, revelation is necessary to instigate action.[97] The faculties of the soul need to be raised by the work of the passions. But not too passionately. Watts recoils from those passions that turn toward the anti-social: "Reason and revelation agree to require social religion," he writes. As Isabel Rivers has argued, Watts came to embrace "politeness," along with his age.[98] Yet that turn was not merely a reflex action against the religious controversy against which the ship of state had foundered. It was, indeed a new solution to the same problem. As Watts wrote in his preface to *Hymns and Spiritual Songs* (1707), "I have avoided the more obscure and controverted points of Christianity, that we might all obey the Direction of the Word of God . . . The Contentions and distinguishing Words of Sects and Parties are secluded, that the whole Assembly might assist at the Harmony, and different Churches join in the same Worship without Offence" (viii). If fundamental questions about the relation of the church to the people remained unanswered within the Protestant nation deeply riven by Dissent, still, contemporary ethics could heal the breach, if only in manners not principle. As we have seen in looking at Marvell and Dryden's approaches to Milton, the proposed antidotes to enthusiasm were various. In Watts' case, forging the bonds of sociability would lead to healing; and indeed the moral habits of sociable tolerance could be strengthened by hymn singing, itself a communal action. With Watts, Rational Dissent comes of age as denominational affiliation is seen as an array of options, not one truth.

The psalms of David, for instance, those rousing anthems that served as a touchstone for parliamentary victory as much as for the radical agency of hymn singing, are cast under a shadow: "The cloudy and typical Expressions of the legal Dispensation should be turned into Evangelical Language, according to the Explications of the New Testament."[99] Severing the Old Testament from the New, Watts hails the hymn as tool of a universal truth. Reason and revelation go together, in a rejection of the enthusiasm that fired the English Revolution. With his analysis of David's psalms, Watts presents a clash between the ancient and the modern, in which his own poetics are resolutely coupled with the modern. "I am perswaded," Watts writes, "that St. *Paul* if he lived in our Age and nation, would no more advise us to sing unintelligible Sentences in *London*, than himself would sing in an unknown Tongue at *Corinth*" ("A Short Essay," 251). This is a new direction for the hymn, premised upon a rejection of ancient Israel, eschewing a superstitious, particularist "Jewishness," as Watts calls it, as opposed to a universal, rational, truth. This anti-Judaism is a battle of the Ancients and Moderns like that taking place over classical learning. Watts promises hymns "suited to the present Case and Experience of Christians" (256), confiding "I shall take pleasure in the Release of [singers'] Souls from that part of *Judaism* which they have so long indulged" (275). It is not surprising that Samuel Johnson accords him a special place: "He was one of the first authors that taught the Dissenters to court attention by the graces of language," chiding the rest for their wonted "coarseness" and obscurity.[100] In his rejection of Revolutionary Puritanism, Watts led the direction of nonconformist aesthetics in the eighteenth century, promoting if not a Rational Dissent, then a polite and sociable one. In his rejection of the violence of civil war, of what he deemed the vengeful anger symbolic of an Old Testament theology, Watts makes plain his negotiation of the cultural – not merely theological or political – legacies of radical Dissent. Watts keeps the affective elements, the spontaneity, flexibility, and populism of the hymn, while removing the typological, violent apocalypticism that had been central to the Dissenting literary tradition. By eschewing violence he labels Hebraic, Watts heralds a new age for Dissenting literary values.

There are, of course, many stories to be told of the "four fathers" of the hymn as a genre. "The Hymn" is no monolith; indeed, the variety of purposes and experiences of hymn writing and hymn singing are manifold.

Here I have been interested in exploring the ways that Dissenting literary form did political work and participated in the cultural battles within Restoration England: hymns are a good illustration of how aesthetic form was a key arena for that ideological contest. Dryden in *Annus Mirabilis* mocked those who "sing their Sabbath Notes with Feeble Voice."[101] Here we have seen how hymns contributed to Dissenting experience, embodying the radicalism of nonconformity by their innovation in form, indeed, how they were opposed in theory and in practice to the Anglican church's set prayer book. Hymns certainly provided shapes for the expression of creativity and ingenuity, a new mode that disguises novelty under a crust of repetition, regularity, and allusion, intertextuality and plagiarism: all culturally freighted elements, but whose ideological commitments do not depend solely upon outward signification, but also on inner meaning. Hymns embodied the collective hopes and fashioned a community. Through hymns, Dissenters linked themselves to a past – through citation of apt quotations from the Bible and favored authors – and to the present. Though choosing exclusion, worshiping both in public and within the public space of the family home, Dissenters could through hymns redeem a sense of a collective tradition, a shared voice and form through which the Holy Spirit could move. The story of the hymn in the seventeenth century may be told as a story of a gradual leeching of its radical political content, a shift from Hebraic to Christian emphasis. The hymn also negotiated the translation of radicalism as directed against the state to a radicalization of the family and discipline, from overt ideology to areas of action in which godliness could be wrought out of significant performances.

Coda: enlightenment

Dissenting poetry thus leaves an important, and lasting cultural legacy. To its detractors, Dissenting literary enthusiasm aroused all the dangers of a space outside surveillance and scrutiny, from which ideas – whether social, religious, or political – might spread in an unauthorized manner to a non-elite audience. And these detractors were right, to a certain extent. Literary enthusiasm did indeed offer a radical space from which to challenge the here and now, politics, and earthliness. Literary enthusiasm was not merely a creation of its enemies, but constituted a political practice, a theory of literature, an alternative to the worldly ethos of Augustanism with its catalogues of things, public persons, and politics. With the legacy of dissent, the triumph of secularization can be seen not simply as a question of reason being victorious over faith, but in the variety of ways of reconciling tensions between otherworldly and this-worldly obligations. This involved a process of admitting human mediation in the civil and cultural realms.

If the English Restoration constitutes a great clash of poetic modes, one of the noisiest confrontations in English literary history, we can see how enthusiasm over the course of the Restoration could be transformed into a poetic mode that valued personal experience, the common reader, direct communication with God, and sublime rapture. These were values in direct conflict with the state-sponsored hierarchies of church and land, but vital to the rise of a liberal politics, fostering an interest in the experiences of ordinary individuals, and habitually defending freedoms that were defined as personal, religious, and civil. If we restore to our range of inquiry the voices of those poets most often mocked by mainstream Restoration practice, we recover something of the revolutionary politics that marks the dissenting side, and see how the political transformations of the early modern period were effected through discourses of religion and literature. Something of the jangle is marked in Samuel Butler's *Hudibras*, and the literary variety, threats of democratic unruliness and social disorder are registered in Dryden's plenitude and exuberance. But these satiric voices aim to check and obscure another register of imaginative capacity that was unleashed in the Restoration and bequeathed to the modern period – the Dissenting mode. No less urgent or immediate than the satirists, Dissenters' poetry offered a contrasting literary approach. The English Revolution had opened up a public literary culture in which even the barely literate could claim a place. Dissenters put new pressures on that public culture by specifically appealing to a demotic audience, by their utopian hopes for a better future, and by reclaiming a lyric tradition, with its poetics of inwardness, feeling, as well as the cosmic sublime. For some, Milton may have seemed the end of a line of poetry. But for the others, Milton was a beginning.

To be sure, from the Restoration to the Glorious Revolution, in religion, politics, and in science, radical prophecy would undergo a series of powerful political rebukes. The Royal Society targeted prophecy and belief in miracles, and Locke's *Essay Concerning Human Understanding* devoted pages to downgrading prophetic enthusiasm to merely a kind of persuasive rhetoric; Joseph Glanvill's *Anti-Fanatical Religion* tells it all in his title.[1] As toleration arguments increasingly severed politics from faith, poetic inspiration was understood as a special kind of sanctioned enthusiasm, unleashed in that sphere of action in which private authority, or divine authority, could be permitted to be expressed. There were, of course, theological results as well, as a harsh involuntarist Calvinism gave way to a tempered voluntarism of Arminian theology, and then towards the even more voluntarist and rationalist Socinian and Deistic shades of Protestant religion. With Protestants including Andrew Marvell, John Howe, and Richard Baxter, increasingly drawn to Arminian or even, in Milton's and Locke's cases, anti-Trinitarian, positions, theological understanding of the meaning of divine obscurity changed dramatically.[2]

It seemed also that from within Dissent, there was movement away from radical antinomian positions. Presbyterians, Independents, and other nonconformists became committed to a "rational theology," and the doctrines of Arminianism, in a challenge to the rough Calvinism, helped to give shape to a more sociable Protestantism, based on an ethics of human voluntary action, emphasizing piety over revelation.[3] In *The Interest of Reason in Religion*, for instance, Robert Ferguson radically reformulated inspiration so as to value social order; his aim was "to vindicate the Non-Conformists from the aspersions lately cast upon them; as if they were *defamers* of reason, disclaiming from all concern in religion."[4] The titles of many nonconformist works such as John Owen's *The Reason of Faith*; Richard Baxter's *Reasons of the Christian Religion*; Charles Wolseley's *The Reasonableness of Scripture-Belief*, and others, testify to the importance of reason to nonconformists.

Richard Ashcraft has argued that the Dissenters' notion of reasonableness –
their "willingness to *rely* upon the judgment of the individual as a rational
free agent" – helped to develop a concept of subjective reason, that very
notion the High Anglicans feared as wildly uncontrollable.[5] Even the most
"rational" of these Restoration nonconformists, however, were still committed to an account of human reason as essentially inadequate to comprehend
the mystery of God and as prone to error due to the effects of the Fall whose
indelible mark had tainted reason: thus the need for Christ's expiating grace.
Revelation, and the assistance of the Holy Spirit, were still central to the
human capacity to understand. With Locke, however, that formulation
was to suffer attack as his reading of the consequences of the Fall led to
a rethinking of the nature of reason, and a challenge to the influence of
the Holy Spirit.[6] This Coda sketches the way Dissent, combustible in the
Restoration, gave power to eighteenth-century writers who worked with its
unfinished projects.[7]

LITERARY-POLITICAL AFTEREFFECTS

The taming of enthusiasm and the coming of Toleration in 1689 did not
settle dissenting literature quietly into the private sphere. Dissenters may
have found themselves at liberty to conduct worship as they pleased; Isaac
Watts may have dismissed biblical prophecy and severed literary creation
from political enthusiasm; John Locke may have excluded enthusiasm from
legitimate rational discourse; and new theologies may have hived off Dissent
from Calvinist predeterminism, but that was not the end of the story for
the Dissenters' literary engagement with politics. The social radicalism
of a Dissenting literary tradition was one lasting consequence of radical
religion, as creative writing and reading spread downward on the social
scale to the barely literate. The strong use and defense of print was another;
as Christopher Ness put it in a pamphlet dedicated to the Whig leader
Shaftesbury, "God Graciously bestowed this *Art of Printing* on Mankind,
for the *Unvailing* and *Unmasking* of this *Mystery of Iniquity* to the world . . .
Printing is like a *Wing*, on which *knowledge flies* throughout the *Habitable
World*, and is at this day a *famous Instrument* of God's holy spirit, to publish
his sacred and *Infallible Truth*." Ness understood there were two sides to
this coin, "though Satan do use it also to spread his *damnable Errors*."[8]
With that democratization of literature also came a set of literary values
prizing openness and accessibility, but also obscurity and transcendence, a
poetics often derided by its enemies, in Pope's *Dunciad*, or Swift's *Tale of a
Tub* and *Mechanical Operations of the Spirit*, for instance.

Full toleration would be a long time in coming, and the pains of Dissenters in the Restoration era were revived in arguments throughout the eighteenth century on behalf of wider tolerance. In his novels and especially his polemic, Daniel Defoe, raised a Dissenter, inherits the urgency, popularity, and directness of the Dissenting mode, stripped of its enthusiasm. The legacy of persecution was ever in his mind, erupting in political satire and polemic all through his writing life. Often Defoe summoned memories of the era of Charles II, daring his contemporary church to refrain from like persecution, to avoid those "*Knocking-down-Arguments* of Goal [sic] and Fine, *Ultra tenementum* which were used in those Arbitrary times, [that] were but the sure Refuge of a Cause by no other Arguments to be Defended," and to eschew the "Indelible Scandal of the Clergy of those Times."[9] Several times, Defoe took up the favored nonconformist genre, the eulogistic life of a persecuted minister, in order to make topical political comment, though leeching that genre of its apocalyptic overtones.[10] His *Shortest Way with Dissenters* (1702) angered both nonconformists and government, as Defoe showed himself the master of the tools of Augustan satire to make the case for toleration through irony.

Dissenters did remain engaged with politics, often closely allied with the Whigs, and over time their various sectarian affiliations became less strident. The main strands of Dissent, Independency, and Presbyterianism, had already sought rapprochement, sharing lectures for instance at Hackney in 1669 and Pinners' Hall in 1672.[11] Quakers were ever the exception; the Quaker William Penn was loyal to the Catholic James II, even when most Dissenters rushed to welcome William III. Come the Revolution, Dissenters allied with the Whigs. A triumph of the Independent concept of toleration rather than the Presbyterian hope for comprehension, the Revolution brought freedom to worship for Dissenters, even if there were still civic limitations, on office-holding for instance.[12] With the death of William III, the Tories quickly moved to suppress Dissenters, and the reign of Anne brought new debates about and measures against occasional conformists and the legacy of Dissent. After the accession of George I, Dissenters were more secure in a Whig-led ministry, though by the 1730s there were new waves of religious fervor, pietism, and Methodism.

Though Dissenting literature in the early eighteenth century eschewed the violence of apocalyptic prophecy, its poetry still sustained a political outlook. A new generation of Whig nonconformist authors, including Elizabeth Singer Rowe, John Hughes, Isaac Watts, and Henry Grove, drew fire from the sources of nonconformist devotion, and their poetry coexisted with the worldly balance of Augustan literary adventure and political topicality. Fervent, passionate, and personal, as well as generically adventurous and aimed for a public, these Dissenting poets maintained a legacy of inspired writing, wearing their religious fervor one day, and their politically engaged modes the next. I can only gesture here towards how we might enlarge our understanding of eighteenth-century poetry by considering the political and aesthetic afterlife of Restoration Dissent.

The Dissenters' legacy coursed powerfully through the writing of Elizabeth Singer Rowe. Her poetry developed from youthful lyric effusions published by John Dunton to the mature writing of a ten-book biblical heroic poem; she was enamored of Milton and the Italians, translated bits of Tasso, adapted Ovid, Crashaw, Drayton, and made a biblical paraphrase of the Song of Songs. With her poetic meditations and experiments in narrative fiction, Rowe bridged the genres of poetry and prose. Well regarded in her own day, hailed by the "Athenians" as William III's laureate, Rowe was seen by Elizabeth Carter as a spokesperson for all women. Born in Somerset in 1674, Rowe was daughter to Walter Singer, a nonconformist minister, and his wife Elizabeth Portness. Her father, who had a fair estate in the neighborhood of Frome, had been imprisoned in his early life for nonconformity and he first met his wife when she was visiting prisoners there as an act of charity. Their daughter Elizabeth was educated religiously, practiced music and drawing, and wrote verse from an early age, including a feminist screed defending her authority as a poet against traditional "polite" women's learning.[13] In 1694 and 1695 she was anonymously published in John Dunton's *Athenian Mercury*, and her *Poems on Several Occasions by Philomela* was brought out, also anonymously, in 1696. When she married, it was in 1710 to Thomas Rowe, thirteen years her junior, son and grandson of ejected nonconformist ministers. The couple moved to London; her husband died in 1715 and was buried at Bunhill Fields. A devout Dissenter, Rowe spent half her yearly income on charity in support of her Rook Lane Congregational Meeting at Frome, where she spent most of her life after her husband's death and where she was buried next to her father.[14]

Rowe was omnivorous in her reading and wrote in the genres of prose and poetry, with her *Devout Exercises* remaining popular and being reprinted until the mid-nineteenth century. Though she is now being rehabilitated in the history of the novel, her poetry, politics, and dissenting engagement deserve much more attention.[15] Above all literary aims, Rowe prized the poetic rapture, a sign of divine presence, and kept returning to the biblical book of the Song of Songs throughout her writing life. Such enthusiastic rapture lies at the heart of devotional poetry itself: the best Dissenting poetry in the early modern period concerns itself with resisting mediations, breaking forms, and spontaneous, immediate relation with the divine. The pleasures of the world are reworked to point to otherworldly ones, as a traditional love-lyric is fused with Canticles 7:2:

> Thou object of my highest bliss,
>   And of my dearest love,
> Come, let us from this tiresome world,
>   And all its cares remove.
>
> Among the murm'ring crystal streams,
>   The groves, and flow'ry fields,
> Let's try the calm and silent joys
>   That blest retirement yields.[16]

We cannot but hear echoes of the rhymes of "The passionate Sheepheard to his love," that Marlovian secular love lyric, in "Come live with mee and be my love" (except rather than *proving* all the worldly pleasures by love, Rowe's speaker seeks a *removing* from them). Under the sign of the Song of Songs, the translation signals a non-worldly approach.

Rowe herself aspires to be enveloped in the boundlessness of divine presence, and her Song of Songs spells out the conditions of such enthusiastic experience:

> Oh! How his pointed Language, like a Dart,
> Sticks to the softest Fibres of my Heart,
> Quite thro' my Soul the charming Accents slide,
> Which from his Life-inspiring Portals glide;
> And whilst I, the inchanting sound admire,
> My melting Vitals in a Trance expire.[17]

This poem is remarkable for its representation of the sensuousness of inhabiting, or being inhabited by, God's "Pointed Language." To evoke the dart is to evoke the wounded Christ, as the speaker takes on the bloodied persona; but in another measure, the wounding is a common enough image for being sexually penetrated, as Rowe's effusion conveys the physical and emotional state induced by sexual receptivity. As Rowe's poem solicits the Word, it also registers how inspired language alone can gratify. The divine presence enters the female body via divine language, but it is her language that reports this presence.[18]

In literary terms, moreover, Rowe continued the iconoclastic methods of Dissenting writing. A rare eighteenth-century champion of the blank verse form, Rowe bore the influence of her beloved Milton. Not only did she write several poems in imitation of Milton, but her forty-two "Devout Soliloquies" transformed his epic medium into a personal, devotional mode.[19] The sequence of these poems, like that in a traditional sonnet sequence, traces a romance between a lover and a beloved. In Rowe's case, the beloved is Jesus: "I've known the names of father, husband, friend;/ But when I think of thee, these tender ties,/ These soft engagements vanish into air."[20] Pledging fidelity to the love that is beyond earthly attachment, Rowe reaches for divine transport:

> Thou art my first desire, my warmest wish:
> These restless motions, these repeated sighs
> Are all addrest to thee; at thee I aim,
> In these imperfect flights, these upward views,
> These frequent glances at the distant stars.[21]

Earnest, simple, and filled with unbounded yearning, Rowe chooses her literary measures to stretch her transports, ambitiously matching her poetic and religious desires. Breaking with the current literary practice of rhyme, her blank verse sequence, with its highly irregular rhythms and its abrupt pauses, maintains the spontaneity of a spoken voice. In reworking the verse form of Milton's great poem, they elevate the drama of spiritual longing to an epic scale.

Rowe's piety made her a well-regarded figure throughout the eighteenth century, but her writing also offered a sharp political edge. In a poem commemorating the great Whig martyr John Hampden – "his soul with freedom fir'd" – Rowe protested against political tyranny and thwarted those who would destroy his good name:

> Tho' impious Priests maliciously defame,
> With servile toungues, th'Immortal Soldier's name;
> Yet shall it live with blooming honours grac'd,
> While liberty in Britain's Isle shall last.[22]

Her *History of Joseph* (1736) was a publishing success, with seven editions, including a German translation. Expanded to an ambitious, ten-book epic, in its second edition of 1737, the work chooses a biblical theme from the time of Pharaoh, evoking a long dissenting tradition of figuring in that familiar type a religious and political arbitrary power. Her hero Joseph moves from slavery to freedom, rising to become a prophet and a royal counsellor, and protesting the "tyrant's yoke." A classic Dissenting transposal, Joseph is seen as an imprisoned hero speaking for the will of the people and prophesying a king's downfall:

> Poor vassals by th'Egyptians are distress'd,
> And by a royal tyrant's yoke oppress'd:
> To heav'n they cry, an aid that never fails,
> Heavn'n hears the cry, the potent pray'r prevails.
> A mighty prophet, by divine command,
> Does bold before the raging monarch stand.[23]

With her experiments in literary form and her themes of liberty, especially religious liberty, Rowe bridges Enthusiasm with Enlightenment. An early appreciator of Thomson's poetry, through her work we can see the transformation of enthusiasm into a pre-Romantic mode.

Literary and political dissent made their mark in a different way on John Hughes (1677–1720), whose exact religious affiliations are unknown, but whose Dissenting background should be further explored. Most importantly remembered for creating the first critical edition of Edmund Spenser, published by Tonson in 1715, Hughes was the grandson of the ejected minister William Hughes, who had maintained his congregation illegally in woods and fields after Uniformity. John was educated at the Dissenting Academy at Newington Green along with Isaac Watts. He wrote a pro-toleration pamphlet in 1705, compiled a Whig history of England, and also pursued a polite literary career, writing plays and poetry of minor success, and collaborating with the Anglican Sir Richard Blackmore in a periodical (which considered such topics as women's education, Newton's colors, and divine prescience).[24] "Too grave a poet for me," as Swift confided to Pope, Hughes paid homage to Milton in his Pindaric "Ode to the Creator of the World," and was author of a "Venus and Adonis" set to music by Handel.[25]

In his edition of Spenser, Hughes knew that *The Faerie Queen* had come under attack for its lack of unity. Yet Hughes admired Spenser for his aberrent, gothic style, his "Mixture of Beauty and Barbarism."[26] By his approval of the non-uniform "Gothic" as against the "Grandeur and Simplicity," of classical Rome, we can perceive an ideological wink: his architectural metaphors become readily available for political import, with the English "Gothic" constitution vaunted at the expense of a uniform neoclassicism (think Uniform Church here), an iconoclastic sensibility born from the experience of Dissent. Hughes was also an enthusiastic poet, registering the boundlessness of creation in *An Ode to the Creator of the World. Occasion'd by Fragments of Orpheus* (1713), a philosophical poem that is a Pindaric, that loose and irregular form itself offering a mimetic representation of the shapeless expanse that is God's extension. As he contemplates God in heaven, his comprehension fails:

> Here Wonder only can take Place; –
> Then Muse, th'adventrous Flight forbear!
> These Mystick Scenes thou canst no farther trace;
> Hope may some boundless Future Bliss embrace,
> But *What*, or *When*, or *How*, or *Where*,
> Are Mazes all, which Fancy runs in vain;
> Nor can the narrow Cells of human Brain
> The vast immesurable Thought contain.[27]

As the poet's control is torn away from him, the words give way to wonder, and then to silence. The dash breaks off attempts to order what is seen, to know one's location: "Here Wonder only can take Place; –". Place, sight, and with these, language, have reached their limits. It is no wonder that the poet clings to his muse, urging her to go no further. The strict rhyme and meter of the last three lines put the reins on the journey, closing with *Brain, contain*: words that put a cap to motion. Whether or not he remained within the Dissenting religious tradition his parents and grandparents bequeathed to him, still in Hughes we can see the impact of Dissenting literary devotion and engaged political activity.

AESTHETIC AFTEREFFECTS

With the works of John Bunyan and Benjamin Keach republished regularly through the eighteenth century, Dissenters bequeathed a legacy of sturdy narrative and writing targeted at the many. Children's literature was a popular genre amongst Dissenting authors. In poetry, among the "polite," those who continued a Dissenting literary tradition did not evict the divine from literary expression, as can be seen in the writing of Rowe and Hughes. And early eighteenth-century non-Dissenting critics such as the Whig third Earl of Shaftesbury and John Dennis offered defenses of enthusiasm as a sublime literary mode.[28] Dennis married two languages in his 1701 treatise, *The Advancement and Reformation of Modern Poetry*, the title punning slyly on a "reformation" that could be both religious and poetic. Dennis asserted: "Poetical Genius, in a Poem, is the true Expression of Ordinary or Enthusiastick Passions proceeding from Ideas to which it naturally belongs; and Poetical Genius, in a Poet, is the power of expressing such Passion worthily: And the Sublime is a great Thought, express'd with the Enthusiasm that belongs to it."[29] Dennis merged a neoclassical sensibility with an appreciation for the fiery emotions aroused by divine presence. For some writers, aesthetic experience could itself be a surrogate for the experience of the divine.[30] Finding Longinus assimilable to their age, many poets and critics, orthodox or not, renovated sublime language to express their confidence, directness, and experimentation.[31] Anglican devotional writers also took up a religious literary mode: Samuel Wesley (the elder) composed a ten-book epic on the life of Jesus published in 1693; and John Norris, Lady Mary Chudleigh, and that butt of Pope's wit, Sir Richard Blackmore, all wrote religious verse.[32] Many of these Anglican poets seemed to prefer New Testament themes, as if following Watts' recommendations to leave behind the violence of the Hebrew Bible. A common enemy for Dissenters and these Anglican religious poets was the atheist.

The influence of Herbert, and with it, the reworking of the aesthetic legacy of Dissent would be captured by the Presbyterian Henry Grove (1684–1738). Grove was a philosophy tutor at the Dissenting Academy at Taunton, probably the author of the life of Elizabeth Rowe published in her miscellaneous works in 1739, and his contributions to *The Spectator* and *St. James's Journal* merited praise from Samuel Johnson.[33] In his harrowing poetry, however, he discards the urbanity of his journalism. In "The Divine Immensity. An Ode," the vastness of the cosmos, measured against a dust mote, cannot but bring on a melancholy, stuttering, perspective. Admitting God's condescending kindness towards human fragility amidst this grand spectacle, he imitates George Herbert's famous poem, "The Altar":

> This slender Altar, Lord, I raise,
> Compos'd of Wonder, to thy Praise;
> Accept what Gratitude demands.
> Amidst Earth's blended Tongues, with th'Ocean's Roar,
> 'Midst countless multitudes who thee adore
> Thou hear'st my feeble Voice, and se'st my lifted Hands.[34]

Despite the cacophony of human languages and the power of nature's "*Roar*," the lone voice of the poet merits audition. With the final line's repetition of the long "e" sounds in "*hear'st . . . feeble . . . se'st*" there is an interchange as the first and last in this series denote God's actions. At the center is the weak human, nested between God's verbs. God's power is to create, and also to hear even the weakest noise. Instead of Herbert's dolorous admission of self-criticism ("A broken ALTAR, Lord, thy servant reares,/ Made of a heart, and cemented with teares"), Grove's poem departs from the original to assume a more confident pose. Thematically, this is not such a different poem; both Herbert and Grove offer praise to their Maker. But Grove's vision is broader, cosmopolitan, and finally surer of God's responsiveness. Theologically, he swerves from the Herbertian notion of sacrifice, and eschews its restlessness (Herbert: "these stones to praise thee may not cease"), withdrawing from the sharper Calvinism of the original. Instead, Grove's poem offers a static emotional register of awe at the vastness of space. The altar is not *broken*, as is Herbert's, but *slender*, the Herbertian conceit of workmanship replaced by that of dimensionality. The poem ranges into the populous universe rather than into the soul. Here is a transvaluation of the poetics of the Holy Spirit. Rather than serving to effect earthly action, the Spirit instead fashions poetry.

As it did for Grove, the freedom and boldness of the Pindaric would made it an appealing form to poets as diverse as John Dryden, the Earl of Rochester, and Daniel Defoe, who each used it for different purposes.[35] As with all emblems of enthusiasm, its high seriousness of purpose also made it a ripe target for parody. Samuel Butler's "Upon an Hypocritical Nonconformist" assumed the cloak of a Pindaric ode to render a thundering attack against Dissenters. Though the ode was a heroic form, topical and agile, and very public in its intention, in the Dissenters' hands the heroism is deployed to accompany the voyager to the heavens, to mark the travails of the spirit. With the Pindaric, seeking to become God's instrument, for example, the great hymn writer Isaac Watts becomes a divine poet instead of a radical saint. Surrender to God's agency thus entails not the violence of divine wrath against enemies, but instead the hope of sublime communication:

> I.
> Far in the heav'ns my God retires,
> My God, the mark of my desires,
>   And hides his lovely face:
>   When he descends within my view,
>   He charms my reason to pursue,
> But leaves it tir'd and fainting in th'unequal chase.
>
> II.
> Or if I reach unusual height
>   Till near his presence brought
> There floods of glory check my flight,
> Cramp the bold pinions of my wit,
>   And all untune my thought;
> Plung'd in a sea of light I roll,
> Where wisdom, justice, mercy, shines;
>   Infinite rays in crossing lines
> Beat thick confusion on my sight, and overwhelm my soul.[36]

The poet moves jarringly through space and time to reach his God. As if daring to suffer the fate of Icarus, whose foolish ambition to fly to the sun led to his destruction, Watts' poetic aspiration also leads to unknown dangers, violence felt all the more acutely by the recurrent trochaic inversions and halting revisits of regular iambic meter. Here the form of the poem itself allegorizes the flight of the spirit, with its irregular meter portraying the boundlessness of enthusiastic moments, the panting efforts of the poet's reason to pursue his God. Line 15 presents an instance of poulter's meter, as if two lines of a hymn are crushed together to portray the soul's being overwhelmed by his ecstatic experience. The movement of the lines downward on the page works in a contrary motion to the poet's desired motion of ascent to meet his deity. The words "crossed lines" imitate the crossing between the last two lines of the second stanza, calling attention to the meter, refusing orderly succession of verse, as the panting poet drops into that rolling chaos of God's presence. This Pindaric, with its loose line lengths and irregular stanzas, surprises readers with each turn, making it an adventure to seek "The Incomprehensible," the title of the poem. In his first edition of *Horae Lyricae* (1706), Watts himself praised "the free and unconfined measures of *Pindar* [which] would also best maintain the Dignity of the Theme, as well as give a loose to the Devout Soul, nor check the Raptures of her Faith and Love." By the second edition, Watts added Milton to the Pindaric models to imitate, claiming that "the free and unconfin'd Numbers of *Pindar*, or the noble Measures of *Milton* without Rhime, would best maintain the Dignity of the Theme."[37] As Milton became assimilable to the sublime mode, he took his place along with Pindar as champion of breaking poetic bounds.

If this book has revived an unjustly neglected literary tradition, I have also hoped to show how the category of "enthusiasm" was constructed in a pivotal contest over religion and political legitimation.[38] In hailing legitimate authority from the divine, in making a bid for immediate presence, the inspired prophet seemed to challenge human institutions and communicative norms, to open the door for holy war. Yet it is also true that in the Restoration there were few resources other than apocalypticism to fire so powerful a challenge to hierarchy and persecution in the period, and to provide the emotional and social resources for brave acts of defiance and solidarity. There were of course, other, secularizing, languages of political theory in early modern England, whether republican, ancient constitution, common or natural law. It would be a major practical task of early political thinking to negate enthusiasm's instrumental role in politics and to find grounds other than holy war in which to voice a political challenge to an authoritarian church and state. Early liberals did find alternate ground for these campaigns by developing a civil science of politics and by settling on an aesthetic framework for the discourse of enthusiasm. The concept of the sublime would become crucial in constructing a place for divine inspiration, providing a means of secluding so-called "enthusiasm" from the sphere of politics and into art.[39] By cordoning off a sphere of legitimate enthusiasm into the private or the aesthetic, early Whigs also did the political work of liberalism in cordoning off religion as an area outside the interest of the state.

The period saw a shift in political poetry from the typological iconoclasm of radical prophecy to a range of styles and modes: Whig political verse; earthy journalism; experimental or devotional poetry; a rapturous, sublime mode; and the novel, that open, plain-speaking form that pursued self-scrutiny within a providential scope. The Romantics would inherit the Dissenters' literary tradition, bringing to it their own renewed political commitments. As the great Whig poet, James Thomson, would put it, "let POETRY, once more, be restored to her antient Truth, and Purity; let Her be inspired from Heaven, and, in Return, her Incense ascend thither."[40] If the Enlightenment bid to contain enthusiastic religion by the discipline of reason was its central gift to modernity, then one aspect of this feat was the securing of enthusiasm into the realm of art, with a new name: the sublime. Yet that mode is no mere aesthetic category; rather, it bears a powerful memory of oppositional force, Dissent's ongoing project. Dissent, what E. P. Thompson calls a "slumbering radicalism," would erupt to become the backbone of workers' reform movements in the eighteenth century.[41] Its literary, cultural, and political habits, shaped in the Restoration under persecution and despair, would prove a rich lode for the generations to come.

Appendix: Milton's burial place

The place of Milton's burial has been taken as evidence for his reconciliation with the Restored Anglican church.[1] This evidence, however, needs to be reconsidered so that a clearer portrait of the great poet's relation to Dissent may emerge. I will thus spend a moment on the burial place to examine this evidence of Milton's only clear institutional religious affiliation.

When Milton's father was buried in March 1647, Cripplegate's ministerial leadership was Independent, after the ousting of royalist prelate William Fuller in 1641. In 1647, Cripplegate churchyard was used for a military marching ground, and a number of innovations in governance were introduced in the 1640s, although the living remained vacant until Richard Cromwell appointed the Presbyterian Samuel Annesley in 1658. That appointment caused controversy. There circulated against him a parish petition headed by a powerful church patron, who had long ago performed the role of Elder Brother in Milton's *Comus* and had been its dedicatee. In the early 1680s the Earl repeatedly gave large sums of money to augment the Cripplegate church ornaments and for new bells to be installed in the recently renovated tower.[2] This was the Earl who had inscribed in the copy of Milton's *First Defense*, "Liber igni, Author furca, dignissimi" (The book is most deserving of burning, the author of the gallows).[3] After 1662, Cripplegate church moved swiftly to put its service in line with the new prayer book, and records show the purchase of a surplice and the receipt of money for rails around the communion table in 1662: that these elements of "the beauty of holiness" were absent until that moment tells us that the church had been rather "Low" before.[4]

Yet Cripplegate parish is an interesting and probably not-uncommon instance of the way that Restoration Uniformity was not uniform. Though ousted, Annesley did nonetheless continue to preach and publish in the area with a great following.[5] Succeeding the nonconformist Annesley were two royalist appointments, the second of whom, Dr. Pritchett, fled the parish during the Great Plague and removed to one of his other livings during the later part of his tenure, which ended in 1681. During that period – a sort of interregnum – it looks as if the mice played whilst the cat was away. Church records show that Dissenting ministers, including the Independent Samuel Slater, were paid to preach at Cripplegate church even after their ejection.[6] The church's then curate William Smythies, who served the parish from 1673 until 1704, had, it turns out, a sideline as a lecturer at local Dissenting meetings, and was accused of being an "Oliverian," attacked for his actions and views by Sir Roger L'Estrange. This would probably have been the church's leadership at the time of Milton's funeral. The Presbyterian Thomas Vincent, who ministered to the City of London during the plague, was, like Milton, buried in the church in 1678, with a Congregational minister preaching his funeral sermon there. In 1681, Edward Fowler was appointed vicar. Fowler is on record for breaking a stained-glass window at Gloucester Cathedral, in protest against high churchiness during the Popish plot, as "a vile relic of popish superstition."[7] He protected seditious Dissenters during his ministry, was a friend to John Locke, and became an ardent supporter of the Revolution of 1688, soon being elevated to a bishopric under William. St. Giles Cripplegate of Milton's day was a church in flux, a conduit through which the tensions between Anglicanism and varieties of Dissent were filtered, and it is clear from the records that sympathies remained largely on the side of Dissent.

Milton's headstone, removed in 1679, made way for steps to be built up to the altar: this was part of a process of the Anglicanization of Cripplegate.[8] It is simply perfect and ghastly too that Milton's memorial was demolished in the name of enhancement of ceremony and sacrament in this process. At Milton's funeral, "All the learned and great Friends in *London*, not without a friendly concourse of the Vulgar, accompany'd his Body to the Church of S. *Giles* near *Cripplegate*, where he lies buried in the Chancel, and where the Piety of his Admirers will shortly erect a Monument becoming his worth," wrote John Toland in 1688.[9] By the time Jonathan Richardson composed his life in 1734, that monument still had not been erected. Plans are currently underway for a memorial to be placed there.

Notes

1 READING DISSENT

1. Anthony à Wood, *Athenae Oxonienses*, ed. P. Bliss, 5 vols. (1813–20), III, 682.
2. Richard Baxter, *Reliquiae Baxterianae*, ed. Matthew Sylvester (1696), Part 2, 386; Anon., *Master Edmund Calamies Leading Case* (1663).
3. Laurence Womock, *Aron-bimnucha: Or, An Antidote to Cure the Calamites of their Trembling for Fear of the Ark* (1663), 85.
4. Thomas Rugge, *Mercurius Politicus Redivivus*, BL Add. MS 10117, fols. 58v, 61.
5. [John Birkenhead], *Cabala, or an Impartial Account of the Non-Conformists Private Designs, Actings and Ways. From August 24. 1662. to December 25 in the same year* (1663), 26, 28.
6. Anon., *Hudibras on Calamy's Imprisonment, and Wild's Poetry* [1663?], single-sheet fol.
7. See for example, Folger MS v.b.94, 200; Henry Newcome's commonplace book, Folger MS v.a.232; Folger MS v.a.148, fol. 16, and fols. 46–48. Satirical response: *Poor Robbin's Parley with Dr. Wilde* (1672); *Dr. Wild's Squibs Returned* (1672). Oldham mocks Wild in the prologue to his "Satires upon the Jesuits," 31, in Elias F. Mengel, Jr., *Poems on Affairs of State*, 7 vols. (New Haven, 1965), I, 20.
8. Robert Wild, "A Poem upon the Imprisonment of Mr. Edmund Calamy in Newgate," *Iter Boreale* (1668), 73. Laurence Womock, *Anti-Boreale* (1663) a riposte to Wilde's poem on Calamy; and see Anon., *Your Servant Sir, or, Ralpho to Hudibras Descanting on Wilds Poetry* (1663).
9. *CSPD* 1663–64, LXII, 10. However, the Church Wardens' accounts of St. Mary Aldermanbury note Calamy was paid for his impromptu speaking; Guildhall MS 3556.2, St. Mary the Virgin Aldermanbury Church Wardens' Accounts, 5 May 1662–5 May 1663.
10. *Mercurius Publicus* (1–8 January 1662), 16. See also Richard L. Greaves, *Saints and Rebels: Seven Nonconformists in Stuart England* (Macon, GA, 1985), 9–62.
11. Greaves, *Deliver*, 221.
12. Thomas Gilbert to Lord Wharton 29 October 1663, Bodl. Rawl. MS 53, fol. 22.

13. Baxter, *Reliquiae Baxterianae*, Part 2, 386.

14. On the political importance of cultural forms, see Eric Hobsbawm and Terence Ranger, eds., *The Invention of Tradition* (Cambridge, 1994), 1–14; and Raphael Samuel, *Theatres of Memory* (1994).

15. Keeble, *LC*, vii.

16. Watts, *Dissenters*, 221–62.

17. On Dissenters' rapprochement with James, see John Miller, *Popery and Politics in England, 1660–1688* (Cambridge, 1973), 214–28; Mark Goldie, "James II and the Dissenters' Revenge: The Commission of Enquiry of 1688," *Historical Research* 66, 159 (1993), 53–88.

18. Nicholas Tyacke, "The 'Rise of Puritanism' and the Legalizing of Dissent, 1571–1719," in Ole Peter Grell, Jonathan I. Israel, and Nicholas Tyacke, eds., *From Persecution to Toleration: The Glorious Revolution and Religion in England* (Oxford, 1991), 17–49; Gordon Schochet, "From 'Persecution' to 'Toleration,'" in J. R. Jones, ed., *Liberty Secured? Britain Before and After 1688* (Stanford, 1992), 122–57; John Spurr, *The Restoration Church of England, 1646–1689* (New Haven, 1991); Tim Harris, Paul Seaward, and Mark Goldie, eds., *The Politics of Religion in Restoration England* (Oxford, 1990).

19. A good summary of this longer history and the theological spectrum is Rivers, *RGS*, 90–109.

20. Blair Worden, "Toleration and the Cromwellian Protectorate," in W. J. Sheils, ed., *Persecution and Toleration*, Studies in Church History 21 (Oxford, 1984), 199–233.

21. Hill, *Defeat*, 17; Tim Harris, *London Crowds in the Reign of Charles II* (Cambridge, 1987), 63; Watts, *Dissenters*, 219; John Coffee, *Persecution and Toleration in Protestant England, 1558–1689* (2000).

22. John S. Coolidge, *The Pauline Renaissance in England: Puritanism and the Bible* (Oxford, 1970); Geoffrey F. Nuttall, *The Holy Spirit in Puritan Faith and Experience* (Chicago, 1992).

23. John Spurr, *England in the 1670s* (Oxford, 2000), 80.

24. Watts, *Dissenters*, 267–89; 227–38.

25. W. A. Speck, *Stability and Strife: England, 1714–1760* (Cambridge, MA, 1977), 100–01.

26. E. P. Thompson, *The Making of the English Working Class* (New York, 1977), 28–58. However, political exclusion was offset by loopholes; see R. K. Webb, "From Toleration to Religious Liberty," in J. R. Jones, ed., *Liberty Secured? Britain Before and After 1688* (Stanford, 1992), 158–98; 175.

27. Greaves, *Deliver* and *Enemies*, and Hill, *Defeat*, have unearthed the Restoration radical underground, that shadowy world of plotters, who were motivated by millenarianism or by anti-Stuart ideology. See also Wilbur Cortez Abbot, "English Conspiracy and Dissent, 1600–1674," *American Historical Review* 14 (1908–09), 503–28 and 696–722; at the other end of the spectrum, J. A. I. Champion, *The Pillars of Priestcraft Shaken: The Church of England and its Enemies, 1660–1730* (Cambridge, 1992).

28. The classic study is Douglas R. Lacey, *Dissent and Parliamentary Politics in England, 1661–1689: A Study in the Perpetuation and Tempering of Parliamentarianism* (New Brunswick, NJ, 1969); see also J. T. Cliffe, *The Puritan Gentry Besieged, 1650–1700* (1993), 176–90; Tim Harris, *Politics under the Later Stuarts: Party Conflict in a Divided Society, 1660–1715* (1993), 105–06; H. Horwitz, "Protestant Reconciliation in the Exclusion Crisis," *Journal of Ecclesiastical History* 15 (1964), 201–17. On Puritan royalists, see Harry Grant Plum, *Restoration Puritanism* (Chapel Hill, 1943).

29. "Most of the sects followed Muggletonians and Quakers into pacifism and abstention from politics. Their God now presided over a provincial, stunted culture; he was no longer capable of transforming nations," muses Christopher Hill, "God and the English Revolution," in *The Collected Essays of Christopher Hill, Vol. 2: Religion and Politics in 17th Century England* (Amherst, 1986), 335.

30. Keeble, *LC*, 47.

31. Keeble insists that in Dissent, there was a "heterogeneity scarcely regarded by the authorities," *LC*, 39. Spurr stresses the constant "self-invention" of the Restoration church, *The Restoration Church*, xiv; Roger Thomas, "Comprehension and Indulgence," in Geoffrey Nuttall and Owen Chadwick, eds., *From Uniformity to Unity, 1662–1962* (1962), 195–206.

32. See Thomas Crosby, *History of the English Baptists*, 4 vols. (1738–40); C. G. Bolam, Jeremy Goring, H. L. Short, and R. Thomas, eds., *The English Presbyterians from Elizabethan Puritanism to Modern Unitarianism* (1968); C. E. Whiting, *Studies in English Puritanism from the Restoration to the Revolution* (New York, 1931); George R. Abernathy, Jr., *The English Presbyterians and the Stuart Restoration, 1648–1663, Transactions of the American Philosophical Society* n.s. 55 (1965), part 2; W. C. Brathwaite, *The Beginnings of Quakerism*, 2nd. ed. (Cambridge, 1955); Hugh Barbour, *The Quakers in Puritan England* (New Haven, 1964); Luella M. Wright, *The Literary Life of the Early Friends, 1650–1725* (New York, 1932).

33. See Earl Miner, *The Restoration Mode from Milton to Dryden* (Princeton, 1974).

34. Hoxie Neale Fairchild, *Religious Trends in English Poetry, 1700–1740*, 6 vols. (New York, 1949), 1, 98–120, on Anglican poets.

35. See Barbara Kiefer Lewalski, *Protestant Poetics and the Seventeenth-Century Religious Lyric* (Princeton, 1979); Louis L. Martz, *The Poetry of Meditation: A Study of English Religious Literature* (New Haven, 1962), insufficiently explains the Puritan strand; Lawrence A. Sasek, *The Literary Temper of the English Puritans* (Baton Rouge, 1961), ignores these poetic forebears.

36. Samuel Parker, *A Discourse of Ecclesiastical Politie* (1670), iv; and cf. xii, xiii, xvii–xviii.

37. Samuel Parker, *A Reproof to the Rehearsal Transprosed* (1673), 9.

38. Thomas Hobbes, *Behemoth*, ed. Ferdinand Tonnies, and with an Introduction by Stephen Holmes (Chicago, 1990), 96, 164.

39. Parker, *Discourse*, xiii.

40. David Lloyd, *Cabala: Or, the Mystery of Conventicles Unvail'd* (1664), frontispiece.

41. John Dryden, *The Hind and the Panther*, in Dryden, *Works*, III, 132 (310, 311, 314).
42. Dryden, *Religio Laici*, in Dryden, *Works*, II, 121 (391, 394–95).
43. Samuel Butler, *Hudibras*, ed. John Wilders (Oxford, 1967), Third Part, II, 8–18.
44. Robert Whitehall, *The Coronation* (1661).
45. R. O., prefatory poem to Samuel How, *The Sufficiencie of the Spirits Teaching without Human Learning* (1683), fol. A3v.
46. Lawrence Stone, cited in Joan Thirsk, ed., *The Restoration* (1976), 172.
47. Whiting, *Studies in English Puritanism*, 75.
48. Butler, *Hudibras*, 16, First Part, I, 497, 501–02; Third Part, II, 603–08.
49. Dryden, *Works*, II, 48 (164–66).
50. Benjamin Laney, *Five Sermons* (1669), 44.
51. [Birkenhead], *Cabala*, 1–2, 12.
52. Joseph Besse, *An Abstract of the Sufferings of the People Called Quakers*, 3 vols. (1738); Joseph Besse, *A Collection of the Sufferings of the People Called Quakers*, 2 vols. (1753).
53. Edmund Calamy, *An Abridgment of Mr. Baxter's History of his Life and Times* (1702); reworked in Samuel Palmer, ed., *The Nonconformist's Memorial* (1775); revised as A. G. Matthews, *Calamy Revised* (Oxford, 1934). Calamy's list was controversial from the time of its publication, when a contest over memory of persecution was central to the politics of toleration in the early modern period. See, for example, the "Advertisement" appended to the Prefatory Discourse to Mary Astell, *Moderation truly Stated: Or, A Review of a late Pamphlet, entituled, Moderation a Vertue. With a Prefatory Discourse to Dr. D'Avenant concerning his late Essays on Peace and War* (1704), n.p.
54. Max Weber, *The Protestant Ethic and the Spirit of Capitalism*, tr. Talcott Parsons (1996); William Lamont, *Puritanism and Historical Controversy* (1996), 103–29; and on the political stakes of that historiography, see Raphael Samuel, "The Discovery of Puritanism, 1820–1914: A Preliminary Sketch," in J. Garnett and C. Mather, eds., *Revival and Religion since 1700: Essays for John Walsh* (1993), 201–47.
55. Thompson, *Making*, 30.

2 MEMORY

1. A. G. Matthews, ed., *Abstracts of Wills of Ejected Ministers* (1934), DWL MS 38.59, fol. 971.
2. Ronald Hutton, *The Restoration* (Oxford, 1987), 132–35.
3. John Dryden, "To His Sacred Majesty, A Panegyrick on His Coronation," 25–26, in Dryden, *Works*, I, 33 (25–26).
4. Paula R. Backscheider, *Spectacular Politics: Theatrical Power and Mass Culture in Early Modern England* (Baltimore, 1993), 7.
5. Edward Whiston, *The Life and Death of Mr. Henry Jessey* (1671), 94. Jessey's burial is recorded in the register of St. Stephen's Ward, Coleman Street, 8 September 1663.

6. Thomas Rugge notes for 7 September: "there was sold in the presse a libell that the people may put their king to death and that the law of God scruples the king not more than any other person the law commanding his saints to take a two edged sword in their hands to execute Judgment," *Mercurius Politicus Redivivus*, in BL Add. MS 10117, fol. 79. On 14 September, covering the previous week's news, *The Kingdoms Intelligencer*, no. 3, commented on a paper "that has justifi'd the Murther of the Late King since the Act of Indemnity, and undertaken by a *Printer* . . . the president of Ehud's stabbing Eglon, is Recommended to the pretending sufferers under the Present Government." Citing Judges 3, the pamphlet was probably *A Treatise of the Execution of Justice*, for which the printer John Twyn's shop was raided on 7 October, the printer later tried and executed for high treason on 24 February 1664. See Greaves, *Deliver*, 224.

7. B. R. White, "Henry Jessey in the Great Rebellion," in R. Buick Knox, ed., *Reformation, Conformity and Dissent* (1977), 132–53; 152; *CR*, 298.

8. Greaves, *Deliver*, 61.

9. *CSPD* 1663–64, LXII, 278; Greaves, *Deliver*, 173.

10. Whiston, *Life*, 95–96.

11. *The Newes*, no. 2 (Thursday 10 September 1663). Anthony à Wood takes his account of Jessey's funeral from this report, *Fasti Oxonienses*, ed. Philip Bliss, 2 vols. (London, 1815), 1, 436.

12. Daniel Defoe, Preface, *De Laune's Plea for the Nonconformists* (1706), i, x, xi.

13. The early modern period brought decisive changes in attitudes towards death. Puritan individualism and falling mortality rates gave rise to an appreciation of the value of life, according to Lawrence Stone, *The Family, Sex and Marriage in England, 1500–1800* (New York, 1977), 66; G. W. Pigman sketches the emergence of "less anxious" personal and psychological attitudes towards grief, in *Grief and the English Renaissance Elegy* (Cambridge, 1985). See also Keith Thomas, *Religion and the Decline of Magic* (New York, 1971), 602–05; Lucinda McCray Beier, "The Good Death in Seventeenth-Century England," in Ralph Houlbrooke, ed., *Death, Ritual, and Bereavement* (1989), 43–61. Stone is challenged by Anne Laurence, "Godly Grief: Individual Responses to Death in Seventeenth-Century Britain," in Houlbrooke, ed., *Death*, 62–76.

14. In the modern period, death has become "invisible," according to Philippe Ariès, *The Hour of Our Death*, tr. Helen Weaver (New York, 1982); Clare Gittings propounds the individualism thesis in *Death, Burial and the Individual in Early Modern England* (1984); Peter Burke, "Death in the Renaissance, 1347–1656," in Jane H. M. Taylor, ed., *Dies Illa: Death in the Middle Ages* (Liverpool, 1984), 59–66; 62. On death's commercialization, see David Cannadine, "War and Death, Grief and Mourning in Modern Britain," in Joachim Whaley, ed., *Mirrors of Mortality: Studies in the Social History of Death* (1981), 187–242; and Thomas Laqueur, "Bodies, Death, and Pauper Funerals," *Representations* 1,1 (1993), 109–31.

15. Henry, *Diary*, 242.

16. Royal Commission on the Historical Monuments of England, *Nonconformist Chapels and Meeting-Houses: Buckinghamshire* (1986), 3; C. G. Crump, ed., *The History of the Life of Thomas Ellwood* (1900), 139–40. Ellwood, along with Isaac Pennington and eight others were there arrested and imprisoned in Aylesbury gaol for a month; W. H. Summers, in *Memories of Jordans and the Chalfonts and the Early Friends in the Chiltern Hundreds* (1904), vii. It is tantalizing to note that Milton resided in the neighborhood in Chalfont St. Giles at this time, in a house that Ellwood had arranged for him. Ellwood, immediately upon his release, visited him there and was shown his manuscript of *Paradise Lost* (Crump, *Ellwood*, 145). See also David Masson, *The Life of John Milton*, 6 vols. (1881–94), VI, 490, 495–96.

17. Keeble, *LC*, 110–20, for nonconformist responses to censorship.

18. On variances from the prescribed service, see Horton Davies, *Worship and Theology in England: From Andrewes to Baxter and Fox, 1603–1690* (Cambridge, 1996), 410.

19. *Directory for the Publique Worship of God* (1644), 73–74.

20. Gittings, *Death, Burial and the Individual*, 56.

21. Benjamin Keach, *A Summons to the Grave . . . a Sermon Preached at the Funeral of . . . Mr. John Norcot* (1676), fol. B1.

22. *DNB.*

23. *The Newes*, no. 2 (Thursday 10 September 1663).

24. D. H. Atkinson, *Ralph Thoresby, the Topographer: His Town and Times*, 2 vols. (Leeds, 1885), 1, 56. See also Robert Wild's generous epitaph for Manton in *Dunton's Whipping Post* (1706), 79: "Here lies a Great Divine, a Learned Man,/ Smart Disputant, well read Historian,/ Accurate Textman, Orthodox avow'd, /If our Church Articles may be allow'd." Manton's teachings were epitomized in a single-sheet folio, probably prepared for his funeral: *Words of Peace: Or Dr. Mantons Last Sayings. Many of them taken from him on his Death-Bed, or observed on other Remarkable Occasions; Tending very much to the Edification of Christians* (1677).

25. [John Birkenhead], *Cabala, or an Impartial Account of the Non-Conformists Private Designs, Actings and Wayes. From August 24. 1662. to December 25 in the Same Year* (1663), 15–16.

26. E. H., *The Mock-Elogie* [sic] *on the Funeral of Mr. Caryl* (1672/73). Also see the satirical broadside for the Presbyterian William Jenkyn, *The Elegy On that Reverend Presbyter Mr. William Jenkins* (1685).

27. Other ministers specifically resisting Anglican burial practices in their wills include: William Bagshaw (1701), Edmund Calamy (1666), Sampson Carel (1667), A. Ackworth, J. Birdwood, G. Benson, S. Fisher, J. Fuller, A. Jackson, P. Kambe, W. Low, R. Steele. In Matthews, ed., *Abstracts*, fols. 52, 184, 200, 2, 121, 105, 358, 377, 666, 603, 639, 924. On the "will as a literary genre," see Ariès, *Hour*, 198–201.

28. Whiston, *Life*, 95.

29. Lucy Hutchinson, *Memoirs of the Life of Colonel Hutchinson*, ed. Neil Keeble (1995), 333–34.

30. David E. Stannard, *The Puritan Way of Death: A Study in Religion, Culture, and Social Change* (New York, 1977), 101–02; Ariès claims requests for simplicity are *always* a feature of wills, especially after the seventeenth century, in *Hour*, 322.

31. Philip Anderton of Kingsland, DWL, MS 38.59, fol. 26. See also *CR*, 11.

32. *DNB*.

33. Whiston, *Life*, 96; *The Last Will of Mr. Henry Stubbs . . . Published at the desire of his Widow* (1678).

34. Another minister explained his nonconformity in his will dated 1667: Rowland Stedman (d. 1673) explained "in my not Conforming to the Ceremonies and other impositions I have not beene led by Humour faction or any carnall Interest whatsover But as Really Judging such Conformity sinfull," Matthews, ed., *Abstracts*, fol. 921. Wills of Edmund Colby (1668), Richard Steele (1691). DWL MS 38.59 fols. 246; 924. On Steele, *CR*, 461; and Bagshaw (1701), *CR*, 22.

35. Henry, *Diary*, 116.

36. H. M. Margoliouth, *The Poems and Letters of Andrew Marvell*, 3rd. edn., 2 vols. (Oxford, 1971), 11, 356.

37. Henry, *Diary*, 231.

38. Richard Baxter, *A True Believers Choice and Pleasure* (1680), fol. A2.

39. Henry, *Diary*, 201.

40. Thomas Watson, *The Fight of Faith Crowned* (1678), 9.

41. Samuel Annesley, *A Sermon Preached at the funeral of . . . Will. Whitaker* (1673), 17–19.

42. On Theodosia Alleine, see Dewey D. Wallace, Jr., *The Spirituality of the Later English Puritans* (Macon, GA, 1987), 53.

43. Whiston, *Life*, 107.

44. *An Elegy on the Death of that Learned, Pious, and Famous* DIVINE, *Doctor* JOHN OWEN (1683).

45. S. T., in *Elegies . . . Mr. William Taylor . . . 1661*, Yale Osborn MS b.88. Taylor's funeral sermon was preached by William Spurstowe, *A Crown of Life . . . Funeral of William Taylor* (1662).

46. Joseph Roach, *Cities of the Dead: Circum-Atlantic Performance* (New York, 1996), 2.

47. *Farewel Sermons Preached by Mr. Calamy, Dr. Manton . . .* (1663), 229.

48. Likewise in his diary Owen Stockton allayed his own fears of arrest for his illegal preaching by reminding himself of the story of Daniel in the lion's den, DWL, MS 24.7, fol. 19.

49. John Goodwin, *On Being Filled with the Spirit* (1670), 531. Goodwin also explicates Elijah, 532.

50. Greaves, *Deliver*, 218.

51. *Farewel Sermons*, 233.

52. *Farewel Sermons*, 240.

53. Watson, *Fight of Faith*, 28.

54. *Saints Memorials: Or, Words fitly Spoken* (1674).

55. Lazarus Seaman to Lord Wharton 16 July 1666, Bodl. Rawl. MS 53, fol. 73.

56. Hill, *Bible*, 206–08, 388. Richard Baxter, *Cain and Abel Malignity* (1689), but written four years earlier, his preface tells us.

57. John Owen, *A Continuation of the Exposition of the Epistle of Paul the Apostle to the Hebrews* (1684), 19.

58. Lucy Hutchinson, *Order and Disorder* (1679), ed. David Norbrook (Oxford, 2001), VI, 235–300, 331; and see Norbrook's introductory discussion of the Cain story, xxxvii–xxxviii.

59. John Bunyan, *An Exposition on the Ten First Chapters of Genesis*, ed. W. R. Owens; Bunyan, *MW*, XII, 165, 166. Compare also Lucy Hutchinson, "in one martyr's bed a church is born" (*Order and Disorder*, VI, 434); Whiston, *Life* takes Hebrews 11:4, "He being Dead, yet speaketh" as an epigraph; Ralph Venning's homiletic sayings were published in a pamphlet entitled *The Dead Yet Speaking* in 1674.

60. William Lloyd, *A Sermon at the Funeral of Sr Edmund-Berry Godfrey* (1678), 1–2.

61. Owen, *Hebrews*, 20.

62. *CR*, 189.

63. J[ohn] F[airfax], *The Dead Saint Speaking, Or, a Sermon Preached Upon Occasion of the Death of that Eminent Man, Mr. Matthew Newcomen* (1679), 11. Newcomen died in 1668 or 1669, and this sermon was preached at that time, though not printed until 1679, safe in the Popish plot avalanche of publications, perhaps.

64. "How long": Henry, *Diary*, 156 (27 October 1664) remembering the 24 August ejections; the inscription for Vavasor Powell in Bunhill repeats this phrase; see Edward Bagshaw, *The Life and Death of Vavasor Powell* (1671), 208; Christopher Ness ends his apocalyptic treatise, *A Distinct Discourse and Discovery of the Person and Period of Antichrist* (1679), 236, with a threefold invocation of "How long."

65. Matthews, ed., *Abstracts*, fol. 184. And see the Appendix for the circumstances of St. Giles Cripplegate at the time of Milton's burial.

66. Benjamin Keach, Postscript to Samuel How, *The Sufficiencie of the Spirits Teaching without Human Learning* (1683), 41.

67. Royal Commission on the Historical Monuments of England, *Nonconformist Chapels and Meeting-Houses: Buckinghamshire*, 7; David M. Butler, *Quaker Meeting Houses* (Kendal, Cumbria, 1995), 18–19; Robert Huxter, *Jordans Meeting* (1989), 28–30. In her will, Mary Pennington specifies her desire to be buried at Jordans "very near my dear and precious husband Isaac Pennington, and I would only be accompanied with the friends of our own meeting privately," *Experiences in the Life of Mary Penington (Written by Herself)*, ed. Norman Penney (Philadelphia, 1911; repr. London, 1992), 111.

68. Thomas Gutteridge, *The Universal Elegy, or a Poem on Bunhill Burial Ground* (1745), 13. On the history of Bunhill Fields, see Alfred W. Light, *Bunhill Fields* (London, 1915).

69. Ann Overton, in Robert Overton, *Gospel Observation*, cited in David Norbrook, "'The Blushinge Tribute of a Borrowed Muse': Robert Overton and his Overturning of the Poetic Canon," in Peter Beal and Jeremy Griffiths, eds., *English Manuscript Studies, 1100–1700* 4 (1993), 220–66; 227. The precise location of the Overton graves is unknown.

70. See Nicole Loraux, *The Invention of Athens: The Funeral Oration in the Classical City* (Cambridge, 1986), and James E. Young, *The Texture of Memory: Holocaust Memorials and their Meaning* (New Haven, 1993).

71. John Weever, *Ancient Funeral Monuments* (1631; repr. Norwood, NJ, 1979), 125.

72. Achsah Guibbory explores the complex relation of this text to the Laudian defenses of ceremony, "'A Rationall of Old Rites': Sir Thomas Browne's *Urne Buriall* and the Conflict over Ceremony," *Yearbook of English Studies* 21 (1991), 229–41.

73. Secretary Nicholas, writing on 1 February in *CSPD 1660–61*, LX, 500. On the exhumations, see Hutton, *Restoration*, 134; and the account in Laura Lunger Knoppers, *Historicizing Milton: Spectacle, Power, and Poetry in Restoration England* (Athens, GA, 1994), 51–53.

74. Anne Fleetwood, in Antonia Fraser, *Cromwell: The Lord Protector* (New York, 1973), 689; On Elizabeth Cromwell, who died in 1665, a visitor to her burial place in Peterborough in 1710 remarked on its lacking "any monument or inscription." BL Landsdowne MS 986, fol. 70.

75. Fraser, *Cromwell*, 693–97.

76. *The Inscriptions upon the Tombs, Grave-stones, etc. In the Dissenters Burial Place near Bunhill Fields* (1717), 79.

77. *Inscriptions upon the Tombs*, 27.

78. Peter Toon, *God's Statesman: The Life and Works of John Owen, Pastor, Educator, Theologian* (Exeter, 1971), 128.

79. Committee of the Corporation of London, *History of the Bunhill Fields Burial Ground* (1902), 54.

80. Michael Mullett, *Sources for the History of English Nonconformity, 1660–1830*, British Records Association no. 8 (1991), 34.

81. London. 11. Civic and Municipal, *Bunhill Fields Burial Ground* (1867), 83.

82. *Inscriptions upon the Tombs*, 17.

83. Milton, *SA*, 53–54.

84. Christopher Hill, *Milton and the English Revolution* (1977), 435, 437, 441; Jackie DiSalvo, "'The Lord's Battels': *Samson Agonistes* and the Puritan Revolution," *Milton Studies* 4 (1972), 39–62; Mary Ann Radzinowicz, *Towards Samson Agonistes: The Growth of Milton's Mind* (Princeton, 1978), 178. Mary Ann Radzinowicz, "*Samson Agonistes* and Milton the Politician in Defeat," *Philological Quarterly* 44 (1965), 454–71.

85. Joseph Wittreich, *Interpreting Samson Agonistes* (Princeton, 1986), 369.

86. Stella Revard, "Dalila as Euripidean Heroine," *Papers on Language and Literature* 23,3 (1987), 291–302; see also Heather Asals, "In Defense of Dalila: *Samson Agonistes* and the Reformation Theology of the Word," *Journal of English and Germanic Philology* 74 (1975), 183–95; and Thomas Kranidas, "Dalila's Role in

Samson Agonistes," Studies in English Literature 6 (1966), 125–37; Hope Parisi helpfully points to the biblical precedents in "Discourse and Danger: Women's Heroism in the Bible and Dalila's Self-Defense," in Charles W. Durham and Kristin Pruitt McColgan, eds., *Spokesperson Milton: Voices in Contemporary Criticism* (1994), 260–74.

87. See John Guillory, "Dalila's House: *Samson Agonistes* and the Sexual Division of Labor," in Maureen Quilligan, Margaret W. Ferguson, and Nancy J. Vickers, eds., *Rewriting the Renaissance: The Discourses of Sexual Difference in Early Modern Europe* (Chicago, 1987), 106–22.

88. See the Appendix on Milton's grave.

89. Emile Durkheim, *The Elementary Forms of Religious Life* (New York, 1965), 435–46; Richard Huntington and Peter Metcalf, *Celebrations of Death: The Anthropology of Mortuary Ritual* (Cambridge, 1979); and Maurice Block and Jonathan Parry, eds., *Death and the Regeneration of Life* (Cambridge, 1982), 1–44.

90. Richard Baxter, *A Breviate of the Life of Margaret, the Daughter of Francis Charlton* (1681), 93–94.

3 PRISON

1. Greaves, *Deliver*, 32.
2. Watts, *Dissenters*, 223.
3. Thomas Rugge, *Mercurius Politicus Redivivus*, BL Add. MS 10117, fols. 42, 51.
4. Greaves, *Deliver* and *Enemies*, and Hill, *Defeat*, discuss the Restoration radical underground. See also Wilbur Cortez Abbot, "English Conspiracy and Dissent, 1600–1674," *American Historical Review* 14 (1908–09), 503–28 and 696–722.
5. On political outlets, see Douglas R. Lacey, *Dissent and Parliamentary Politics in England, 1661–1689: A Study in the Perpetuation and Tempering of Parliamentarianism* (New Brunswick, NJ, 1969); see also C. E. Whiting, *Studies in English Puritanism from the Restoration to the Revolution, 1660–1688* (New York, 1931), 474–544; Richard Ashcraft, *Revolutionary Politics and Locke's Two Treatises of Government* (Princeton, 1986), 17–38; John Spurr, *England in the 1670s* (Oxford, 2000), 214–41; Tim Harris, *Politics under the Later Stuarts: Party Conflict in a Divided Society, 1660–1715* (1993), 93–94.
6. John Bunyan, *Prison-Meditations, Directed to the Heart of Suffering Saints and Reigning Sinners*, first published at the end of *Christian Behaviour: or the Fruits of True Christianity* (1663), 149, in Bunyan, *MW*, VI, 47. Bunyan also published the poem at the end of the third edition of *One Thing is Needful* (1683); there *Prison-Meditations* was dated 1665. On the importance of dissenting publishing for collective identity, see Keeble, *LC*, 82–92, and *passim*.
7. Francis Bugg, *The Quaker's Charm Discovered* (1702), 2.
8. Christopher Hill, *A Tinker and a Poor Man: John Bunyan and His Church, 1628–1688* (New York, 1989), 121–22; George Fox, *The Journal of George Fox*, ed. Nigel Smith (Harmondsworth, 1998), 284, 286.

9. John Bunyan, *The Pilgrim's Progress*, ed. Roger Sharrock (Harmondsworth, 1987), 77–78. Perhaps this is the image firing Max Weber's thought in figuring the "iron cage" of capitalism.

10. See Hill, *Tinker*, 119. On the melancholic who feels forsaken by God, see Richard Baxter, *Christian Directory*, 2nd. edn. (1677), 261–62.

11. Bunyan, *Pilgrim's Progress*, 78–79.

12. Bunyan, *Prison-Meditations*, 47.

13. Elias Pledger, *Diary of Elias Pledger*, DWL, MS 28.4, 30.

14. Richard Baxter, *A Sense of Repentance* (1660), 3.

15. Baxter, *Christian Directory*, 262. On pastoral therapy against despair, see *Christian Directory*, 261–68; 295–98. On nonconformist ministers' "religious therapy," see Michael MacDonald, *Mystical Bedlam: Madness, Anxiety, and Healing in Seventeenth-Century England* (Cambridge, 1981), 227–28.

16. [Johsua Kirby?], "A Prisoners Verdict," BL Add. MS 4460, fol. 82b. Life details in *CR*, 310.

17. "A Letter from W. L.," in Benjamin Antrobus, *Buds and Blossoms of Piety; with some Fruit of the Spirit of Love*, 2nd. edn. (1691), 99.

18. Denzil Holles, *The Long Parliament Dissolved* (1676), 4. See also Marchamont Nedham, *A Second Pacquet of Advises and Animadversions sent to the Men of Shaftesbury* (1677), 41.

19. John Reeve, To the Reader, *Hymns and Spiritual Songs* (1682), fol. A2v. Reeve was General Baptist minister at Bessel's Green, Kent (not the Muggletonian of the same name). Henry R. Plomer, *A Dictionary of the Printers and Booksellers, 1668–1725* (Oxford, 1968), 141.

20. Reeve, prefatory poem, "To the chast and pure Virgin-Souls, that love the Lord Jesus," in *Spiritual Hymns upon Solomon's Song* (1684), n.p.

21. Reeve, Hymn 14, 1, 6, in *Spiritual Hymns*, 16–17.

22. Reeve, Hymn 15, 1, 6, in *Spiritual Hymns*, 17.

23. Max Weber, *The Protestant Ethic and the Spirit of Capitalism*, tr. Talcott Parsons (1996), 105.

24. Richard Baxter sees the conjunction of self-scrutiny and despair; "These poor men cry out of sin and the wrath of God, when the main cause is in the bodily distemper," he writes in *Saints Everlasting Rest* (1650), 423; see also Samuel Clifford, *The Signs and Causes of Melancholy . . . Collected out of the Works of Mr. Richard Baxter* (1716), 7. Baxter noted that in 1671 in particular, "I was troubled this year with multitudes of melancholy Persons, from several Parts of the land, some of high Quality, some of low, some very exquisitely learned, some unlearned," in *Reliquiae Baxterianae*, ed. Matthew Sylvester (1696), Part 3, 85.

25. Reeve, Hymn 54, III, 8, in *Spiritual Hymns*, 66.

26. Reeve, Preface, *Spiritual Hymns*, n.p.

27. Baxter, *Right Rejoycing, or, the Nature and Order of Rational and Warrantable Joy* (1660), 25, 10, 37.

28. David Norbrook, "*Order and Disorder*: The Poem and its Contexts," in Lucy Hutchinson, *Order and Disorder*, ed. David Norbrook (Oxford, 2001), xv–xxi.

29. David Norbrook, "Lucy Hutchinson's 'Elegies' and the Situation of the Republican Woman Writer (with text)," *English Literary Renaissance* 27 (1997), 468–521. Citations are to this text.

30. Rachel Jevon, "Exultationis Carmen: To the Kings Most Excellent Majesty Upon his Most Desired Return," in Peter Davidson, ed. *Poetry and Revolution* (Oxford, 1999), 492.

31. Christopher Ness, *A Distinct Discourse and Discovery of the Person and Period of Antichrist* (1679), 198.

32. Bryan W. Ball, *A Great Expectation: Eschatological Thought in English Puritanism to 1660* (Leiden, 1975); Paul Christianson, *Reformers and Babylon: English Apocalyptic Visions from the Reformation to the Eve of the Civil War* (Toronto, 1978); William Haller, *Foxe's Book of Martyrs and the Elect Nation* (1963); John R. Knott, *Discourses of Martyrdom in English Literature, 1563–1694* (Cambridge, 1993).

33. John Owen, *Ouranon Ourania: The Shaking and Translating of Heaven and Earth*, in William H. Goold, ed., *The Works of John Owen*, 23 vols. (1966), VIII, 242; cited in Peter Toon, *The Correspondence of John Owen* (Cambridge, 1970), 29; cf. Milton's opening to *Lycidas*.

34. Mary Mollineux, "On Daniel," in *Fruits of Retirement* (1702), 123.

35. Robert Overton, *Gospel Observations and Religious Manifestations*, 56–57, Princeton MS (1666?).

36. George Wither, *The Improvement of Imprisonment* (1661), 5.

37. Mollineux, "Meditations concerning our Imprisonment only for Conscience Sake," in *Fruits*, 123.

38. Baxter, "The Resolution," in *Poetical Fragments* (1681), 56. Baxter himself would languish in prison from February 1685 to November 1686 for a "seditious" *Paraphrase of the New Testament* (1685).

39. Samuel Butler, "Upon a Hypocritical Nonconformist," in René Lamar, ed., *Samuel Butler: Satires and Miscellaneous Poetry and Prose* (Cambridge, 1928), 143.

40. J. Milton French, "George Wither in Prison," *Papers of the Modern Language Association* 45 (1930), 959–66.

41. Charcoal: Lyle H. Kendall, Jr., "An Unrecorded Prose Pamphlet of George Wither," *Huntington Library Quarterly* 20 (1996–97), 190–95; smuggled: Wither, *The Improvement of Imprisonment* (1661), t.p.; George Wither, *The Triple Paradox* (1661), 1.

42. John Bunyan, *Seasonable Counsel*, in Bunyan, *MW*, x, 92.

43. Keeble, *LC*, 190.

44. Jean Delumeau, *Sin and Fear: The Emergence of a Western Guilt Culture*, tr. Eric Nicholson (New York, 1990), 523.

45. John Owen, *A Continuation of the Exposition of the Epistle of Paul the Apostle to the Hebrews* (1684), 16.

46. George Wither, *The Hymnes and Songs of the Church* (1623), 72. On the political uses of Jeremiah, see Hill, *Bible*, 344–46. Royalists mourning the fall of Charles I had also adopted Jeremiah as their spokesman; e.g. [Anon.], *Lamentations of the Prophet Jeremiah Paraphras'd. Suitable to the Exegencies of these Times* (1647).

47. Greaves, *Deliver*, 30, 40; Hill, *Defeat*, 67.
48. Vavasor Powell, [Hebrew: *Tsofer Bepah*] or *The Bird in the Cage* (1661), 20; cf. Lamentations 3:64–66.
49. Powell, *Bird*, 7, 16, 17; from his adaptation of Lamentations 1:20; 3:12; 3:22.
50. Powell, *Bird*, 26; reading Lamentations 5:20–21.
51. Powell, *Bird*, 17, reading Lamentations 3:25–26.
52. Powell, *Bird*, fols. A6–A6v.
53. Benjamin Antrobus, "Some Lines written by the Author, in the Time of his Imprisonment," in *Buds and Blossoms* (1691), 97, 96.
54. Theophilus Gale, prefatory poem, "Upon this ELABORATE Work," in *The Court of the Gentiles*, 2nd. edn. (Oxford, 1672), n.p.
55. Frances Owen, "A Testimony Concerning my dear Friend and Cousin Mary Mollineux," in Mollineux, *Fruits*, fol. A4.
56. Bugg, *The Quaker's Charm*, 2.
57. Hilary Hinds surely misses the radical tenor of Mollineux's biblicisim in "'Who may Binde where God hath Loosed?': Responses to sectarian women's writing in the second half of the seventeenth century," in S. P. Cerasano and Marion Wynne-Davis, eds., *Gloriana's Face: Women, Public and Private in the English Renaissance* (New York, 1992), 205–27; 208.
58. Mollineux, "A Meditation (1668)," in *Fruits*, 21–22.
59. *Most Holy and Profitable sayings of that Reverend divine Dr. Thomas Goodwin. Who departed this Life, Feb 23, 1679/80* (1680).
60. The diaries of ministers during this period are rich with the ambiguities and complexities of these decisions. See, for example, the Presbyterian Ralph Josselin, who had been a chaplain in the parliamentary army, in Alan Macfarlane, ed., *The Diary of Ralph Josselin* (Oxford, 1991), 493, 498, 548, 505; Owen Stockton, *Diary*, DWL, MS 24.8, 64, 74; Henry, *Diary*, 94, 98–101, 117, 177, 246. See also Hill, *Defeat*, 207–19.

4 VIOLENCE

1. John Bunyan, *Grace Abounding to the Chief of Sinners*, ed. W. R. Owens (Harmondsworth, 1987), 1.
2. Hill, *Bible*, 4, 5.
3. Barbara Kiefer Lewalski, *Protestant Poetics and the Seventeenth-Century Religious Lyric* (Princeton, 1979), ix.
4. Paul Christianson, *Reformers and Babylon: English Apocalyptic Visions from the Reformation to the Eve of the Civil War* (Toronto, 1978).
5. Matthew Henry, *An Account of the Life and Death of Mr Philip Henry* (1699), fol. A7v; and see Keeble, *LC*, 237, for this kind of praise of ordinary lives.
6. Henry, *Diary*, 245.
7. Henry, *Diary*, 145. Cf. Jer. 1:3; 2 Kings 25:8–26.
8. Geoffrey F. Nuttall, *The Holy Spirit in Puritan Faith and Experience* (Chicago, 1992), 95; see also B. A. Gerrish, "Sign and Reality: The Lord's Supper in the

Reformed Confessions," in *The Old Protestantism and the New: Essays on the Reformation Heritage* (Chicago, 1982), 118–30.

9. See John Owen, *Sacramental Discourses*, in William H. Goold, ed., *The Works of John Owen* 23 vols. (1966), IX, 572.

10. Richard Baxter, *The Poor Man's Family Book*, cited in Stephen Mayor, *The Lord's Supper in Early English Dissent* (1972), 128.

11. Mayor, *The Lord's Supper*, 120, 139, 145; Nuttall, *Holy Spirit*, 90–101.

12. Owen, *Sacramental Discourses*, 573.

13. John Perrot, *The Mistery of Baptism and the Lord's Supper and Spirit of Jesus* (1662), 8. On Quaker rejection of sacraments, see W. C. Brathwaite, *The Beginnings of Quakerism*, 2nd. edn. (Cambridge, 1955), 137.

14. Henry, *Diary*, 148.

15. René Girard, *Violence and the Sacred*, tr. Patrick Gregory (Baltimore, 1977), 31.

16. See also Deborah Shuger, *The Renaissance Bible: Scholarship, Sacrifice, and Subjectivity* (Los Angeles, 1994), 90, 98, 99.

17. Christopher Hill, *Puritanism and Revolution* (Harmondsworth, 1986), 315.

18. Daniel Defoe, *Review* 2,125 (22 December 1705), 498.

19. Against the topical application of the prophecies of Daniel, see John Owen, *Exercitations on the Epistle to the Hebrews . . . Two First Chapters* (1668), 168–69.

20. Hill, *Puritanism and Revolution*, 311, 313. William Lamont, *Godly Rule: Politics and Religion, 1603–1660* (1969), 106; B. Capp, *The Fifth Monarchy Men: A Study in Seventeenth-Century English Millenarianism* (1972), 23–49; K. R. Firth, *The Apocalyptic Tradition in Reformation Britain, 1530–1645* (Oxford, 1979). Nigel Smith, *Perfection Proclaimed: Language and Literature in English Radical Religion, 1640–1660* (Oxford, 1989), 229–67; Christopher Hill, " 'Til the Conversion of the Jews," in *Millenarianism and Messianism in English Literature and Thought, 1650–1982*, ed. R. Popkin (Leiden, 1988), 12–36; William Lamont, *Puritanism and Historical Controversy* (1996), 129–58.

21. Richard Baxter, *Christian Directory*, 2nd. edn. (1677) t.p. Thomas Watson, *Heaven Taken by Storm* (1670), 5–6; cited in Gary De Krey, "Rethinking the Restoration: Dissenting Cases for Conscience, 1667–1672," *Historical Journal* 38,1 (1995), 53–83; 71–72.

22. Greaves, *Enemies*, 180.

23. Christopher Jelinger, *Heaven Won by Violence . . . Sacred Violence* (1665); Jeremiah Bourroughs, *Four Books on the Eleventh of Matthew* (1659); Watson, *Heaven Taken by Storm* (1670), all focused on Matthew 11.

24. John Pocock, "Time, History and Eschatology in the Thought of Thomas Hobbes," *Politics, Language, and Time: Essays on Political Thought and History* (Chicago, 1989), 148–201; 169.

25. Richard Baxter, *The Saints Everlasting Rest* (1650), 440.

26. Richard Baxter, *Reliquiae Baxterianae*, ed. Matthew Sylvester (1696), Part 1, 10; Part 3, 174; see also Part 1, 9–11; Part 1, 80–83; Part 3, 60. And see Neil Keeble, *Richard Baxter: Puritan Man of Letters* (Oxford, 1982), 11; Baxter, *Saints Everlasting Rest* (1650), fol. A2v. N. H. Keeble, "The Autobiographer

as Apologist: *Reliquiae Baxterianae* (1696)," in Thomas N. Corns, ed., *The Literature of Controversy* (1987), 105–19.

27. Baxter, *Saints Everlasting Rest* (1650), 123. By 1662, this personal grief had became a collective mourning, as Baxter changed all the personal pronouns from singular to plural in this passage to speak a common loss. See *Saints Everlasting Rest* (1662), 115. On the civil war context of *Saint's Everlasting Rest*, see Keeble, *Baxter*, 94–100. On Baxter's army career, see Baxter, *Reliquiae Baxterianae*, Part 1, 43–46; Anne Laurence, *Parliamentary Army Chaplains, 1642–1651* (Woodbridge, 1990), 96–97. On the legacy of his work, see J. T. Wilkinson, ed., *The Saint's Everlasting Rest* (1962), 12–22. The best biography is G. F. Nuttall, *Richard Baxter* (1965); for the Restoration period, see Frederick J. Powicke, *The Reverend Richard Baxter under the Cross, 1662–1691* (1927).

28. Richard Baxter, *A Breviate of the Life of Margaret, the Daughter of Francis Charlton* (1681), 8, 27–28, 90–92.

29. Richard Baxter, *The True History of Councils* (1682), 43; see also 143.

30. Andrew Marvell, *The Rehearsal Transpros'd: The Second Part* (1673), in D. I. B. Smith, ed., *The Rehearsal Transpros'd and The Rehearsal Transpros'd: The Second Part* (Oxford, 1971), 256; citing Hooker, *Laws*, book VIII. On the radical uses of Hooker, see Robert Eccleshall, "Richard Hooker and the Peculiarities of the English: The Reception of the *Ecclesiastical Polity* in the Seventeenth and Eighteenth Centuries," *History of Political Thought* 2,1 (1981), 63–117; 72–75.

31. Baxter, *Reliquiae Baxterianae*, Part 1, 39.

32. Laurence, *Chaplains*, 96–97.

33. William Lamont, "*A Holy Commonwealth* as a Love Poem to Richard Cromwell," in Richard Baxter, *A Holy Commonwealth*, ed. William Lamont (Cambridge, 1994), ix.

34. Richard Baxter, *Christian Directory*, in *The Practical Works of Richard Baxter*, 4 vols. (1707), 1, 173, 174.

35. Richard Baxter, "Love Breathing Thanks and Praise," in *Poetical Fragments* (1681), 2.

36. On Baxter's apocalypticism, see William B. Lamont, *Richard Baxter and the Millennium: Protestant Imperialism and the English Revolution* (1979).

37. Baxter's *Poetical Fragments* appeared in the November 1681 Term Catalogue, for sale bound at 1s; see Edward Arber, ed., *Term Catalogues 1668–1709*, 3 vols. (1906), 1, 462–63.

38. Joan Webber, *The Eloquent "I": Style and Self in Seventeenth-Century Prose* (Madison, 1968), 147; 115–48.

39. Baxter, *Reliquiae Baxterianae*, Part 1, 39; see also Lamont, *Godly Rule*, 98.

40. Baxter, *Reliquiae Baxterianae*, Part 1, 46.

41. On Baxter's Arminianism, see Lamont, *Puritanism and Historical Controversy*, 90; and William Lamont, "Arminianism: The Controversy that Never Was," in Nicholas Phillipson and Quentin Skinner, eds., *Political Discourse in Early Modern Britain* (Cambridge, 1993), 45–66.

42. Baxter, *Saints Everlasting Rest* (1650), 455.
43. John R. Knott, "Bunyan and the Cry of Blood," in David Gay, James G. Randall, and Arlette Zinck, eds., *Awakening Words: John Bunyan and the Language of Community* (Newark, 2000), 51–67; 60.
44. Richard L. Greaves, *John Bunyan and English Nonconformity* (1993), 177–83; and Richard L. Greaves, "'Let Truth be Free': John Bunyan and the Restoration Crisis of 1667–1673," *Albion* 28,4 (1996), 507–605.
45. The sufferings of the Bedford congregation, and the ethic of suffering are presented in Anon., *A True and Impartial Narrative of some Illegal and Arbitrary Proceedings* (1670).
46. W. R. Owens, "John Bunyan and English Millenarianism," in Gay, Randall, and Zinck, eds., *Awakening Words*, 85.
47. So argues Richard L. Greaves, "Conscience, Liberty, and the Spirit: Bunyan and Nonconformity," in N. H. Keeble, ed., *John Bunyan: Conventicle and Parnassus* (Oxford, 1988), 29. See also Greaves, *Bunyan and English Nonconformity*, ch. 10.
48. See Roger Sharrock and James F. Forrest, Introduction, in John Bunyan, *The Holy War* (Oxford, 1980). For the political contexts see Barrie White, "John Bunyan and the Context of Persecution," in Anne Laurence, W. R. Owens, and Stuart Sim, eds., *John Bunyan and His England, 1628–88* (1990), 51–62. On *The Holy War*'s spiritual agon see Rivers, *RGS*, 144–51.
49. Greaves, *Bunyan and English Nonconformity*, 115–17; 170–83.
50. Greaves, *Bunyan and English Nonconformity*, 103; 102–26. Christopher Hill, *A Tinker and Poor Man: John Bunyan and His Church, 1628–1688* (New York, 1989), 153, suggests that armed resistance is implicit in Bunyan's millenarian writing.
51. Bunyan, *Holy War*, xx.
52. Bunyan, Holy War, xxxvii.
53. Bunyan, *Holy War*, xxxiii–xxxiv. E. P. Thompson, *The Making of the English Working Class* (New York, 1977), 34–36.
54. Rivers, *RGS*, 146.
55. Bunyan, Holy War, 93; and see pp. 215–17 below for Dissenters' songs of violence.
56. Knott, "Bunyan and the Cry of Blood," 63–64.
57. John Bunyan, *An Exposition on the Ten First Chapters of Genesis*, ed. W. R. Owens, Bunyan, *MW*, XII, 223.
58. John Bunyan, *Pilgrim's Progress*, ed. Roger Sharrock (Harmondsworth, 1987), 165–66.
59. John Bunyan, *Seasonable Counsel*, in Bunyan, *MW*, X, 72, 97.
60. On Bunyan as a radical millenarian, see Michael A. Mullett, *John Bunyan in Context* (Keele, 1996), 92, 283; and Aileen M. Ross, "Paradise Regained: The Development of John Bunyan's Millenarianism," in M. van Os and G. J. Schutte, eds., *Bunyan in England and Abroad* (Amsterdam, 1990), 73.
61. Bunyan, *Grace Abounding*, 1.
62. Bunyan, *Holy War*, 5.

63. See Vincent Newey, "'With the Eyes of my Understanding': Bunyan, Experience, and Acts of Interpretation," in Keeble, ed., *John Bunyan*, 189–216.

64. John Bunyan, *Of Antichrist, and His Ruine*, ed. W. R. Owens, in Bunyan, *MW*, XII, 458.

65. Cf., Anon., *Annus Mirabilis, or the Year of Prodigies* (1661), fol. A3.

66. Bunyan, *Antichrist*, 479.

67. See Gary S. De Krey, "London Radicals and Revolutionary Politics, 1675–1683," in Tim Harris, Paul Seaward, and Mark Goldie, eds., *The Politics of Religion in Restoration England* (Oxford, 1990), 133–62.

68. Bunyan, *Seasonable Counsel*, 35.

69. De Krey, "London Radicals," 142.

70. Greaves, *Enemies Under his Feet*, ch. 6; and Greaves, *Bunyan and English Nonconformity*, 17, 117, 167. Bunyan also associated with Owen and Griffith, accused in the Monmouth rebellion.

71. John Lilburne, *The Resolved Man's Resolution* (1647); Joseph Wittreich, *Interpreting Samson Agonistes* (Princeton, 1986), 193–238.

72. John Milton, *Areopagitica*, in *CPW*, II, 558; also *CPW*, I, 858–59.

73. Edward Sexby, *Killing Noe Murder* (1659), 9, cited in Wittreich, *Interpreting*, 213.

74. Andrew Marvell, "On *Paradise Lost*," in Hughes, *John Milton*, 209.

75. Bunyan, *Holy War*, 182.

76. Rivers, *RGS*, 115.

5 MILTON

1. Jonathan Richardson, "The Life of the Author," from *Explanatory Notes and Remarks on Milton's Paradise Lost* (1734), in Helen Darbishire, ed., *Early Lives of Milton* (1931), 198–330; 232.

2. J. M. French, *The Life Records of John Milton*, 5 vols. (New Brunswick, NJ, 1949–58), IV, 398–99; compare William Riley Parker, *Milton's Contemporary Reputation* (Columbus, 1940), 47; George F. Sensabaugh, *That Grand Whig Milton* (Stanford, 1952), 22. Godfrey Davies, "Milton in 1660," *Huntington Library Quarterly* 18 (1954–55), 351–63; 356.

3. Tim Harris, *London Crowds in the Reign of Charles II* (Cambridge, 1987), 59, 66, 222; David Masson, *The Life of John Milton*, 6 vols. (1881–94), VI, 416.

4. Mark Goldie and John Spurr, "Politics and the Restoration Parish: Edward Fowler and the Struggle for St Giles Cripplegate," *English Historical Review* 109 (1994), 572–96; 578.

5. Masson, *Life*, VI, 485.

6. Cited in Caroline Gordon and Wilfrid Dewhirst, *The Ward of Cripplegate in the City of London* (Oxford, 1985), 117.

7. David Masson, "Local Memories of Milton," *Good Words* 34 (April 1893), 232–41; 232; Gordon and Dewhirst, *Cripplegate*, 46–47, 101.

8. Royal Commission on the Historical Monuments of England, *Nonconformist Chapels and Meeting-Houses: Buckinghamshire* (1986), 7; Masson, "Local Memories," 240.

9. Geoffrey F. Nuttall, "Milton's Churchmanship in 1659: His Letter to Jean de Labadie," *Milton Quarterly* 35 (2001), 227–31; 230; Barbara Lewalski, *The Life of John Milton* (Oxford, 2000), 364.

10. John Toland, *The Life of John Milton* (1698), cited in Darbishire, *Early Lives*, 83–197; 195.

11. John Phillips, "The Life of John Milton," in Darbishire, *Early Lives*, 34.

12. For details concerning Milton's burial place, see the Appendix. William B. Hunter sees this burial place as evidence for Milton's conforming, in *Visitation Unimplor'd: Milton and the Authorship of De Doctrina Christiana* (Pittsburgh, 1998), 14.

13. David Norbrook, *Writing the English Republic* (Cambridge, 1999), 435.

14. George Sikes, *The Life and Death of Sir Henry Vane* (1662), 13. See Blair Worden, "Milton, *Samson Agonistes*, and the Restoration," in Gerald Maclean, ed., *Culture and Society in the Stuart Restoration* (Cambridge, 1995), 111–36.

15. Sikes, *Vane*, 138.

16. [John Milton], "Vane, Young in Years," Sikes, *Vane*, 94.

17. Sikes, *Vane*, 98.

18. Darbishire, *Early Lives*, 13; Thomas Ellwood, *The History of the Life of Thomas Ellwood* (1714), 233; French, *Life Records*, IV, 417.

19. On *Paradise Lost* and Milton's backward glance, see Hill, *Defeat*, 302, 309–12; Christopher Hill, *Milton and the English Revolution* (1977), 402–12; Sharon Achinstein, *Milton and the Revolutionary Reader* (Princeton, NJ, 1994), 182–210; and John N. King, *Milton and Religious Controversy: Satire and Polemic in Paradise Lost* (Cambridge, 2000); on its republican and tragic elements, Norbrook, *English Republic*, 438–67; on the poem's engagement with the radical religion of the Revolution and Restoration, see Keeble, *LC*, 84–86; David Loewenstein, *Representing Revolution in Milton and his Contemporaries* (Cambridge, 2001). On the toleration context, see Nicholas von Maltzahn, "The First Reception of *Paradise Lost* (1667)," *Review of English Studies* 47 (1996), 479–99.

20. Hugh Wilson, "The Publication of *Paradise Lost*: The Occasion of the First Edition: Censorship and Resistance," *Milton Studies* 37 (1999), 18–41.

21. On Milton as Abdiel, see Perez Zagorin, *Milton: Aristocrat and Rebel* (Rochester, NY, 1992), 126. Abdiel is usually placed in a Revolution, not Restoration, context; see Joan Bennett, *Reviving Liberty: Radical Christian Humanism in Milton's Great Poems* (Cambridge, MA, 1989), 87; Roger Lejosne sees him as a royalist, "Milton, Satan, Salmasius and Abdiel," in David Armitage, Armand Himy, and Quentin Skinner, eds., *Milton and Republicanism* (Cambridge, 1995), 114; though David Loewenstein, *Representing*, 235–39, notes the Restoration context.

22. Allan H. Gilbert, *On the Composition of Paradise Lost* (Chapel Hill, 1947), 123–27; and Allan H. Gilbert, "The Theological Basis of Satan's Rebellion and the Function of Abdiel in *Paradise Lost*," *Modern Philology* 40,1 (1942), 19–42.

23. Sikes, *Vane*, 137. Andrew Marvell, *Rehearsal Transpros'd and The Rehearsal Transpros'd: The Second Part*, ed. D. I. B. Smith (Oxford, 1971), 62, 53, also accuses Samuel Parker of reducing grace to prudence.

24. John Milton, *Considerations Touching the Likeliest Means to remove Hirelings* (1659), in *CPW*, VII, 321.

25. See, for instance, John Collens, *A Word in Season* (1660); *Plain English . . . Or, A Word in Season* (1660); Vavasor Powell, *A Word in Season*, in [*Tsofer Bepah*]: *or The Bird in the Cage* (1661); Cf. John Bunyan, *Seasonable Counsel*, p. 107 above.

26. Sikes, *Vane*, 121; and see Loewenstein, *Representing*, 236–37.

27. See Janel Mueller, "Milton on Heresy," in Stephen Dobranski and John Rumrich, eds., *Milton and Heresy* (Cambridge, 1998), 21–38.

28. See Bennett, *Reviving Liberty*, 94–118, for the best account of the uneasy tensions between reason and compulsion in this scene.

29. C. S. Lewis, *A Preface to Paradise Lost* (Oxford, 1942), 125. Achsah Guibbory insightfully sees *Paradise Lost* as a "history of idolatry," in *Ceremony and Community from Herbert to Milton: Literature, Religion, and Cultural Conflict in Seventeenth-Century England* (Cambridge, 1998), 195; and see 195–202.

30. John Milton *Lycidas*, in *Poems of John Milton* (1645), with headnote, 127, 125.

31. Milton, *Of Reformation*, (1641), in *CPW*, I, 537, 545.

32. On Milton and apocalypse, see Leland Ryken, *The Apocalyptic Vision in Paradise Lost* (Ithaca, 1970), and William G. Madsen, "From Shadowy Types to Truth," in Joseph Summers, ed., *The Lyric and Dramatic Milton* (New York, 1965), 95–114.

33. John Locke, "Essay on Toleration" (1667), in David Wootton, ed., *Political Writings of John Locke* (New York, 1993), 205.

34. Algernon Sidney, *Court Maxims* (1665–66), 203; cited in Jonathan Scott, *Algernon Sidney and the English Republic, 1623–1677* (Cambridge, 1988), 186.

35. Cedric Brown, "Great Senates and Godly Education," in Armitage, Himy, and Skinner, eds., *Milton and Republicanism*, 59.

36. Richard Ashcraft, *Revolutionary Politics and Locke's Two Treatises of Government* (Princeton, 1986), 39–74.

37. John Milton, *Of True Religion, Haeresie, Schism, Toleration* (1673), in *CPW*, VIII, 417–40. Ray Tumbleson, "Of True Religion and False Politics: Milton and the Uses of Anti-Catholicism," *Prose Studies* 15 (1992), 253–70. R. M. Sanchez softens the anti-Catholicism in, "Milton's *Of True Religion* and the Issue of Religious Tolerance," *Prose Studies* 9 (1986), 21–38; Martin Dzelzainis, "Milton's *Of True Religion* and the Earl of Castlemaine," *The Seventeenth Century* 7 (1992), 53–69 disagrees. Don M. Wolfe, "Limits of Miltonic Toleration," *Journal of English and Germanic Philology* 60,4 (1961), 834–46, considers Milton on Catholics and Jews.

38. Nicholas von Maltzahn, "The Whig Milton, 1667–1700," in Armitage, Himy, and Skinner, eds., *Milton and Republicanism*, 229–53; 247; and his "*Paradise Lost* (1667)."

39. Richard Baxter, *A Paraphrase to the New Testament*, 2nd. edn. (1695), fol. 14v; see EEE2v where Baxter mentions this passage as one in the case against him.

40. Gary De Krey, "Rethinking the Restoration: Dissenting Cases for Conscience, 1667–1672," *Historical Journal* 38,1 (1995), 53–83; 80, 67. See also De Krey,

"The First Restoration Crisis: Conscience and Coersion in London, 1667–73," *Albion* 25,4 (1993), 565–80; Richard L. Greaves, "'Let Truth be Free': John Bunyan and the Restoration Crisis of 1667–1673," *Albion* 28,4 (1996), 587–605; Richard L. Greaves, "Great Scott! The Restoration in Turmoil, or, Restoration Crises and the Emergence of Pary," *Albion* 25,4 (1993), 605–18.

41. John Spurr, *The Restoration Church of England, 1646–1689* (New Haven, 1991), 57–61; *Journals of the House of Commons*, 55 vols. (1803), IX; *Journals of the House of Lords*, 42 vols. (1803), XII; *A Complete Collection of State Trials*, ed. T. B. Howell, 36 vols. (1808), IV, 444–47.

42. Greaves, *Enemies*, 154–59.

43. Masson, *Life*, VI, 651, notes the volume was licensed on 21 July but not entered into the Stationers' Registers until 20 September 1670. Parliament went into session on 24 October 1670; one of its topics was to establish a committee to inspect the April Law against Conventicles. See *The Parliamentary Diary of Sir Edward Dering, 1670–1673*, ed. Basil Duke Henning (New Haven, 1940), 7.

44. Hill, *Milton and the English Revolution*, 435, 437, 441; Jackie DiSalvo, "'The Lord's Battels': *Samson Agonistes* and the Puritan Revolution," *Milton Studies* 4 (1972), 39–62; Mary Ann Radzinowicz, *Towards* Samson Agonistes: *The Growth of Milton's Mind* (Princeton, 1978), 178.

45. Joseph Wittreich reads *Samson Agonistes* as one of those "how-*not*-to live poems," in *Interpreting Samson Agonistes* (Princeton, 1986), 379.

46. Barbara Kiefer Lewalski, "Milton's *Samson* and the 'New Acquist of True [Political] Experience,'" *Milton Studies* 24 (1988), 233–51.

47. A pre-Restoration date for the composition of *Samson Agonistes* is posited by W. R. Parker, "The Date of *Samson Agonistes* Again," in Joseph Anthony Wittreich, ed., *Calm of Mind: Tercenentary Essays on Paradise Regained and Samson Agonistes* (Cleveland, 1971), 163–74. Restoration topical allusions have been analyzed by Hill, *Defeat*, 310–19; Worden, "Milton, *Samson Agonistes*"; Nicholas Jose, *Ideas of the Restoration in English Literature, 1660–1671* (Cambridge, MA, 1984), 142–63; and Laura Lunger Knoppers, *Historicizing Milton: Spectacle, Power, and Poetry in Restoration England* (Athens, GA, 1994); David Loewenstein, "The Kingdom Within: Radical Religious Culture and the Politics of *Paradise Regained*," *Literature and History* 3,2 (1994), 63–89; 82–83.

48. For Milton's positive commitment to political activism in *Paradise Regain'd* see Hill, *Defeat*, 313–16; Loewenstein, "The Kingdom Within"; Knoppers, *Historicizing Milton*, 123–41; and Bennett, *Reviving Liberty*, 161–204.

49. See Leah Marcus, *Unediting the Renaissance: Shakespeare, Marlowe, Milton* (New York, 1996), 215–16, 224–25.

50. Harris F. Fletcher, *John Milton's Complete Poetical Works, Reproduced in Photographic Facsimile*, 4 vols. (Urbana, 1943–48), I, 177.

51. On the relationship between the two poems, see Wittreich, *Interpreting*, 329; William Kerrigan, *The Prophetic Milton* (Charlottesville, 1974); Arthur E. Barker, "Calm Regained through Passion Spent," in Balachandra Rajan, ed., *The Prison and the Pinnacle* (Toronto, 1973), 3–48; and Loewenstein, "The Kingdom Within."

52. See Sharon Achinstein, "*Samson Agonistes* and the Drama of Dissent," *Milton Studies* 33 (1996), 133–58.
53. In the 1640s, Milton had thought of writing a tragedy on Ahab, "beginning at th[e] synod of fals profets," in "Outlines for Tragedies," *CPW*, VIII, 556; he wrote of Charles I as an Ahab, *CPW*, III, 216, 234; and specifically lanced at Ahab's priests in *Eikonoklastes*, *CPW*, III, 365, 550; dissidents compared Charles II to Ahab, according to Hill, *Bible*, 420.
54. John Milton, *On Christian Doctrine*, in Columbia Milton, XIV, 387; cf. Columbia Milton, XVII, 71.
55. Mark Goldie, "Priestcraft and the Birth of Whiggism," in N. Phillipson and Q. Skinner, eds., *Political Discourse in Early Modern Britain* (Cambridge, 1993), 209–31.
56. Milton, *Christian Doctrine*, Columbia Milton, XIV, 3. The shape of the primitive church was a key subject for those debating the legitimacy of the Anglican regime; see, for instance, Andrew Marvell, *A Short Historical Essay Touching General Councils* (1676); John Owen, *An Enquiry into the Original, Nature, Institution, Power, Order and Communion of Evangelical Churches* (1681); Richard Baxter, *Church-History of the Government of Bishops* (1680); Edward Stillingfleet, *Irenicum* (1661), 170; the Anglican Henry Bagshaw, *The Excellency of Primitive Government* (1673); William Prynne, *The Unbishoping of Timothy and Titus ... Proving Timothy and the Angel to be no first, sole, or Diocesan Bishop of Ephesis* (1636; rpr. 1661); see Gary De Krey, "Reformation in the Restoration Crisis, 1679–1682," in Richard Strier and Donna Hamilton, eds., *Religion, Literature and Politics in Post-Reformation England* (Cambridge, 1996), 231–52.
57. Edward Tayler, *Milton's Poetry: Its Development in Time* (Pittsburgh, 1979), 155; Barbara Lewalski, *Milton's Brief Epic: The Genre, Meaning, and Art of Paradise Regained* (1966), 356.
58. See above, pp. 41, 42, 47. Mary Ann Radzinowicz, *Milton's Epics and the Books of Psalms* (Princeton, 1989), 74–76.
59. John Bunyan, *The Holy War*, ed. Roger Sharrock and James F. Forrest (Oxford, 1980), 250.
60. James Livesey, *Pneumat-apologia: Or, an Apology for the Power and Liberty of the Spirit* (1674), 53.
61. Livesey, *Pneumat-apologia*, 113.
62. Milton, *Hirelings*, in *CPW*, VII, 303, 314.
63. Keeble, *LC*, 188–89; Knoppers, *Historicizing Milton*, 43; Worden, "Milton, *Samson Agonistes*." David Loewenstein, in *Milton and the Drama of History* (Cambridge, 1990) examines such rites in considering the theme of anti-idolatry in Milton.
64. John Kenyon, *The Stuart Constitution, 1603–1688*, 2nd. edn. (Cambridge, 1986), 353–56; see also Harris, *London Crowds*, 62–95.
65. Kenyon, *Stuart Constitution*, 355.
66. Kenyon, *Stuart Constitution*, 353–56.
67. Benjamin Laney, *Five Sermons* (1669), 14. Mark Goldie brilliantly shows how Luke 14 was used in the Anglican defense of compulsion in "The Theory of

Religious Intolerance in Restoration England," in Ole Peter Grell, Jonathan I. Israel, and Nicholas Tyacke, eds., *From Persecution to Toleration: The Glorious Revolution and Religion in England* (Oxford, 1991), 331–68.

68. Hugo Grotius, *The Most Excellent Hugo Grotius his Three Books Treating the Rights of War and Peace*, tr. William Evats (1682), 390.

69. Sir Charles Wolseley, *Liberty of Conscience upon its True and Proper Grounds Asserted and Vindicated* (1668), 29. See also Robert Ferguson, *A Sober Enquiry into the Nature, Measure, and Principles of Moral Virtue* (1673), 175; Greaves, *Enemies*, 124.

70. Richard Baxter, *Paraphrase on the New Testament*, 2nd. edn. (1695), fol. N 5.

71. Wolseley, *Liberty of Conscience*, 24.

72. Ashcraft, *Revolutionary Politics*, 65.

73. John Owen, *Truth and Innocence Vindicated* (1669), in William H. Goold, ed. *The Works of John Owen*, 23 vols. (1966), XIII, 442.

74. John Owen, *A Discourse concerning Liturgies, and their Imposition* (1662), *Works*, XV, 21.

75. See Hugh MacCallum, "*Samson Agonistes*: The Deliverer as Judge," *Milton Studies* 23 (1987), 259–90; 279.

76. As has argued Stanley Fish, in "Spectacle and Evidence in *Samson Agonistes*," *Critical Inquiry* 15,3 (1989), 556–86; 567, 586; "Question and Answer in *Samson Agonistes*," *Critical Quarterly* 11 (1969), 163–85; 237; and "Things and Actions Indifferent: The Temptation of Plot in *Paradise Regained*," *Milton Studies* 17 (1983), 180.

77. Dewey Wallace, Jr., *Puritans and Predestination: Grace in English Protestant Theology, 1525–1695* (Chapel Hill, 1982), 178.

78. Stephen Fallon, "'Elect above the rest': Theology as Self-representation in Milton," in Dobranski and Rumrich, eds., *Milton and Heresy*, 93–116.

79. Lewalski, "'New Acquist,'" 248.

80. See also John R. Knott, Jr., *The Sword of the Spirit: Puritan Responses to the Bible* (Chicago, 1980), 121; and Maurice Kelley, *This Great Argument: A Study of Milton's De Doctrina Christiana as a Gloss upon Paradise Lost* (Princeton, 1941), 167.

81. See John Bunyan, *I will Pray with the Spirit* (1662); Henry Lukin, *The Interest of the Spirit in Prayer* (1674). On the history of prayer book controversies, see Horton Davies, *Worship and Theology in England: From Andrewes to Baxter and Foxe, 1603–1690* (Cambridge, 1996), 340–44; 363–94; Ramie Targoff, *Common Prayer: The Language of Public Devotion in Early Modern England* (Chicago, 2001), 36–37.

82. See Fallon, "'Elect above the rest,'" an excellent presentation that is careful to distinguish Arminian salvific theology from the practices of the Laudian Church. On Milton's theology, see Dennis Danielson, *Milton's Good God: A Study in Literary Theodicy* (Cambridge, 1992).

83. Psalm 6, cited in Hughes, *John Milton*, 165.

84. On Milton's psalms and covenant, see Radzinowicz, *Towards Samson Agonistes*, 205–08. On the political context of the psalm translations, see Norbrook, *English Republic*, 299.

85. Goodwin's *Prelatique Preachers None of Christ's Teachers* (1663) urged people to avoid state churches, and was burned in 1663. Goodwin was arrested by L'Estrange on charges of seditious writing in 1664. Greaves, *Deliver*, 223, discredits the assignment of *Mene Tekel* to Goodwin; see Greaves, *Enemies*, 168.
86. John Goodwin, *On Being Filled with the Spirit* (1670), 528.
87. Milton has recently been seen as a nascent anti-Trinitarian, but this analysis does not explain how the Holy Spirit intersects with the other attributes of the Godhead. As I see it, the language of the Holy Spirit is distinct in Milton's writing from the other aspects of God's power, but more work is needed here. I take the authorship of *Christian Doctrine* to be Milton's; See William B. Hunter, "The Provenance of the *Christian Doctrine*," *Studies in English Literature* 32 (1992), 129–42; followed by a "Forum" which includes responses by John T. Shawcross, 155–62; Barbara Lewalski, 143–54; and a reply by Hunter, 163–66. See also Introduction, Dobranski and Rumrich, eds., *Milton and Heresy*; and William Kolbrener, *Milton's Warring Angels: A Study of Critical Engagements* (Cambridge, 1997), 63–83.
88. On the king's theft, see Achinstein, *Milton and the Revolutionary Reader*, 163–68.
89. Cf. John Owen, *Preumatologia, or, A Discourse Concerning the Holy Spirit* (1674), in *Works*, III, 149.
90. Stephen B. Dobranski, "Samson and the Omissa," *Studies in English Literature* 36 (1996), 149–69.

6 ENTHUSIASM

1. Nathaniel Lee, "To Mr. Dryden, on his Poem of Paradice," in Montague Summers, ed., *Dryden: The Dramatic Works*, 6 vols. (1932), III, 415.
2. Steven Zwicker, "Milton, Dryden, and the Politics of Literary Controversy," in Gerald Maclean, ed., *Culture and Society in the Stuart Restoration* (Cambridge, 1995), 137–58.
3. Samuel Parker, *A Discourse of Ecclesiastical Politie* (1670), xvii–xviii.
4. Daniel Defoe, *A Dialogue between a Dissenter and the Observator* (1703), in P. N. Furbank and W. R. Owens, eds., *Daniel Defoe: The True-Born Englishman and other Writings* (1997), 154.
5. J. M. French, *The Life Records of John Milton*, 5 vols. (New Brunswick, NJ, 1949–58), IV, 22, 329.
6. Milton, *PL*, 7:27–28.
7. [Richard Leigh, attr.], *The Transproser Rehears'd* (1673), 72, 147, 55. On Milton's political afterlife, see George F. Sensabaugh, *That Grand Whig Milton* (Stanford, 1952) and Nicholas von Maltzahn, "The Whig Milton, 1667–1700," in David Armitage, Armand Himy, and Quentin Skinner, eds., *Milton and Republicanism* (Cambridge, 1995), 229–53.
8. Samuel Parker, *A Reproof to the Rehearsal Transprosed* (1673), 55.
9. Parker, *Reproof*, 212.

10. G. S. Holmes, "Religion and Party in Late Stuart England," in *Politics, Religion and Society in England, 1679–1742* (London, 1986), 181–216; Michael Heyd, "The Reaction to Enthusiasm in the Seventeenth Century: Towards an Integrative Approach," *Journal of Modern History* 53 (1981), 258–80.

11. J. G. A. Pocock, *Virtue, Commerce, and History* (Cambridge, 1985), 219.

12. See G. F. Parker, "Marvell on Milton: Why the Poem Rhymes Not," *Cambridge Quarterly* 20,3 (1991), 183–209; Judith Scherer Herz, "Milton and Marvell: The Poet as Fit Reader," *Modern Language Quarterly* 39,3 (1978), 239–63.

13. Andrew Marvell, *The Rehearsal Transpros'd and The Rehearsal Transpros'd: The Second Part*, ed., D. I. B. Smith (Oxford, 1971), 135. Hereafter Marvell, *RT*.

14. Christopher Hill, "Milton and Marvell," in C. A. Patrides, ed., *Approaches to Marvell: The York Tercentenary Lectures* (1978), 1–30; 1. See also Austin Woolrych, "Milton and the Good Old Cause," in Ronald G. Shafer, ed., *Ringing the Bell Backward: The Proceedings of the First International Milton Symposium* (Indiana, PA, 1982), 135–50.

15. Greaves, *Enemies*, 174–75, 232; Henry R. Plomer, *A Dictionary of the Printers and Booksellers, 1668 to 1725* (Oxford, 1968), 144, 230.

16. Marvell, *RT*, 4.

17. Frederick S. Siebert, *Freedom of the Press in England, 1476–1776* (Urbana, 1952), 221–63. Christopher Hill, "Censorship and English Literature," in *The Collected Essays of Christopher Hill, Vol. 1: Writing and Revolution in 17th Century England* (Amherst, 1985), 32–71; 51.

18. Greaves, *Deliver*, 221–24; see also Siebert, *Freedom*, 267.

19. See Hughes, *John Milton*, 210. Regarding language of the "Good Old Cause," see Annabel Patterson, *Reading Between the Lines* (Madison, 1993), ch. 7.

20. See Christopher Kendrick, *Milton: A Study in Ideology and Form* (New York, 1986), 83; Hill, "Censorship," 34.

21. Hill, "Milton and Marvell," 23.

22. Hill, "Censorship," 56.

23. Annabel Patterson, *Censorship and Interpretation: The Conditions of Writing and Reading in Early Modern England* (Madison, 1984), 18; and her *Reading between the Lines*, 256–75.

24. Douglas R. Lacey, *Dissent and Parliamentary Politics in England, 1661–1689: A Study in the Perpetuation and Tempering of Parliamentarianism* (New Brunswick, NJ, 1969), 168–72.

25. Robert Ferguson, *A Sober Enquiry into the Nature, Measure, and Principles of Moral Virtue* (1673), 141–42.

26. Contrast the view of Ferguson in Richard Ashcraft, *Revolutionary Politics and Locke's Two Treatises of Government* (Princeton, 1986), 55–61; John Marshall, *John Locke: Resistance, Religion and Responsibility* (Cambridge, 1994), 128 n. 11.

27. Geoffrey Nuttall, *The Holy Spirit in Puritan Faith and Experience* (Chicago, 1992), 7.

28. Debora Shuger, *The Renaissance Bible: Scholarship, Sacrifice, and Subjectivity* (Los Angeles, 1994), 46–48.

29. George Fox, *The Journal of George Fox*, ed. Norman Penney, 2 vols. (Cambridge, 1911), I, 66, 257; cited in Nuttall, *Holy Spirit*, 26 n. 5. Nigel Smith, *Perfection Proclaimed: Language and Literature in English Radical Religion, 1640–1660* (Oxford, 1989), explores Continental mystical influences.

30. Richard Kroll, *The Material Word: Literate Culture in the Restoration and Early Eighteenth Century* (Baltimore, 1991), 240, 248; 239–75.

31. On rational religion, see Rivers, *RGS*, 25–88.

32. J. G. A. Pocock, "Enthusiasm: The Antiself of Enlightenment," in Lawrence E. Klein and Anthony J. La Vopa, eds., *Enthusiasm and Enlightenment in Europe, 1650–1850* (San Marino, CA, 1998), 7–28.

33. John Owen, Preface to the Reader, *Pneumatologia, or A Discourse Concerning the Holy Spirit* (1674), in William H. Goold, ed., *The Works of John Owen*, 23 vols. (1966), III, 7.

34. Peter Toon, *God's Statesman: The Life and Works of John Owen, Pastor, Educator, Theologian* (Exeter, 1971), 166–67.

35. Owen, *Holy Spirit*, 131. For the differences between Owen's Calvinist and Baxter's Arminian notions of grace in relation to Bunyan, see Rivers, *RGS*, 132–40.

36. William Clagett, *A Discourse Concerning the Operations of the Holy Spirit, Together with a Confutation of Some Part of Dr. Owen's Book upon that Subject* (1678), 283–84.

37. Clagett, *Discourse*, 283–84.

38. George Hickes, *The Spirit of Enthusiasm Exorcised* (1680), 39.

39. Clagett, *Discourse*, 162.

40. Clagett, *Discourse*, 282; referring to Owen, *Holy Spirit*, 254, 269; 283–84: italics in original.

41. Clagett, *Discourse*, 284; and see Jonathan Swift, *A Discourse Concerning the Mechanical Operation of the Spirit* (1710).

42. Richard Baxter, *An Answer to Mr. Dodwell and Dr. Sherlocke*, cited in Nuttall, *Holy Spirit*, 169.

43. Baxter, *An Answer*, in Nuttall, *Holy Spirit*, 179.

44. Olive M. Griffiths, *Religion and Learning: A Study in English Presbyterian Thought from the Bartholomew Ejections (1662) to the Foundation of the Unitarian Movement* (Cambridge, 1935), 94; and see Dewey D. Wallace, Jr., *Puritans and Predestination: Grace in English Protestant Theology, 1525–1695* (Chapel Hill, 1982), 185.

45. John Howe, *The Reconcileableness of God's Prescience of the Sins of Men* (1677), 37.

46. Andrew Marvell, *Remarks upon a Late Disingenuous Discourse*, in Alexander B. Grosart, ed., *The Complete Works in Verse and Prose of Andrew Marvell*, 4 vols. (1872–75), IV, 195–96.

47. John Locke, *An Essay Concerning Human Understanding*, ed. Peter H. Nidditch (Oxford, 1975), XIX.16, 705.

48. See, for example, Richard Baxter, *The Reasons of the Christian Religion* (1667); see Rivers, *RGS*, 149–50.

49. Derek Hirst, "Making all Religion Ridiculous: Of Culture High and Low: The Polemics of Toleration, 1667–1673," *Renaissance Forum* 1,1 (1996), http://www.hull.ac.uk/renforum/v1no1/hirst/htm; George McFadden, "Political Satire in *The Rehearsal*," *Yearbook of English Studies* 4 (1974), 120–28. The publisher has used its best endeavors to ensure that the URL for the external website referred to in this book is correct and active at the time of going to press. However, the publisher has no responsibility for the website and can make no guarantee that a site will remain live or that the content is or will remain appropriate.

50. George Villiers, Duke of Buckingham, *The Rehearsal* (1672) Epilogue, 18.

51. Marvell, *RT*, 10. Warren Chernaik, *The Poet's Time: Politics and Religion in the Work of Andrew Marvell* (Cambridge, 1983), 120, 122. On the context of Marvell's tract, see Neil Keeble, "Why Transprose *The Rehearsal*? "in Martin Dzelzainis and Warren Chernaik, eds., *Marvell and Liberty* (1999), 249–68; Annabel Patterson, *Marvell and the Civic Crown* (Princeton, 1978), 189–210; John Wallace, *Destiny his Choice: The Loyalism of Andrew Marvell* (Cambridge, 1968), 184–207; Gordon Schochet, "Between Lambeth and Leviathan: Samuel Parker on the Church of England and Political Order," in Nicholas Phillipson and Quentin Skinner, eds., *Political Discourse in Early Modern Britain* (Cambridge, 1993), 189–208.

52. Andrew Marvell, "On *Paradise Lost*," in Hughes, *John Milton*, 209.

53. *The Transproser Rehears'd* (1673), 147, 43. On the context, see Martin Dzelzainis, "An Allusion to Milton in *The Transproser Rehears'd* (1673)," *Notes and Queries* n.s. 41 (1994), 172–73.

54. *A Common-place Book out of the Rehearsal Transpros'd* (1673), 44.

55. *Transproser Rehears'd*, 72, 123, 9.

56. Keeble, *LC*, 82–88.

57. *Transproser Rehears'd*, 43, 29.

58. John Dryden, "An Essay of Dramatick Poesie" (1668) Dryden, *Works*, XVII, 73.

59. Quoted in Hill, "Censorship," 51.

60. Dryden, Preface to "The Medall," in Dryden, *Works*, II, 42.

61. *Transproser Rehears'd*, 41.

62. Samuel Parker, *A Free and Impartial Censure of the Platonick Philosophie* (Oxford, 1666), 27.

63. Parker, *Discourse*, liii.

64. Parker, *Discourse*, xi.

65. John Dryden, *Sir Martin Mar-All*, IV:i, 122–26, in Dryden, *Works*, IX, 253. For an astute survey of anti-Puritan rhetoric in the English Renaissance, see Kristen Poole, *Radical Religion from Shakespeare to Milton: Figures of Nonconformity in Early Modern England* (Cambridge, 2000).

66. Parker, *Reproof*, 56–57; Derek Hirst warns against conflating Dryden and Parker, in "Samuel Parker, Andrew Marvell, and Political Culture, 1667–73," in Derek Hirst and Richard Strier, eds., *Writing and Political Engagement in Seventeenth-Century England* (Cambridge, 1999), 145–64; 151–52.

67. *Transproser Rehears'd*, 41.
68. William Davenant, "Author's Preface to his Much Honor'd Friend, M. Hobbes," in David F. Gladish, ed., *Sir William Davenant's Gondibert* (Oxford, 1971), 22.
69. See Patterson, *Reading Between the Lines*, 256–75; George Williamson, "The Restoration Revolt against Enthusiasm," in his *Seventeenth-Century Contexts* (1960), 202–39.
70. Cf. John Dryden, Preface to *The State of Innocence*, in Summers, ed., *Dramatic Works*, III, 423. See George Williamson, "Dryden's View of Milton," in his *Milton and Others* (Chicago, 1970), 103–21, and Anne Davidson Ferry, *Milton and the Miltonic Dryden* (Cambridge, MA, 1968).
71. Though the play was not published until 1677, it was circulating in manuscript as early as 1673 and 1674, according to James Winn, *John Dryden and his World* (New Haven, 1987), 294.
72. Winn, *Dryden*, 266–67. See also Morris Freedman, "The 'Tagging' of Paradise Lost: Rhyme in Dryden's *The State of Innocence*," *Milton Quarterly* 5 (1971), 18–22; Steven Zwicker, "Politics and Literary Practice in the Restoration," in Barbara Lewalski, ed., *Renaissance Genres* (Cambridge, MA, 1986), 268–98; 284.
73. Dryden, "Essay," in Dryden, *Works*, XVII, 79–80.
74. Parker, *Free and Impartial Censure*, 76.
75. Dryden, "Essay," 80.
76. Caroline Robbins, "Marvell's Religion: Was he a New Methodist?" *Journal of the History of Ideas* 23,2 (1962), 268–72; 272; Grosart, ed., *Prose Works*, III, 518; William Lamont, "The Religion of Andrew Marvell," in Conal Condren and A. D. Cousins, eds., *The Political Identity of Andrew Marvell* (Aldershot, 1990), 135–56.
77. The tract is *Remarks upon a Late Disingenuous Discourse* (1678), in Grosart, ed., *Prose Works*, IV, 165–242. See Pierre Legouis, *Andrew Marvell: Poet, Puritan, Patriot* (Oxford, 1968), 206–07.
78. Marvell, *Remarks*, in Grosart, ed., *Prose Works*, IV, 188.
79. Marshall, *Locke*, 149.
80. Andrew Marvell, Letter to Sir Edward Harley, 3 May 1673, in H. M. Margoliouth, ed., *Poems and Letters of Andrew Marvell*, 3rd. edn., 2 vols. (Oxford, 1971), II, 328. Are those five miles a confidential allusion to the Five Mile Act (in abeyance)?
81. Marvell, *RT*, 1st. part, 45. Marvell is shocked by the same passages in Parker that worried John Locke; see John Locke MS "Qs on S. P.'s discourse of toleration 69," in Mark Goldie, ed., *Locke: Political Essays* (Cambridge, 1997), 212. This bears further inquiry.
82. Marvell, *RT*, 2nd. part, 268.
83. Andrew Marvell, "On *Paradise Lost*," 6.
84. Andrew Shifflett, *Stoicism, Politics, and Literature in the Age of Milton* (Cambridge, 1998), 110–13.

85. Dryden, "Absalom and Achitophel," in Dryden, *Works*, II, 210–11.
86. Dryden, "The Medall," in Dryden, *Works*, II, 199–200.
87. Benjamin Laney, *Five Sermons* (1669), 31.
88. Ferguson, *A Sober Enquiry*, fol. A6v.
89. Parker, *Discourse*, xi.
90. Marvell, *Mr. Smirke, Or the Divine in Mode*, in Grosart, ed., *Prose Works*, IV, 12.
91. John Locke, *A Letter Concerning Toleration*, ed. James H. Tully (Indianapolis, 1983), 36, 35.
92. John Locke, "Essay on Toleration" (1667) in David Wootton, ed., *Political Writings of John Locke* (New York, 1993), 189.

7 POETICS

1. John Milton, *Reason of Church Government*, (1641), in *CPW*, I, 816.
2. [Edmund Spenser], *The Shepheardes Calender*, ed. William A. Oram et al., *The Yale Edition of the Shorter Poems of Edmund Spenser* (New Haven, 1989), 170.
3. Richard Baxter, *A Treatise of Self-Denial* (1659), in *The Practical Works of Richard Baxter*, 4 vols. (1707), III, 377.
4. Richard Baxter, *Poetical Fragments* (1681), fol. A8.
5. Theophilus Gale, *The Court of the Gentiles*, 2nd. edn. (Oxford, 1672), 8–9.
6. Baxter, *Fragments*, fol. A3v.
7. Francis Bugg, *The Quaker's Charm Discovered* (1702), 2; see also 14.
8. E. Turll, *The Life and Character of the Reverend Benjamin Coleman* (1749), 30; Bryon Dale, *The Good Lord Wharton* (1906), 83.
9. Richard Baxter wrote a MS attack, his "Animadversions on Gale's Court of the Gentiles" (1679), DWL, Baxter MS 349–50.
10. For forerunners, see Nigel Smith, *Perfection Proclaimed: Language and Literature in English Radical Religion, 1640–1660* (Oxford, 1989), 185–225.
11. Gale, *Court*, 8.
12. Thomas Gilbert, *Mr. Wm Brownings Verses: Being a Translation of Mr. Gilberts Laudatory Poem on Dr. Owens Book of the Holy Spirit*, BL Add. MS 29,921, fol. 108v.
13. Dorothy White, *A Call from God out of Egypt, by his Son Christ the Light of Life* (1662), 7–8.
14. Anon., "A Hymn," in Thomas Ellwood, *A Collection of Poems on Various Subjects* (1730?), 62.
15. Jackson Cope, "Seventeenth Century Quaker Style," in Stanley Fish, ed., *Seventeenth-Century Prose: Modern Essays in Criticism* (New York, 1971), 200–35.
16. Thomas Ellwood, "Divine Worship," in *Poems*, 3–4.
17. Katharine Evans and Sarah Chevers, *This is a Short Relation of Some of the Cruel Sufferings (for Truths sake) of Katharine Evans and Sarah Chevers* (1662), 44.

18. John Kelsall, "O! Thou Almighty," in Luella M. Wright, *The Literary Life of the Early Friends, 1650–1725* (New York, 1932), 135.

19. Benjamin Keach, "A Mystical Hymn of Thanksgiving," in *War with the Devil*, 4th. edn. (1676), 116.

20. Barbara Kiefer Lewalski, *Protestant Poetics and the Seventeenth-Century Religious Lyric* (Princeton, 1979), 39–53.

21. Baxter, "On David's Psalms," in *Fragments*, 63.

22. On literary images in earlier poetry, see Stanley Stewart, *The Enclosed Garden: The Tradition and the Image in Seventeenth-Century Poetry* (Madison, 1966), 3–30, and Noam Flinker, *The Song of Songs in the English Renaissance: Kisses of their Mouths* (Cambridge, 2002).

23. John Lloyd, *Shir ha Shirim, Or the Song of Songs* (1682), fol. A4; John Speed, prefatory poem to *Shir ha Shirim*, n.p.

24. John Milton, *Reason of Church Government*, in *CPW*, 1, 815. On Milton's use of the Song of Songs, see Flinker, *Songs*, 148–59.

25. John Robotham, *An Exposition on the whole booke of Solomons* SONG, *Commonly called the Canticles* (1651), 10, 9.

26. See, for example, Thomas Beverley, *An Exposition of the Divinely Prophetick Song of Songs* (1687), 49, 51; Robert Fleming, *The Mirrour of Divine Love* (1691), fol. A4v; and John Brayne, *An Exposition upon the Canticles* (1651), fol. A2v.

27. *"The Centuries" of Julia Palmer*, ed. V. Burke and E. Clarke (Nottingham, 2001), 250. J. Collinges, *The Intercourses of Divine Love Betwixt Christ and the Church . . . Second Chapter of Canticles* (1676), fol. A3v.

28. Collinges, *Intercourses*, fol. A4.

29. William Guild, *Loves Encounter between the Lamb and his Bride, Christ and his Church* (1657), fol. A2v; James Durham, *Clavis Cantici* (Edinburgh, 1668), 2.

30. Richard Turner, *The Song of Solomon Rendred in Plain and Familiar Verse* (1659), fol. A4.

31. There were also apocalyptic and political interpretations of the Song of Songs; see Bryan W. Ball, *A Great Expectation: Eschatological Thought in English Puritanism to 1660* (Leiden, 1975), 239–42.

32. See James Grantham Turner, *Libertines and Radicals in Early Modern London: Sexuality, Politics, and Literary Culture* (Cambridge, 2002), 171.

33. Peter Brown, *The Body and Society: Men, Women, and Sexual Renunciation in Early Christianity* (1988), 428–47; see Richard Rambuss, *Closet Devotions* (Durham, NC, 1998) on devotion as desire.

34. Robotham, *An Exposition*, 19. On Robotham, see *CR*, 413–14; Robotham, whose radicalism had stirred objections to his ordination to the 4th London Classis in 1647, was ousted from his rectorship in Essex in 1660.

35. Turner, *Song*, fol. A3.

36. John Reeve, Hymn 4, 1, 2, in *Spiritual Hymns upon Solomon's Song* (1684), 4.

37. Benjamin Keach, *Spiritual Songs*, 2nd. edn. (1700) (there is no first edition).

38. Reeve, Preface, *Spiritual Hymns*, n.p.

39. Christopher Jelinger, *Christ and the Saints* (1656), 35.

40. John Bunyan, "Of the Spouse of Christ," in *A Book for Boys and Girls*, in Bunyan, *MW*, VI, 258.

41. Benjamin Keach, *Sion in Distress*, 2nd. edn. (1682), 119.

42. See, for example, J. C., "Untitled," in B[enjamin] A[ntrobus], *Buds and Blossoms of Piety, with some Fruit of the Spirit of Love*, 2nd. edn. (1691), 91; Beverley, "A Table of the Grand Events Relating to the Kingdom of Christ . . . given in this Song," in *An Exposition*, n.p.; Keach, *Sion*.

43. Michael A. G. Haykin, *Kiffin, Knollys and Keach* (Leeds, 1996), 84–87.

44. John Dunton, *The Life and Errors of John Dunton* (1818), 177.

45. Beverley, Preface, *An Exposition*, n.p.

46. Benjamin Keach, *The Glorious Lover* (1679), frontispiece. The diptych fronting Keach's *War with the Devil* (1678), presents a double image of a young man; see p. 20 above.

47. Keach, Proem, *Glorious Lover*, n.p.

48. Keach, Proem, *Glorious Lover*, n.p.; cf. 263.

49. Thomas Ager, *A Paraphrase on the Canticles or Song of Songs* (1680), fol. A3.

50. David and Jonathan as ideal friends in Dissenting literature are common; cf. Thomas Ellwood, *Davideis* (1712), 53–61, 94, 143; Mary Mollineux, "On David and Jonathan," in *Fruits of Retirement* (1702), 142–44.

51. Westminster Assembly of Divines, *Annotations upon all the Books of the Old and New Testament* (1657), fol. 7G3. Yet the Revolution's radicals such as the Ranters were choosing a carnal interpretation, according to Flinker, *Songs*, 120–39.

52. Ellwood, "An Epistle to a Friend," in *Poems*, 55; Mollineux, "Another Letter to a Friend," in *Fruits*, 159.

53. See, for instance, Anne Wentworth, *The Revelation* (1679), Palmer, *The "Centuries*," 72–74; 271; 308–09; and Lucy Hutchinson, *Order and Disorder* (1679), ed. David Norbrook (Oxford, 2001), 47, 111, 477–92. See Sharon Achinstein, "Female Sexuality and Religious Desire in Early Modern England," *English Literary History* 69 (Summer 2002), 413–38; and Rambuss, *Closet Devotions*, 78–82.

54. Helen Vendler, *The Poetry of George Herbert* (Cambridge, MA, 1979), 138.

55. Richard Baxter added the allusion to Herbert in his second edition of *Saints Everlasting Rest* (1651), Part 3, 199. See F. E. Hutchinson, ed., *The Works of George Herbert* (Oxford, 1972), xliii–xliv. See also Robert H. Ray, *The Herbert Allusion Book: Allusions to George Herbert in the Seventeenth Century*, Texts and Studies, 1986, *Studies in Philology* 83,4 (1986); Ray, "Herbert's Seventeenth-Century Reputation: A Summary and New Consideration," *George Herbert Journal* 9,2 (1986), 1–15; 7. Helen Wilcox, "Something Understood: The Reception and Influence of George Herbert to 1715" (D. Phil. dissertation, Oxford, 1984), 199–251; Sebastian Köppl, *Die Rezeption George Herberts im 17. und 18. Jahrhundert* (Heidelberg, 1978). John T. Shawcross has compiled later allusions in "Additional Seventeenth- and Eighteenth-Century Allusions to George Herbert," *George Herbert Journal* 15,1 (1991), 68–72; and in "More Early Allusions to Donne and Herbert," *John Donne Journal* 13,1–2 (1994), 113–23.

56. John Dunton, *The Athenian Mercury* (24 October 1693), cited in Helen Wilcox, "Women, Reading, and Devotion in Seventeenth-Century England," in Donna B. Hamilton and Richard Strier, eds., *Religion, Literature and Politics in Post-Reformation England* (Cambridge, 1996), 187–207; 193.

57. Baxter, *Saints Everlasting Rest* (1650), 853–56.

58. *Transcript of the Registers of the Worshipful Company of Stationers, 1640–1708*, 3 vols. (1913), II, 419.

59. Kathleen Lynch, "Devotion Bound: A Social History of the Temple," in Jennifer Andersen and Elizabeth Sauer, eds., *Books and Readers in Early Modern England* (Philadelphia, forthcoming).

60. See, for instance, John Bryan, *Dwelling with God, the Interest and Duty of Believers. In Opposition To the Complemental, Heartless, and Reserved Religion of the Hypocrite* (1670).

61. Ray, *The Herbert Allusion Book*; see also Sidney Gottlieb, "A Royalist Rewriting of George Herbert, *His Majesties Complaint to his Subjects* (1647)," *Modern Philology* 89 (1991), 211–24.

62. See Sharon Achinstein, "Reading George Herbert in the Restoration" (forthcoming); and see Jessica Martin, *Walton's Lives: Conformist Commemorations and the Rise of Biography* (Oxford, 2001), 203–09.

63. J. R. Watson, *The English Hymn: A Critical and Historical Study* (Oxford, 1997), 104; Stanley Stewart, *George Herbert* (Boston, 1986), 142.

64. Vendler, *George Herbert*, 109. More balanced is Wilcox, *Something Understood*.

65. John Perrot, "To the Children of the Day," in *A Sea of the Seed's Sufferings* (1661), 23. On Perrot's civil war poetry, see Nigel Smith, "John Perrot and the Quaker Epic," in Thomas Healy and Jonathan Sawday, eds., *Literature and the English Civil War* (Cambridge, 1990), 248–64.

66. Robert Rich, *Hidden Things Brought to Light* (1678), 7–8; cited in Kenneth Cane Carroll, *John Perrot: Early Quaker Schismatic, Friends Historical Journal Supplement* 33 (1971), 51–52; Richard Bauman, *Let Your Words be Few: Symbolism of Speaking and Silence among Seventeenth-Century Quakers* (Cambridge, 1983), 140–44.

67. Nicholas Billingsley, "The Invocation," in *Treasury of Divine Raptures* (1667), n.p.

68. Baxter, *Fragments*, fol. A7v.

69. Baxter, "Divine Love's Rest," in *Fragments*, 61.

70. Ellwood, *Davideis* (1712), xi, xiii.

71. Ellwood, "Love's Caveat," in *Poems*, 26.

72. Thomas Forde, *Fragmenta Poetica: Or, Poetical Diversions* (1660), 17–18.

73. Overton's compilation dates possibly from as early as 1666 and continues through to 1671; see David Norbrook, "'The Blushinge Tribute of a Borrowed Muse': Robert Overton and his Overturning of the Poetic Canon," in Peter Beal and Jeremy Griffiths, eds., *English Manuscript Studies, 1100–1700*, 4 (1993), 220–66; 221; see also Sidney Gottlieb, "Allusions to George Herbert in Robert Overton's *Gospell Observations & Religious Manifestations*," *Studies in Philology* 90,1 (1993), 83–99; and Sidney Gottlieb, "George Herbert and Robert

Overton," in Jonathan F. S. Post and Sidney Gottlieb, eds., *George Herbert in the Nineties* (Fairfield, CT, 1995), 185–200.

74. On *The Temple* as Psalter, see Lewalski, *Protestant Poetics*, 300.

75. "Aaron," in *Select Hymns Taken out of Mr. Herbert's Temple* (1697), Augustan Reprint Society 98 (Los Angeles, 1962), 29 (italics mine).

76. *Select Hymns*, "Praise," 23.

77. *Select Hymns*, fol. A2.

78. *Select Hymns*, fol. AA2.

79. Elizabeth Rowe, "Soliloquy 1," in *Miscellaneous Works in Prose and Verse*, 2 vols. (1739), 1, 175.

8 HYMN

1. Henry Newcome, Commonplace Book (c. 1669) , Folger MS V.a.232, fol. 63.

2. As does Donald Davie, *The Eighteenth-Century Hymn in England* (Cambridge, 1993), 7, 8. See the recent fine study by J. R. Watson, *The English Hymn: A Critical and Historical Study* (Oxford, 1997).

3. For example, William Barton, *A Century of Select Hymns* (1659), fol. A6.

4. Benjamin Keach, *Spiritual Melody, Containing near Three Hundred Sacred Hymns* (1691), fol. A3.

5. William Geddes, Preface, *The Saints Recreation, Third Part* (Edinburgh, 1683), n.p.

6. Elias Keach, Hymn 62, in *A Banquetting-House Full of Spiritual Delights* (1696), 79.

7. George Wither, Hymne 1, in *Halleluiah or, Britans* [sic] *Second Remembrancer* (1641).

8. Joseph Stennett, *Hymns in Commemoration of the Sufferings of our Blessed Saviour Jesus Christ*, 2nd. edn. (1705), fol. A3.

9. On the tradition of English hymns, see Madeleine Forell Marshall and Janet Todd, *English Congregational Hymns in the Eighteenth Century* (Lexington, 1982); Frederick John Gillman, *The Evolution of the English Hymn* (1927); John Julian, *Dictionary of Hymnology* (1908); Edna D. Parks, *Early English Hymns: An Index* (Metuchen, NJ, 1972). Hill, *Bible*, 351–62, explores the political uses of psalms; Nigel Smith, *Literature and Revolution in England, 1640–1660* (New Haven, 1994), 260–75, on civil war hymns.

10. Thomas Carlyle, ed., *Cromwell's Letters and Speeches*, cited in Percy A. Scholes, *The Puritans and Music in England and New England* (Oxford, 1934; repr. 1969).

11. *Acts of the General Assemblies, 1638–49* (1691), 354; cited in Louis F. Benson, *The English Hymn: Its Development and Use in Worship* (New York, 1915), 57.

12. William B. Hunter, "Milton Translates the Psalms," *Philological Quarterly* 40 (1961), 485–94.

13. Tessa Watt, *Cheap Print and Popular Piety, 1550–1640* (Cambridge, 1991), 47; Patrick Collinson, *The Birthpangs of Protestant England: Religious and Cultural*

Change in the Sixteenth and Seventeenth Centuries (New York, 1988), 106–12; Smith, *Literature and Revolution*, 260.

14. Patrick Collinson, "From Iconoclasm to Iconophobia: The Cultural Impact of the Second English Reformation," in Peter Marshall, ed., *The Impact of the English Reformation, 1500–1640* (1997), 291–92.

15. J. A. Birrell, "Sarbiewski, Watts, and the Later Metaphysical Tradition," *Review of English Studies* 37 (1956), 125–32.

16. Diane Kelsey McColley, *Poetry and Music in Seventeenth Century England* (Cambridge, 1997), 50–52.

17. George Wither, *The Hymnes and Songs of the Church* (1623), 2.

18. Anne Laurence, "Two Ranter Poems," *Review of English Studies* 31 (1980), 56–59; 58.

19. *Three Hymns, Or Certain excellent new Psalmes, composed by those three Reverend, and Learned Divines, Mr. John Goodwin, Mr. Dasoser* [sic] *Powel, Mr. Appletree* (1650).

20. John Goodwin, *Two Hymns, or Spiritual Songs* (1651).

21. William Barton, HALLELUJAH. *Or Certain Hymns, Composed out of Scripture, to celebrate some special and Publick Occasions… Upon Occasion of those two Glorious and most Remarkable Appearances of God for them, at Dunbar and Worcester: both upon that Memorable Day Septemb. 3 {1650/1651}* (1651).

22. Barton, *Hallelujah*, A3r–A3v.

23. These texts are: Eph. 5.19–20; Mark 14:26; Col. 3:16; and James 5:13, cited in Milton, *On Christian Doctrine*, in *CPW*, VI, 683; cf. E. Keach, *A Banquetting-House*, t.p.; Matthew Sylvester, ed., *Mr. Richard Baxter's Paraphrase on the Psalms of David in Metre, With other Hymns* (1692), fol. A11v; Barton, *A Century*, t.p.; Keach, *Spiritual Melody*, t.p.; Geddes, *Saints Recreation*, t.p.; Arthur Hildersham, Preface, *The Canticles, or Song of Solomon Paraphrased* (1672), n.p.; Isaac Watts, "A Short Essay Toward the Improvement of Psalmody," in *Hymns and Spiritual Songs* (1707), 234–39; Stennett, *Hymns*, n.p.

24. "The Song of Deborah, Judg. 5," in Hildersham, *The Canticles*, 150.

25. Anon., *A Door of Hope* (1660), t.p; Mary Mollineux, *Fruits of Retirement* (1702), t.p. Miriam's song was also used as defense of women's singing in mixed congregations in the controversy between Benjamin Keach and Isaac Marlow in the 1690s; see John Cotton, *Singing of Psalmes a Gospel Ordinance* (1647), 43; cf. Benjamin Keach, *The Breach Repair'd in Gods Worship* (1691), 141; Isaac Marlow, *Truth Soberly Defended* (1692), 91.

26. Barton, *Hallelujah*, 11–13.

27. Lucy Hutchinson, *Order and Disorder*, ed., David Norbrook (Oxford, 2001), 26, 11, 197–98; Hill, *Bible*, 407; Margaret Aston, *Lollards and Reformers: Images and Literacy in Late Medieval Religion* (1984), 55–56.

28. Katharine Evans and Sarah Chevers, *This is a Short Relation of Some of the Cruel Sufferings (for Truths Sake) of Katharine Evans and Sarah Chevers* (1662), 46.

29. Thomas Ellwood, "Awake, Awake," in C. G. Crump, ed., *The History of the Life of Thomas Ellwood* (1900), 138.

30. Parks, *Early English Hymns*, 75–82.
31. Edwin Welch, "William Barton, Hymnwriter," *The Guildhall Miscellany* 3,4 (1971), 235–41. Watson, *Hymn*, 104. The political contours of this conflict merit further attention.
32. *Baxter's Paraphrase*, fol. A6v: the preface is by Baxter.
33. Greaves, *Enemies*, 149.
34. *Baxter's Paraphrase*, fols. A7r–A7v.
35. "A Wigg Psalm," Folger MS v.a.399, fol. 26v.
36. *Baxter's Paraphrase*, fols. A5v–A6r.
37. See Leah S. Marcus, *Childhood and Cultural Despair: A Theme and Variations in Seventeenth-Century Literature* (Pittsburgh, 1978), 244.
38. B. Keach, *Spiritual Melody*, fol. A4.
39. *Baxter's Paraphrase*, fol. A9v.
40. B. Keach, *Spiritual Melody*, fols. A3r–A3v.
41. E. Keach, Dedicatory Epistle, *A Banquetting-House*, n.p.
42. Matthew Henry, *Family-Hymns* (1702), fol. A3v.
43. William Tong, *An Account of the Life and Death of Mr. Matthew Henry* (1716), 95.
44. See Patricia Crawford, "Katharine and Philip Henry and their Children: A Case Study in Family Ideology," *Transactions of the Historic Society of Lancashire and Cheshire* 134 (1984), 39–73.
45. Tong, *An Account…Mr. Matthew Henry*, 82.
46. Samuel Crossman, *The Young Man's Calling* (1678), fols. A7v–A8r.
47. Hugh Martin, ed., *A Companion to the Baptist Church Hymnal* (1953), xviii; Michael Haykin, *Kiffin, Knollys and Keach* (Leeds, 1996), 85.
48. See Watson, *Hymn*, 110–14. Keach, *Breach Repair'd*, 139–41.
49. Mary Pennington, *Experiences in the life of Mary Penington (Written By Herself)*, ed. Norman Penney (Philadelphia, 1911; repr. 1992), 26.
50. George Fox, *The Journal of George Fox*, ed. Nigel Smith (Harmondsworth, 1998), 248.
51. Evans and Chevers, *Short Relation*, 44.
52. John Bunyan, *Grace Abounding to the Chief of Sinners and The Pilgrim's Progress*, ed. Roger Sharrock (Oxford, 1966), where hymns and songs communicate joy and celebration (170, 182, 291–92, 379); doctrine (e.g. 226, 229, 238, 246, 307, 310, 315, 331–32, 335); utterances of faith in times of trouble (192, 199, 392); and commemoration (218, 235, 248). On Bunyan's singing, see Christopher Hill, *A Tinker and a Poor Man: John Bunyan and His Church, 1628–1688* (New York, 1989), 264–65.
53. *Baxter's Paraphrase*, fol. A9v.
54. *Baxter's Paraphrase*, fol. A10.
55. Richard Baxter, *Poetical Fragments* (1681), fol. A6v.
56. Joseph Boyce, *Sacramental Hymns* (Dublin; repr. London, 1693), 51–52. Boyse (1660–1728), was the father of Samuel, and after training at Richard Frankland's famous academy near Kendal, preached in Amsterdam and then took up a post in Dublin in 1683, writing polemics defending nonconformity and

Presbyterianism, including *Vindiciae Calvinisticae* (1688). His *Family Hymns* appeared in 1701.

57. E. Keach, Dedicatory Epistle, *A Banquetting-House*, n.p.
58. Watts, *Hymns and Spiritual Songs*, viii–ix.
59. Theodosia Alleine, *The Life and Death of that Excellent Minister of Christ Mr. Joseph Alleine* (1672), 89.
60. *Baxter's Paraphrase*, fols. A12r–A12v.
61. Barton, *A Century* (1659), A3v.
62. *Baxter's Paraphrase*, 231–34, 234–37; cf. William Barton, *Four Centuries of Select Hymns* (1668), 249; 369–370,
63. Samuel Bury, "A Spiritual Song, for Saturday Morn, 51st Psalm," in *A Collection of Psalms and Hymns* (1707), 69.
64. Henry, *Family-Hymns* (1702), fols. A5v–A6r.
65. Joseph Boyse, *A Collection of Divine Hymns upon Several Occasions*, 2nd. edn. (1704), fol. A2.
66. Boyse, *Sacramental Hymns*, 43; Mr. Patrick is not the Anglican Latitudinarian, but his brother John, who published *A Century of Select Psalms* (1679).
67. Boyse, *A Collection*, fol. A2.
68. *Baxter's Paraphrase*, fol. A8v.
69. *Baxter's Paraphrase*, fol. A3.
70. *Memoirs of the Life and Writings of Isaac Watts, D.D.* (1806), 75–76; and see also Thomas Gibbons, *Memoirs of the Rev. Isaac Watts, D.D.* (1780), 254. See V. De Sola Pinto, "Isaac Watts and the Adventurous Muse," *Essays and Studies* 20 (1934), 86–107.
71. Watts, "A Short Essay," 263–64.
72. Baxter, "Love Breathing Thanks and Praise," in *Poetical Fragments*, 1.
73. Boyse, *Sacramental Hymns*, fol. A4.
74. Boyse, *Sacramental Hymns*, fol. A4.
75. Boyse, *A Collection*, fol. A2v.
76. Geddes, Preface, *Saints Recreation*, n.p.
77. *Select Hymns, Taken Out of Mr. Herbert's Temple* (1697), fol. A3.
78. Elizabeth Hincks, *The Poor Widows Mite, Cast into the Lord's Treasury* (1671), 46.
79. Stennett, *Hymns* (1705), fol. A4.
80. Boyce, *Sacramental Hymns*, fol. A4.
81. T. S., *The Book of the Song of Solomon in Meeter* (1676), fol. A2v.
82. Thomas Ellwood, "Divine Worship," *A Collection of Poems on Various Subjects* (1730?), 9.
83. Haykin, *Kiffin, Knollys and Keach*; Hugh Martin, *Benjamin Keach, 1640–1704* (1961); Hugh Martin, "The Baptist Contribution to Early English Hymnody," *Baptist Quarterly* 19 (1961–62), 195–208; David W. Music, "The Hymns of Benjamin Keach: An Introductory Study," *The Hymn* (July 1983), 147–54; Alan Clifford, "Benjamin Keach and Nonconformist Hymnology," in *Spiritual Worship* (1985), 69–93.

84. John Dunton, cited in Henry R. Plomer, *A Dictionary of the Printers and Booksellers, 1668 to 1725* (Oxford, 1968), 97.

85. Keeble, *LC*, 113, 130; Greaves, *Deliver*, 218; Greaves, *Enemies*, 172.

86. Plomer, *Dictionary 1668–1725*, 141.

87. Plomer, *Dictionary 1668–1725*, 144–6.

88. See D. F. McKenzie, "Printers of the Mind: Some Notes on Bibliographical Theories and Printing-House Practices," *Studies in Bibliography* 22 (1969), 1–75.

89. Adrian Johns, *The Nature of the Book* (Chicago, 1998), 120–24.

90. Reported of a Mr. John Hardy by Nicholas Billingsley [the younger], *Rational and Christian Principles the Best Rules of Conduct* (1721), 90.

91. Gibbons, *Memoirs... Watts* (1806), 76.

92. Watts, *Hymns and Spiritual Songs*, iv.

93. Watts, *Hymns and Spiritual Songs*, v.

94. De Sola Pinto, "Isaac Watts," 89.

95. Watts, "A Short Essay," 251.

96. M. Watts, *Dissenters*, ch. 4.

97. Isaac Watts, "Philosophical Essays on Various Subjects, with some Remarks on Mr. Locke's Essay on Human Understanding" (1733), in *The Works of the Late Reverend and Learned Isaac Watts, D. D.*, ed. D. Jennings and P. Doddridge, 6 vols. (1753), v, 500–633; 548; and his *The Doctrine of the Passions*, 5th. edn. (1770). See Rivers, *RGS*, 188.

98. Watts, "The Rational Foundation of a Christian Church" (1747), in *Works*, vi, 1–30; 1; Rivers, *RGS*, 176.

99. Watts, "A Short Essay," 246.

100. Samuel Johnson, *Lives of the English Poets*, ed. George Birkbeck Hill, 3 vols. (Oxford, 1905), iii, 306.

101. John Dryden, "Annus Mirabilis," in *Works*, i, 93, st. 223.

CODA: ENLIGHTENMENT

1. Joseph Glanvill, "Anti-fanatical Religion and Free Philosophy," in *Essays on Several Important Subjects in Philosophy and Religion* (1676), 1–58, fols. M mir–T t2v. See Jackson I. Cope, " 'The Cupri-Cosmits': Glanvill on Latitudinarian Anti-Enthusiasm," *Huntington Library Quarterly* 17 (1954), 269–86. See also R. K. Webb, "The Emergence of Rational Dissent," in Knud Haakonssen, ed., *Enlightenment and Religion: Rational Dissent in Eighteenth-Century Britain* (Cambridge, 1996), 12–41; and B. R. White, "The Twilight of Puritanism in the Years Before and After 1688," in Ole Peter Grell, Jonathan I. Israel, and Nicholas Tyacke, eds., *From Persecution to Toleration: The Glorious Revolution and Religion in England* (Oxford, 1991), 307–30.

2. Olive M. Griffiths, *Religion and Learning: A Study in English Presbyterian Thought from the Bartholomew Ejections (1662) to the Foundation of the Unitarian Movement* (Cambridge, 1935), 100; Dewey D. Wallace, Jr. *Puritans*

and Predestination: Grace in English Protestant Theology, 1525–1695 (Chapel Hill, 1982), 180; Rivers, *RGS*, 97–98; Roger Thomas, "Presbyterians in Transition," in C. G. Bolam, Jeremy Goring, H. L. Short, and Roger Thomas, eds., *The English Presbyterians from Elizabethan Puritanism to Modern Unitarianism* (1968), 113–20.

3. Lawrence E. Klein, "Sociability, Solitude, and Enthusiasm," in Lawrence E. Klein and Anthony J. La Vopa, eds., *Enthusiasm and Enlightenment in Europe, 1650–1850* (San Marino, CA, 1998), 153–77; 164; Richard Ashcraft, "Latitudinarianism and Toleration: Historical Myth versus Political History," in Richard Kroll, Richard Ashcraft, and Perez Zagorin, eds., *Philosophy, Science, and Religion in England, 1640–1700* (Cambridge, 1992), 151–77.

4. Robert Ferguson, *The Interest of Reason in Religion* (1675), 62, 272; cited in Richard Ashcraft, *Revolutionary Politics and Locke's Two Treatises of Government* (Princeton, 1986), 161.

5. Ashcraft, "Latitudinarianism," 167; Ashcraft, *Revolutionary Politics*, 51–67.

6. On Locke's Socinianism, see John Marshall, *John Locke: Resistance, Religion and Responsibility* (Cambridge, 1994); Richard Ashcraft, "Faith and Knowledge in Locke's Philosophy," in John W. Yolton, ed., *John Locke: Problems and Perspectives* (Cambridge, 1969), 194–223; and Richard Ashcraft, "Anticlericalism and Authority in Lockean Political Thought," in Roger Lund, ed., *The Margins of Orthodoxy: Heterodox Writing and Cultural Response, 1660–1750* (Cambridge, 1995), 73–96.

7. Other studies opening up the early eighteenth-century Dissenting literary legacy are Donald Davie, *A Gathered Church: The Literature of the English Dissenting Interest, 1700–1930* (1978); A. G. Matthews, *Mr. Pepys and Nonconformity* (1954); Hoxie Neale Fairchild, *Religious Trends in English Poetry, 1700–1740*, 6 vols. (New York, 1949), 1.

8. Christopher Ness, *A Distinct Discourse and Discovery of the Person and Period of Antichrist* (1679), 96.

9. Daniel Defoe, Preface, *De Laune's Plea for the Nonconformists* (1706), vii, ii.

10. E.g. Daniel Defoe, *The Character of the Late Dr. Samuel Annesley* (1697); *Memoirs of the Life and Eminent Conduct of that Learned and Reverend Divine, Daniel Williams* (1718).

11. John Spurr, "From Puritanism to Dissent," in Christopher Durston and Jaqueline Eales, eds., *The Culture of English Puritanism, 1560–1700* (1996), 251.

12. Watts, *Dissenters*, 260.

13. Elizabeth Singer Rowe, "To A Friend who Persuades me to leave the Muses," in *Poems on Several Occasions by Philomela* (1696), 6–9.

14. See *DNB*; Henry F. Stecher, *Elizabeth Singer Rowe, the Poetess of Frome* (Bern, 1973); and Henry Grove in his Introduction to Elizabeth Rowe, *Miscellaneous Works in Prose and Verse*, 2 vols. (1739), 1, i–xcvii.

15. See the excellent overview of her prose career by John J. Richetti, *Popular Fiction before Richardson: Narrative Patterns, 1700–1739* (Oxford, 1992), 240–59.

16. Rowe, "Come, my Beloved...Cant. vii.11," in *Miscellaneous Works*, 1, 43–44.

17. Elizabeth Singer Rowe, "On CANTICLES. Ch. v.vi.&c," in *Philomela: Or, Poems by Mrs. Elizabeth Singer, now Rowe* (1738), 22.

18. Rowe's writing did attract comment for its overtones of erotic and spiritual effusiveness, as Isaac Watts notes in the Preface to Elizabeth Singer Rowe, *Devout Exercises of the Heart in Meditation and Soliloquy, Prayer and Praise. Review'd and Published at her Request, by I. Watts, D.D.* (1738), xiii–vi (paginated incorrectly: should be xiii–xiv). See also Madeleine Forell Marshall, ed., *The Poetry of Elizabeth Singer Rowe, 1674–1737* (Lewiston, 1989), 77.

19. See Sharon Achinstein, "'Pleasure by Description': Elizabeth Singer Rowe's Enlightened Milton," in John T. Shawcross and Mark Kelley, eds., *Milton and the Grounds of Contention: Essays in Honor of Joseph Wittreich* (Pittsburgh, forthcoming).

20. Elizabeth Singer Rowe, "Soliloquy VI," in *Devout Soliloquies. In Blank Verse*, in *Miscellaneous Works*, 1, 198.

21. Elizabeth Singer Rowe, "Soliloquy XIII," in *Miscellaneous Works*, 1, 205.

22. Elizabeth Singer Rowe, "On Hampden," cited in Stecher, *Elizabeth Singer Rowe*, 198.

23. Elizabeth Singer Rowe, *The History of Joseph* (1739), 60.

24. John Hughes and Richard Blackmore, *The Lay-Monastery* (1714), a compilation of their essays published serially.

25. Jonathan Swift to Alexander Pope, 3 September 1735, as reported in Samuel Johnson, *Lives of the English Poets*, ed. George Birkbeck Hill, 3 vols. (Oxford, 1905), II, 164.

26. John Hughes, ed., "Remarks on the Fairy [sic] Queen," in *The Works of Mr. Edmund Spenser*, 6 vols. (1715), 1, lx.

27. [John Hughes], *An Ode to the Creator of the World. Occasion'd by Fragments of Orpheus*, 2nd. edn. (1713), 7–8.

28. Anthony Ashley Cooper, third Earl of Shaftesbury, *A Letter Concerning Enthusiasm* (1708), in *Characteristics*, ed. John M. Robertson, 2 vols. (Gloucester, 1963), 1, 37–38.

29. John Dennis, "The Advancement and Reformation of Modern Poetry," in *The Critical Works of John Dennis*, ed. Edward Niles Hooker, 2 vols. (Baltimore, 1939), 1, 222. See John Morillo, "John Dennis: Enthusiastic Passions, Cultural Memory, and Literary Theory," *Eighteenth-Century Studies* 34, 1 (2000), 21–41.

30. Ernest Lee Tuveson, *The Imagination as a Means of Grace: Locke and the Aesthetics of Romanticism* (Berkeley, 1960), 91–102.

31. Margaret Doody, *The Daring Muse: Augustan Poetry Reconsidered* (Cambridge, 1985), 18–20; David B. Morris, *The Religious Sublime: Christian Poetry and Critical Tradition in Eighteenth-Century England* (Lexington, KY, 1972), 28–38.

32. Fairchild, *Religious Trends in English Poetry*, 1, 98–120. See Lily B. Campbell, "The Christian Muse," *Huntington Library Bulletin* 8 (1935), 29–70.

33. 10 April 1776 and again in 1780, James Boswell, *The Life of Samuel Johnson, LL.D.* (1965), 740, 1089.

34. Henry Grove, "The Divine Immensity. An Ode," *Poems on Several Occasions*, in *Miscellanies in Prose and Verse* (1739), 109.

35. See Stella P. Revard, "The Seventeenth-Century Religious Ode and its Classical Models," in Claude J. Summers and Ted-Larry Pebworth, eds., *"Bright Shootes of Everlastingnesse:" The Seventeenth-Century Religious Lyric* (Columbia, MO, 1987), 173–91; Robert Shafer, *The English Ode to 1660: An Essay in Literary History* (New York, 1966), 1; and Doody, *Daring Muse*, 249–58.

36. Isaac Watts, "The Incomprehensible," in *Horae Lyricae* (1709), 27, 1–15.

37. Isaac Watts, Preface, *Horae Lyricae* (1706), n.p.; *Horae Lyricae* (1709), xvi.

38. J. G. A. Pocock, "Enthusiasm: The Antiself of Enlightenment," in Lawrence E. Klein and Anthony J. La Vopa, eds., *Enthusiasm and Enlightenment in Europe, 1650–1850* (San Marino, CA, 1998), 7–28; restricting his interest to the aesthetic element, is Shaun Irlam, *Elations: The Poetics of Enthusiasm in Eighteenth-Century Britain* (Stanford, 1999).

39. George Williamson, "The Restoration Revolt Against Enthusiasm," in *Seventeenth-Century Contexts* (1960), 202–39; Clement Hawes, *Mania and Literary Style: The Rhetoric of Enthusiasm from the Ranters to Christopher Smart* (Cambridge, 1996); Attracta Anne Coppins, "Religious Enthusiasm from Robert Browne to George Fox: A Study of its Meaning and the Reaction against it in the Seventeenth Century" (D.Phil. dissertation, University of Oxford, 1983), 34.

40. James Thomson, Preface to "Winter" (1726), in *The Seasons* ed. James Sambrook, (Oxford, 1981), 304.

41. E. P. Thompson, *The Making of the English Working Class* (New York, 1977), 30; and see 26–54.

APPENDIX: MILTON'S BURIAL PLACE

1. William B. Hunter, *Visitation Unimplor'd: Milton and the Authorship of De Doctrina Christiana* (Pittsburgh, 1998), 14.

2. Caroline Gordon and Wilfrid Dewhirst, *The Ward of Cripplegate in the City of London* (Oxford, 1985), 107, 115–17.

3. William Riley Parker, *Milton: A Biography*, 2 vols. (Oxford, 1968), 11, 975.

4. Guildhall MS 6047.1, p. 286, St. Giles Cripplegate Church Wardens' Accounts, 14 August 1662–25 August 1663; Guildhall MS 6047.1, 18 St. Giles Cripplegate Vestry Minutes Book, p. 18, 5 September 1662 (surplice), and p. 19, 18 November 1662 (rails).

5. Daniel Defoe limned his life in *The Character of the Late Dr. Samuel Annesley* (1697).

6. Guildhall MS 6047.1, p. 287, St. Giles Cripplegate Church Wardens' Accounts, 14 August 1662–25 August 1663.

7. See Mark Goldie and John Spurr, "Politics and the Restoration Parish: Edward Fowler and the Struggle for St Giles Cripplegate," *English Historical Review* 109 (1994), 572–96.
8. John Aubrey, "Minutes of the Life of Mr. John Milton," in Helen Darbishire, ed., *Early Lives of Milton* (1932), 1–15; 5.
9. John Toland, *The Life of John Milton* (1698), in Darbishire, *Early Lives*, 83–197; 193.

Index

Printed in the United Kingdom
by Lightning Source UK Ltd.
134148UK00001B/104/A